C000002931

'It is a great pleasure to me to recommend this tril[...]
to the continuing intellectual contribution of the '[...]
efforts to improve human relations in organizations.'

Manfred F. R. Kets de Vries, *distinguished clinical professor of Leadership Development and Organizational Change*

'Through a series of diverse contributions, the authors sensitise us to the nature of the many challenges, not always sufficiently recognised, with which organisational change practitioners must tussle, and possible ways of overcoming them.'

David Shaw, *independent researcher in the philosophy of management*

'In the second volume of a trilogy on a Tavistock systems psychodynamics paradigm, David Lawlor and Mannie Sher have excelled themselves in producing a volume that details the emergence and development of The Tavistock Institute of Human Relations – something that is essential if one is inclined to harness the richness of the Tavistock Institute.'

Anton Obholzer, *member, British Psychoanalytic Society*

'If much systems psychodynamics theory has focused on explicating the persistence of dysfunction in groups and organizations, this book reminds us that an equally important focus of this approach is its ability to cast a light on, and facilitate, the emergence of the new in social systems.'

Gianpiero Petriglieri, *associate professor of Organisational Behaviour, INSEAD*

Systems Psychodynamics

In the second of this three-volume series, the authors expand on the theory and practice of systems psychodynamics – which integrates psychoanalytic thinking, open systems theory and complexity theory – in its applications to consultancy work in organisations and wider social contexts.

Multidisciplinary and multitheoretical in nature, the systems psychodynamics paradigm develops from the understanding that no single theory or approach explains the complex nature of organisational systems. Replete with explanations of key theories, practical guidance and exercises, this book demonstrates how systems psychodynamics can be used by consultants to plan and put into action organisational changes in four main areas: change planning and management; action research and evaluation; leadership and whole systems; and professional development and next steps. In light of systems psychodynamics, rather than functioning as a leader of change processes, the role of an organisational development consultant is one of providing containment, understanding and facilitation for others to take up *their* leadership roles responsibly in *their* change processes.

With a focus on practical application in real situations, this book will be invaluable for psychoanalysts, managers, policymakers, consultants and researchers in a wide range of professional and clinical settings.

David Lawlor is professional partner at the Tavistock Institute of Human Relations, specialising in research and consultancy practice; co-director on *Organisational Consultancy: Working with the Dynamics;* visiting lecturer at the Tavistock and Portman NHS Trust; group relations consultant; formerly, head of the Social Work Discipline at the Tavistock and Portman NHS Trust; and principal consultant at Tavistock Consultancy.

Mannie Sher is principal social scientist at the Tavistock Institute of Human Relations; formerly, director of Group Relations Programme; formerly, chair of British Association of Psychotherapists; former board member of International Society for the Psychoanalytic Study of Organisations (ISPSO); author of *The Dynamics of Change: Tavistock Approaches to Improving Social Systems* (2013); and editor of *Dynamics at Boardroom Level: A Tavistock Primer for Leaders, Coaches and Consultants; Lawlor, D. & Sher, M. (2022)* and *An Introduction to Systems Psychodynamics: Consultancy, Research and Training*, Routledge.

Systems Psychodynamics

Innovative Approaches to Change, Whole Systems and Complexity

David Lawlor and Mannie Sher

With contributions from Eliat Aram, David Armstrong, Anne Benson, Mee-Yan Cheung-Judge, Camilla Child, Jonathan Gosling, Dione Hills, Olya Khaleelee, Susan Long, Anton Obholzer, Carolyn Ordowich and Bert Painter

Routledge
Taylor & Francis Group

LONDON AND NEW YORK

Designed cover image: irabell © Getty Images

First published 2023
by Routledge
4 Park Square, Milton Park, Abingdon, Oxon OX14 4RN

and by Routledge
605 Third Avenue, New York, NY 10158

Routledge is an imprint of the Taylor & Francis Group, an informa business

© 2023 David Lawlor and Mannie Sher

The right of David Lawlor and Mannie Sher to be identified as authors of this work has been asserted in accordance with sections 77 and 78 of the Copyright, Designs and Patents Act 1988.

All rights reserved. No part of this book may be reprinted or reproduced or utilised in any form or by any electronic, mechanical, or other means, now known or hereafter invented, including photocopying and recording, or in any information storage or retrieval system, without permission in writing from the publishers.

Trademark notice: Product or corporate names may be trademarks or registered trademarks, and are used only for identification and explanation without intent to infringe.

British Library Cataloguing-in-Publication Data
A catalogue record for this book is available from the British Library

Library of Congress Cataloging-in-Publication Data
Names: Lawlor, David, 1949– author. | Sher, Mannie, author.
Title: Systems psychodynamics : innovative approaches to change, whole systems and complexity / David Lawlor and Mannie Sher.
Description: 1 Edition. | New York, NY : Routledge, 2023. | Includes bibliographical references and index. |
Identifiers: LCCN 2022056707 (print) | LCCN 2022056708 (ebook) | ISBN 9781032437392 (hardback) | ISBN 9781032437408 (paperback) | ISBN 9781003368663 (ebook)
Subjects: LCSH: Organizational sociology. | Organizational behavior. | Organizational change. | System theory—Social aspects.
Classification: LCC HM786 .L39 2023 (print) | LCC HM786 (ebook) | DDC 302.3/5—dc23/eng/20230203
LC record available at https://lccn.loc.gov/2022056707
LC ebook record available at https://lccn.loc.gov/2022056708

ISBN: 9781032437392 (hbk)
ISBN: 9781032437408 (pbk)
ISBN: 9781003368663 (ebk)

DOI: 10.4324/9781003368663

Typeset in Garamond
by codeMantra

Homage to Eric Trist (1909–1993) and Fred Emery (1925–1997)

Eric Trist and Fred Emery were formidable social scientists, and their collaboration at the Tavistock Institute proved extremely fruitful.

Fred Emery, a psychologist by training, had his initial academic appointment at Melbourne University, where he made significant contributions to rural sociology, and the effects of film and television viewing. Constantly drawn towards testing social science theory in field settings, in 1958 he joined Eric Trist, one of his closest intellectual collaborators, at the Tavistock Institute of Human Relations in London.

Over the next 10 years, he, with Trist and other colleagues, established 'open socio-technical systems theory' as an alternative paradigm for organisational design – field-tested on a national scale in Norway – in partnership with Einar Thorsrud. Two of Emery and Trist's key publications were *The Causal Texture of Organisational Environments* (1965) – which became a citation classic – and *Towards a Social Ecology* (1972).

On Emery's return to Australia, he continued his action research in industry and the public sector and developed new tools for the diffusion of democracy in organisations and in communities. The three books that perhaps best convey the extraordinary breadth and depth of his thinking are *Toward a Social Ecology* (1972, with Trist), *On purposeful systems* (1972, with Russ Ackoff) and *Futures We're In* (1977).

He also edited for Penguin two volumes of readings called *Systems Thinking* (the initial volume was reprinted six times), which will long remain a staple resource on the origins and development of open systems thinking throughout the life sciences. In the final two years of his life, he co-edited the third and final volume of the 'Tavistock Anthology' being published by the University of Pennsylvania Press – *The Social Engagement of Social Science*.

Eric Trist's discipline of origin was psychology, but the title of the three chairs he held in North American universities between 1966 and 1983 offers a succinct statement of his central contribution to the social sciences: 'Professor of Organizational Behavior and Social Ecology'. And the titles of his best-known books, both written with colleagues from the Tavistock Institute, were *Organizational Choice* (1964) and *Towards a Social Ecology* (1973).

Trist joined up with a group of psychiatrists and others from the Tavistock Clinic, who told him what they were doing in the army, and he decided to join them. Through this, Trist broadened his theoretical repertoire to include psychoanalysis and anthropology. He and other Tavistock colleagues wished to apply their army experience to the problems of post-war reconstruction. The outcome, in 1947, was the Tavistock Institute of Human Relations, of which Trist was a key founder member. As deputy chairman and later as chairman, Trist was a major driving force throughout his 20 years at the Institute.

Trist's research in coalmining established his international reputation. His concept of the 'socio-technical system' made it possible to think of work organisation as a meeting of two systems, technological and psychosocial. To optimise the one at the expense of the other was a recipe for sub-optimal performance. Instead of technological determinism, there was a real possibility of 'organisational choice'. The semi-autonomous workgroup, internally led and self-regulatory, was likely to be more productive and more satisfying to the workers than the conventional hierarchy. The idea spread rapidly in different kinds of enterprises in many countries. In continental Europe, especially Scandinavia, it was a significant ingredient of industrial democracy and it opened the way for the world-wide 'quality of working life' movement. Famous though it became, the socio-technical concept was but one of Trist's many contributions to the Tavistock Institute's work. In 1946, with Kurt Lewin, he was active in launching a new journal, *Human Relations*, at the Research Center for Group Dynamics at Ann Arbor. He was instrumental in developing two new institutes under the Tavistock Institute umbrella: the Family Discussion Bureau (now the Institute of Marital Studies) and the Institute for Operational Research.

Trist was ambivalent about leaving the Tavistock for an appointment at UCLA. The precipitating factor was that his wife, Beulah, was advised by doctors to move to a warmer climate. Although he had many American friends, he was not really happy until he moved to the Wharton School at Philadelphia in 1969, alongside Russ Ackoff, of operational research fame. From then his career continued its upward trajectory. He extended his interest in work organisation to wider social systems. Later, at York University, Toronto, he initiated a programme of future studies.

He conceived a massive anthology of work, and the title 'The Social Engagement of Social Science' captured the focus of his life's work. What these volumes do not display is the Eric Trist who had a great sense of humour and was the life and soul of parties, in which, in his younger days, he could be persuaded to give a spirited rendering of a Navaho rain dance. He was a man of many parts.

Contents

Figures

Acknowledgements

Writing one book, let alone three, is a big task. It was a labour of love to describe, in a systematic way, the ideas, constructs and theories of systems psychodynamics, and their application, to which we have been attached for over half a century and which forms essential parts of our individual and professional identities. In this task, we were assisted by colleagues, collaborators, contributors and endorsers who helped these volumes appear in print. We also had our critics. To all, we offer our grateful thanks because through their support and challenge, they influenced the shape and content of these volumes.

We set out to write a 'how to' book for organisational development consultants and social science researchers, but inevitably, at times, we were drawn back to the theories of organisations and social institutions. We realised then that theory and practice are two indivisible elements of the same thing, and we accepted Lewin's message that there is nothing so practical as a good theory. The theories that have emerged from the field of psychoanalysis and the Tavistock Institute of Human Relations have stood the test of time. We are grateful to the 'giants' of psychoanalytic thinking like Sigmund Freud, Melanie Klein, Wilfred Bion and Donald Winnicott, and the 'early pioneers' of the Tavistock Institute like Eric Trist, Fred Emery, Cyril Sofer, Elliott Jaques, Isobel Menzies Lyth, Kenneth Rice, Eric Miller, Pierre Turquet, Robert Gosling, the Balint's, Evelyn Cleavely, Tim Dartington, Gordon Lawrence, Larry Hirschhorn, Larry Gould, Margaret Rioch, Jim Krantz and Susan Long, for the legacies they have left us, which sustained our confidence when the going got rough. We were spurred on by their demands for 'more and better research' and 'building on the foundations' laid by them. It is easy to rest on the laurels of others. We were often forced away from a tendency to worship our ancestors. We needed to acknowledge that we had to move forward. This led us to examine and think how changing circumstances and conditions in the world challenge cherished ideas. We had to let go of some of them or refresh them to be relevant for the contemporary world and to make room for the new. We hope our books adequately reflect that struggle and that they are refreshing to read and act as stimuli to new thinking and action.

We offer a special thank you to Eliat Aram and to the Council and members of staff at the Tavistock Institute who continue to support thought leadership in the Institute and all who associate with it. 'Thought leadership' is to become recognised as experts, without being expert, and used as a go-to resource in particular fields, areas or topics. Eliat overseas the environment of the Institute where everyone faces challenges and finds their own ways to address them. The ideal of academic freedom is an enshrined value at the Institute, and while it can sometimes lead to sharp differences between people, there is enough shared agreement on principle and practice to unify the Institute into a healthy working environment. This enables individual creativity, which continues to flourish despite the demands of an increasingly competitive environment. At the same time, we can see across the globe that systems psychodynamics is an evolving discipline. For instance, it has deep roots in the USA via Group Relations and the A K Rice Institute, in Australia via The National Institute of Organisation Dynamics, Australia, and its innovative group relations programme, in India via Group Relation India, in Europe and South Africa, in Israel via OFEK and in China via Tavistock Institute China, to name a few. Systems psychodynamics is seen as helpful to what seem to be intractable social problems. In the UK, the Organisation Promoting the Understanding of Society (OPUS) continues to thrive and grow and is now established as an international organisation, and the Tavistock Clinic continues with its advanced academic programmes. The International Society for the Psychoanalytic Study of Organisations (ISPSO) acts as an important forum for debate and intellectual work.

I would like to thank Barbara Williams, Nuala Dent and Annie Boland for their help in editing and refining this Foreword.

Authors

David Lawlor is professional partner at the Tavistock Institute of Human Relations, where he specialises in research and consultancy practice. He is a co-director on the *Organisational Consultancy: Working with the Dynamics* programme. David is a visiting lecturer at the Tavistock and Portman NHS Trust. He is an experienced international Group Relations Conference consultant. He was head of the Social Work Discipline at the Tavistock and Portman NHS Trust and a principal consultant at Tavistock Consultancy. David has extensive experience managing and working in local authority settings, voluntary organisations and psychiatric hospitals. At the Tavistock Clinic, he trained in organisational consultancy and psychoanalytic psychotherapy. He has delivered a wide range of training and staff development programmes in the care sector. As part of his PhD research, he has evaluated consultancy interventions and examined how to improve the outcome for the client. He is particularly interested in the impact of stressful environments on staff functioning. He is author of *Test of Time: A Case Study in the Functioning of Social Systems as a Defence Against Anxiety: Rereading 50 Years on, Clinical Child Psychology and Psychiatry, Vol. 14 No. 4, 2009;* and with Liz Webb: 'An Interview with Isabel Menzies Lyth with a Conceptual Commentary', *Organisational and Social Dynamics, Vol. 9 No. 1* (2009).

Mannie Sher is principal social scientist at the Tavistock Institute of Human Relations, London. He manages a portfolio of organisational development and change assignments and consults to boards and executives on their strategic and leadership challenges. His research and consultancy work focuses on the impact of thought on the dialectic relationship between social constructivism, the unconscious and liberal democracy. Mannie is a practising psychoanalytical psychotherapist. He has published on subjects of consultancy, leadership, organisational development, social dreaming, ethics and corruption. His latest books are *The Dynamics of Change: Tavistock Approaches to Improving Social Systems* (2013) with David Lawlor, published by Karnac Books, and *Dynamics at Boardroom Level: A Tavistock Primer for Leaders, Coaches and Consultants* (2020), edited by Leslie Brissett, Mannie Sher and

Tazi Smith, published by Routledge. Mannie is the former director of the Tavistock Institute's Group Relations Programme (1997–2017) and a former member of the Board of the International Society for the Psychoanalytic Study of Organisations (ISPSO).

Contributing Authors

Eliat Aram has been the CEO of the Tavistock Institute of Human Relations (TIHR) for 14 years. Eliat is a chartered scientist psychologist (BPS), a UKCP registered gestalt psychotherapist, and has been one of the pioneering members of the CMC (Complexity & Management Centre) of Hertfordshire University. She holds a diploma in Company Directorship from the IoD and is a companion of the British Academy of Management. She is a keen practitioner of Group Relations, the Institute's core 'learning through experience' practice. She consults to senior leadership teams and organisational diversity and transformation programmes internationally.

David Armstrong is associate consultant at Tavistock Consulting, a unit of the Tavistock and Portman NHS Foundation Trust. He trained as a social psychologist at the Tavistock Institute of Human Relations from 1959 to 1967, working with Eric Trist, Hugh Murray and Eric Miller on action research projects into the impact of automation on relations at work. David worked in action research and organisational consultancy at the University of London and The Grubb Institute before returning to the Tavistock in 1994 to join a newly established consultancy service at the Tavistock Clinic. A distinguished member of the International Society for the Psychoanalytic Study of Organizations (ISPSO), he is the author of *Organization in the Mind: Psychoanalysis, Group Relations and Organizational Consultancy* (Karnac, 2005), and with Michael Rustin, co-editor, of *Social Defences Against Anxiety: Explorations in a Paradigm* (Karnac, 2015).

Anne Benson is an organisational consultant, executive coach and UKCP-accredited psychotherapist, and currently head of Professional Development Programmes at the Tavistock Institute. Anne began her career as a nurse, establishing her interest in the interdependencies between physical and mental health and her curiosity about dynamics in the workplace. For the last 30 years, she has been working in practice-based consultancy, education and development, in the field of organisational and system change, leadership and team development, supervision and coaching. She has worked extensively with the Public Sector and not-for-profit sector, specifically the NHS and Local Authorities in the UK, as well as internationally in Germany, The Netherlands, China, and Trinidad & Tobago. She has a small private practice as a cognitive analytic psychotherapist.

Mee-Yan Cheung-Judge (d. 2022) was a *'scholar-educator-practitioner'* in the field of organisational development (OD). She worked across sectors alongside clients in global transformation programmes. She started and held the dean role in the NTL OD Certificate programme in Europe for 11 years. She was the author of many OD articles, books and research reports and a recipient of two *Lifetime Achievement Awards* (ODN, 2013; IODA, 2016) in acknowledgement of her outstanding contribution to the field of OD globally. *Human Resources* Magazine in the UK voted her as the top influential thinker in HR 2018, 2019.

Camilla Child is a principal consultant and researcher at the Tavistock Institute, engaged in organisational consultancy, evaluation research and coaching practice, aiming to help organisations, teams and individuals learn and develop through gaining a broader understanding of context, role and dynamics. Camilla works extensively in and with the public sector including local government, health and social care, children's services and education, housing, community and voluntary sectors. She has researched and worked on social policy related issues, such as social inclusion, young people and their risky behaviours, role of public libraries, employment and health promotion.

Jonathan Gosling is interested in active citizenship and is lead faculty of The Forward Institute promoting a movement for responsible leadership. He is an emeritus professor of Leadership at Exeter University and runs a consultancy for world thinkers called Pelumbra.com. He hosts writing retreats on the beautiful and wild island of *Lambay*, off the coast of Ireland. Jonathan was chair of ILA's 2011 Annual Conference in London.

Dione (Sanji) Hills (1948–2021) was a founder member of the Evaluation Development and Review Unit (EDRU) at the Tavistock Institute, undertaking complex, programme-level evaluations in community care, support for disabled people and health education at a community level. Her evaluations included HELIOS II, an EU programme for equal rights and integration of disabled people; London Lighthouse, a centre for people with HIV and AIDS; the DHSS Training Support Programme for Older People; and the Healthy Living Centre Initiatives to address health inequalities. Dione contributed to the field of evaluation in her use of theory-based, realistic and contribution analysis evaluation approaches and took a methodological lead in evaluations. She also developed evaluation frameworks with and for clients to support their learning. Dione was a great collaborator, and a valued member of many working partnerships.

Olya Khaleelee is a corporate psychologist and organisational consultant with a particular interest in leadership, and organisational transition and transformation. She was director of OPUS, an Organisation for Promoting Understanding of Society from 1980 to 1994, and is the current chair of the Trustees. Olya is a professional partner of the Tavistock Institute and was the first female director of the Leicester Conference on the theme of Authority, Leadership and Organisation. She has published extensively in the areas of leadership and system psychodynamics in organisations, and beyond, into society. Recently, she has co-written a book with Halina Brunning: *Danse Macabre and Other Stories: A Psychoanalytic Perspective on Global Dynamics*.

James Krantz is an organisational consultant and researcher from New York, where he is managing principal of Worklab, a consulting firm focusing on strategy implementation and leadership development. His principal interests are with the impact of emerging trends on the exercise of leadership and authority; the social and technical dimensions of new forms of work organisation; and the unconscious background to work and organisational life. Currently, Jim serves as honorary professor at the Higher School of Economics in Moscow; chair, Editorial Committee of the *Journal of Organisational and Social Dynamics*; and faculty, Dynamics of Consulting at the Wharton School.

Susan Long is an organisational consultant and executive coach. Previously, professor of Creative and Sustainable Organisation at RMIT University, she is now a professor and director of Research and Scholarship at the National Institute for Organisation Dynamics Australia (NIODA); associate of the University of Melbourne Executive Programmes; and teacher at INSEAD, Singapore, and the University of Divinity, Melbourne. Susan has over 35 years of experience in group relations, having been on staff or directing many conferences. Susan has authored 10 books and many articles in books and scholarly journals; she is a general editor of *Socioanalysis* and an associate editor of *Organisational and Social Dynamics*. She is a member of the Advisory Board for Mental Health at Work at Comcare and a past member of the Board of the Judicial College of Victoria. Susan is a distinguished member of ISPSO.

Anton Obholzer is a member of the British Psychoanalytic Society; emeritus senior faculty member, INSEAD Global Leadership Centre, Paris, France, 2000–present; founder and director, Tavistock Centre Consulting to Institutions workshop, 1980–2002; director and chief executive, Tavistock Centre, London, 1985–2002; visiting professor, Universities of Vienna and Graz, Austria; formerly, chair, Tavistock Institute of Medical Psychology, London. By training a medical doctor, psychiatrist, psychoanalyst and group and organisational consultant, Anton has increasingly moved into the application of psychological understanding in the management of organisations. His consultancy experience covers a wide range of commercial, banking and public sector organisations with the main emphasis of work and publications being on 'under-the-surface'/unconscious factors causing resistance to change. He has worked and is presently engaged in projects in the UK, Germany, Austria, France, Italy and Spain. His work with chief executives and senior management staff takes the form of mentoring, coaching and role consultancy. The emphasis is on the multiplicity of factors playing a role in personal and institutional creativity. His publications include *Workplace Intelligence* (2021) Routledge, and with Vega Roberts, *The Unconscious at Work*, Routledge.

Carolyn Ordowich is founder and president of STS Associates, Inc. since 1976, first in Montreal and Toronto, Canada and then in Princeton, New Jersey. She is an organisation design practitioner using socio-technical systems (STS) theory, organisation development, design thinking and participation-based change technologies with a wide range of industries in North America and internationally. Her career has included three 'greenfield' state-of-the-art STS designs, including a long running example, at 36 years, for Canadian General Electric Aviation, Bromont, Quebec. Her focus is on *collaborative, high-performing, ethical organising* of complex systems.

Bert Painter is an independent consulting social scientist and documentary filmmaker who has facilitated STS design of work organisations across Canada and internationally since 1975. Current consulting involves digital transformation of manufacturing processes and support for organisational design of virtual work. He has served as faculty associate in Leadership Studies at Royal Roads University and taught in the Department of Engineering at the University of British Columbia. As a filmmaker, Bert has produced over 20 documentaries on innovative workplaces in North America. For further information, see: www.moderntimesworkplace.com

Foreword by James Krantz

Centenaries are the perfect moment to reflect on where we have been, where we are now and where we are going. It is a pleasure to introduce a volume that testifies to the richness of the past, the strength of the present and the promise of the future for systems psychodynamic thinking.

The Tavistock Institute is celebrating its centenary of creating a sea change in how individuals, groups, organisations and communities can be understood and developed. Chief among the tributaries that feed this enormous reservoir of creativity were developments in psychoanalytic thinking beyond the clinic, most closely associated with Melanie Klein and Wilfred Bion, and the use of systems thinking to understand living systems, pioneered by Eric Trist and Fred Emery among others. Integrating the two standpoints revealed new, reciprocal interconnections between individuals and their social contexts. Many of the ideas and methods emerging from this remarkable moment went on to irrigate other fields of study.

Because so many have been deeply touched by this tradition, it is no surprise that there are many Tavistocks – or maybe it should be said 'Tavistocks-in-the-mind'. Mine can be traced to group relations conferences, beginning in 1976, and to a personal connection with Eric Trist, which began in 1982 at the Wharton School. I had the exceptionally good fortune of working with Eric while pursuing a PhD and was deeply influenced by his mentoring. Of his many reminiscences, the one that comes to mind for this Foreword was his observation that one of the Institute's greatest achievements was containing three geniuses without tearing itself apart with envy (not counting himself amongst this trio). In the mid-80s, I went to 'sit at the feet of my gods', so to speak, where I had further opportunities to work with Eric Miller, Isabel Menzies and others. The enduring impact of this tradition is why it is also an honour, as well as a pleasure, to write this Foreword.

Of course, for any tradition to thrive each generation must relate it anew to its present moment. Many following in the footsteps of these remarkable thinkers have given this legacy new vitality by adapting it to new challenges, resisting the temptation of safeguarding a cherished past but facilitating the encounter of systems psychodynamics with changing circumstances – the spirit that is animating this volume.

The challenges facing today's practitioners are daunting. Existential crises cast a shadow across a world that so often seems upside down. Increasingly, it resembles what used to be seen as the terrain of the unconscious – illogical, primordial, cruel and passionate. Ever more dominated by paranoid-schizoid states of mind, tribalism and polarisation, we seem to be besieged by splitting dynamics that are fragmenting our social systems.

Such irrationality is understandable in light of the upheaval of social and natural conditions. The world, as we have known it, is crumbling while, at the same time, we are on the cusp of extraordinary (possibly cataclysmic) change. Familiar habits of thought no longer hold in the face of shifting realities. Simultaneously coping with the impact of losing the familiar world, while confronting uncertainties of an unknown future, leaves many in a state of acute anxiety.

In my view, we are in transition from a world organised around industrial logic (e.g. linear cause-and-effect thinking) to one that will be organised around an 'information logic' (e.g. systems thinking). I would argue that today's societal regression represents the destabilising experience of liminal space between the lost social order of the past and the sometimes frightening outlines of a future we are only beginning to perceive but cannot comprehend, *futures we are in* as Fred Emery referred to elements of the future that are already present.

The intermingling of these two trajectories produces dynamics to which, I believe, systems psychodynamics can provide a unique and constructive voice. How can we help people cope thoughtfully with the loses and engage meaningfully with what is emerging? How can we support the development of humane social systems that are suited to the emerging world?

Looking back, the decline of the world as we've known it has left a fragmented, disoriented society. Symbol systems of family, social and political authority, sexuality, birth, death and the life cycle are in disarray, precipitating intensely felt grief, despair and anguish. Repeated betrayals by organisations, failed dependency, massive social trauma and fragmentation of the self have stimulated deep yearning for renewal, leaving many searching for connection and meaning through cults, tribal solidarity, conspiracy theories, etc. Formerly connected social groups and individuals are becoming alienated from one another, forming polarised camps, and turning former compatriots into strangers or threats.

Trusted institutions are losing their legitimacy. Confidence in them is waning and, somehow, they seem increasingly ill suited to our needs. Following Menzies' groundbreaking work, a core contribution of the Tavistock tradition has been understanding how institutions contain anxiety, and through the roles they provide, offer meaning by connecting people to larger social purposes. Disruptive change erodes the containing structures which people rely upon to function in the Kleinian depressive position of concern and compassion.

Politics are progressively dominated by a breakdown of the national discourse. On the left is the religion of 'Wokism', sanctimonious, obsessed with political correctness, and absolutely certain about the answer to injustice. Its totalitarian impulses are revealed through cancel culture, it's version of the inquisition. On the (US) right, the relationship to political reality pushes people deeper into paranoid fantasies. The cult of victimhood convinces believers that sadistic desires are virtuous, further legitimising authoritarian inclinations. On both sides, the symbolism of virtuous superiority and the rhetoric of victimhood create a toxic polarisation resembling the final scene in *Oedipus Rex* where Oedipus and Tiresias, both blind and exiled, furiously rage – each seeing himself as the seer and the other as transgressor.

Turning towards the future presents equally daunting challenges, though one crucial difference is that the future contains fresh possibilities. I have no doubt that the new and exploding technologies – genetics, informatics, robotics and nanotechnologies, the internet – will offer tremendous gifts and provide vast opportunities for social and economic development. Utopian voices focus on the promises of quantum computing, hydrogen fuels, medical treatments at the molecular level, artificial intelligence and so many other dazzling developments. But as we are learning, they come with serious risks as well.

The dawn of the internet revolution also envisioned utopian possibilities. Democracy would become an irresistible force as social media made it impossible for autocrats to maintain control. Knowledge would be universally accessible, politics more objective and less polarised. Citizens would be better informed and more involved, making them less subject to manipulation.

Yet, the opposite has often proved true. Technology has made autocrats stronger, not weaker. It has increased the spread of disinformation and lies, which often drown out genuine information. Our devices and systems unsettle the subjective experience of being human. The virtual and real are enmeshed in ways that confuse our sense of context, proportion and experience of self.

Advanced technologies and globalisation have created dense interdependence and great complexity that, in turn, produce problems that industrial-type thinking cannot address. Trist and his colleagues were prescient in recognising that the kinds of problems we are facing today required new approaches and mind-sets. Today's complexity is beyond our conventional approaches to understanding. In Einstein's terms, one cannot solve problems with the same thinking that created them.

Problems have a different character now. They are deeply embedded in the complex interactions of multiple forces. These are problems for which there is no solution and can only be addressed at the level of the field or domain, not by independent organisation or even sovereign nations. We need other people and groups to confront our difficulties. Many of our challenges will require the skills to manage loosely coupled networks and discover how to enable nations and enterprises to collaborate rather than to compete, what Eric Trist termed 'New Directions of Hope'.

The political realities arising from our interdependence bring to mind Bion's observation that we are group animals because we can only meet our needs through others. Addressing our most challenging issues will require us to embrace our interdependence – something our survival may depend on understanding. In systems terms, it means recognising the essential unit of analysis is not the bounded individual, organisation or nation, but rather each of these elements in conjunction with their environments, together and inseparable.

Global interconnectedness exposes us to the unknown and large numbers of unfamiliar people. It subjects us to a frightening helplessness and confronts us with the recognition that our destiny is not in our own hands alone. It also confronts us with otherness in new and extreme ways, setting the stage for ever more toxic splitting.

The 'other' so often carries the terror, disgust and hatred stirred up by loss of the familiar and frightening confrontation with the new. Repudiating the unknown in order to preserve a sense of mastery leads to policies of dehumanisation and exclusion. That sense of certainty, achieved by excluding or dominating 'the other', undergirds totalitarianism and fundamentalism. Democracy implies a kind of relatedness to the other that is under great assault these days.

Technology has supercharged our hubristic, God-like drive to create and destroy without regard to the social contract, wellbeing or the physical environment. The Latin proverb *'Those who would be Gods will be destroyed on* the *Lathe of Heaven'* seems particularly apt. Our lathe is climate. The darker realities force us to recognise that human nature is not developing alongside technology. Rather, in many ways it empowers and accentuates our destructive and aggressive drives, overriding our reach for creativity.

Artificial intelligence supplants large swaths of human agency and has now developed to the point that algorithms can learn and adapt on their own. Its derivative of surveillance capitalism transforms us from being customers to being raw material, turning our experience into a commodity that is translated into data then used to predict and manipulate our behaviour. The sense of being governed by a class of experts who cannot be addressed or held accountable undoubtedly contributes to populist anger.

Psychodynamic thinking calls our attention to the unconscious sources of meaning, connectedness and identity. Systems thinking brings complexity and interdependence into sharp focus. Systems psychodynamics shows how both are indispensable for understanding social, organisational and community life. It leads us to embrace the importance of understanding unconscious dynamics as a moral choice – it is how we tolerate uncertainty, accept the other within and recognise that the 'other' is essential to our wellbeing.

System psychodynamics has so much to offer for understanding the impact of these dynamics and for informing strategies to address them. Newer forms of systems thinking accounting for a degree of complexity and uncertainty that was unimaginable for the founding generations hold great promise, as does the potential of psychoanalytic thinking to help us understand how unconscious forces shape and are uniquely shaped by today's fresh challenges.

Together, these perspectives provide an avenue for exploring what sorts of anxieties are stimulated in emerging social systems and how they are expressed in organisations, networks and eco-systems. What does containment mean in loosely bounded systems? What are the psychodynamics of complexity? How do we understand the psychic dimensions of our 'liquid society?' How do we discover the social defences that are baked into algorithms and that reside in the digisphere? What does our thinking contribute to understanding decentralised work and workplaces that are on the rise with freelancing, gig work and remote work?

Thinking and the capacity to occupy reflective spaces are, of course, the first casualties of regressive dynamics. Systems psychodynamics offers ways to mitigate this downward spiral by helping people reclaim their capacity to think amidst turbulent and unstable conditions. We desperately need to learn how to create spaces in which paradox, conflict and difference can be played with creatively and constructively. We know something about designing facilitating environments in which people can think, imagine, discuss and coalesce.

We can certainly contribute to the redesign of tools, models and approaches to fulfil basic human needs for belonging. These chapters point to ways that we might develop new approaches to restore the basic human need for meaningful connection in the face of loneliness, alienation and exclusion.

It is the legacy of the Tavistock tradition and the thinkers now carrying it forward, as this volume so aptly illustrates, that fuels my hope. Hope that systems psychodynamic thinking will remain relevant by adapting foundational ideas to emerging conditions. That it will find a way to strengthen peoples' sense of belonging and discover greater meaning in their roles. And that it will help organisations be effective while helping shape new, more humane, social systems that will support a generative transition to the Information world.

Introduction

David Lawlor and Mannie Sher

This series of books coincides with the centenary of the founding of the Tavistock 'Family' in 1920, which initially was the Tavistock Institute of Medical Psychology (which led to the establishment of the Tavistock Clinic, now known as the Tavistock and Portman NHS Trust), the parent body of the post-World War II Tavistock Institute of Human Relations. This series of books is creative testimony to the continuing intellectual contribution of the Tavistock Institute to improving human relations.

Volume 1, which is termed 'Dawn', introduces the reader to systems psychodynamics theory and its application for organisations and consultancy.

This volume explores the current state of knowledge about the practice and application of the systems psychodynamics paradigm, illustrated by several case studies, and an account of its historical and theoretical development. We describe the work of the main theorists who have developed the theory and practice and how these ideas have been advanced. The authors (Lawlor and Sher with contributing authors) show how systems psychodynamics methods and models are attempts to understand the nature of organisational life and at the same time demonstrate practical application insofar as the models have a built-in problem-solving approach. The authors demonstrate that the work of professionals associated with systems psychodynamics methods has a multidisciplinary, multitheoretical and holistic approach to organisational and social problems.

Volume 2, which we have termed 'Emergence', continues with our in-depth exploration of the application of the following sets of theories, also illustrated with many case studies and an exercise at the end of each chapter. The volume's authors and guest authors Eliat Aram, David Armstrong, Anne Benson, Mee-Yan Cheung-Judge, Camilla Child, Jonathan Gosling, Dione Hills, Olya Khaleelee, Susan Long and Anton Obholzer cover socio-technical systems and change (Chapter 2), socio-technical systems in the 21st century (Chapter 3), the application of action research (Chapter 4), evaluation of systems psychodynamics consultancy (Chapter 6), planning and conducting an organisational development evaluation (Chapter 7), varieties of action research (Chapter 8), working with large complex collaborative partnerships – whole systems (Chapter 9),

DOI: 10.4324/9781003368663-1

complexity theory (Chapter 10), the systems psychodynamics view of leadership (Chapter 11), social dreaming (Chapter 12), systems psychodynamics and the impact of digitalisation, AI and virtual working on the eco-system (Chapter 13), professional development for systems psychodynamics consultants (Chapter 14), and systems psychodynamics – developments and definitions (Chapter 15) and concludes with theoretical developments in the systems psychodynamics paradigm (Chapter 16).

In Volume 3, we present the work of prominent practitioners and clients who are implementing the systems psychodynamics paradigm and developing in their practice.

Throughout the series, the authors strenuously hold the view that the systems psychodynamics paradigm means taking a view of and working as far as possible with the total system and not just one part of it; nor does one theory or approach explain the complex nature of organisational systems, and domains. The systems psychodynamics paradigm eschews the idea of the individual consultant working alone heroically to effect change. The paradigm in effect changes the function of the organisational development consultant from a leader of change processes to a provider of containment, understanding and facilitation of others to take up their leadership roles responsibly in their change processes.

The multidisciplinary and multitheoretical nature of *systems psychodynamics* makes for a complex and sophisticated set of theories and interventions available for a consultant to draw upon. The model is a complex interweaving of different theories that are brought to bear when a consultant is working with a client system. Using the different concepts that make up the model can lead to discussions on the application of psychoanalytic theory and the appropriateness of open systems thinking for organisational theorising. But this would be dissembling the parts that make up the totality of the model. *Systems psychodynamics* could be thought of as akin to a menu that attempts to achieve balance and equilibrium in its constituent parts. By examining only one part of the menu and losing sight of the whole ends up with an incomplete picture of the whole system, or in this case, the *systems psychodynamics* model.

'Emergence'

David Lawlor and Mannie Sher

As we said in our first book, *DAWN* (Lawlor and Sher, 2021), systems psychodynamics, both theory and practice, is an evolving field within the social sciences and consultancy practice. We introduced the reader to some of the key theories and practices that make up the model. A significant aspect of the systems psychodynamics model is the combining of systems concepts and psychoanalytic concepts.

In this volume, 'EMERGENCE', we want to suggest that systems psychodynamics is an emergent set of theories and practices that can be situated within the *Theory of Emergence* (Goldstein, 1999), which is a term used in philosophy, art and science to describe how new properties and features are created as we put things together. Emergence describes a process whereby component parts interact to form synergies; these synergies then add value to the combined organisation, which gives rise to the emergence of a new macro-level of organisation that is a product of the synergies between the parts and not simply the properties of the parts themselves. Emergence involves the creation of something new that could not be expected from a description of the parts prior to its creation. We believe systems psychodynamics does involve the creation of a new way of understanding organisations and the task of organisational consultancy.

In philosophy, systems theory, science and art, emergence occurs when an entity is observed to have properties its parts do not have on their own, properties or behaviours, which emerge only when the parts interact in a wider whole. We believe that systems psychodynamics as a transdisciplinary and multidisciplinary discipline exhibits properties that its constituent parts do not have separately. The combination and integration of the theories and practices is a truly emerging entity. Systems psychodynamics can be situated within the broad field of organisational development.

Organisation development as a practice involves an ongoing, systematic process of implementing effective organisational change. Organisation development is both a field of applied science focused on understanding and managing organisational change and a field of scientific study and inquiry. It is interdisciplinary in nature and draws on sociology, psychology, particularly industrial and organisational psychology, and theories of motivation, learning and

DOI: 10.4324/9781003368663-2

personality. Although behavioural science has provided the basic foundation for the study and practice of organisation development, new and emerging fields of study have made their presence felt.

The perspective of experts in systems thinking, in organisational learning, in the structure of intuition in decision-making, and in coaching, to name a few, is not limited to the behavioural sciences, but covers a wider multidisciplinary and interdisciplinary approach to organisation development. Systems psychodynamics draws upon psychoanalysis, psychodynamics, social anthropology, complexity theory, action research, open systems theory, systems thinking, systems theory and socio-technical systems (STS), which in organisational development is an approach to complex organisational work design that recognises and studies the interaction between people in their different roles, tasks and sub-systems and the technologies of their workplaces. The term also refers to the interaction between society's complex infrastructures and human behaviour. In this sense, society itself and most of its substructures are complex socio-technical systems. Within these disciplines, there are a variety of methods and methodologies which add choice to how consultants may choose to intervene and work.

Emergent change processes

In the field of group facilitation and organisation development, there have been several new group processes that are designed to maximise emergence and self-organisation, by offering a minimal set of effective initial conditions. The forerunner of these was the Search Conference developed by Eric Trist and Fred Emery (1960) of the Tavistock Institute.

Over the ensuing years, many varieties of large group and self-organising methodologies have been developed. Examples of these processes are SEED-SCALE, (Taylor et al., 2012), appreciative inquiry (Barrett and Fry, 2005), Future Search (Weisbord, 1995), World Cafe (Steier et al. 2015) and open space technology (Harrison, 2008, and Holman, 2010).

How to understand emergent behaviour in the physical, biological and social sciences? The short answer is a new starting point: recognising that understanding emergent behaviour requires a focus on the emergent collective properties that characterise the system as a whole and a search for their origin. It means identifying emergent collective patterns and regularities through experiment or observation, and then devising models that embody collective organising concepts and principles that might explain them. These patterns, principles and models are the gateways to emergent behaviour observed in the system under study. Only through studying these gateways can we hope to grasp emergent behaviours on a grand, unifying scale. We believe that systems psychodynamics can be truly seen as an emergent and evolving paradigm.

Part I

Change

Chapter 1, *Vicissitudes of Change*, covers the development of organisational theory and change during the 1940s and 1950s at the Tavistock Institute of Human Relations (TIHR) that focused mainly on manufacturing industries. Eric Trist's and Ken Bamforth's work in the long-wall coal mining studies produced the theory of socio-technical systems and design (STSD) making the case for innovation and loose rather than tight management. Ken Rice's and Eric Miller's work with cotton weaving mills in Ahmedabad in India gave us the concepts of task systems and sentient systems, meaning that organisational systems of relationships are based on commitment and understanding of the task and feelings of loyalty, belonging, shared identity, all of which need understanding and management. Elliott Jaques' studies in the Glacier Metal Co identified *culture* as the key element in organisational life.

In the 1960s, Emery and Trist introduced the term 'turbulent fields' for organisations. Chapter 1 describes how these concepts influenced the next phase in the development of organisational theory at the Tavistock Institute, with Emery and Trist's attention to more complex, diverse structures, and rapid change and resistance, that required a different approach to studying organisations: an analysis of the component technical aspects and the working relationship structures – how internal coordination and control systems are created.

Chapter 1 addresses three interlocking and overlapping domains – system psychodynamics, group relations and organisational development theories with an emphasis on unconscious processes linked to the interpretation of overt behaviour. Systems theory defines organisations as relatively stable in a changing environment – 'stabilising the differences between their interior and exterior worlds'. But Tavistock Institute social scientists argued that successful change initiatives depend on participation of all players in the technical and social change process.

Chapter 1 includes a section on the huge and ongoing influence of Kurt Lewin on the work of the Tavistock Institute. Lewin was a humanitarian who believed that only by resolving social conflict and introducing democratic values could the human condition be improved. The chapter describes Lewin's ideas about planned change through learning to enable people to understand and restructure their perceptions of the world around them. Lewin's four elements

DOI: 10.4324/9781003368663-3

of planned change are described: field theory, group relations, action research and the 3-step model of change.

Chapter 1 introduces readers to the contribution of psychoanalytic theory, developmental psychology, family systems theory and cognition to organisational development work. These theories describe the irrational or latent processes underlying organisational dynamics and show how they can be surfaced, understood and addressed. The work of Isobel Menzies Lyth and Kets de Vries is shown to be particularly relevant to the work with organisations.

Chapter 2, *Socio-technical Systems and Change*, moves to a more detailed description of socio-technical systems and change with a contribution from the late Mee-Yan Cheung-Judge of the Oxford Business School on the future of organisational development and change. Socio-technical systems consider the impact of technology and how people in the social system make use of the technology. The characteristics of joint optimisation are described, as are autonomous work teams, job enrichment, job enlargement, job rotation, task analysis, and job design, with an example of the UK Track and Trace system for COVID-19. Sentient and task systems and inter-group relations are described, with an example from a global hi-tech giant. The concepts of social defence systems of splitting, denial and projective identification describe the obstacles to achieving sophisticated change, as well as ideas about the depressive position and its role in avoiding primitive type change.

Chapter 2 concludes with Kolb and Frohman's stage models of consultancy from a systems psychodynamics viewpoint, which includes discussions on entry and contracting, data gathering, data analysis (diagnosis), sense-making and hypothesis development, evaluating, and ending and transitioning. The chapter rounds off by stating that systems psychodynamics consultants need the capability to identify and clarify the nature of the task, to work with conscious and unconscious processes evoked by the task, and to work with the interplay between the task and sentient system.

Chapters 3 and 4, *Socio-technical Systems in the 21st Century*, bring us up to date with the latest developments in socio-technical systems theory. Interactions of linear cause-and-effect relationships are contrasted with contemporary non-linear, complex and unpredictable relationships. Bert Painter and Carolyn Ordowich describe the concept of human-computer interaction (HCI) and social informatics, and their bearing on ethical computer use. These chapters include the concept of the 'network society', which has replaced the antiquated metaphor of the organisation as machine. Network SoC, digitalisation, globalisation and technological developments have introduced changes in socio-technical systems theory towards the smart organisation. The chapters describe developments of socio-technical systems from factory and office environments to computing systems in systems of organisations. A case is presented of a global hi-tech company struggling to develop the sentient emotions of people in a highly technical environment and how easy it is for the balance to be tipped in favour of either technology or sentience. The chapters end on arguing for balance and ability to adapt and change, rather than just cope with it. The whole ecosystem needs to feel welcomed, included, valued and connected.

Chapter 1

The vicissitudes of change

David Lawlor and Mannie Sher

Change, the individual and work

The development of organisational theory and change from the late 1940s and early 1950s at the Tavistock Institute centred mainly on the manufacturing industries. Three early strands of work had a remarkable impact on the development of organisational theory:

1 Eric Trist, in collaboration with the ex-miner Ken Bamforth (1951), discovered what later came to be termed by Emery and Trist (1965, 1969) as *socio-technical systems (STS) design*. In the long-wall coal-mining studies, they noted that when faced with the need for innovation, loose rather than tight management was required. Ken Rice (1958, 2001) introduced the STS design characteristics into cotton weaving mills in Ahmedabad in India. This had an immediate impact on the weaving mills, and in association with Eric Miller (1967), further understanding was generated of organisations as *task systems and sentient systems*; that is, the mills were made of systems of relationships based on feelings of loyalty, belonging, and shared identity, all needing understanding and managing.

2 Elliott Jaques (1951), in studies in the Glacier Metal Company, identified *culture* as a key element in organisational life.

   These two approaches found ready audiences among social scientists working in organisational development and change. The post-war period provided fertile soil for these developments in industrial sociology and industrial psychology in the USA and in the UK. In the USA, Davis (1993, p. 303) at the University of California, Los Angeles (UCLA) was an important collaborator. In Europe, and particularly in Scandinavia, willing collaborators emerged, including the Works Research Institute in Norway. Einar Thorsrud (1977) applied these findings in other Scandinavian countries.

3 A third approach developed by Emery and Trist (1965) considered the organisation in its environment, which included the notion of the *turbulent environment*. This concept had broad resonance and is used today in organisational studies, for example, where ideas of complex systems and emergent structures are studied and drawn upon. The spread of these new ideas

DOI: 10.4324/9781003368663-4

generated further applications, often involving the active participation of a wide range of stakeholders in planning their organisational structures, their environments and futures. Emery and Trist (1965, p. 21) state, 'A main problem in the study of organisational change is that the environmental contexts in which organisations exist are themselves changing at an increasing rate and towards increasing complexity'.

The Tavistock Institute attempted to categorise organisations into three types, which had distinctive patterns and may be described as follows:

Type A: Centres of basic research associated with major teaching facilities, located within universities as autonomous departments undertaking both undergraduate and graduate teaching. Here, research problems are determined by the needs of theory and method and express a research/teaching mix.

Type B: Centres of professional social science activity that undertake work on immediate practical problems, located within user organisations or in external consulting groups. User organisations require a means of identifying areas of social science knowledge relevant to their interests and need social science professionals in continuous contact with administrators. In such centres, research problems are determined by client needs. They express a research/service mix.

Type C: Centres of applied research associated with advanced research training. They may be regarded as a resultant of Types A and B and supply the necessary link between them. They may be located either on the boundaries of universities or outside them as independent institutes. They are problem-centred and interdisciplinary but focus on generic rather than specific problems. They accept professional and scientific responsibility for the projects they undertake and contribute both to the improvement of practice and to theoretical development. Their work expresses a research/action mix.

These three types of institution form an interdependent system. One type cannot be fully effective without the others since the feedback of each into the others is critical for the balanced development of the whole. The boundaries of A and B can easily extend into C, and those of C into either A or B. For a detailed description of the types, see: http://www.moderntimesworkplace.com/archives/ericsess/tavis3/tavis3.html

The world of work and change

The world of work is changing. It is more complex, more diverse, changes are inconceivably more rapid and with more unevenness among parts, a source both of innovation (e.g. Emery and Trist's idea of the 'leading part') and of resistance.

Emery and Trist (1965) state that the first function of a socio-technical systems concept is as a frame of reference – a general way of ordering the facts. It directs attention to the following groups of problems as the focus of the main stages in the analysis of the enterprise – (i) the analysis of the component parts to reveal the way each contributes to the performance of the enterprise and (ii) creates or meets the requirements of other parts. The components to analyse are as follows:

1 The technical – an analysis of the ways raw materials and technical systems inter-relate to produce products or services
2 The 'work relationship structure' and its occupational roles – an analysis of the inter-relation of these parts with particular reference to the problems of internal coordination and control thus created, the detection and analysis of the relevant external environment of the enterprise and the way the enterprise manages its relation to it

The same frame of reference may be applied to the study of parts of an enterprise. For primary work groups, the relevant environment is provided by the enterprise itself, since it defines the ends of these groups, controls the input of people and materials and constantly influences group performance. Analysis of parts of an enterprise also involves attention to details usually disregarded in an analysis of the enterprise as a whole. To analyse structure, 'no more is required than the whole from which the analysis starts and two levels of analysis' – the roles and the interpersonal actions (Feibleman and Friend, 1945, p. 42). Both levels require decisions to be made – deciding overall objectives for the set of roles and deciding who should perform which roles at a given time. The analysis then would help to discover 'the leading part' that is pertinent to the change process and any resistance to it.

This current structural analysis should happen hand in hand with well-documented changes to work roles and the dynamics of organisational life in which politics, global relationships and speed of transactions are all proliferating – with a generational inversion in which the old are challenged to understand and adapt to the young.

The dynamics of change need to be applied to the ecological context: What are the boundaries of the system? What, if anything, aligns interests? How are differences worked through, if at all? How is authority negotiated? Is it taken, imposed or exercised within a shared legitimate structure?

Among the features of emerging and changing patterns of work in organisations that require new ways of thinking, including unconscious processes and social defences, are:

1 The diminished role of small groups and of stable, clearly bounded social entities
2 Networks, rather than group and inter-group relations, as increasingly forming the basis for connection

3 Negotiated, rather than delegated, authority
4 Horizontal rather than vertical sources of authorisation
5 A pervasive reliance on computer-mediated relationships (Harrison et al., 2011)

Krantz (2010) suggests that new information technologies in the world of work function as social defences when they enable the speed of work to undermine organisational capacity for reflective thought. Our intellectual traditions emphasise the importance of reflection and the creation of reflective space, as a critical path to Kleinian 'depressive position functioning', which regards teamwork, partnership and cooperation as optimal levels of functioning. Extreme speed closes off reflection or careful analysis. As the UK financial crisis in 2008 suggested, speed may interfere with forming moral judgements and help shield people from awareness of the consequences of their actions.

Domains of work and change

According to Trist (1983), the unbounded nature of work groups and the complex patterns of interconnection forming the networks, which are becoming the backbone of new organisations, create conditions whereby social defences arise less from organisational practices and more at the domain level. Inter-organisational domains are concerned with field-related organisational populations. An organisational population becomes field-related when it engages with a set of problems, or a societal problem area, which constitutes a domain of common concern for its members. Inter-organisational domains are functional social systems that occupy a position in social space between the society as a whole and the single organisation. In one perspective, a society may be said to construe itself in terms of domains, which tend to actualise themselves in concrete settings. The financial crisis illustrates this point since the social defence system existed at the level of the domain system rather than arising from any single organisation. It is a truism to say that domain change is inevitable and continuous in our contemporary world and in its institutions and organisations. Change management and organisational change are central to organisational development theory (Burke et al., 2008).

System psychodynamics, group relations and organisational development, according to Burke (2017), have some similarities, but there are differences. They rely on open systems theory and their value systems overlap, such as human relations, resolving intra-personal and inter-personal conflicts, group dynamics and working at change to improve social and organisational systems. But the differences are that systems psychodynamics and group relations *emphasise unconscious processes linked to the interpretation of overt behaviour.* The focus is on the underlying dynamics that are under the surface in the interactions between individuals and groups, whereas organisational development practitioners tend to focus on the *overt behaviours*, taking at face value what people say and do. Burke compares the two foci in at least four dimensions:

1 Theoretical focus – Bion for group relations and Lewin for organisational development
2 Diagnostic focus – the group unconscious for group relations; norms and values for organisational development
3 The 'invisible leader' – Mary Parker Follett's (1998) notion that the 'leader' to be followed is the *purpose*, which is consistent with organisational development, whereas for group relations, the 'leader' is the *task*.
4 Primary concern is authority and authorisation for group relations; power and politics for organisational development.

Within the systems psychodynamics model, change too is a central preoccupation. Systems theory works with the concept of homeostasis and defines organisational entities, which are relatively stable in a changing environment. 'Organisations are entities that maintain themselves in complex and changing environments by stabilising the differences between their interior and external worlds' (Luhmann, 1984, p. 143). Organisations change and the interesting question is how and why they change. Pusic (1999, p. 81) states that:

> *change is the outcome of differentiating organisational structure or of a change in its internal integrating framework. It is caused by forces in the environment. An emphasis on internally caused processes of change will assign greater weight to the interests of internal participants, members of the organisation in any capacity. Seeing change as primarily caused by external forces leads to paying more attention to external participants- suppliers, customers, consumers, users, etc., and their evolving interests.*

Emery and Purser (1996) argue that successful change initiatives depend on some form of participation by those subject to the change. Systems psychodynamics consultants, researchers and social scientists associated with the Tavistock Institute have long been interested in how to help individuals and organisations work and manage change. They have shown interest in both the technical *and* social aspects of systems. The original work stemmed from two action research projects – one with an engineering company and the other with the mining industry. The first project was a comprehensive application of the socio-clinical and socio-therapeutic ideas concerning groups that were being developed at the Tavistock (Jaques, 1951). Trist (1981) describes the second project, which included the technical *and* the social system in the factors to be considered. Trist argued that this constituted a new field of inquiry that led to the development of socio-technical systems concepts. The aspect that both projects had in common was the notion of participation. In the Glacier Metal Company, Wilfred Brown, the Managing Director, engaged Elliott Jaques, a psychoanalytically oriented consultant from the Tavistock Institute, to introduce a participative, humanistic type of organisation.

The work of Kurt Lewin

Kurt Lewin (1939, 1943–1944, 1943a, 1943b, 1946, 1947a, 1947b, 1951) had a strong influence on the work of the Tavistock Institute. Neumann (2004) has drawn out both the history and the impact of Lewinian ideas and practice in her paper; *Kurt Lewin at the Tavistock Institute*. She shows that Lewin, although often unacknowledged, had a strong impact on the culture and work practices, especially Tavistock's adherence to action research as a method both for research and for consultancy.

Burnes (2004a, 2004b, 2000c, 2012) states that Lewin was a humanitarian who believed that only by resolving social conflict, whether it be religious, racial, marital or industrial, could the human condition be improved (Marrow, 1969; Lewin, 1992; Tobach, 1994; Cooke, 1999). He believed that only the permeation of democratic values into all facets of society could prevent the worst extremes of social conflict that he had seen in his lifetime (Lewin, 1943b). Lewin believed that the key to resolving social conflict was to facilitate planned change through learning, and so enable individuals to understand and restructure their perceptions of the world around them. A unifying theme of much of his work is the view that '... the group to which an individual belongs is the ground for his perceptions, his feelings and his actions' (Allport, 1948, p. vii). As Burnes (2004b) has shown, Lewin's planned approach to change comprised four elements: field theory, group dynamics, action research and the 3-step model of change. Though these tend, now, to be treated as separate elements of his work (Back, 1992; Gold, 1992; Hendry, 1996; Wheelan et al., 1990), Lewin saw them as a unified whole with all of them necessary to bring about planned change (Allport, 1948; Bargal and Bar, 1992; Kippenberger, 1998a, 1998b; Smith, 2001; Neumann, 2005). Neumann (2004) sums up Lewin's field theory:

> as applying 'field theory' for organisational change and consulting requires an acceptance of its central premise. People and their surroundings and conditions depend closely on each other. In Lewin's words, 'to understand or to predict behaviour, the person and his environment must be considered as one constellation of interdependent factors' (1946:338). Thus, the notion of 'field' refers to: (a) all aspects of individuals in relationship with their surroundings and conditions; (b) that apparently influence the behaviours and developments of concern; (c) at a particular point in time.

Hall and Lindzey (1978, p. 386) summarise the central features of Kurt Lewin's field theory as follows:

1   Behaviour is a function of the field that exists at the time the behaviour occurs. Analysis begins with the situation as a whole, from which the component parts are differentiated, and

2 The concrete person in a concrete situation can be represented mathematically.

Kurt Lewin's (1890–1947) work had a profound impact on social psychology and, more particularly for systems psychodynamics, on our appreciation of experiential learning, group dynamics and action research.

The clinical orientation and change

Balas and Kets de Vries (1997a, 1997b; 1999a, 1999b) describe how concepts from psychoanalytic theory, developmental psychology, neurology, family systems theory and cognition provide a clinical orientation to organisational development work. They describe the irrational or latent processes underlying organisational dynamics and show how they can be surfaced, understood and addressed. This is opposed to the traditional approaches of organisational development that tend to focus on observable behaviours and processes. They make the case that the identification of cognitive and affective distortions in an organisation's leaders and followers can help recognise and acknowledge the extent to which unconscious fantasies and out-of-awareness behaviour affect decision-making and management practices in an organisation. They cite psychoanalysts such as Melanie Klein (1948), Wilfred Bion (1959) and Donald Winnicott (1975) who first applied Freud's theories to the workplace. The ideas of these psychoanalysts have been further explored by clinically informed scholars of organisations (Baum, 1987; Czander, 1993; Diamond, 1993; Gabriel, 1999; Hirschhorn, 1988; Jaques, 1951; Kernberg, 1998; Kets de Vries 1984, 1991, 2000, 2004, 2006; Balas and Kets de Vriess, 1999; Kets de Vries and Schein, 2000; Levinson, 1972, 1982; Maccoby, 1976; Obholzer and Roberts, 1994; Schwartz, 1990; Zaleznik, 1966; Zaleznik and Kets de Vries, 1975). The insights of these authors give a rich and deep meaning to the life of organisations. Manfred Kets de Vries and Katherine Balas (1997, 1998, 1999) describe how organisational consultancy informed by a clinical orientation takes place. They state that the original stated problem is often not the real problem but only a signifier of other, deeper problems – often covering up something more complex.

Menzies Lyth (1990, p. 361) enunciates this dynamic process within institutions that consultants will meet in their work with organisations. She writes of the ways in which the presenting symptoms in an assignment may appear discrepant with the emotional charge that accompanies them, and which has led the organisation to seek consultancy in the first place:

> *I think what may be happening is something like this. There is within the job situation a focus of deep anxiety and distress. Associated with this there is despair about being able to improve matters. The defensive system collusively set up against these feelings consists, first, in fragmentation of the core problem so that it no longer exists in an integrated and recognisable form consciously and openly among those*

concerned. Secondly, the fragments are projected onto bits of the ambience of the job situation, which are then consciously and honestly, but mistakenly, experienced as the problem about which something needs to be done, usually by someone else. Responsibility has also been fragmented and projected often into unknown others, 'Them', the authorities. One meets this same process frequently in psychoanalysis when a patient feels himself to be up against an intractable problem and believes he cannot manage the feelings associated with it. Such defensive reactions to institutional problems often mean the institution cannot really learn. The solutions tried before had failed, but they will work this time – as though there is a kind of magic about them. Effective resolution can only come when the institution, with or without the help of a consultant, can address itself to the heart of the matter and not only to its ambience, and introduce relevant changes there.

The clinical paradigm

The clinical paradigm as outlined by Kets De Vries (2016) is the framework through which a psychodynamic lens is applied to the study of behaviour in organisations. Kets De Vries proposes that by making sense out of leaders' deeper wishes and fantasies and showing how these fantasies influence behaviour in the organisational world, this paradigm offers a practical way of discovering how leaders and organisations really function (Kets de Vries and Miller, 1984).

The clinical paradigm consists of four basic premises:

1   There is a rationale behind every human act, a logical explanation, even for actions that seem irrational. All behaviour has an explanation. The explanation may be elusive, inextricably interwoven with unconscious needs and desires.
2   A great deal of mental life, feelings, fears and motives lies outside of conscious awareness, but still affects conscious reality and even physical well-being. We all have blind spots.
3   The third premise states that nothing is more central to whom a person is than the way he or she regulates and expresses emotions.
4   The fourth premise is that human development is an inter- and intrapersonal process. Our past experiences, and those experiences, including the developmental experiences provided by our early caregivers, continue to influence us throughout life (Emde, 1980; Erikson, 1950; Kagan, 1994; Kohlberg, 1981; Oglensky, 1995; Piaget, 1952; Pine, 1985).

Balas and Kets de Vriess (1999) suggest that the task of the systems psychodynamics consultant or, as they characterise the role, the 'clinically oriented consultant', is to go beyond pointing out the salient issues and collusive processes that may be in play. The issues must be made more explicit, and this may mean a confrontation. The source of the data for the consultant is the experience that the consultant has of the organisation. This shows itself in the way the organisational members interact with them. This is specifically the skill in paying attention to transferential experiences, that is client feelings that are transferred from earlier relationships onto the persons of leaders and consultants; and countertransferential expressions, that is feelings evoked in consultants and leaders in response to the context they are in. Balas and Kets de Vries s(1999) cite Etchegoyen, (1991), Greenson, (1967), Malan (1972) and Malan and Osimo (1992) who emphasise these experiences as diagnostic tools:

> *The ever-present triangle of relationships – in these situations, the person, the significant past, the person, the significant 'other', and the consultant – provides a conceptual structure for assessing patterns of response, enabling them to point out the similarity of past relationships to what is happening in the present. Anyone hoping to make sense of interpersonal encounters on anything but a superficial level needs to understand these transferential processes that are part of the consultant's intervention toolbox.*
>
> *Furthermore, as in any form of organisational consultation, multiple resistances are at play. After making a list of the primary symptoms and problems, the consultant needs to move on to what we call resistance interpretations, pointing out the varipus defence mechanisms (social and individual) used by power holders to prevent unpleasant insights from coming to the fore. The consultant works backwards from there, going behind symptoms and defences to offer conjectures and interpretations about the roots of any dysfunctional processes that come to light'.*
>
> (Kets de Vries and Balass, p. 98)

All this requires the consultant to have time to reflect on what is emerging and not be pushed or feel under pressure to come up with a quick fix. In this model of psychoanalytically oriented consultation, Kets de Vries and Balas suggest that there is little difference between the diagnostic and intervention stages. Interpretations that are offered are usually put as working hypothesis to be tested. The work on the hypothesis can give further diagnostic material and deepen the consultant's understanding of the problems in the system. As Levinson says, the mere fact of data gathering implies that the intervention has begun (Levinson, 1972).

Therefore, the working relationship between roles is central to understanding how well or how poorly an organisation is functioning. Additionally, roles carrying authority and decision-making powers at fulfilling the primary task contribute to understanding an organisation's effectiveness. In a well-functioning organisation, there will be a capacity among staff and managers to think about the emotional impact and significance of the work undertaken with respect to the primary task. Individuals in role make use, in a psychological sense, of other individuals within the organisation as repositories for anxiety, criticism, blame or denigration or other unwanted feelings. Emotional experience is understood as an expression of the relatedness between individual, group and organisation. This organisational experience, frequently referred to as *culture*, can be ascertained by the 'accepted' way that work is done.

Transitions, change and resistance

A system going through an important change process – a transition – becomes under-bounded as the boundaries shift and change. There is simply no other way for change to take place. During change, people become nervous, unsettled and resistant. Comfortable dependencies are upset. People may become angry, stressed out and ill. Thinking of others and loyalty can give way to short-term thinking and selfishness. In theoretical terms, what is happening is that the boundaries have become threatened and there is risk to the established identities, rewards and roles of the people in the system. There are high ambiguity, unclear goals, more stress, more inter-group conflict and less information, performance results are at risk, and there is less control. Not surprisingly, these are not happy circumstances. This all becomes more intense if there is no one really managing the change. The systems psychodynamics model recognises the legitimacy of the strong feelings of everyone associated with change in the enterprise.

Vince and Broussine (1996) argue that both emotional and political forces are occurring together in organisations (Vince and Martin, 1993) and that such forces are particularly relevant in relation to the possibilities for and defences against change. Their intention is to add to the different ways of looking at and working with change in organisations. They suggest a set of working propositions that move away from problem-solving or planning-based approaches to change, towards a method that focuses primarily on organisational members' emotions and relations, and on forces of uncertainty and defensiveness. They highlight the dynamic nature of change, and point towards some key issues, often avoided, for engaging with aspects of change. The boundary is an essential element in individual, group or organisational identity. It not only provides a sense of being an entity, but also contains the sense-making processes that continually shape and redefine, in practice, the individual, group or organisation. This relatedness is seen as central to organisational change. Vince and Broussine (1996) state the following:

> There are many models of change in organizations that are based on the idea that change is a problem to be solved through appropriate diagnosis, often of forces of 'resistance', followed by appropriate readjustment or strategy. This usually involves a given number of 'steps', for example, in the literature of resistance to change: 10 critical factors' (Matejka and Ramona 1993), '8 basic patterns' (Conner 1993), '4 distinct stages' (Reynolds 1994), '10 key principles' (Kyle 1993) and '5 common causes' (O'Connor 1993), these being just the recent

additions. Such perspectives on change in organizations are based on the idea that change is primarily a strategic issue, shaped by internal politics and individual interests (Kotter and Schlesinger 1979). Change can be planned for and resistance dealt with through a variety of possible strategies on a continuum (in Kotter and Schlesinger's model ranging from communication to coercion) and the underlying assumption of these approaches is that there will be an appropriate strategy to fit an identified problem of change.

The difficulty with problem-based models of change is that they overemphasize the rational and consequently do not take into account the complexity, ambiguity and paradox acknowledged to be an integral part of organization.

(Dawson, 1992; Johnson, 1987; Morgan, 1986)

Vince and Broussine (1996) from their research with managers suggest the following four-staged process, which can be described as follows:

1 **Working with complexity and uncertainty in the change process**: Their approach encouraged managers to stay with the uncertainty long enough not to automatically deny or avoid the feelings associated with it.
2 **Reviewing the boundary**: It struck them that managers perceived the boundaries between different groupings within an organisation as clearer and more separate than they actually are. It seemed to be important to encourage managers to reflect on the issues that exist on the boundary between organisational groups.
3 **Relatedness**: Once managers had become aware of an emotional level of interaction existing underneath their everyday perspective on inter-personal behaviour, they were able to assess the extent to which feelings about change were based on defensive reactions or actual differences.
4 **Working through**: The realisation of underlying emotions or processes between groups did not seek to deny or shift managers away from their true feelings about the change process – that is, the process did not set out to conjure up, for example, optimism where there was none.

Obholzer (2021) suggests that with change, we enter an area of uncertainty; a new, different and not previously managed uncomfortableness. He then shows how resistance as a defence mechanism is mobilised by individuals and groups. The nature of change means having to cope with the experience of confusion, of giving up the certainty, or, more accurately, the pseudo-certainty of the past. It means unlearning; giving up ideas of the past and taking on board new ideas about which we are unsure. Obholzer (2021) observes that when struggling with the issue of having to accommodate to new facts or different ways of seeing things, it is not unusual for the individual, or for that matter the institution, to seek out other 'like-minded individuals and to use them to bolster our defences against change'. He argues that individuals and groups who are faced with change unconsciously form collusive groups to resist the change. Through the process of projection, the 'other' is seen as the enemy who must be resisted.

> *The enemy also serves the useful function of being a dumping ground for all sorts of personal negative qualities. These are difficult to deal with within oneself, and, therefore, one prefers to see them in others instead... In a state of mind of self-idealization and of the denigration of others, there is a price to be paid: one loses touch with reality. It is, therefore, difficult to deal with any related issues and to update one's work functioning accordingly.*

(Obholzer, 2021, pp. 34–35)

Obholzer (2021) then proposes the following as a way forward.

> *What is, therefore, required of all is the patience to sit down with each other and, on a regular basis, to observe other social, mental and work attitudes. Then, one can discuss how they might affect work workplace processes and routines. Instead, I suggest a process of providing a thoughtful space in which observation of the other and their way of working is open for discussion and evaluation. Arising from this process the hope is that some agreed way of proceeding is arrived at. The process is available for constant observation and open for modification as learning is applied….. this learning process is not without its problems, for it means that all concerned need to have a certain capacity to give up their cherished views on the way business should be done, and have an open mind for trying the unfamiliar…… Finding an accommodation using the above-described processes, means branching out for oneself, having one's own ideas, and abandoning, or at least modifying, the 'tablets of truth' handed down to us by our elders.*

A real life story

A Northern Health Trust sought consultancy on how to assist a group of cardiac surgeons, working across three hospitals, to implement a better level of cardiac surgery services in the Trust, and lessen the risk of decisions about their future being taken elsewhere.

The Health Trust had a well-developed range of cardiac surgery services and procedures, which were difficult to maintain in day-to-day operations due to internal conflict in the group of surgeons. Senior management regarded the available services as good but not working well in practice.

In our view, the reasons for this were complex and were discussed in our interviews from individual, inter-personal and systemic perspectives. We thought that problems surrounding the cardiac surgery service were linked to uncertainties about the function and nature of the discipline which was organised along Hub and Network lines. The Hub and Network relationships were ambiguous, and all attempts to resolve them were deflected by the conflicts in the surgeons' group.

Management's attempts to integrate cardiac services in the main and satellite hospitals were undermined by ineffective communication and decision-making by both the cardiac surgical consultants and the management, and a mutually antagonistic relationship between the consultants (riven with internal conflicts) and the Trust management (that was unnecessarily bureaucratic). The consequences were intense mutual blame and defensiveness – consultants blamed by management for not getting their act together; and management staff blamed by the consultants for ignoring their concerns about changes to the services. It appeared that the two groups 'used' each other to 'export' and 'import' wrong-doing and failure into the other. Both groups, under pressure, used all the means possible to protect themselves from feelings of helplessness and hopelessness by blaming the other.

The Tavistock Institute consulting team was asked to work with the cardiac surgeons to identify and process the different thoughts and feelings evoked by the situation with a view to developing ways of working better as a team. We met and talked to the surgeons and their colleagues across the wider cardiology network. Our joint work was intended to draw together what we were told and serve as a stimulus for discussion, not a definitive version of events.

Context

The surgeons spoke about there being difficulties in the team for some years. The difficulties arose from a complex interplay between individual and inter-personal dynamics and systemic issues. As well as complaints about behaviour, concerns around the formation and operationalisation of the cardiovascular network all evoked powerful thoughts and feelings. In listening to the cardiac surgeons and other colleagues, we heard about:

- A passion for and commitment to the work
- A high level of clinical competence
- A strong focus on the patient and providing an excellent quality service
- A general commitment and desire to make the network work and be the best that it could be, while recognising there was a way to go

Some acknowledgement and recognition of feelings

Clearly difficult inter-personal relations evoked powerful emotions, which at times felt paralysing and impossible to move beyond. Different people felt different things powerfully. However, hurt, anger, fury, frustration, despair, fear, anxiety, disbelief, outrage, concern and shock were all present. These emotions were also alive in relation to working relationships in the network generally.

Building Trust

We were told about a lack of trust in the cardiovascular teams across the Trust. There were different relationships, alliances and allegiances within the teams; some of which were open and known, others remaining rather shadowy. We got a sense of the teams rarely speaking openly and directly to each other about the actual problems they faced or the feelings they evoked, although many of the issues were known to everyone. This made relationships mysterious or opaque. The culture did not support mechanisms for getting or giving clear information, asking directly or holding to account. Mystery also had a rather absorbing and compelling seductive quality.

Developing the network

The surgical consultants knew the network was their future reality, not their individual hospital departments, but establishing the network and how it would work left them with many unresolved feelings. There were tensions between the main and satellite hospitals, a fear that the satellites would be deprived of resources and how the different working practices across the network would be affected. Each location felt that the other locations did not understand their context or concerns. The central general hospital was experienced as predatory, competing with other cities for prime position. Satellite sites feared being 'gobbled up' and losing something of themselves in the wake of this powerful tide. The interplay of these wider systemic issues left the cardiac surgical teams struggling to establish and maintain high-quality, effective, efficient and agreed working practices across the cardiovascular network.

The locus for the different struggles

The following were areas causing tension:

*   **Competition and status:** Who worked harder than whom; who was more in the right than whom; who earned more than whom. These related to job plans and PAs, as well as the different contractual arrangements across the network and the different working practices. The dynamics of status and competition were at play at every level.

- **Tensions between managers and clinicians:** Difficulties in the cardiovascular teams had been reported to managers years before; these were not addressed and left to drift. Managers in turn felt unable to fulfil their role due to the internal strife among the clinicians and what felt like consultants' refusal to support the managers in their roles. In our experience, systemic issues arise when two parties involved subvert each other's work and a state of frustration, apathy and helplessness ensues. These feelings characterised the culture, which developed between the managers and clinicians.
- **Leadership and followership:** Refusal by colleagues to authorise those in leadership roles and, in turn, affecting how they took up followership roles. In this atmosphere, none of the consultants wished to take on formal leadership roles.
- **Private practice:** Feelings around those who had and those who did not have a private practice; when, where and how private practice dovetailed with NHS commitments.

What others say about the team of cardiovascular consultants

As individuals, the consultants were liked and highly respected for their work. They were regarded as highly skilled, talented clinicians who focused on the needs of patients. Colleagues enjoyed working with them as individuals. There was appreciation for the support they provided, the expertise they shared and the developments they encouraged. However, as a team, people did not see the cardiovascular surgeons working well together. The group was regarded as strong, quirky and ruthlessly competitive with individuals whose behaviour in meetings, on many occasions being rude, divisive and inappropriate, made their non-consultant colleagues and the service's management fill with embarrassment, frustration and despair. They feared that the cardiovascular surgeon's behaviour would impact negatively on the service's quality and safety and hence on the service's future survival.

What we did

The consultant team

A series of meetings was held bringing the cardiovascular surgeons together with the purpose to (i) provide time and space for the team to come together to listen to and talk with each other about some of the difficulties they were facing; and (ii) for the team to work together around the concepts critical to effective team working such as leadership and followership, role, boundary, authority, unconscious group processes – projection, splitting and valency.

The wider cardiovascular network

Meetings were held with the senior leaders – CEOs, Medical Directors, Chief Operating Officers from the three hospitals to consider the challenges and think about the future direction of the network.

Coaching

Individual coaching was undertaken with members of the network.

Result

This piece of consultancy work and the deep discussions involved between members of the cardiovascular consultants, allied professionals and senior management led to agreement to develop and observe new work practices and rotas, and improved relationships with management and the Trust's leadership.

Summary

New information technologies function as social defences when they enable the speed of work to undermine organisational capacity for reflective thought. Extreme speed closes off reflection or careful analysis. Speed may interfere with forming moral judgements and help shield people from awareness of the consequences of their actions. The unbounded nature of work groups and the complex patterns of interconnection that form networks are the backbone of current organisations, creating conditions whereby social defences arise less from organisational practices and more at the domain or ecosystem level.

Inter-organisational domains are concerned with field-related organisational populations. An organisational population becomes field-related when it engages with a set of problems, or a societal problem area, which constitutes a domain of common concern for its members. Inter-organisational domains are functional social systems that occupy a position between society as a whole and the single organisation. The social defence system exists at the level of the domain system rather than arising from any single organisation.

System psychodynamics, group relations and organisational development rely on open systems theory. Their value systems overlap, such as human relations, resolving intra-personal and inter-personal conflicts, group dynamics and working at change to improve social and organisational systems.

Systems psychodynamics and group relations emphasise unconscious processes linked to the interpretation of overt behaviour.

Organisations are entities that maintain themselves in complex and changing environments by stabilising the differences between their interior and external worlds. Change is caused by forces in the environment. An emphasis on internally caused processes of change will assign greater weight to the interests of internal participants. Seeing change as primarily caused by external forces leads to attention on external participants – suppliers, customers, consumers, users, etc. – and their evolving interests. Successful change initiatives depend on participation by those subject to the change.

Exercise

1 Explain why an understanding of both *'task systems'* and *'sentient systems'* is important for the management of an enterprise and for consultancy practice.
2 What technical and ethical problems are likely to be encountered if the emphasis is given to only one of these elements?
3 What is the relation between the notion of the *'turbulent environment'* and the active participation of the widest possible range of stakeholders?
4 How do the *'rate of change'* and *'increasing complexity'* influence organisational function and leadership capability?
5 Comment on the apparent contradiction that change can be source of both *'innovation'* and *'resistance'*.

Chapter 2

Socio-technical systems and change

David Lawlor and Mannie Sher with Mee-Yan Cheung-Judge

Socio-technical systems

From socio-technical systems theory, we can see how change can be understood both from the impact of technology and from the social system required to make use of such technology. Therefore:

1 How organisations are designed impacts both their performance and the satisfaction of their members.
2 Changing the design of the technical system affects the social system and vice versa.
3 The most effective arrangements will be those that integrate the demands of both.
4 This dual concern with the social and technical system is known as *joint optimisation;* peak performance can only be achieved when the needs of both systems are met.
5 In organisational design (OD), *work design* is the application of socio-technical systems principles and techniques for the humanisation of work.
6 The aims of work design are:
   a   Improved job satisfaction
   b   Improved through-put
   c   Improved quality
   d   Reduced employee problems, for example grievances and absenteeism

Characteristics of joint optimisation

Below are some brief descriptions of what is considered through a socio-technical lens when looking at organisational design.

Joint optimisation entails commitment to self-managing work teams. Here, work groups take collective responsibility for performing a set of tasks and some self-management. There is more delegation of decision-making. Whole tasks mean that work is not broken up into many operations. The task is organised into a meaningful whole. Tasks are made whole by incorporating functions

DOI: 10.4324/9781003368663-5

that previously were performed by other services or units. There is greater flexibility in work assignments. This creates and aids more individual skill development. Mutual learning helps reinforce coordination and team-wide planning activities. The team determines how its members rotate through or learn a larger set of tasks.

Autonomous work teams: Autonomous work teams also called self-managed teams are an alternative to traditional assembly line methods. Rather than having a large number of employees each do a small operation to assemble a product, the employees are organised into small teams, each of which is responsible for assembling an entire product. These teams are self-managed and are independent of one another (Oldham and Hackman 2010).

Job enrichment: Job enrichment in organisational development, human resources management and organisational behaviour is the process of giving the employee a wider and higher level scope of responsibility with increased decision-making authority. This is the opposite of job enlargement, which simply would not involve greater authority. Instead, it will only have an increased number of duties (Steers and Porter 1991). Mumford (2006) with regard to the concept of minimal critical specifications states that workers should be told what to do but not how to do it. Deciding this should be left to their initiative. She says they can be involved in work groups, matrices and networks. The employee should receive clear objectives, but they decide how to achieve these objectives.

Job enlargement: Job enlargement means increasing the scope of a job through extending the range of job duties and responsibilities. This contradicts the principles of specialisation and the division of labour whereby work is divided into small units, each of which is performed repetitively by an individual worker. Some motivational theories suggest that the boredom and alienation caused by the division of labour can actually cause efficiency to fall.

Job rotation: Job rotation is an approach to management development, where an individual is moved through a schedule of assignments designed to give them the breadth of exposure to the entire operation. Job rotation is also practised to allow qualified employees to gain more insights into the processes of a company and to increase job satisfaction through job variation. The term job rotation can also mean the scheduled exchange of persons in offices, especially in public offices, prior to the end of incumbency or the legislative period.

Process improvement: Process improvement in organisational development is a series of actions taken to identify, analyse and improve existing processes within an organisation to meet new goals and objectives. These actions often follow a specific methodology or strategy to create successful results.

Task analysis: Task analysis is the analysis of how a task is accomplished, including a detailed description of both manual and mental activities, task and element durations, task frequency, task allocation, task complexity, environmental conditions, necessary clothing and equipment, and any other unique factors involved in or required for one or more people to perform a given task. This information can then be used for many purposes, such as personnel selection and training, tool or equipment design, procedure design (e.g. design of checklists or decision support systems) and automation.

Job design: Job design or work design in organisational development is the application of socio-technical systems principles and techniques to the humanisation of work, for example, through job enrichment. The aims of work design are improved job satisfaction, improved throughput, improved quality and reduced employee problems, for example grievances, absenteeism.

Sentient systems and task systems

As a task system, groups and organisations survive and adapt through interaction with their environments. The environment includes members of other groups and organisations. The task system must engage in inter-group relations if it is to continue to exist. The task system is made of two interlinked processes – the primary task and the sentient system. The sentient system refers to the needs of the individuals, feelings, beliefs, and stories and the practices in which they invest feelings. The strength of the sentient system may mean that members seek to preserve it from change. This may cause conflict between the activities of the task system, which demand openness to the environment and to other groups, and those of the sentient system, directed towards protecting itself from disruption and invasion.

Inter-group relations and change

Vertical inter-group relations exist between top management groups and subordinate departments in many organisations. As a task system, the senior management group requires information and advice from the main sub-systems to formulate policy and regulate the work. Similarly, the sub-systems require information from senior management to do their jobs and coordinate their activities with those of other sub-systems. In practice, interaction between different levels can be guarded and manipulative since each has the power to frustrate the objectives of the other, objectives in which the respective sentient group has invested a great deal, financially and emotionally. People in roles as heads of department who are members of one of the sub-systems and members of the senior management group are in the central position in relation to this dynamic.

Case example

Three years after the purchase of an American high-tech R&D company by a European manufacturing giant, there were difficulties in leadership, management and production of new essential technology. The technical experts said the new technology could be developed, but in practice, conflicts about ways of doing things led to delays and frustrations throughout the workforce, and for investors and customers. Complex machinery, sometimes involving different measurements in millimetres and other miniscule dimensions, led the boards of the two companies to dig their heels in, each one claiming that their approach, measurements and operations were better than the other's. Cultural and national differences were offered as explanations for the ongoing difficulties, for example adherence to metric versus British imperial systems of measurement. National pride and personality differences were offered as explanations as to why deadlines could not be met and technical breakthroughs could not be achieved.

When technical specialists from the two sides were brought together, the tone of their interactions was either overtly aggressive or passively sullen. Consultancy was offered over three days of off-site meetings, which included joint workshops based on action learning, face-to-face individual meetings, use of dreams (see Chapter 12) and careful arrangement of seating at mealtimes to promote easy socialising. It emerged that the people from the purchased company feared losing their sentient systems, losing their identity to the European giant and their specialist skills not being recognised. The meetings significantly reduced some of these fears.

The gathering of the two teams raised other threats too, viz. failure to develop the new technology and thereby losing their leadership of the market to their competitors, who were only two to three years behind in developing rival technologies. Among the technical experts of the two companies, three years seemed a reasonable lead time, until one of the team leaders told the gathering about a dream he had had the night before in which he is driving a car along an icy road; the car going into a slide on the ice, approaching an overhead bridge under which there was not enough room for the car to pass. The car slid under the bridge and had its top sliced off, crashing into a river and sinking. The dream, it was suggested, mirrored the company's dilemma of continuing as a single-product company in a volatile market or diversifying product development. But diversification was high risk, involving gambling huge amounts in new products, which would represent 'sliding away' from its main product, and possibly 'having its head sliced off' as lead in the market. The dream was thought of as a metaphor for the conflict in strategy – single product or diversification – and how positions in this conflict were taken up by different team members and by different groups. In the event, the workshop examined all options in small groups and in a full group. The result was that everyone renewed their commitment to continue the two companies' existing path of working together to develop the new technology, address the different stances of the European and American teams and devise better and improved integrated working arrangements.

Within two years, there was a breakthrough; the new technology had been perfected and installed in the product, resulting in strong commercial success and expansion of the companies.

Major change efforts, which often involve altering many facets of an organisation including structures, policies, procedures, technologies, role design and
cultural patterns, are increasingly common as organisations adapt to competitive pressures and accelerating rates of change in markets, technologies. While
turbulent operating environments may necessitate such changes, they are also
profoundly disruptive both to the organisations and to the people functioning
within them.

Pasmore (1994) argues that change, radical, unrelenting and ever-accelerating
change, is the dominant issue for organisations. He argues that what is needed
is a set of guidelines for designing, implementing and managing the fundamental changes that companies need to make. Using socio-technical design and
thinking, he shows how to help people become participants in change; how to
design and implement more flexible work systems; how to implement a more
flexible approach to the way technologies are managed; and how to apply bold
new nonlinear organisational models.

Krantz (2001) considers the interplay between the modes of functioning that
people adopt to cope with the experience of change and the way in which the
change efforts are designed and conducted. Systems psychodynamics researchers have illuminated the importance of anxiety and related defences to the functioning of both individuals and institutions.

Social defence system and change

The meaning of relatedness is changing in contemporary organisations. The
world of work is changing – more complex, more diverse, changes are inconceivably more rapid and, with more unevenness among parts, a source both of
innovation and of resistance.

Krantz (2010) argues that major organisational change efforts pose great
psychic challenges to their members and require, in response, distinctive conditions to adequately contain the profound anxieties evoked by such upheaval.
In the absence of these conditions, change efforts are likely to fail, in part
because members will tend to employ primitive and destructive defences to
protect themselves from the painful anxieties and fears that attend disruption
and turmoil.

An organisation's social defence system will support the capacity of its members to function effectively by helping them contain, and put into useful perspective, the more primitive fears and anxieties evoked through membership
and confrontation with complex tasks. Otherwise, people will rely on primitive
defences, like splitting and projection to protect themselves from the persecutory anxieties that result from change.

According to Krantz (2010), reverting to splitting, denial and projective
identification to cope with distressing anxiety leads to genuinely disturbing and
psychically threatening organisational environments. The source of unacceptable emotions, like vulnerability, competition and rivalry, sense of loss, may be

attributed to individuals or groups as a means of gaining relief. Where the qualities of thoughtfulness and collaborative competence give way to blame-ridden, rigid, concrete thinking, an escalating downward spiral of fragmentation and persecutory functioning can come to dominate and paralyse an organisation.

Effective change

Effective change requires sophisticated effort, diagnosis, conceptualisation, planning, implementation, etc. Yet, it is these features of organisational life that protect them from the intrusion of primitive processes – its social defence system – that are at the same time being dismantled. Just as Menzies Lyth (1990) has shown how an important source of resistance to change is the reluctance of members to give up features of organised life that help keep painful anxieties at bay, organisations undergoing major change can lose the capacity to contain primitive emotional states as social defence systems are dismantled. Consequently, efforts to implement change and to innovate confront organisations with a paradox; that is, change undermines features of organisational life that are meant to foster the very qualities of functioning required to make change succeed.

What are the qualities of change efforts that can help people function, despite heightened exposure to anxiety-producing factors? Thoughtfully developed approaches to change often include features that fill the 'social defence vacuum' and support members' efforts to protect themselves. Efforts to provide containment fall along a parallel continuum to that of ordinary social defences: some promote a more integrated, mature and sophisticated approach to coping with the emotional challenge, while others evoke more primitive responses that rely on splitting defences.

For example, Krantz (2010) lists among common elements of change efforts that can take on social defence functions:

1 Transition planning structures that are effectively authorised to manage the complex issues that arise during change.
2 Outplacement support helps moderate both the persecutory anxieties stimulated in relation to some people losing their jobs, as well as moderating the guilt of those continuing with the organisation.
3 Articulation of vision, purpose and goal. This can be done in a way that helps people take an integrated and realistic stance towards change and the future, or in a way that is not based on glib clichés and grandiose platitudes.
4 Communication strategies aimed at providing information.

Sophisticated change and the depressive position

Effecting significant change in organisations is, to be sure, a daunting challenge and one that requires skill and subtlety on several dimensions simultaneously.

Krantz (2010) categorises sophisticated features that are consistent with realistic, grounded, thoughtful functioning, including organisational change efforts, as follows:

1 Genuine investment in structures designed to 'contain' and address issues pertaining to the change effort
2 Realistic assessment of the time required to effect significant change
3 Appreciation of how much time people must devote to bringing change about and the impact of this redirection of energy on productivity
4 Respectful recognition of the anxiety evoked by major change efforts and recognition that certain segments of people may be significantly disadvantaged and hurt
5 Opportunities for people to acknowledge their complex feelings about such change efforts, including both the depressive and angry dimensions of losing the familiar
6 Toleration of learning from inevitable mistakes and a corresponding ability to make mid-course adjustments as a result
7 Articulation of a plausible and compelling picture of the future that is commonly shared and understood
8 Clarity about how the change effort represents continuity and discontinuity – how it is linked to the past
9 Carefully planned and thoughtfully executed, with an appreciation of the human and economic and technical factors that intermingle to produce successful outcomes

Characteristics of a primitive type change effort include:

1 Extreme expectations of change in unrealistically short time frames
2 Inconsistent leadership, often marked by changing, and often implausible, images of a sought-after future
3 Clever epithets and superficial ideologies are used to avoid struggle or sidestep the painful difficulties involved in change
4 Grandiose, self-idealising leadership that is susceptible to the magic elixirs and simple solutions that emerge from efforts to popularise and promote various change technologies
5 The great complexity of organisational reality and of change efforts get reduced to superficial nostrums or panaceas which, when recited like mantras, stop thought

The contribution of psychoanalysis to change

Halton (1994) states that an individual's personal unconscious plays only a subsidiary role in organisational functioning. The links between personal behaviour and organisational dynamics are the psychoanalytic concepts of projective identification and introjective identification. Freud (1921) used the concept of identification to explain the relationship between leaders and followers. Followers 'take in' the leader through identification, and the leader takes the place of their ego-ideal. Projection and projective identification are more fully taken up in organisational dynamics literature. Elliott Jaques (1951) clearly links the two processes and demonstrates how they operate in social and organisational relationships.

Introjection and introjective identification are complementary to the mechanism of projection and projective identification. Through introjection, the individual takes attributes of other people into themselves and the introjection becomes part of their personality. In introjective identification, the personality is made up of a whole configuration of internal objects which are composed of experiences and relationships and based on early development. According to the object relations school of psychoanalysis, and Kleinian theory, the emphasis is on the individual's relations with actual (external) and phantasised (internal) objects. The term *object* is used, rather than *person*, because the object is not always a person; it can be an organisation, a group, an idea or a symbol. These processes begin in infancy in relation to the infant's body and the mother's body.

The basis of integration, steadiness and inner security (Klein, 1957), is the consequence of 'the introjection of an object who loves and protects the self and is loved and protected by the self'. Bion (1967) developed Klein's theory, stressing the *function* of this introjected object, which is essentially to make feelings thinkable, understandable and therefore tolerable. He describes how it is necessary, for a healthy emotional development, to have the experience of a parental object (it is often the mother) who can receive a cluster of sensations, feelings and discomforts that the child cannot give a name to and is therefore unable to think about. In adult relationships, this steadiness is found at work through a mature management system.

Alpha function and change

Bion (1962a) introduces the terms: 'alpha function', 'alpha elements' and 'beta elements' to designate certain aspects of this process of integration and steadiness and inner security. *Alpha function* refers to the ability to *create meaning* out of raw, unprocessed sensory data, which he called 'beta elements'. The mother's 'reverie' is her alpha function and represents the ability to modify her child's tensions and anxieties. The mother and the child form a 'thinking couple', which is the prototype of the thinking process that continues developing throughout life. It is our contention that in organisational change, ideally, leaders, managers and supervisors provide alpha functioning; that is, they contain and process the distress that employees are subject to during change initiatives.

According to Bion, the alpha function works on the unprocessed beta elements and transforms them into alpha elements similar to a chemical transformation – indeed, Bion compares it to the digestive process, thinking being 'alimentary'. The 'beta elements' (which are fit only for projection and splitting) are so modified that they become absorbable and quite literally, *food for thought*. The alpha element represents the link between our innate preconceptions (intuitions) and raw experience of the external world. They form the building blocks of thought upon which more complex systems can be built. Therefore, leaders and managers receive the raw fear and catastrophic feelings, which are the consequence of change processes, which are the beta elements, acknowledging them, taking them in, digesting and processing them and feeding them back to the workforce in a more digestible and rational way. This is the management equivalent of the alpha function, which provides security and stability in the change process.

The function of 'alpha function' or 'reverie' (Bion, 1967) is keeping in mind, giving a meaning and making thinkable those feelings for the child or, in the case of organisations, the employee. After repeated experiences of this type of holding or containment, such a function can be internalised and gradually dealt with. Czander (1993) suggests that for organisational theorists, the most significant aspect of Kleinian theory is her conceptualisation of how one perceives. Klein (1959b) suggests that the external world is seen in terms of internal concerns, and one's experiences in the world reinforce some anxieties and diminish others. This suggests that organisations, as an external reality, will have a significant impact on the psychodynamics process of employees.

When working with change effort, the systems psychodynamics consultant uses interpretation to help the system become aware of these processes and how they are inhibiting the development of more mature and sophisticated working relationships.

Denial of the consequences and impact of change

Denial shows up as the absence of a structure to 'contain' change processes or artificial organisational change structures, such as project teams, change management teams. These structures are invariably not vested with genuine authority or meaning; they are paid 'lip service' by senior managers or consultants who conduct the change process in alternative, often a largely covert, fashion. As change is happening at an accelerated rate, staff are constantly required to understand the changes, cope with the challenges and ultimately adapt. The typical response is to resist change, for instance, cognitively, 'I think you have got it wrong'; emotionally, 'my gut tells me this is wrong'; and behaviourally, 'I'm not going to behave in the way you want me to'.

The reasons for resistance are: staff do not understand why changes are occurring, do not understand what they entail, do not know how they will be affected; skills may become obsolete and new ones required; organisational structures, systems, rewards and recognition do not fit with the change; and there is a culture of mistrust due to prior ineffective changes. Resistance can be brought about by fear regarding what the change may bring and the lack of control of the process of change.

Ways of thinking about reactions to change

Ending, losing and letting go

All organisational development involves change, and change, inevitably, involves loss. This can lead to defensive behaviour. The success of organisational change is directly related to the extent to which leaders and staff are aware of the link between perceived loss and their potential resistance to change. During this stage, people are dealing with letting go of the way things were before the change. People need to let go of what has been before. Emotional reactions often resemble the grief process (Kübler-Ross, 1969).

Working below the surface and above the surface

During change, systems psychodynamics practitioners have in mind two interlinked processes. They are often characterised as working below the surface and above the surface. Above the surface, phenomena are functional leadership, the rational system, the organisational structure, strategies, policies and procedures, operations, goals and commitments. Below the surface, phenomena are inter-personal and developmental leadership, culture (how things are done here), user or customer experience, the emotional impact on staff of the task, inter-personal, inter-group and intra-group tensions, hopes and aspirations, creativity and potential.

Future of organisation development and change

By Mee-Yan Cheung-Judge

In the 1990s, Peter Drucker published a series of articles for *Management Today*, which were compiled into a two-part book called ***Managing for the Future***. He predicted what organisations would face in the future and what leaders would need to do to survive.

Two decades later, his predictions were proved accurate: the world economy has changed with the rise and fall of economic integration through the European Union, the rise of the East, particularly China, and the emergence of a new international economic order supported by the rise of the knowledge society in which ICT and technology make a big difference to how organisations manage knowledge and run operations. He asserted that in times like these, innovation and entrepreneurship would make the difference between which organisations survived and thrived and which did not, and that effective leaders would need to engage in 'organised abandonment' and 'transformative learning' to make way for innovation.

Now in the mid-2020s, the seismic shock of the impact of COVID-19 pandemic on the whole of humanity has not only revealed the dark underbelly of societies, but also no one and nothing has been spared. The collective suffering at every level – individual, community, societal – is gut-wrenching. Paradigms, basic beliefs, and ways of being have all been challenged to the core. No wonder there is bewilderment about what 'recovery' will be like. For most organisations, there is a stark realisation that their organisation has been 'burnt to the ground' and the rebuilding process will need to start with asking who we are and what are we here to do; and who are the people we serve and how to change the way we engage with users and clients. There is a glimmer of hope. During the crisis, we have witnessed new patterns of behaviour being elicited with speed to navigate through the crisis, but there is uncertainty as how to leverage these new ways of working when changes are continuing. We ask what does a 'just in time' and yet also 'just in case' recovery pathway look like.

The three questions from Adaptive Action will guide our discussion: What? So what? (implications) and Now what?

What is happening in the world of work?

Here are some of the future work trends that all organisations will need to reckon with: (note 1)

- An increase in remote working – 50% of employees will likely remain working remotely post-pandemic (Google has said a majority of their employees can work from home during COVID; Twitter's CEO told employees that they will be allowed to work from home permanently, even after COVID-19). This will be accompanied by the expansion of data tracking employees' work output.
- Various surveys show that 30% of organisations will replace full-time employees with contingent workers as a cost-saving mechanism, as well as a contingent worker deployment strategy. The gig economy is on a rapid rise.
- Designing for efficiency is no longer sufficient: organisations need to know how to design for resilience and to ask what flexible structures will help them cope with further uncertainty.

- Past human resource management models need radical re-examination as virtual working will stay, and critical skills will become more important than roles. Rapid deployment of the right skills to form bubbles to extract rapid solutions will become not just a good thing to do, but a critical approach for survival. Talent data will be required to enable rapid redeployment.
- Organisations' old business models no longer work, at least not in the way they used to. The accepted model of supply chains has fallen apart during the crisis. Customers' anxiety requires careful management – but how can that be balanced with volume of trade and profit? 'Scale' and 'density' have now become liabilities. Not to mention the move towards a contact-free economy, the rise of digital commerce, telemedicine, automation, etc. All these cause anxiety among those who are leading recovery, as they know preserving legacy strategies and business models or maintaining the status quo will undo the viability of their organisations.
- Organisations also need to adapt to more public scrutiny, with greater regulations, not just because the public requires transparency and guarantee of safety, but also because of the financial interventions that governments have imposed on the commercial sector.
- For most employers, the crisis has shown that a 'new social contract' will be required, which will need to be more human-centred, honouring not just the contractual obligation but the social safety and wellbeing of their employees. This type of relational contract will require a rewiring of the relationships between the individual and organisation, and the organisation and society – which is much more than 'social responsibility'.
- Organisations need to work to balance their own advantage with those of the broader ecosystem; and shareholder values need to go beyond money, to a 'quadruple bottom line' – people, planet, profit and diversity/equity, which in turn affirms the tight interconnectedness between all things.
- A deep realisation that band-aid solutions will only prolong the pain.

So what? – Implications for OD and change

The above 'contextual WHAT' has major implications for the way change will be handled, which we briefly capture under two categories:

Workforce-related matters: Need Rethinking as how to…

1 Rethink manpower planning – calculating the need for what human resources in what type of circumstances.
2 Organise and coordinate distributed workforces.
3 Rethink performance and accountability in virtual circumstances.
4 Go from lines, solo to networks, informal groups, with on-the-spot accountability.
5 Build a strong sense of affiliation when people are not co-located.
6 Rethink how to support effective team working in temporary bubbles and in virtual and hybrid working.
7 Accelerate practices around collaboration, flexibility, inclusion and accountability and how to track whether they are happening or not.
8 What to provide, for example, smartphones, cloud-based collaboration tools to offer constant connectivity to encourage a connected way of working.
9 Address the equity issue of some having permanent contracts and some on temporary contracts or from the gig economy.
10 Develop the middle managers who need to help people feel supported, as well as being clear in tasks performance as required.
11 Work out how functions like HR, communication, supply chain, marketing and sales need to work together to support the value creation for the organisations.
12 Build conditions that will help to boost a sense of wellbeing among those who work in the organisation.
13 Embed diversity, equality, inclusion and equity into the organisation fabric as a way of being – infusing all that the organisation is doing as an HR policy.

Organisation practices: Need Rethinking as how to…

14 Learn how to lock in the transition to agility and other good practice which the company has achieved with speed during the pandemic.
15 Build and encourage a much faster, flatter, decision-making process to support agility with governance.
16 Embrace working with the whole ecosystem, conscious of how all the parts fit together.
17 Re-examine how hierarchy, power and politics work.
18 Help organisations to see environmental management not as a compliance issue, but a core management and financial issue – from making trade-offs to embedding sustainability.
19 Accelerate digital adoption to enable reimagination.
20 Support the strength of partnership between multiple agencies in terms of collaboration, for example government, public sector, state, national and local agencies.
21 Combine agility, innovation and speed to work out what the organisation has to offer.
22 Work with the workforce to decide what type of cultural mind-set, as well as behaviour patterns, that will support the organisation to survive the future.
23 Fertilising the ground for more cross-boundary ways of working with sufficient diversity and collective intelligence to create solutions for big problems.
24 Build integrative service-delivery models with commissioning organisations, suppliers and other third parties working together.

The above is neither an exhaustive nor a new listing of implications. Since the 1990s, a lot of the above has begun to happen though the speed of adoption is very slow. It is the pandemic and all its associated consequences that have forced many organisations to adapt in haste to survive (Cheung-Judge, 2017; note 2).

NOW WHAT?

No one knows what will be the 'right' shifts in our change approach, but the following conjectures may give us a steer as to what we may need to keep, adapt, rework and experiment.

- **Team intervention change work**: We will see the need for team intervention work to continue, but innovative team development work will need to emerge because (a) more individuals will belong to multiple temporary teams in the 'bubble' fashion doing agile projects; (b) intact teams will be interacting mainly in a remote or hybrid fashion.

    The critical thing is to hold on to the basic needs of individuals of wanting to belong, to contribute, to be seen, to have a voice and to be part of a bigger agenda. Any methodology that (a) acknowledges those needs; (b) allows multiple levels of work – for individuals, subgroups within the team and the whole team, supported by technology, will have a future.

- **Large group system change work**: As Weisbord (1987) said recently, with virtual technology, it may be easier for us to bring the whole system into the room. I predict large group methodology will still stand as an important change intervention. In seeking adaptation, some large group methodology may be more suitable for virtual working, for example the conference model. Ongoing experimentation has begun with global organisations experimenting how to manage large staff gatherings (with over 500 people) doing co-construction of the future of the organisation both in the same room and in small groups.

- **Large-scale transformation change work**: The large-scale transformation change work will continue as multinational corporations will continue to reconfigure the way they organise work at the global level. I predict there will continue to be a project management focus using the big consultancy firms as extra pairs of hands to support them as long as the financial resources are available.

    The amount of 'task'-focused work will continue to take centre stage: for example risk factor calculation, mitigation work, multitiered project planning system work, financial monitoring work, tracking value of different strands of change work. However, a progressive recognition is taking place among some corporations that without people-centric principles being built into their methodology, sustainable success during implementation of change will be compromised.

- **Change methodology will evolve towards being simpler and more accessible**: As changes continue to evolve, organisations will ask for simpler methodologies, and more accessible change tools which untrained local line leaders will be able to adapt for 'just in time' application in their local context. Glenda Eoyang's (2013) work is an example of such methodology.
- **Innovate on the 'C' methodology**: As systems are encouraged to be more self-sufficient in change, there will be a joint effort between us and clients to innovate along the C methodology: building Cross-functional interaction, becoming a more Connected workforce, enabling their own Co-construction and Co-creation of the future they want, making Cross-boundary work and Collaborative learning a norm. Clients may need more help to surface Collective intelligence within their own system, and to make growth strategy to become an occasion for Co-venturing, using Co-Creativity as a tool for innovation.

While we continue to adapt change approaches, we must also keep true to our core in the following areas:

- Teaching and upping the clients' understanding of some of the OD core theories to enable them to work out how to turn theories into intervention. The theories that are useful include systems theory, social constructionism, dialogue, social discourse, complexity and chaos, Lewin's 3 key theories, especially action research, economic behaviour. There are more applied behaviour science theories that will help to equip local change leaders to understand what and how to shift their systems.
- Working on the dual purpose of organisation development: so that all change efforts will aim to build a healthy organisation while increasing the effect performance of the system. Making change synonymous with development is always our goal.
- Passing on effective working group skills to members of the client system, as it is in groups that transformation work begins.
- Always showing the client the input-throughput-output dynamics (open system) so that the external focus will become the reference point for survival – and to show how the organisation needs to adapt themselves continuously to the changing needs of those whom they serve.
- Continuing to base our change work on Weisbord's concept about building community in the workplace, because when there is mutual support to harness energy, productivity will go beyond imagination through community. Regardless of which new way of 'organising', relationships remain the top work for all.

- Teaching our clients to know how to work in the dynamics of tensions and polarity management – often holding the polarity of keeping what is core to the business values and practices while acquiring something new and different to build on what we have, while discarding obsolete practices.
- We will uphold the core OD values in our change work, for example helping the system to reveal itself to itself (action research) – and to raise the client's ability to self-organise, encourage people in the system to be 'expert' in their own areas of concern, passing on skills and know-how to clients so that they will have sufficient ability to sustain their own change.
- We will need to continue to stretch our intervention repertoire by learning from other disciplines, for example IT, economic behaviour and network mapping – and working in partnership with colleagues from HR, LD, communication, etc. We will practice and teach the importance of the rapid learning and prototyping cycle, the action-reflect-revise-action and plan cycle, the emphasis on action, small experimentation and ongoing developmental evaluation.

Being Future Ready is an exciting and complex topic for both organisations and us, the practitioners. We are facing new scenarios, which we have never encountered before. However, we are confident that the field of OD is equipped to come alongside leaders to work things out as long as we remain faithful learners in the field of applied behavioural science.

Note:

Note 1: From work done by McKinsey, Deloitte, Gartner.com, the Institute of Leadership and Management, etc., published between March and July 2020
Note 2: 'Future of Organisations and Implications for OD Practitioners' in ODP Vol. 49 No. 1 2017

The reality of the consulting process and change

Reviewing the Kolb & Frohman stage model of consultancy from a systems psychodynamics consultancy viewpoint

The stage model of consultancy can give a somewhat unrealistic view of the process of entry into an organisational system. The working reality of most organisational consultancies is that they prove to be far messier and inchoate than the stages model would lead one to believe (Figures 2.1–2.4).

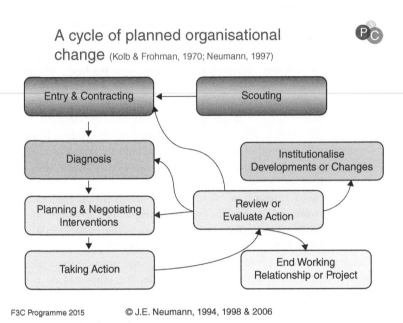

Figure 2.1 Cycle of Planned Organisational Change. © J.E. Neumann (1996, 1998, 2006). Reproduced with permission from the Tavistock Institute of Human Relations.

Figure 2.2 Reality of 'Planned' Change. Reproduced with permission from the Tavistock Institute of Human Relations.

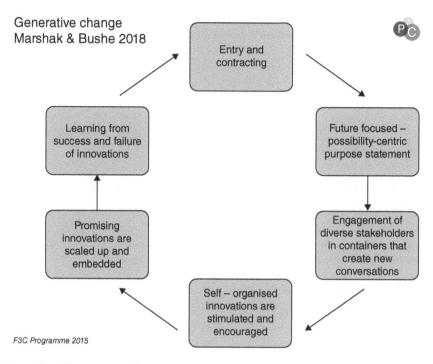

Figure 2.3 Generative Change (Marshak and Bushe, 2018). Reproduced with permission from the Tavistock Institute of Human Relations.

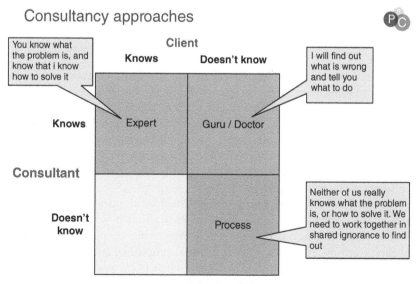

Figure 2.4 Consultancy Approaches. Reproduced with permission from the Tavistock Institute of Human Relations.

According to Pasmore (2015), failing at change is all too common. Change efforts fail 50-70% of the time. He states that most of the advice about leading change and the models we have is based on dealing with a single change effort or change initiative. But in reality, change is ongoing and simultaneous. A single change cannot be teased out or isolated from everything else in the organisation or divorced from other changes taking place at the same time. We are surrounded by turbulence. Change is multifaceted, complex and continuous. What seems to be a single change is anything but it is a complex change that competes for time, attention and resources with other changes that are already underway, and those changes yet to be conceived.

What makes complex, continuous change so hard?

Leading single change efforts can be challenging. Even seemingly simple changes can get out of hand, demanding more time, money and attention than predicted. Those challenges are magnified when leaders and organisations are faced with multiple, ongoing changes. Complex, continuous change always involves adjusting the approach and priorities as new information becomes available. While single changes can be 'rolled out', continuous change is always 'a work in progress'.

According to Pasmore (2015), there are four key actions to take, and each requires a specific mind-set. He offers a four-part model and four mind-sets that allow leaders to deal with multiple changes simultaneously without drowning in the turbulence.

The first step, Pasmore says, is to **discover**, which involves stepping back, scanning and visioning which external pressures for change are the most necessary to address. The key here is to pinpoint the highest impact options.

The second step is to **decide** how many change efforts the organisation can manage, which involves diagnosing, focusing and prioritising, scoping and designing.

He then describes the third step **doing**, which is communicating, engaging, piloting and implementing. In complex, continuous change, executing is always happening. Helping people understand what to pay attention to and why, at any given moment, requires constant communication. Tapping the collective intelligence of the organisation helps the overall change process be faster and more effective and requires engagement. Piloting using rapid prototyping saves enormous time and energy so that the careful work that leads to successful implementation can take place.

The fourth step is **discerning**, which involves aligning and integrating, assessing and adjusting. He suggests we must discern what is working as intended and what is not. Aligning and integrating change efforts requires real-time learning. Assessing what is being accomplished compared with what was expected requires reflection. Finally, the whole point of learning is to adjust actions going forward so that more can be accomplished with less.

Also, activities in the consulting practice may occur simultaneously, some are returned to at different points, while others are constant throughout. For example, when contracting, we want to understand the purpose of the consultancy, which will influence evaluation. We return to contracting when circumstances change, the work loses its way or difficulties arise. Data gathering is constant; we are always alert to our own feelings and responses and those of others as we work. These give us data about the system. Entry and contracting are valuable sources of data, how we are approached for the work, who we are invited to meet and what response our curiosity evokes. Review is also constant, in keeping with action research principles we work in repeated cycles of reflection, sense-making and action with the client.

As practitioners, we view everything as an intervention (Tschudy 2014). There are 'boxes' for intervention design and implementation in the diagrams above. These refer to specific interventions, for example Action Learning Sets, team coaching, open space events. However, we work with the principle that every action within a system is an intervention and will influence the system in some way (Checkland 1991). From our first contact with the client, we are intervening. The process and impact of these first contacts are influenced by what has gone before, what we know of the client and what they know of us, the assumptions we make and projections we exchange.

Scouting involves keeping alert to what is happening in the world, noticing and understanding trends, anticipating what may be over the horizon and knowing where you can access different resources. It involves relationship and networking skills alongside technical skills to keep abreast of and make use of advancing technology.

Entry and contracting involves:

1 Establishing our relationship with the client
2 Clarifying who is the main client
3 Understanding the client's objectives and motives
4 Agreeing objectives and overall scope for the consulting work
5 Agreeing any metrics to assess progress towards objectives or outcomes
6 Planning the broad sequence and duration of the work
7 Agreeing budget, logistics, frequency of contact and issues of confidentiality
8 Agreeing how the work will be communicated to others
9 Considering who might be in steering roles in relation to data gathering, sense-making and mutual planning of an intervention
10 Agreeing who and where you need access to and how you will get that access
11 Clarifying the roles of all involved

Data gathering

(Here is a link to the importance of diagnosis: https://www.youtube.com/watch?v=y-vn9CE2sow&t=28s)

As stated above, data gathering is a constant and holistic process; any and every event associated with a piece of consultancy work gives us data. In addition to this, we will also undertake specific data-gathering activities. There are a wide range of these including:

1 Observations of meetings, spaces, customer or client-facing work. Field notes should be taken at the time or soon afterwards
2 Interviews and focus groups
3 Surveys and questionnaires
4 Review of documents, policies, for example staff satisfaction surveys, exit interviews, complaints, strategies, business plans, reports from regulatory bodies, progress against KPIs

What data you need to gather by what methods is driven by the purpose of the consultancy, the scope of the project including issues of access, time and budget.

Analysis, sense-making and hypothesis development

Once gathered, data needs to be analysed. Methods of analysis depend again on the purpose of the consultancy and on the type of data you have. Sense-making and hypothesis development is the process of framing your ideas about what is going on. The 'what is going on' considers how people are relating to the primary task, the conscious and unconscious dynamics at play and the inter-relationship between these. Decisions need to be made about who is involved in these sense-making processes and how the information is shared with others in the system. Miller's (1995) working note remains a practical, meaningful and containing artefact to work with in this stage of consultancy. A working note is a live document; it brings together a synthesis of the data gathered to date. In addition, it offers ideas for what might be happening in the system, organisation or team and suggestions for the next steps. This working note is shared and discussed and next steps agreed with relevant stakeholders.

Planning and intervention design

Like data gathering, intervening is constant and holistic. Everything is an intervention, who you communicate with, how you do it and how you set up a room. Again, there is a wide range of specific interventions you might use. Your choice of intervention depends on the purpose of the consultancy, the hypotheses developed, the acceptability of the intervention to the audience, the scope, timescale and budget of the project. There are too numerous interventions to name here, but to give a flavour, they might include:

1 Workshops/masterclasses/seminars
2 Working with the 'here and now'
3 Social dreaming matrices
4 Arts-based interventions
5 Team coaching
6 Role consultancy
7 Action learning
8 360 feedback
9 System-wide events
10 Listening post
11 Leadership or organisational exchanges
12 Shadowing
13 Mentoring

Implementation

This stage involves the actual doing of the different interventions planned. You need to consider who participates in which intervention, the different timings for them and how they inter-relate.

Reviewing and learning

These are also constant activities, which take place through: supervision; the keeping of field notes or reflective notes; and debriefing with colleagues and the client. They can also be marked by specific moments or activities scheduled into the overall project plan: for example review meetings with the client; learning events in the client system; and internal team meetings.

Evaluating

This needs to be thought about at the outset of any consultancy project. You need to consider with the client what outcomes or impact they are hoping for, what you want to evaluate, the metrics and methods you want to use, how any data will be gathered, timescales and how and with whom the evaluative information will be presented and used.

Ending and transition

It is important to pay attention to this aspect of a consultancy project. The ending of an organisational consultation is the beginning of next steps in the change or development process. The transitions from the consultant being present and active, to them leaving and those within the organisation continuing are important developments. As consultants, we work towards client ownership and sustainability of changes and development (Neumann et al 1997). Endings can bring complex, frequently unconscious ghosts from our past, echoes of previous endings. They can force us into liminal or transitional spaces, which can be both confusing and destabilising, and spaces of great creativity, change and development.

Benson (2018) suggested paying attention to the physical, emotional and intellectual aspects of endings. This is helpful in enabling losses to be acknowledged and processed and the creative possibilities to be realised. The physical aspect includes the different tasks or activities involved, have they been completed, are more to be done, what is left? How shall the ending be marked or noted, the performance of ritual is important here. The emotional aspect requires attention to the ending of the relationships developed, the feelings about the work done, the next steps. It includes the acknowledgement of the influence of previous endings for both the consultant and the client. The intellectual part of ending involves making sense of the work done, what has been achieved, the evaluation against hoped-for outcomes, what needs to happen next, how can changes be sustained and what needs to stop or be let go of.

In addition, there are the different layers of task identified by Lawrence (1997); the normative primary task: the stated purpose of the system; what it exists to do; the existential primary task: what people believe they are doing; and the phenomenological primary task: what people appear to be doing as evidenced by their behaviour and actions. The phenomenal primary task is frequently driven by the unconscious processes of individuals and groups. These layers of primary task apply to any of the tasks identified in the paragraph above.

Associated with these different aspects of task is the idea of the task and the sentient system. The task system is those rational conscious aspects of the work or the job, what needs to be done. The sentient system includes the social, human processes: the symbols, meanings, emotional experiences, attitudes, and beliefs based on the needs, fantasies and patterns of identification for an individual, within a role and an organisation. This is where politics and dynamics of organisational life take place. The activities within the sentient system are driven by both conscious and unconscious processes, and they interact powerfully with the task system.

Thus, systems psychodynamics consultants need the capacity and capabilities to identify and clarify the nature of the task, to work with conscious and unconscious processes evoked by the task, and to work with the interplay between the task and the sentient system.

Summary

In systems thinking, increases in understanding are believed to be obtainable by expanding the systems to be understood, not by reducing them to their elements.

Understanding proceeds from the whole to its parts, not from the parts to the whole as knowledge does.

Ackoff (1972)

The strength of the sentient system of feelings, belonging, beliefs and stories may mean that members of groups and organisations may seek to preserve them from change and retain the vertical inter-group relations that exist between top management groups and subordinate departments. However, sub-systems require information from senior management to do their jobs and coordinate their activities with those of other sub-systems.

The world of work is changing, in more complex, more diverse and inconceivably more rapid ways, with, more unevenness among parts, a source both of innovation and of resistance. Change is also comprehensive – major change efforts may involve altering structures, policies, procedures, technologies, role design and cultural patterns as organisations adapt to accelerating rates of change in markets, technologies and competitive pressures. Therefore, major organisational change efforts pose great psychic challenges to their members and require distinctive conditions to contain the anxieties evoked by such upheaval. The psychological defence mechanisms such as splitting, denial and projective identification, which are used to cope with distressing anxiety, can lead to a genuinely disturbing and psychically threatening organisational environment. The link between personal behaviour and organisational dynamics is tied to the concepts of *projective identification* and *introjective identification* because all organisational development involves change, and change, inevitably, involves loss.

Exercise

1 Describe the social system that you work in from the vantage point of the sentient and the task system.
2 How do you think joint optimisation could be achieved in the task system and sentient system of your work group?
3 How does your technology interface with the work group and its sentient system?
4 Describe the impact of COVID-19 on your task and sentient system. What has been positive? What has been negative?
5 How do you imagine the future development of your work group in terms of change and change processes?

Chapter 3

Socio-technical systems in the 21st century (part 1)

David Lawlor and Mannie Sher with Bert Painter and Carolyn Ordowich

Socio-technical refers to the inter-relatedness of *social* and *technical* aspects of an organisation. Socio-technical theory is founded on two main principles:

1 One is that the interaction between social and technical factors creates the conditions for successful (or unsuccessful) organisational performance. This interaction consists partly of linear cause-and-effect relationships (the relationships that are normally 'designed') and partly of non-linear, complex, even unpredictable relationships (the good or bad relationships that are often unexpected). Whether designed or not, both types of interaction occur when social and technical elements are put to work.

2 The corollary of this, and the second of the two main principles, is that optimisation of each aspect alone (social or technical) tends to increase not only the quantity of unpredictable, 'un-designed' relationships, but also those relationships that are injurious to the system's performance.

Therefore, socio-technical theory is about *joint optimisation* (Cooper and Foster, 1971), that is, designing the social system and technical system in tandem so that they work smoothly together. Socio-technical theory is usually based on designing different kinds of organisation, ones in which the relationships between social and technical elements lead to the emergence of productivity and wellbeing, rather than the all too often case of new technology failing to meet the expectations of designers and users alike. Socio-technical theory has at its core the idea that the design and performance of any organisational system can only be understood and improved if both 'social' and 'technical' aspects are brought together and treated as interdependent parts of a complex system.

Organisational change programmes often fail because they are too focused on one aspect of the system, commonly technology, and fail to analyse and understand the complex interdependencies that exist.

Painter (2009) suggests that socio-technical systems thinking survived prior to and after the turn of the century in traditional manufacturing applications, but, more particularly, in three new streams of development. One

DOI: 10.4324/9781003368663-6

of the strongest applications has been in social principles for design of information technology. Illustrating this approach has been concepts of 'human-computer interaction' (HCI), or those aspects of information science dealing with the social impacts of computerisation, that is 'social informatics' (Kling, 2000); and, closer to the original STS thinking, has been 'ethical computer use' and the 'ETHICS' method of system design (Mumford, 1996, 2003; Porra and Hirscheim, 2007). The focus on technology is also implied in an oft-quoted definition of socio-technical systems as 'technical works involving significant social participation, interests, and concerns' (Maier and Rechtin, 2000). Also, in social computing, socio-technical systems are defined as 'systems of people communicating with people that arise through interactions mediated by technology' (Whitworth, 2009, pp. 394–400).

At the same time, there is growing understanding that information technology, though integral, is insufficient for the development of knowledge work and knowledge management (McDermott, 1999, pp. 103–116; Shani and Sena, 2000). This conclusion is based upon a distinction between 'information' and the discretionary and social dimensions of 'knowing'. Information systems enable a knowledge economy, and yet, it takes human systems to achieve it. Experience in the design of such systems like 'communities of practice' to leverage knowledge across disciplines or business units has revealed that this process involves technical, social and socio-technical challenges (McDermott et al., 2002).

Network organisations

Manual Castells (2000) devised the term 'network society' to describe societal developments at the millennium and argued that the present age may be described as 'replacing the antiquated metaphor of the machine with that of the network' (2000, p. 3). This fits well with contemporary discourses on the digitalisation of work life and society. Aside from the network society, globalisation, digitalisation and technological developments, other reconfigurations are also taking place. The traditional distinctions between different forms of business and different sectors of society are transcended or blurred, for example when manufacturing industries are 'servitised', when service sectors are 'industrialised', when public administration takes on governance principles from the business sectors (such as 'new public governance' and 'lean') in management, and how all this produces distinctive socio-technical problematisation.

The network society, globalisation, digitalisation, technological developments, and the blurring of previously clean demarcations between various societal subsystems all these have again made organisations and work life a highly focused and debated ground. Two developments, information/communication technology (ICT) and an economy based on knowledge and innovation, have spawned a third effect, the emergence of 'network organisations' (Van Alstyne, 1997) that span the boundaries of individual teams and organisations. The need for societies and single organisations to develop an 'inter-organisational capability' was anticipated very early in socio-technical systems literature that built upon von Bertalanffy's (1950) theory of 'open systems' and profiled the 'causal texture of organisational environments' (Emery and Trist, 1965). The increasing 'turbulence' in the real world of organisational environments and the emergence of issues 'too extensive and too many-sided to be coped with by any single organisation' has led to a new theory for 'referent organisations and development of the inter-organisational domain' (Trist, 1983). Thus, socio-technical systems theory and its 'socio-ecological' perspective (Trist et al., 1997) provide foundational understanding for 'institution-building' and design.

In 2005, members of the STS Roundtable (an association of academics and STS practitioners – http://stsroundtable.com/wiki/STS_Roundtable) chose to launch an STS 'Discovery' initiative, a true action research process to be carried out on two levels, to examine the causes of the decline and develop ways to apply STS concepts and methodologies to problems of the 21st century. At the higher level, a framework/model was developed with a set of hypotheses about key lines (tracks) of potential innovation in STS theory and practice. On a second level, along eight tracks of modern 'STS Design Challenges', project information is shared, to help build a database of emerging STS applications and develop further understanding in how to continue to apply its principles in a world driven by technology and knowledge work. This 'action-on-the-ground' as reported in member projects contributes to a body of new knowledge in STS concepts and methodologies.

Digital transformation changes the conceptual foundation of STS towards *SmarT Organisation Design*

By Bert Painter and Carolyn Ordowich

> This essay on renewal of the conceptual foundation of STS Design is a product of the 'collective intelligence' of organisation design practitioners, academics, students, and organisational leaders within the STS Roundtable (North America: www.stsroundtable.com) and Global Network for SmarT Organization Design.
> (21st century STS Design community in Europe, Scandinavia, U.K., Australia: www.smartorganization.com)

Humanity is at a fork in the road. The 21st-century world we live in has become hyper-turbulent and interconnected. Challenges for organisations and society have become increasingly *complex*. Exponential and disruptive digital transformation in all sectors of work and life creates significant new opportunities, as well as threats of technological hegemony, 'surveillance capitalism' (Zuboff, 2019), and 'mass extinction' of jobs and corporations (Siebel, 2019). For humankind to achieve 'whole' outcomes with humane and effective results, this era calls for institutions and society to choose new ways of 'organising' for action.

Fortunately, Tavistock social scientists left us a philosophical guide to help us 'see' a **new way to adapt** through *systemic learning* **that is adaptive** versus simply *coping* with change. This adaptive (eco) systemic learning is based upon **THREE PERSPECTIVES** or lenses that focus one's attention on fundamental axioms of social ordering for our 'whole' system choices.

Moreover, what enables a whole transformational learning experience and helps people transition from one perspective to another is an integral system **PARTICIPATIVE DESIGN** process. The process is dynamic and able to shift as people decide how to transform and adapt in a continuously changing environment. The goal is not to design only one intervention in one perspective, but to design a flow of interventions woven into a meaningful and comprehensive organisational design journey.

The aim is to have all in the 'ecosystem' feel welcomed, included, valued and connected through the continuous practice of awareness of the three perspectives, that is learning about their choices in being, thinking and acting so that they can make informed, collective choices about what to change in their world. The explanatory power of a coherent fundamental theory, such as the three perspectives, helps make the design function knowable to all participants in the ecosystem so all can participate fully. The result is a continuously evolving 'wholistic learning system' with information flow between experts and non-experts who experiment with different transformations in a world of exponential change.

Originally, the three perspectives were presented in the order of the Tavistock scientists' own learning (Trist et al., 1990–1997), with the socio-psychological as the first, defining how 'group relations' are central to the development of thriving individuals and for our humanity in the form of culture. This was followed by a novel perspective, socio-technical systems, about how social and technical choices for value creation enhance or constrain individual and organisational ability to thrive. The final perspective was the socio-ecological, where organisational viability in turbulent environments depends on collaborative interaction with the macro-institutional level of society.

In this digital era of exponential change, we have renewed this conceptual foundation of STS to address contemporary and future organisational realities in 'SmarT Organization Design'. We start with the socio-ecological perspective to discover the 'edges' (Hagel, 2009) upon which to grow a new framework of institutional adaptive logic, then move to the socio-technical systems perspective to design an agile healthy work system framework to create value and conclude with the socio-psychological perspective to support a thriving culture at the heart of both a bounded organisation and its collaborative ecosystem.

We have also reframed the three perspectives to describe an overarching contemporary need for social innovation *and* social order in a paradoxical organisational context of self-adaptive 'dynamic stability', a cycle of continuous learning and experimenting at pace with the current of change. One STS theorist, Cal Pava, called this learning the new nature of work – non-linear– and defined its new form as 'deliberations' within networks of diverse participants (Pava, 1983). Competence in deliberation design is now essential for achieving a 'sense-and-respond' capability so that each social entity – at micro/meso/macro-levels – can participatively design its own fit for its context in an integrated way (Austrom and Ordowich, 2019).

The three perspectives as a fundamental theory is an important guide regarding the philosophical questions of design in complex systems (generating much deeper insight than the traditional STS Philosophy Statement) before we get into the details of the operational design. OUR CHOICES – the culture we create, the scenarios we imagine, the stories we tell and our decisions about which technologies to fund or buy, which products or services to provide and how to use automation to develop our processes and people will determine our future. These are the topics that we must carefully deliberate, using the 3 perspectives to guide us, supported by effective deliberation design to make sure the culture we create in the process of design includes all voices (Figure 3.1).

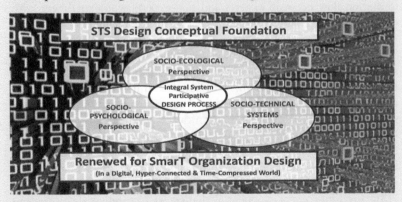

Figure 3.1 STS Design Conceptual Foundation, reprinted with permission from the author.

In our 21st-century reinvention of an STS position, the meaning of the **socio-ecological perspective** has shifted from being a static context (or monolithic macro-environment) for a bounded organisation to a multi-organisational complex system (of systems), an ecosystem in continuous evolution. Furthermore, the work systems of individual bounded organisations now extend into the expanse of the ecosystem to include gig workers, project teams, and whole organisations and subunits – all networked in a dense pattern of interaction to advance their own viability and create value together.

Ecosystems are the new 'field of organising' for dealing with exponential change. These complex systems can be adaptive or maladaptive, but they are always made up of interconnected, autonomous entities, acting and reacting to one another, without centralised control, pursuing both an emergent shared 'negotiated order' and individually specific 'alternate futures'. Emery and Trist left us with what might be described as key design parameters for collaborative ecosystems, now enabled by new digital technologies and an economic prototype called a 'platform'.

The **socio-technical systems perspective** is still focused on 'structures' and 'processes' for value creation but structures are now very fluid, temporary, and often self-organising networks of interaction. Tasks are continually changing, defined roles may be non-existent, and relationships need to become more peer-to-peer in 'discretionary coalitions' formed to do the work of resolving problematic issues required to move 'non-routine' knowledge work forward. The process of sustained value creation also takes on new meaning. Organisations must embrace the paradox of ambidexterity – with a learning infrastructure to optimise present performance while developing disruptive potential for longer term growth.

At the micro-level of organisation, the 'technology' concept has also changed in the digital age. In the cyber-physical relationship, or what may be called the digital-technical relation, information from the physical world is captured and creates a digital record that is shared with information from other sources, allowing for advanced analytics, to which algorithms and human decisions are applied for a new series of movements in the physical world. In this digital form, the relationship between humans and technology is changing, from one of complementarity to 'symbiosis' – a much more 'entangled' relationship (Kramer, 2019) where the human can be augmented by the machine, while machines are trained or sustained by humans.

How the human-machine relationship develops depends greatly upon the **socio-psychological perspective**, the 'heart and mind' of organisational life defining the patterns for human identity and agency. These patterns are nurtured by a framework of rules and norms (culture) that now pertains to both the bounded organisation and the larger ecosystem. Values are still central to 'culture', but the importance of purpose, passion and 'ideal-seeking' has increased. This is a development consistent with the foresight of Eric Trist who anticipated that 'we are entering the Age of the Person' when under Type IV environment conditions, (s)he will become 'the agent of change ... rather than any institution or system' (Trist, 1979).

Furthermore, the relevant nature of the 'leadership' function as the carrier and transmitter of culture has also changed, with an emphasis on 'cultivation', engaging people in the continual reinvention of work. A culture that promotes an agile mind, a lifetime love of learning, a capacity for self-understanding and awareness and an ability to connect with others can provide a stable bridge to help manage the inherent tension in organisational ambidexterity. However, today, there is also a need for culture as a disruptive force, to build new bridges to people with different thinking for a rapid pace of innovation.

This **conceptual foundation of three perspectives** is a fundamental theory, providing a discovery and understanding phase for the designing process where actual organisational choices are made. Now, the STS Roundtable through its global network, annual meetings, and webinars is championing application of these renewed STS perspectives in current innovations: in digital STS design of healthcare (Winby and Mohrman, 2018), integrated care ecosystems (Mohr and Dessers, 2019), catalyst organisations for open innovation (Majchrzak and Griffith, 2018), 'braided' organisations for digitally enabled collaboration (Pasmore et al., 2019), reinventing jobs in automation of work (Jesuthasan and Boudreau, 2018), human-centred smart service systems (Spohrer et al., 2016) and relevant to effects of the COVID-19 pandemic – STS design of virtual teamwork (Painter et al., 2016) based on studies funded by the National Science Foundation (USA).

The STS Roundtable's central purpose is to be an open learning community advancing knowledge and practices that create healthy, powerful organisations and communities. Our 'big idea' is to build on this conceptual foundation to collaborate on and discover a next generation of organisational design technology to match the speed and dimension of our digitised VUCA world while making a choice for humanity.

Phases in the development of the theory and the practice of socio-technical systems design (STSD) to the present-day era

Pasmore et al (2018) note that others added to the principles of socio-technical design (Cherns, 1976; Emery, 1959; Pasmore, 1988), summarised in the table below:

Classical socio-technical systems design principles

Principle	Explanation
Wholeness	The work system should be conceived as a set of activities making up a functioning whole, rather than a collection of individual jobs.
Teams	The work group should be considered more central than individual jobholders.
Process control	Variances (problems or deviations from expectations) should be identified and handled as close to their point of origin as possible, preferably by those who can prevent them from occurring, without requiring supervisory intervention.
Self-direction	Internal regulation of the work system is preferable to external regulation of individuals by supervisors.
Multiskilling	The underlying design philosophy should be based on a redundancy of functions rather than on a redundancy of parts (multiskilling vs. single-skilling).
Discretion	The discretionary component of work is as important to the success of the system as the prescribed component.
Joint optimisation	The individual should be viewed as complementary to the machine rather than as an extension of it.
Adaptation	The design of work should be variety increasing rather than variety decreasing, meaning that individual and organisational learning is essential to allow organisational adaptation to change.
Meaning	At the level of the individual job in a socio-technical system, there should be for each person an optimal level of variety, learning opportunities, some scope for setting decisions that affect the outcomes of work, organisational support, a job worthy of societal recognition and the potential for a desirable future.
Incompletion	Since the context of the organisation will continue to evolve over time, no design can be considered 'finished'.

Eijnatten (1998) proposes a history of socio-technical systems design (STSD) by showing the phases in the development of the theory and the practice. He states that STSD is a series of major and minor discoveries, projects, conceptualisations and developments of methodologies. He references Merrelyn Emery (1993) who distinguishes several important turning points that form sequential steps in the democratisation of the workplace:

1   As a first important fact – no more than a starter – he mentions Lewin's leadership experiments just before the Second World War (Lippit and White, 1939). These laboratory studies pointed to three basic types of

organisational structures: the autocracy, the democracy and the 'laissez-faire' type (variant without structure).

2   The first turning point of STSD is the set of British mining studies (Trist et al., 1963). In these field studies, researchers discover an alternative form of work organisation (the so-called 'semi-autonomous work group') and applied it on a limited scale.

3   The second turning point of STSD is the Norwegian 'Industrial Democracy Project' (Emery and Thorsrud, 1964). Here, employers, employees and the government jointly carried out research into and improved the democratic content of industrial sectors for the first time.

4   The third turning point of STSD covers the so-called 'participative design' methodology in Australia (Emery and Emery, 1974) in which workers themselves carried out the whole trajectory of socio-technical analysis and redesign by means of 'participative design workshops and search conferences'.

5   Van Beinum (1990) points out a fourth turning point in the development of STSD: 'large scale and broad-based organisational change process with democratic dialogue as the leading element on the conceptual as well as the operational level' (Gustavsen, 1985) as practiced on a national scale in Sweden. Eventually, the Dutch approach to integral Organisational Renewal (De Sitter et al., 1990) may become a competitor. This approach not only combines a structure and process option, but also looks for the happy medium between the expert and participative approach.

Eijnatten (1998) distinguishes three development trajectories:

1   Phase 1 (1949–1959 +): the period of the Socio-Technical Pioneering Work;
2   Phase 2 (1959–1971 +): the period of classical STSD; and
3   Phase 3 (1971- present): the period of modern STSD.

STS design (STSD) and virtual relationships – socio-technical systems and its contemporary application: the Internet and working in virtual organisations

Winby and Moorman (2018) point out that the steady advancement of digital technology that has enabled global connection and integration across populations and organisations has catalysed fundamental change in societal norms, behaviours and expectations. Examples that commonly enter into the public discourse include the integration of social media into the lives of populations everywhere, easy access to and expectations of transparency of information, and the impact of the internet on awareness and expectations of people around the world. The designs of organisations have changed fundamentally to reflect the technical and social realities of our times. Among the impacts are horizontal organisation and industry models characterised by virtual relationships to and among customers: partnerships along the value stream, outsourcing, the increasing use of contract and transaction-based workers replacing loyalty, and commitment-based relationships; and the building of work systems that include robotics, artificial intelligence and machine learning.

These approaches have been made possible by the generation of powerful internet-enabled digital platforms, such as those employed by gig-based businesses like Uber and Amazon, as they relentlessly pursue complements to their original e-commerce platforms; and by Facebook as it persistently grows its power and role in connecting people, information, advertisers, employers and customers. Airlines are another example of companies that rely on big data and digital platforms to make continual pricing, service and route decisions to optimise revenue. They have decomposed the elements of air travel and connected customers through self-service web platforms where they create itineraries tailored to their willingness and ability to pay for the services they want and the amount of space they and their luggage will take up.

Communication and coordination

One clear implication is that digital platforms have become major enablers of the communication and coordination underpinning economic transactions and work systems. They are co-evolving with the strategies and designs of organisations and work systems and of economies and societies. The scope for relevant technical and market optimisation, integration and design now extends well beyond company boundaries to include industry and cross-industry ecosystems, with significant impacts for all of us. Large elements of the global economy are now linked together by technology platforms that enable the members of the ecosystem to operate in a complementary way and generate product and service innovations with sweeping involvement of and impact across many stakeholders. IT platforms, often developed, owned and controlled by particular economic entities, become the information processors and the integrators (and in many ways provide the direction and supervision) of activities that often are carried out by customers and by temporary teams cutting across organisational, sector and geographic boundaries.

We label these teams 'smart' because the technology provides unprecedented access to data, information and analyses that provide the foundation for coordinated and complementary activity. In effect, the capabilities inherent in the digital platforms are integral to significantly increased collective intelligence (Hutchins, 1991; Wegner et al., 1987). Meanwhile, work relationships are increasingly transactional, contractual, temporary and virtual. Many organisations are populated by a small core of mission critical employees, connected to contractors and outsourcers, all with tasks and roles defined by the ecosystem-wide network that is defined through various connections to an IT platform (Weber, 2017).

Socio-technical systems and its contemporary application: the Internet and working in virtual organisations

The STS concept originated from studies of British coal mining methods by the Tavistock Institute (Trist and Bamforth, 1951). Early STS studies observed that employee behaviour and work design were so intertwined that technical processes could not be understood without understanding social processes (Emery, 1959; Trist and Bamforth, 1951). The original theory focused on how work practices could increase productivity without large capital expenditures (Trist, 1981). Researchers have since applied STS theory to many fields: human relations (Cherns, 1976; Emery, 1959; Miller, 1959; Pasmore et al., 1982; Rice, 1958; Trist et al., 1963); ergonomics (Clegg, 2000); applied psychology (Cooper and Foster, 1971); engineering design (Griffith and Dougherty, 2001); organisational behaviour (Fox, 1995; Pasmore, 1988; Seiler, 1967; Susman and Chase, 1986); information technology (Mumford, 2006); knowledge management (Pan and Scarbrough, 1998); and general management (Cummings, 1978; Woodward, 1958).

Winter et al. (2014) review STS theory and practice and state that the socio-technical systems (STS) approach provides a framework that is well-suited to grappling with many issues of work in organisations. The socio-technical approach to understanding the interplay between the organisation and those working there that stems from research in British coal mines in the 1950s (Trist and Bamforth, 1951) and industrial relations needs a recalibration for a better fit with the digital paradigm. There is a need to be clear on the implications of digitalisation and automation as specific and technology-based organisational changes, which can be both technologically and organisationally driven.

Digitalisation and automation represent a giant leap from the mechanistic work systems of the 1960s, and a shift of attention from work design to organisation design, with a focus on motivation, productivity and industrial democracy (De Sitter et al., 1997). Newer research on socio-technical systems design (STSD) has leaned more and more towards design theory as in organisation re-design, a retake often referred to as the Dutch tradition, built through the interactions of researchers, practitioners, consultants and organisation managers in close interaction with the Scandinavian tradition (Thorsrud and Emery, 1969). There is, however, a significant difference between these two; the Scandinavian tradition embraces to a greater extent participants' understanding and involvement, if not over that of external experts, at least as equal. A main argument of modern STSD is that technology, work and employees should not be conceived as either separate systems or subsystems that need to be adapted to one another to obtain an optimal fit. These components constitute together the larger organisational work system and need to be studied in terms of how they are connected, interact and produce effects: that is their functional and interactive relations (De Sitter et al., 1997). The Dutch tradition in this conceptualisation of integral design relies heavily on expert design of structural parameters in production structures ('the grouping and coupling of performance functions') and in control structures ('the allocation and coupling of control functions') (De Sitter et al., 1997).

By conceiving of work systems as mutually shaping social and technological systems, the STS approach has provided decades of researchers and practitioners with robust analytical tools to consider both the social and the technical elements of organisational contexts. However, they identify two areas where the conceptualisation of socio-technical systems must be updated to reflect the role of information infrastructures as an enabler of trans-organisational work arrangements. First, with its view of nested systems, the STS approach encapsulates work and the infrastructure used to do it within organisations (either explicitly or implicitly), often leading to a 'container' view of organisations as the context of work and a venue for joint optimisation of the social and the technical. Second, because work is generally treated as encapsulated within superordinate, nested systems, elements of that work are inherited from those superordinate systems. In their paper, de Sitter et al. (1997) characterise the limitations of industrial age assumptions of organisational encapsulation and inheritance that, rooted in the STS approach, underlie much of traditional information systems scholarship. They theorise an updated socio-technical framework (Neo-STS) and apply it to examples of contemporary work situations to highlight the importance and implications of trans-organisational information infrastructures and multidirectional inheritance.

Developments in socio-technical theory and design (STSD)

As we see in Introduction, the Tavistock Institute for Human Relations discovered the concept and practice of STS design, beginning in the 1940s. Then, the Institute's focus was directed at the design of work systems in factories and offices and initially focused on traditional non-computing manufacturing systems (Emery and Trist, 1960). STS design, social psychology and social ecology were the three major foci of the Institute's concern with fostering and improving relations between people who were otherwise seen as 'dehumanised' by modern industrial society.

By the 1970s, the Institute had begun to focus attention on the design and introduction of computing systems as STS for use in organisational settings.

Holding on to the social *and* the technical

Even though Trist and Bamforth (1951) introduced the term socio-technical in a production system context, there has been a shift away from the technical towards the social aspects of socio-technical in recent decades. Today, socio-technical systems theory typically deals with topics such as motivation, process improvement, and job satisfaction, self-managing teams, job design and enrichment, job rotation and empowerment through communicative participation. Along this line, we argue that present STS models have lost its original, and important, perspective. Furthermore, it is crucial to bring the origin into focus again, not by itself, but as a vital part of the two-sided value creation process that will strengthen companies' competitive edge.

Conclusion

The technical in the socio-technical equation has changed fundamentally in scope and impact on social organisation, driving new ways of working together and getting our needs met, or not. Digital platforms have fundamentally changed the relationship between companies and with customers, empowering customers to quickly and conveniently get their needs met, and in effect bringing them into the work system through self-service approaches in which customers carry out the tasks once carried out by employees. Customers provide the data necessary for the company to provide service effectively during transactions and episodes of product and service provision, and knowingly or unknowingly contribute to large databases that enable the organisation to improve services and products, reduce costs and optimise revenue and gain competitive advantage. In many organisations, customers provide input into (help with) product design and provide feedback about employees and the customer experience that may determine performance ratings and even incentives. The implications of these changes are just beginning to be systematically investigated and critically examined (Gazzaley and Rosen, 2016; Medeiros-Ward et al., 2015).

Exercise

1 Analyse a problem work situation and make a personal management map as a preliminary guide to developing a viable strategy for change utilising STS theory.
2 How do you see the change problem and their causes?

Chapter 4

Socio-technical systems in the 21st century (part 2)

David Lawlor and Mannie Sher with Bert Painter and Carolyn Ordowich

Socio-technical systems design for the future

Pasmore et al. (2018) offer the following as the evolving practice of socio-technical design as the reality of the changing world we are in. They suggest that we are moving away from one-time intensive efforts to achieve the internal joint optimisation of a work system towards a 'living' or 'agile' process for continuously redesigning systems within systems in the face of continuous change.

Shifts in socio-technical systems design in future

From	To
Designing an organisation	Designing an organisation and its ecosystem
Designing a static system	Designing a system that is in a continuous state of change
Designing social systems around a fixed technical system to achieve joint optimisation	Designing organisations, ecosystems, technical systems and social systems on an ongoing basis as each element changes to achieve balanced optimisation
Using an internal design team to represent the system being designed	Using design laboratories that bring many voices from inside and outside the system into the design process
Designing the work system	Designing the strategic, operating and work systems
Designing a system with a fixed membership for its current members	Designing a system in which many important contributions are made by people who come and go as their expertise is needed; designing for people who are not yet members of the system
Focusing exclusively on the internal workings of the system	Perfecting collaborative work among entities that compose the value chain
Designing for high performance and variance control	Designing for innovation and agility
Design based on analysis of current systems	Design based on ideas about what is possible

According to Pasmore et al. (2018), there are four levels of design work to be accomplished:

DOI: 10.4324/9781003368663-7

1 Strategic design, which includes the definition of the system in the context of the broader environment in which it is embedded.
2 The focus under strategic design is to examine the governance of the system as it needs to evolve to represent the investments and priorities of key stakeholders.
3 The third focus under strategic design is the ecosystem. In the future, we will design the rough outlines of an ecosystem of partners and contributors who work together in an interconnected fashion using technological platforms to achieve a shared purpose.
4 Finally, there is the design of the core or primary organisation itself. The core organisation is the sun in the ecosystem solar system. It attracts others to a shared purpose and governs their interactions, rewards and ways of working.

Pasmore et al. (2018) argue that the design of the organisation is itself constantly evolving; therefore, it must be designed as an agile, networked, living system rather than a lifeless chart on a piece of paper. The goal of all three levels of design is balanced optimisation of the ecosystem, organisation, technical system and social system. In traditional socio-technical design, the goal was to design the social system around a fixed technical system in a way that maximised throughput and quality while satisfying human needs. In next-generation socio-technical design, the goal of balanced optimisation is predicated on the notion that everything is in motion. As the external environment changes, the design of the four components (ecosystem, organisation, technical system and social system) needs to evolve and align. The goal of balanced optimisation is to produce a better fit between the system and the environment, thereby increasing sustainability. Success can be measured by the system's survival and by the contributions it makes to society, the organisational outcomes achieved and the individual needs satisfied.

Co-designing the design space

A new value proposition for STS designing in the digital era

Austrom, Ordowich and Painter (2022) (https://stsroundtable.com/resources/sodf-materials/) make the case that we live and work in a fragmented, fast-changing societal context that has created serious challenges to collaborative, co-creative organisational designing. This requires a radically different approach both in the role of the designer and in the design process. They propose a renewed systemic mind-set (based on STS legacy) that acts as a starting point helping diverse stakeholders with varied perceptions of reality build a shared understanding about social order, systems intervention and first principles of human-centered organising. This is the foundation for detailed designing, the prelude to specific design projects. They share and continue development of this 'meta-designing' framework and specifically explore the following:

1 Our emerging socio-digital order and the opportunities and challenges for designing
2 Human-centered first principles that provide the foundation for dynamic designing – respect for human dignity, self-determination plus co-determination, reciprocity and mutual flourishing, and whole systems thinking
3 Renewal of the Tavistock Institute's three system perspectives – socio-psychological, socio-technical and socio-ecological systems – and the deliberation topics informed by these perspectives in order to have a truly whole systems approach
4 A meta-design approach based on deliberation designing – topics, forums and participants – which are actually the basis of virtually all approaches to the design of human systems
5 Our role as co-designers of the deliberations by which the people in the system design their collective activity rather than organisation designers, especially in light of the first principles of self-determination and co-determination
6 The importance of embedding the skills of designing and conducting participative deliberation designing so that the members of the social system can do their work and continuously improve their work

The new value proposition for STS designing

The new value proposition for STS they propose is a meta-approach that:

1 Is based on a foundation of explicitly articulated first principles of human-centred designing and organising and is otherwise agnostic about specific approaches and the structured deliberations on which they are based.
2 Is a prelude to detailed designing, helping diverse stakeholders develop awareness of their frequently varied perceptions of reality and then build a common understanding to create a pathway through 'design space', determining together the elements of a meaningful comprehensive design.
3 Builds on the three systems originally expounded by the Tavistock Institute – socio-psychological, socio-technical and socio-ecological – to achieve a 'whole systems' perspective.
4 Recognises that we are not organisation designers, but rather co-designers of the design space in which the system's stakeholders deliberate and dynamically design the organisation.
5 Identifies deliberations are the primary unit of analysis for work in a knowledge era.
6 Assumes that work, especially knowledge work, is continuously being (re-) designed by the people doing the work through a series of deliberations.

Deliberation designing

Deliberations are patterns of reflection, exchange and communication in which people engage to reduce the uncertainty and ambiguity of problematic issues that are critical to advancing knowledge and moving this work forward.

The initiating step in designing a deliberation is to identify the topic(s) or problematic issue(s) about which people must reflect and communicate, and then to address these elements:

1 Sharpen definition of the topic(s), that is challenge, opportunity to be addressed
2 Identify participants – critical stakeholders to the issue; those who should be involved in the reflections and conversations; representative diversity of roles and perspectives
3 Determine data – the information that is needed to effectively address the topic and advance the reflections and communication; physical documents and stored information; databases; analytics, algorithms and machine learning
4 Choose forums – in which they occur, which may be structured, semi-structured, unstructured or ad hoc; in person or online meetings; informal interactions; internet collaboration platforms

Deliberation-based designing methods and tools

In the new value proposition for STS, they are agnostic about specific designing methods and tools as long as they fully embrace the first principles of human-centered designing so that the process is fully participative, co-designed, and co-creative and incorporates the three Tavistock perspectives for seeing and understanding the whole system. There are numerous approaches to designing and change that are in actual practice structured series of deliberations. Here is a partial listing:

1 Participative design workshops
2 Appreciative inquiry
3 Search conferences, future searches, conference model
4 Open space technology
5 Participatory action research

As co-designers of the design space, they encourage a 'mix and match' and use whichever methods and tools that best fit the challenges and opportunities in the systems with which you are working.

Guest et al. (2022) make the following points that the new and residual challenges related to digital technology, COVID-19, precarious employment and scientific management are a reminder of research published in the early years of *Human Relations* that laid the foundation for socio-technical systems theory and its later conceptual offspring, the quality of working life. Analysing the evolution, challenges, legacy and lessons of socio-technical systems and quality of working life, they develop guiding principles for the theoretical development and practical implementation of socio-technical systems and quality of working life for the 21st century. These principles are needed to optimise the benefits of new technology and improve job quality. They would enable an effective and sustained humanisation of work through stakeholder involvement, interdisciplinary partnerships and institutional support, producing positive outcomes for employees and employers, as well as wider society.

Guest et al. (2022), also see https://beyond4-0.eu/news/82, discuss the new digital technology and its effects on worker wellbeing. They argue that if socio-technical systems (STS) and Quality of Working Live (QWL) were a response to the introduction of a new technology to 20th-century workplaces, another new technology – digital technology – is re-igniting interest in the relationship between humans and technology as the 21st century unfolds. This new technology is said to herald a new digital age (Vallas and Kovalainen, 2019) that represents a fourth Industrial Revolution (Schwab, 2016). They note that there are a number of ways in which digitalisation can affect work and employment (Warhurst et al., 2020).

Two types have attracted most attention from researchers and policymakers. The first is the digitalisation of production, sometimes called 'Industrie 4.0'. Although there is no agreed definition of Industrie 4.0, it involves artificial intelligence and advanced automation combined with the emergence of big data, the internet of things and huge and ever-increasing computer power to create 'smart factories' (Davies, 2015). The 'clever robots' used in these factories are capable of undertaking not just physical tasks but, increasingly, cognitive tasks. The second is the digitalisation of work, sometimes known as 'gig work' or 'platform work'. The platform economy uses digital networks (platforms) to coordinate economic transactions through algorithms – usually matching the demand for and supply of resources. The platform mediates worker supply and consumer demand for the completion of a task or 'gig', operating as market intermediary (Friedman, 2014; Gandini, 2019). As such, platform companies present themselves as brokers of tasks, not the employers of those who do the tasks, and these tasks are contingent, occurring 'on-demand' as and when needed by consumers, and payment is for the task.

Guest et al. wonder if we have come full circle: renewing socio-technical systems and revising quality of working life for the 21st century. There is a new wave of researchers concerned to implement digital technology within organisations to jointly maximise the technical and the social; drawing again on socio-technical systems theory (Avis, 2018; Bednar and Welch, 2020). Referencing the past work of the Tavistock, Bednar and Welch state that a contemporary socio-technical perspective should be the 'cornerstone in discussions about smart working in Industry 4.0 and 5.0' (p. 291). They continue that organisational change that maximises technological capacity needs to be based on 'human-centred design' (pg. 292). For Avis (2018), this renewed advocacy of STS rests on technology and social relations mutually 'co-constituting' the development of the 4th Industrial Revolution with both needed to maximise its outcomes. This return to STS is underpinned by broader recognition that there are organisational choices in how digital technology is used and that these choices affect the quality of jobs (Dhondt et al., 2021). This return to STS and QWL (quality of working life) is to be welcomed but will not deliver on effective or sustained humanised workplaces if the lessons from the past are not learnt.

The past challenges suggest six guiding principles for the theoretical development and practical implementation of STS and QWL in the 21st century that might provide the necessary generative mechanisms. Attempts have been made already by Grote and Guest (2017) and Warhurst and Knox (2022) to revise QWL and, reflecting on past QWL experience, together suggest six guiding principles.

Principle 1: It addresses the past ambiguity regarding the purpose of QWL by asserting that QWL is primarily a workplace issue. Both Grote and Guest and Warhurst and Knox take the constitution of jobs to be the key focus of the workplace or organisation. Therefore, the main point of intervention is the site of job, specifically wellbeing and productivity. The focus of interventions has to be tight. This focus should be the workplace. Interventions should improve the quality of working life, not promote wider social change. Jobs and the experience of work have to be the first-order priority. There may well be very welcome spillover effects from workplace interventions based on STS. For example, Marmot et al. (2020) have argued that improving quality of working life would benefit communities, government and society by redressing health inequalities and reducing healthcare costs. However, those benefits would only accrue from first improving job quality. Thus, improving the content of jobs and the experience of work is the first-order priority and potential beneficial extra-organisational outcomes (Guest et al., 2022).

Principle 2: It is that QWL envelops both the work and employment practices that comprise jobs. In seeking to address its past definitional and conceptual fuzziness, Grote and Guest (2017) contemporise the intellectual coherence of QWL by arguing that much of the research has focused on a specific dimension of QWL rather than taking an integrated approach that examines a range of QWL dimensions, including aspects of work and employment. Improving the quality of jobs means focusing on both work and employment practices. Although 'work' and 'employment' are often used synonymously, they are distinct. Work can exist without employment for example. It is the bundle of work practices and employment practices that shape job quality. The UK's Measuring Job Quality Working Group identified seven key practices, representing the dimensions of job quality: terms of employment; pay and benefits; health, safety and psychosocial wellbeing; job design and the nature of work; social support and cohesion; voice and representation; and work-life balance. Humanising work needs to cover all seven and understand how digitalisation effects each, as well as how they interact with each other.

Principle 3: It is that QWL requires institutional support, particularly from governments. Both Grote and Guest and Warhurst and Knox support workplace initiatives to promote QWL. However, the latter call for extra-organisational institutional support both for the diffusion and for the sustainability of QWL. Echoing the Scandinavian experience of STS, they call for statutory intervention to provide minimum standards of job quality. Efforts to humanise work require institutional support, particularly from governments. Workplace initiatives require outside institutional support if they are to be diffused and sustained. Employer organisations and workers' representatives, including trade unions and works councils, have an important role to play here but perhaps the lessons from past STS experiments, particularly in Scandinavia, are that government support is crucial. Voluntary workplace interventions triggered by employer choice or management-union negotiations that aim for best practice should be encouraged and supported by government, including through the provision of evidence-based information and education. However, government should also set minimum standards that ensure decent jobs for all and act as a baseline, based on the dimensions of job quality.

Future research should also examine how the COVID-19 pandemic has affected the QWL (Baum and Hai, 2020; Quinlan, 2021; Wang et al., 2021). The ways in which different industries, organisations and occupations have adapted to the challenges created by the pandemic and its aftermath along with the potentially longer-lasting pressures created by digital technologies will have critical implications for QWL and wider society.

Principle 4: It centres on optimising mutual interests that need to focus on the technical and the social dimensions of STS, rather than with one implying management priorities, while the other gives weight to workers' interests. Workplace initiatives need to optimise mutual interests. While there can be differing interests in the workplace, collaboration is also needed between managers and workers. Focusing only on conflict can overlook the reality of shared workplace interests. The introduction of digital technology has to be based on reconciling the different interests that deliver the joint maximisation of outcomes. A useful human resource management (HRM) approach here is that advocated by Kochan and his colleagues in the US and others in Europe to bring stakeholders together, ensuring voice to explore mutual interests and seek win-win opportunities through STS. It is notable that the OECD is advocating job quality as a route to better employee wellbeing and higher productivity and so in the interests of management and shareholders, not just workers.

Principle 5: It is the need for awareness of a stakeholder ecosystem in which everything is connected to everything else. Beer et al. (1985) have outlined a stakeholder approach to human resource management (HRM) that recognises the need to consider the interests of a range of stakeholders and therefore a range of potentially different outcomes. To better promote balance of focus on both the technical and social and reflecting past evidence of the limited diffusion of STS and QWL initiatives, the need is to recognise a stakeholder ecosystem. Drawing again on the HRM literature, this time the work of Michael Beer and his colleagues, it is useful to recognise the interests of a range of stakeholders and therefore the desire for a range of potentially different outcomes.

Specifically, they identify shareholders, managers, employees, government, the local community and workers' representatives as stakeholders, to which we would add customers. Each stakeholder seeks distinctive but often overlapping outcomes that can be supported through good design of work.

Principle 6: The sixth principle has two parts. First, expert input into interventions has to integrate the voices and experiences of workers, their representatives and managers at the workplace or organisational level. Experts also need to appreciate these non-experts' capacities and capabilities. Interventions need the support of senior management but, in conception and execution, need to be decentralised and negotiated. Second, the expert disciplinary lens brought to bear upon the problem and its solution must be interdisciplinary. There needs to be a balance between the social and technical in terms of expertise and focus, which means a partnership of the social and engineering sciences. However, if improvements in worker wellbeing are to be an outcome, the health sciences should also be partners.

Guest et al. (2022) make the point that these guiding principles should help the new generation of researchers interested in organisational-level change to draw on STS and QWL. The aim has to be an evidence-informed humanisation of work through sustainable interventions that can produce positive outcomes for employees and employers in the first instance and wider society in the second. Achieving these outcomes will require gaining the commitment of stakeholders and institutional support not just at organisational level, but at industry and national levels.

Socio-technical design and ecosystems

In short, because of the capacity to connect, work systems are now complex ecosystems that extend beyond an organisation and its employees. Organisations rely increasingly on technologically enabled integration and optimisation of a network of multifaceted connections that are integral to each involved organisation's ability to perform effectively and carry out its strategy. The design of any organisation extends well beyond the organisation's boundaries to include its lateral connections with many elements within the ecosystem. Organisation designers must expand focus from bounded organisations to the design of ecosystems. The design of the technical system that links together the members of the ecosystem will have to occur interactively with the design of the ecosystem's social system.

The socio-technical systems Roundtable (https://stsroundtable.com/about-us/) is a global network of organisation design practitioners, academics, students and organisational leaders. During 2019, in a series of dialogues, a webinar and their annual meeting at USC in Los Angeles, the STSRT community collaborated to reinvent the SmarT Organization Design Framework (SODF) and bring it into the digital era. Their approach to SmarT Organization Design is based upon a socio-technical systems (STS) conceptual foundation of three interdependent perspectives, socio-psychological, socio-technical and socio-ecological each with its own focus or lens, integrated through a whole systems participative design process.

Case example

Socio-technical systems and the dynamics of value chains – interdependence of organisations – working with the socio-ecological approach

The client, a high-tech company, spent much energy and time on 'conversion systems', the processes that lie between the 'import' and 'export' activities in a chain of suppliers and customers. The goal of 'joint optimisation' was enshrined as a value encompassing activity systems cross the boundaries of several enterprises in the supply chain, such as research and development; procurement and operations; and construction and maintenance. Consultancy was requested to address (i) the disentanglement of equivalent task boundaries in the supply chain; (ii) leadership of temporary and transitional task systems (design and construction); and (iii) managing transactions across organisational boundaries in the value chain (production systems).

The client was a key player in the value chain of a complex and dynamic supply and demand network that added value to their product and service at each step of its development. The client was part of a system of organisations, people, activities, information and resources involved in the transformation of natural resources, raw materials and components into a finished product or service and moving that product or service from supplier to the end user. The client was justifiably proud of its role in a sophisticated value chain system that used products and services in which residual value was recyclable. The value-chain concept extended beyond the client organisation. The client's concern was the efficacy of the whole value chain and its distribution networks. The delivery of a mix of products and services to the end customer mobilised the major part of the client's economic and organisational effort. The industry-wide synchronised interactions of local value chains created an extended global value chain. This larger interconnected system, the 'value system', included suppliers (and their suppliers all the way back), the client organisation itself and its distribution channels, and extended to the buyers and users all the way forward. To achieve and sustain a competitive advantage, the client was concerned that its cadre of operational leaders needed to understand and be skilled in working with every component of this value system. What was difficult to comprehend was that the dynamics of the value chain seemed to be preventing the development of understanding and the consultants were asked to provide explanations for why and how the quest for understanding was undermined.

Forces that oppose high standards of coordination and collaboration were exposed in the consultancy as the fragmenting dynamics of large systems and the presence in them of strong projective processes (the attribution of failings of the client organisation to supplier and customer organisations in the value chain) that constantly threatened the stability of the value chain.

Problems associated with value chain behaviour usually concentrate on studying production-distribution systems. The client requested help with understanding the inter-organisational dynamics and detailed organisational and attitudinal changes that were needed to achieve improvements. The client's mode of addressing production-distribution problematics in the systems concentrated on cognitive, intellectual, rational problem-solving approaches of its scientific-based professions and disciplines. While trust, dependence and social exchange concepts were acknowledged, little attention was given to knowledge derived from complexity theory and group relations theory that could have helped explain the fissile nature of human systems that are dominated by destructive forces that were outside the comprehension of the senior leadership team.

The client claimed that inadequate knowledge about customers' anticipated needs for its product made planning and organising for work a matter of guesswork. Both the client and customer hoped to achieve competitive advantage through cost reduction and quality enhancement – both had much to lose by failed negotiations on cost or persistent difficulties with process and product improvement, as with failed understandings of organisational and inter-organisational projective dynamics.

The consultancy work centred on strategic choice on how the client was operating in different environments and its tendency to respond to user-supplier risk by adopting mitigation strategies in which the relationship between client, customer and supplier was influenced by factors, such as trust and dependence, key elements of social exchange theory. Mitigation strategies varied depending on the environment in which the client was operating. These strategies were influenced by factors that helped in managing supplier-customer risk and enhancing downstream supply chain performance.

The application of systems psychodynamics models to its value chain was relatively new for the client. A global economy and increase in customer expectations in cost and quality put a premium on value chain dynamics and processes of the client and its suppliers. One cause of amplification in the client's supply chain was the time delay incurred by both 'value-added' and 'idle' operations throughout the value chain. Reducing cycle times made sense from the total systems viewpoint, as was the removal of intermediate layers of decision-making within the chain. Moreover, the use of system psychodynamics thinking helped provide qualitative forecasts of predicted performance improvement and enabled the identification of blocking mechanisms that interfered with achieving this objective. Demand amplification, we found, was influenced by communications and interactions as much as by unconscious dynamics of competition and rivalry between businesses and services in the value chain. Through integrating decision-making mechanisms and resulting information flows throughout the chain and attending to organisational

defences against anxiety, substantial improvements to both order amplification peaks and stock-level swings were achieved.

Our views on the systems psychodynamics of the value chain were
derived from material drawn from an 18-month action research–based
organisational development consultancy. The client called for assistance
with challenges in areas like cross-organisational development, systems
reviews, leadership development and culture change, but it soon emerged
that the client was experiencing challenging relationships with its suppliers and customers and users that needed attention. Despite having invested time, money and human resource to improving relationships with
its supply chains, bottlenecks continued troubling the client; solutions
to order amplification peaks and stock-level swings, fluctuating service
droughts and floods remained permanently just out of reach. Improvements that had been achieved frequently unravelled, inter-organisational
relationships deteriorated, and initial enthusiasms for collaborative partnership working with suppliers and customers/users rapidly diminished.

> In one Action Learning Set that was preparing an agenda and partnership
> strategy for a forthcoming meeting with an important, but difficult supplier,
> the leader of the negotiating team, normally a calm, thoughtful and polite
> individual, thumped the table and declared: 'I just don't understand them
> (R&D collaborators)!' His startled colleagues said: 'we can hardly go into the
> meeting tomorrow with our leader feeling like that about our collaborator'.
> The Action Learning Set discussed hitherto unspoken and unacknowledged
> feelings that had to be worked through if the forthcoming meeting with the
> supplier was to have any chance of success. In the event, the meeting with the
> supplier turned out to be one of the most productive ever with both parties
> reaching agreement on all key issues.

Action research–based change consultancy with the client was built
around the creation of small theme-based cross-organisation groups that
worked alongside established work groups in the hierarchy. Membership
of the groups was voluntary and made up of people with (i) a special interest, (ii) specific responsibility in the topic area, (iii) relevant skills, (iv) representing different disciplines, and (v) different sites of the company. The
Action Learning Sets typically met once a month for half a day, and they
were consulted on their internal dynamics and their external relationships. All Sets had a double task to study (a) the organisational, discipli-
nary/professional and business aspects of their chosen theme; and (b) the
dynamics between leadership and followership within the Set, external
relationships to other Sets and relationships to the overall leadership development programme and to the value chain of which the company was a
part. The number of senior leaders involved in the action research–based
consultancy fluctuated around 75. The Sets understood that by working

on their key business and organisational themes or cross-organisational relationships, they were doing so on behalf of the other Sets, the programme and the organisation as a whole and the value chain, that is the total system. Six Action Learning Sets were established covering most, if not all, key organisational challenges. The Action Learning Sets were coordinated and regularly provided feedback on their progress to the rest of the Action Learning Set system, to the rest of the organisation and to parts of the value chain they related to. Joint work, relationship-building, alliances and partnerships and collaboration and cooperation between Sets, departments, divisions, sections, sites and with suppliers and customers were the ultimate objectives of the value chain consultancy interventions. These goals were always achieved to a high degree.

Without pre-determining the six themes of the Action Learning Sets, they inevitably chose to focus on aspects of the company's relationships with suppliers and customers or users. One Set was called 'Improving Value Chain Effectiveness'. The consultancy focus moved from production behaviours of the single enterprise to the behaviours and interdependent relationships of large connected national and global organisations that relied on many actors to accomplish complex tasks.

Findings about the dynamics of value chain management focused on planning for action, followed by recommendations for change, negotiation and implementation, which, in turn, led to reviews of actions taken and thence to new rounds of planning, following a traditional cycle of the planning-implementation-review-planning model of organisational change consultancy. The output of the Action Learning Sets and feedback meetings between the Sets and with different levels of management in the hierarchy was recorded and circulated. Diaries of reflections on the work were kept; questionnaires, interviews and feedback meetings were used to monitor and evaluate the progress of the project.

Persistent difficulties with quality of products or services were traced to defects in raw materials or poor management or leadership, which resulted in high wastage rates and machines standing idle, while technicians attempted to compensate for poor-quality inputs. Therefore, improving relationships between the client and its suppliers has strategic importance. Two options emerged in relation to achieving an effective value chain. The first option involved decreasing the number of suppliers; the second was to identify preferred suppliers and customers with whom special arrangements on price and disclosure were agreed. Agreements on improving quality or reducing cost produced advantages for all parties who benefitted from improved quality, cooperation on price and process improvements, and the pace of new product or service introduction. By breaking down the barriers to sharing information and solving mutual problems, all parties joined together against competitors, thus improving their collective competitive advantage.

Integrating information flows with decision-making required more than engineering and management know-how. We offered the hypothesis that to achieve improvements in the value chain decision-making and behaviour, the players needed to have a good understanding of the 'anxieties' that move up and down the value chain together with the products or services. Organisational anxieties generated organisational defences, and these impeded efficiencies by virtue of negative perceptions and aggressive reactions that influence inter-organisational behaviour in the value chain. Long cycle times, poor-quality products or services, high cost and organisational pressures to stay ahead by developing more and more complex models led companies in the value chain into a push-me-pull-you dynamic that generated suspicion and mistrust between them and reduced the desire for increased interdependent collaboration. Increased anxiety led to increased instability in the value chain.

> *Our company operates in a very open network where customers and suppliers share information on the market. The quality of the information, however, is very poor. Customers do not give us a true picture of when they need our products. The same goes for us when informing our suppliers. Demand is consistently overrated in the system.*
>
> Head, Logistics

Concluding comment: value chain management

The term value chain expresses the need to integrate key business or organisational processes from end user through to original suppliers. Organisations involve themselves in a value chain by exchanging information about market fluctuations and production or service capabilities. If all relevant information is accessible to any relevant part of the value chain, all organisations have the ability to optimise the entire value chain rather than to sub-optimise based on local interest. The aim is to lead to better-planned overall production and distribution pathways and to cut costs and give a more attractive final product or service, leading to better overall results for the organisations in the value chain.

Shared beliefs about their respective company contributions to the value chain are indispensable:

> *Our Customer Service Center integrates real-time information on our worldwide operations and collective analytic expertise enables faster decision-making, improves operational processes, and allows service and value to be brought to customers' fast-paced production lines. Our accelerating knowledge creation helps our customers' productivity and allows real time feedback to our factory and product groups.*
>
> Director, Customer Services Centre

Conclusion

There is growing understanding that information technology, though integral, is insufficient for development of knowledge work and knowledge management. Design of 'communities of practice' to leverage knowledge across disciplines or business units has revealed that this process involves technical, social, and socio-technical challenges. Information/communication technology (ICT), and an economy based on knowledge and innovation have spawned a third effect, the emergence of 'network organisations', which span the boundaries of individual teams and organisations. Increasing 'turbulence' in the real world of organisational environments and the emergence of issues 'too extensive and too many-sided to be coped with by any single organisation' has led to new theory for 'referent organisations and development of the inter-organisational domain'. Socio-technical systems theory and its 'socio-ecological' perspective provide foundational understanding for 'institution-building' and design. Pasmore et al. (2018) state that 'In the years since sociotechnical systems theory and practice first appeared, there have been dramatic advances in technology and developments in society that demand that we reconsider what we know about organisation design'.

The world has become hyper-turbulent and interconnected. Challenges for organisations and society have become increasingly *complex*. Exponential and disruptive digital transformation creates significant new opportunities, as well as threats of technological hegemony, 'surveillance capitalism' and 'mass extinction' of jobs and corporations. For humankind to achieve 'whole' outcomes with humane and effective results, this era calls for institutions and society to choose new ways of 'organising' for action. Tavistock social scientists provide us a philosophical guide to help us 'see' a *new way to adapt* through *systemic learning that is adaptive* versus simply *coping* with change. Whole transformational learning experience helps people transition from one perspective to another and is an integral participative design process. Participative design is a dynamic process and able to shift as people decide how to transform and adapt in a continuously changing environment. The goal is not to design only one intervention in one perspective, but to design a flow of interventions woven into a meaningful and comprehensive organisational design journey. The aim is to have all in the 'ecosystem' feel welcomed, included, valued and connected through the continuous practice of awareness of the three perspectives, that is learning about their choices in being, thinking and acting so that they can make informed, collective choices of what to change in their world.

Exercise

1 Describe your experience of working virtually during the pandemic.
2 How would you apply STS theory to your experiences?

Part II

Action research and evaluation

Chapter 5 describes the introduction of action research and its application as a consultancy skill in the systems psychodynamics framework. The action research model is a step-by-step method and helps consultants conduct interventions geared towards improving an organisational situation. The chapter outlines the approaches to all aspects of an organisational problem and helping an organisation achieve its goals. The organisational development process is an action research model designed to understand known problems, set measurable goals, implement changes and analyse results. The chapter delves into the history of action research, a term coined by the social psychologist Kurt Lewin, in connexion with research, which aims to promote social action through democratic decision-making and active participation of practitioners in their research process. Lewin constructed a theory of action research, which he described as 'proceeding in a spiral of steps, each of which is composed of planning, action and evaluation of the result of action' and 'to understand and change certain social practices, social scientists have to include practitioners from the real social world in all phases of inquiry'. The chapter also describes Lewin's other key maxim, 'the only way to understand the social system is by trying to change it through action research'. Lewin was interested in group dynamics, and he used action research with groups to influence values, attitudes and behaviours to promote social change.

The chapter also addresses the differences between action research and organisational development, emphasising the four aspects of Lewin's approach – field theory, the contemporaneity rule, constructive method rule and countervailing force fields. The chapter ends on a summary of action research as covering diagnosis, data gathering and feedback to the client group, data discussion and work by the client group, action planning and action. The sequence is cyclical with the focus on the new or advanced problems as the client group learns to work more effectively together.

Chapter 6 moves to describing varieties of action research: *Creative Inquiry* involves people who share a common concern for developing understanding and practice in a personal, professional or social arena, integrating four forms of knowing – experiential, presentational, propositional and practical.

DOI: 10.4324/9781003368663-8

Action Science and Action Inquiry – methods for inquiring into and developing congruence between purposes, theories and frames, behaviour and impact in the world. These practices are applied at individual, small group and organisational levels. Their overall aim is to bring inquiry and action together in everyday life, to see inquiry as a 'way of life'.

Learning History records the lived experience of those in an action research or learning situation. Researchers work collaboratively with those involved to agree the scope and focus of the history, identify key questions, gather information through an iterative reflective interview process and distil this information into a form which the organisation or community can 'hear' and facilitate dialogue with organisation members to explore the accuracy, implications and practical outcomes that the work suggests.

Chapters 6 and 7 were written by the late Dione Hills, who was a principal researcher and consultant at the Tavistock Institute of Human Relations for over 35 years and whose enormous imprint on evaluation practice has been recognised by the creation of the Dione Hills Tavistock Institute and UK Evaluation Society Prize for the best short paper on the application of complexity-informed thinking in the field of evaluation. Dione writes that evaluation makes an important contribution to improving organisational development interventions, as well as providing evidence of what works best in different situations. She writes there are growing calls for more evaluation of organisational development initiatives and the seeking of the evidence base of consultation to improve consultancy practice. She describes a wide range of evaluation approaches, methods and tools that would be suitable for the evaluation of consultancy – theory-based, participative or action research–based approaches that can be helpful in supporting a systems psychodynamics-based consultancy. In Dione's second chapter (Chapter 7), she describes planning and conducting an organisational development evaluation by considering the purpose of the evaluation, the characteristics of what is being evaluated and the evaluation resources available, having good evaluation questions, drawing up a theory of change or system map, using care and skill in the design of appropriate data collection tools and in data analysis and feeding evaluation findings back to the client, and finally, Dione warns not to mix up findings, recommendations and actions that come from recommendations.

Chapter 5

The application of action research

David Lawlor and Mannie Sher

Introduction

In this chapter, we will describe the origins of action research and its application as a consultancy skill within the systems psychodynamics framework. The action research model is a step-by-step method that helps organisational development professionals conduct interventions geared towards improving an organisational situation. Since it is systematic, the emphasis is to ensure that all aspects of a problem are considered in a proper order and appropriately addressed. Thus, action research refers to searching of actions with an objective to help the organisation achieve its goals. Action research involves a continuous series of activities to be undertaken in the organisation to find a solution for the problem. Viewed from this perspective, action research is viewed as a process of organisational development. The organisational development process is an action research model designed to understand known problems, set measurable goals, implement changes and analyse results.

The application of action research

Defining action research

Action research is a key aspect of organisational development, fundamental in the theory and practice of the organisational development field. Action research according to French and Bell (1999) can be defined as follows:

> *Action research is the process of systematically collecting research data about an ongoing system relative to some objective, goal, or need of that system; feeding these data back into the system; taking actions by altering selected variables within the system based on the data and on hypotheses; and evaluating the results of actions by collecting more data.*

> (p. 138)

DOI: 10.4324/9781003368663-9

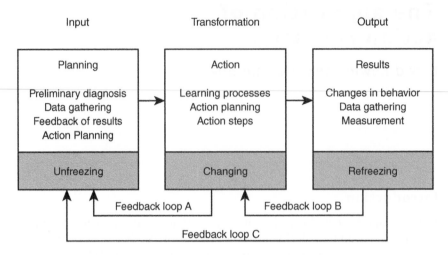

Figure 5.1 Systems Model of Action Research Process. From Matt Bond (2014), https://commons.wikimedia.org/w/index.php?curid=34814552. This file is licensed under the Creative Commons Attribution-Share Alike 4.0 International licence.

French and Bell clarify the model as follows:

> *The key aspects of the model are diagnosis, data gathering, and feedback to the client group, data discussion and work by the client group, action planning and action. The sequence tends to be cyclical, with the focus on new or advanced problems as the client group learns to work more effectively together.*

(p. 23)

According to Coghlan (2011), quoting McArdle and Reason, (2008), organisational development and action research are closely related; they exist independently of one another, and there are important roots and strands of action research existing outside of organisational development.

History

Origins of action research

The term action research was coined by the social psychologist Kurt Lewin in the USA in about 1944 in connection with research, which aimed to promote social action through democratic decision-making and active participation of practitioners in the research process. In the mid-1940s, he constructed a theory of action research, which described action research as 'proceeding in a spiral of steps, each of which is composed of planning, action and the evaluation of the result of action' (Kemmis and McTaggert, 1992, p. 8). Lewin argued that to '*understand and change certain social practices, social scientists have to include practitioners from the real social world in all phases of inquiry*' (McKernan, 1991, p. 10).

Whatever the scenario, action research always involves the same seven-step process:

Step 1 – Selecting a focus
Step 2 – Clarifying theories
Step 3 – Identifying research questions
Step 4 – Collecting data
Step 5 – Analysing data
Step 6 – Reporting results
Step 7 – Taking informed action

Action research is a useful method for facilitating organisational change by collaborating and involving the client in the entire process of diagnostic, problem identification, experiential learning and problem-solving process. The entire process of action research is action-oriented with the objective of making the change happen successfully. The process equally involves experimentation with the various frameworks in practical situations and application of various theories in various contexts, which require change.

In other words, the process of action research requires three distinctive stages, which are consistent with Lewin's model, which describes the three stages of change (also, see below for critical discussion of the theory):

1 Diagnosing the need for change (unfreezing)
2 Introduction of an intervention (moving)
3 Evaluation and stabilisation of change (refreezing)

Action research in organisations

Action research was born when social scientists and practitioners, concerned not only with the generation of scientific knowledge, but also with its usefulness in solving practical problems, worked to bridge the gap between theory and practice. In 1946, Kurt Lewin proposed learning about social systems by trying to change them through action research. Action research in organisations is an inquiry process intended to solve practical problems and generate new knowledge through collaborative efforts by researcher(s) and client(s). Action research is used here as a tool for organisational change and development. Action researchers place a high value on developmental change. They seek to make social systems and organisations more efficient and effective through a consensus-oriented approach.

Action research was originally used to improve race relations at the community level by John Collier (1945) and Kurt Lewin (1946), rather than for purposes of organisational improvement in business and industry. Collier used research as a tool for solving practical problems, with all parties collaborating in the process. He called this method action research.

Kurt Lewin, founding father of action research

Lewin (1946, 1947, 1948, 1951) concluded that traditional social science was not helping to solve social problems. According to Lewin (1948, p. 203) *'research that produces nothing but books will not suffice'*. He was particularly interested in group dynamics, and thus used action research with groups to influence attitudes, values and behaviours to promote social change.

Lewin recognised the importance of participation in planned change processes. He encouraged decision-making by participants based on analysis of available information. Through this process of collective discovery, group members more readily accepted change rather than resisting it. Moreover, such participation had the potential to bridge the gap between social research and social action. Lewin developed his ideas within the field of social psychology, based primarily on his experience with experimental studies on authoritarian, democratic and leaderless groups; food habits in a community; and efforts to reduce prejudice and discrimination suffered by minority groups. Besides being interested in using social science to solve social problems, Lewin further intended to conduct research, which would add to knowledge in the behavioural social sciences. This knowledge would not only deal with problems faced by a client but would be applicable to broader issues, such as the laws of human behaviour and social phenomena, and problems faced by organisations.

Lewin subsequently founded two applied research institutions: the Committee on Community Interrelations for the American Jewish Congress in 1944 and, in 1945, the Centre for the Study of Group Dynamics at the Massachusetts Institute of Technology, later moved to the University of Michigan. The application of action research to social problems, as originally envisioned by Lewin, was gradually abandoned, probably because researchers at the Centre for Group Dynamics were more interested in using group dynamics as a tool almost exclusively for improving work organisations.

Elton Mayo (1933) and William Foot Whyte (1969) were also among the early proponents of action research. Both worked in the field of applied anthropology, bringing anthropological methods and insights to formal organisational settings. Mayo's (1933) work at the Hawthorne Plant of Western Electric Company included most of the characteristics of what is now known as action research. Pickering (2001), Elias (1987), Mayo (1933), Roethlisberger and Dickson (1939) and Sofer (1961) were concerned with what was termed the 'civilising process' through which individuals absorb and internalise social rules through which social life can be understood. Roethlisberger was a key member of the team that studied employee relations at the Western Electric Company Hawthorne Plant in Hawthorne, Illinois. The Hawthorne Studies had started in 1924 under the supervision of MIT's Dugald C. Jackson. Western Electric brought Elton Mayo and the Harvard Business School Industrial Research Group into the studies in 1927. Professor Roethlisberger worked on the studies actively from 1927 to 1936, first as Mayo's assistant and later as his collaborator. The aim of the studies was to explore the relationships between physical working conditions (e.g. lighting levels), worker morale and industrial output. Answers to questions about such relationships proved to be elusive in the early years of the project. Roethlisberger regularly expanded the boundaries of the investigation while searching for deeper insights into the behaviour of employees. Approximately 20,000 employees were interviewed, and many others were observed at their jobs under laboratory conditions measuring productivity, individual physiology and changes in physical working conditions. The studies became a milestone in the development of the Human Relations School of Industrial Management. Roethlisberger and fellow researcher William Dickson (1939) summarised the results of the studies in the classic book, *Management and the Worker*. Pickering describes a post-humanistic sociology of people and things – a reference to the exploration of the inner human experience of technology – 'industrialised consciousness'. Pickering recounts that post-World War II, a post-humanist philosophy developed in operational research, systems dynamics, systems theory, ergonomics, cybernetics, quality of working life, participative design and collaborative work movements that addressed specifically the realm of production. 'All of these are linked to the human and the nonhuman, the interactive tuning between subjects and objects'. Pickering describes his sense of déjà vu when he discovered that as far back as the 1950s, the Tavistock Institute of Human Relations – the home of the quality of working life movement – was thinking seriously about the open-ended practice of cultural transformation, a topic he worked on in the late 1980s. He discovered that the phrase 'socio-technical systems' was coined at the Tavistock (Miller and Rose, 2008; Rose, 1998), leaving him with 'a reaction of distaste' to discover that his own interpretive scheme was actually articulated by others before him. He consoles himself with 'the symmetry principle of the sociology of scientific knowledge'. Flowing from this, understandings that derive from Tavistock socio-technical systems thinking, theory and practice of group relations and psychoanalysis offer the promise of further developments in the study of organisations, social policy and international conflict. Future challenges centre on extending these bodies of knowledge into practical means of moving beyond conference work and organisation-centred consultancy into the realm of uncontained, and sometimes uncontainable, dynamics and forces in society.

Developments occurred in England at the Tavistock Institute of Human Relations, which extended clinical action research methodologies of the Tavistock Clinic. They worked with British prisoners of war experiencing problems during resettlement in their communities. Tavistock Institute researchers relied more heavily on psychoanalysis and social psychiatry than did Lewin whose emphasis was social and experimental psychology. Later in the 1950s, Tavistock researchers applied action research to industrial organisations. Classic case studies in this field include Trist and Bamforth's (1951) work in the coal mines of England, and Rice's (1958) efforts in the textile mills of India. Tavistock researchers typically centred on solving clients' problems. They undertook long-term projects documenting, analysing and taking part in changes that occurred within organisations. They also worked as consultants, contributing to solving organisational problems in different settings and enlarging the body of knowledge in the field of organisational behavioural theory.

This construction of action research theory by Lewin made action research a method of acceptable inquiry (McKernan, 1991, p. 9). Lewin (1947) developed action research at the Research Centre for Group Dynamics (University of Michigan) to study social psychology within the framework of field theory. However, another group, working independently at the Tavistock Clinic (later the Tavistock Institute), developed a similar method, which was a psycho-social equivalent of operational research (see Trist, 1997). The Tavistock Institute of Human Relations in London and the Work Research Institute in Oslo are two organisations that did extensive work in studying and promoting action research.

Action research is one of the distinctive features of organisation development and one of its core origins (French and Bell, 1999). Schein (1989) argues that organisation development grew out of Lewin's seminal work. Lewin was able to combine the methodology of experimentation with bold theory and a concern for action around important social concerns. For Lewin, it was not enough to try to explain things; one also had to try to change them. It was clear to Lewin and others that working at changing human systems often involved variables that could not be controlled as in traditional research methods, developed in the physical sciences. These insights led to the development of action research and the powerful notion that human systems could only be understood and changed if one involved the members of the system in the inquiry process itself. The tradition of involving the members of an organisation in the change process, which is the hallmark of organisation development, originated in a scientific premise of (a) getting better data and (b) effecting change. Action research is not only a methodology and a set of tools but also a theory of social science (Peters and Robinson, 1984).

Organisation development and action research

While organisation development and action research are closely related, they exist independently of one another and there are important roots and strands of action research existing outside of organisational development (McArdle and Reason, 2008). The most used model of action research is Warner Burke's seven-step action research model (2017). These seven steps are:

1 Stage of entry
2 Contracting
3 Data collection

4 Providing feedback
5 Strategic planning
6 Planning
7 Designing interventions and evaluating the success of interventions.

Kurt Lewin discussed action research as a form of experimental inquiry based upon the group's experiences of problems. He argued that social problems should serve as the locus of social science research. Basic to Lewin's model is a view of research composed of action cycles including analysis, fact-finding, conceptualisation, planning, implementation and evaluation of action (McKernan, 1991, p. 9). Chevalier and Buckles (2013, p. 11) describe Lewin's action research model:

> *The first step in the action research spiral is a problem awareness phase that seeks to 'unfreeze' a situation through fact-finding and diagnostic thinking. Shifts in understanding create the possibility of movement and support the formulation of an overall idea or plan of action to dismantle the existing mind-set and overcome the defence mechanisms and inertia. Decisions regarding immediate steps lead in turn to a phase of experimentation with transformative action. Progressive learning from these experiments feeds back into earlier plans and invites adjustments between objectives and actions. Iterative motions of research in action and action under research prepare the last phase, a closing spiral as new plans 'freeze' new forms of behaviour based on corrective action.*

(Lewin, 1948, p. 206)

McNiff, J and Whitehead, J. (2005) summarise Lewin's three-step process of change.

Figure 5.1 summarises the steps and processes involved in planned change through action research. Action research is depicted as a cyclical process of change.

The cycle begins with a series of planning actions initiated by the client and the change agent working together. The principal elements of this stage include a preliminary diagnosis, data gathering, feedback of results and joint action planning. In the language of systems theory, this is the input phase, in which the client system becomes aware of problems as yet unidentified, realises it may need outside help to effect changes and shares with the consultant the process of problem diagnosis.

The second stage of action research is the action, or transformation, phase. This stage includes actions relating to learning processes (perhaps in the form of role analysis) and to planning and executing behavioural changes in the client organisation. As shown in Figure 5.1, feedback at this stage would move via Feedback Loop A and would have the effect of altering previous planning to bring the learning activities of the client system into better alignment with change objectives. Included in this stage is action-planning activity carried out jointly by the consultant and members of the client system. Following the workshop or learning sessions, these action steps are carried out on the job as part of the transformation stage (Johnson, 1976). The third stage of action research is the output or results phase. This stage includes actual changes in behaviour (if any) resulting from corrective action steps taken following the second stage. Data are again gathered from the client system so that progress can be determined and necessary adjustments in learning activities can be made. Minor adjustments of this nature can be made in learning activities via Feedback Loop B (see Figure 5.1).

Major adjustments and re-evaluations would return the organisational development project to the first or planning stage for basic changes in the programme. The action research model shown in Figure 5.1 closely follows Lewin's repetitive cycle of planning, action and measuring results. It also illustrates other aspects of Lewin's general model of change. As indicated in the diagram, the planning stage is a period of unfreezing or problem awareness. The action stage is a period of changing, that is trying out new forms of behaviour to understand and cope with the system's problems. (There is inevitable overlap between the stages since the boundaries are not clear-cut and cannot be in a continuous process.)

The results stage is a period of refreezing, in which new behaviours are tried out on the job and, if successful and reinforcing, become a part of the system's repertoire of problem-solving behaviour. These early researchers developed relatively simple change models that emphasised initial evaluation of an organisation, preparation for change, change actions and securing change into daily organisational operations and culture.

Contemporary researchers have built on this early work by Lewin and others and created multistep models of change that involve varied organisational dimensions such as culture, leadership, communications, motivation, employee engagement, structure, rewards and teamwork, to name a few. Models by Burke and Litwin (1992), Nadler and Tushman (1980), and Tichy (1983) indicate the importance of internal and external influences such as culture, structure, individual needs and values, goal setting and feedback, among others. Conceptualisations by Kotter (1996) and Ulrich (1998) include leadership, shared need, guiding coalitions, commitment, communicating, changing structures, empowering others and making change last. These models have been criticised for their linear supposition and rigid steps, inability to account for the complexities of change, discounting of the human factor and failure to prepare for resistance to change (Gilley, 2005). Doyle et al. (2000) reported that change agents find the numerous models to be too 'pre-packaged' while failing to address the linkages and contradictions in change. Nadler (1998) states that 'the reality of change in the organisational trenches defies rigid academic models as well as superficial management fads' (p. 3). As a result, understanding the individual, group and organisational processes that must occur to drive positive change is critical for leaders, consultants and change agents. As action research is problem-centred, client-centred and action-oriented involving the client system in diagnostic, active-learning, problem-finding and problem-solving processes, it is possible to be flexible to the unpredictable changes in the system.

Lewin's model of action research

In the 1950s and 1960s, action research was used in the study of industry. Action research developed a commitment following in the USA at the Massachusetts Institute of Technology and in the UK at the Tavistock Institute of Human Relations (McKernan, 1991, p. 10; Coghlan, D., and Jacobs, C., 2005; Crosby, G., 2021). According to Frances Abraham (2013), the importance of action research as an orientation strongly pervaded the Tavistock Institute Group and their shared practice. Jaques first constructed for the Glacier Metal Company an action research methodology, which they would all largely adopt and adapt. Trist wrote that 'interdisciplinary collaboration was achieved in an action frame of reference ... A common set of understandings developed, based on a shared core value – commitment to the social engagement of social science' (Trist, 1973, p. 104). The initial studies, most of them reported in the journal, *Human Relations* (a joint venture with Lewin's Research Centre for Group Dynamics at MIT and later University of Michigan), are narrow in focus; the novelty of their findings providing a strong sense of the emergent nature of their theory.

Kurt Lewin's 'field theory' was based on the gestalt understanding of systems: that the whole is more than the sum of its parts and that each part needed to be understood in relation to the whole, drawing attention to 'the dynamics of such interdependencies' (Miller, 1999, p. xv). This can be seen in the early Tavistock's emphasis on what goes on at the boundaries of teams or work groups and their departments, between departments and between the organisation and its environment. After Emery's arrival at the Tavistock Institute in 1957, he brought the Tavistock's attention to the work of von Bertalanffy (1950), systems thinking about organisations as organic and mechanical systems – with inputs, transformative capability and outputs – supported them in analysing work organisation and work processes to effect good job and work design. We can trace a direct stream of related work in action research that follows Lewin and the Tavistock experience. These arise in the field of organisational sociology and social psychology. The essential assumptions underlying planned change are derived originally from Lewin (1947). As we said above, Lewin's model proposes three phases: unfreezing (identifying the need for change); moving, (changing); and refreezing (embedding the change).

But Cummings, Bridgman and Brown (2015) argue that Kurt Lewin's 'changing as three steps' (unfreezing → changing → refreezing) although regarded by many as the classic or fundamental approach to managing change was never articulated by Lewin in such a way. They compare what Lewin wrote about changing as three steps with how this is presented in later works and argue that he never developed such a model, and it took form after his death. They point out that in recent years, some have disparaged Lewin for advancing an overly simplistic model. For example, Kanter et al. (1992, p. 10) claim that 'Lewin's... quaintly linear and static conception – the organisation as an ice cube – is so wildly inappropriate that this is difficult to see why it has not only survived but prospered'. Child (2005, p. 293) points out that Lewin's rigid idea of 'refreezing' is inappropriate in today's complex world, which requires flexibility and adaptation. Clegg et al. (2005, p. 376) are critical of the way in which Lewin's 'simple chain of unfreeze, move, refreeze [which has become] the template for most change programs' is just a repackaging of a mechanistic philosophy behind 'Taylor's (1911) concept of scientific management'. They claim that 'change as three steps' (CATS) represents just a quarter of Lewin's canon and must be understood in concert with his other 'three pillars': field theory, group dynamics and action research (Burnes, 2004a, 2004b), and that contemporary understandings of field theory neglect Lewin's concern with gestalt psychology and conventional topology (Burnes and Cooke, 2012b). Cummings, Bridgman and Brown (2015) point out that Lewin never presented CATS in a linear diagrammatic form, and he did not list it as bullet points. CATS is merely described as a way that 'planned social change may be thought of' (Lewin, 1947, p. 36; 1951, p. 231); an example explaining (in an abstract way) the group dynamics of social change and the advantages of group versus individual decision-making. It appears almost as an afterthought, or at least not fully thought out, given that the CATS (see Figure 5.1 for foundational schema of CATS) metaphor of 'unfreezing' and 'freezing' seems to contradict Lewin's more detailed empirically based theorising of 'quasi-equilibrium', which is explained in considerable depth in *Field Theory* and argues that groups are in a continual process of adaptation, rather than a steady or frozen state.

According to Crosby (2021), critics of Lewin have said this model of change as three steps (dubbed CATS) is too simple. Unfreezing, moving, and freezing is an intentional simplification, to create a framework for the process of planned change. Lewin was aware that the actual effort of changing something is complicated and full of setbacks and surprises, many of which emerge along the way. For changing a social equilibrium, too, one has to consider the total social field: the groups and subgroups involved their relations, their value systems, etc. The constellation of the social field as a whole has to be studied and so reorganised that social events flow differently (Lewin, 1947a, 2008, p. 327).

With such complexity in mind, Lewin devised methods of planned change that address enough of the 'constellation of the social field as a whole', to reliably implement and sustain the desired outcomes.

Freezing at the new level is not some sort of final or permanent condition. Change is continuous. Change and constancy are relative concepts; group life is never without change, merely differences in the amount and type of change exist (Lewin, 1947, 2008, p. 308). Lewin was adamant that group dynamics must not be seen in simplistic or static terms and believed that groups were never in a steady state, seeing them instead as being in continuous movement, albeit having periods of relative stability or 'quasi-stationary equilibria' (1951, p. 199). Lewin never said his idea was a model that could be used by a change agent. He did, however, do significant research and published highly respected articles that argued against Taylor's mechanistic approach (Lewin, 1920; Marrow, 1969).

While extensively accepted and modified, the idea that organisations are frozen and refrozen has been heavily criticised (Dawson, 2003). Burnes (2013), however, accepted Lewin's view that his model should be used with the three other features that comprise planned change – field theory, group dynamics and action research. These make an integrated approach to analysing, understanding and bringing about change, thus providing a sequential prescription for the processes of change (see Figure 5.2).

Since Lewin's death, unfreeze-change-refreeze has sometimes been applied more rigidly than he intended, for example through discarding an old structure, setting up a new one and then fixing this into place. Such an inflexible course of action fits badly with more modern perspectives on change as a continuous and flowing process of evolution, and Lewin's change model is now often criticised for its linearity, especially from the perspective of more recent research on nonlinear, chaotic systems and complexity theory. The model was, however, process-oriented originally, and Lewin himself viewed change as a continuing process, recognising that extremely complex forces are at work in group and organisational dynamics.

The action research cycles

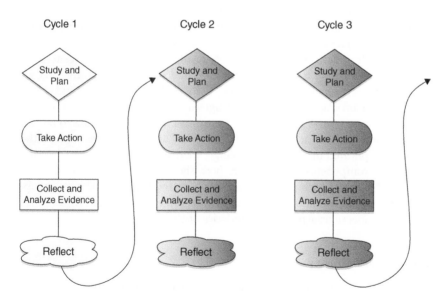

Figure 5.2 Action Research Cycles by Margaret Riel (2006), https://commons. wikimedia.org/wiki/File:Riel-action_research.jpg. This file is licensed under the Creative Commons Attribution-Share Alike 3.0 Unported licence.

Kurt Lewin's field theory

Neumann (2011a, 2011b, 2012, 2013a, 2013b, 2013c, 2018), (https://www.bl.uk/business-and-management/editorials/kurt-lewins-field-theory) describes four aspects of Kurt Lewin's approach that have influenced the Tavistock Institute, viz.:

1 Lewin's dynamic approach rule
2 Field theory
3 Lewin's contemporaneity rule
4 Lewin's constructive method rule
5 Lewin's dynamic approach rule

Lewin's dynamic approach rule

Neumann (2012) summarises the dynamic approach in the following manner:

'The dynamic approach indicates the necessity of discovering multiple forces at work in any situation. This means that no matter where we enter an organisational development or change process we need to be prepared to use many levels of analysis to understand what is going on within the social system. What is affecting the people who are leading, managing and existing amid the change and development?

Lewin's dynamic approach rule states that the 'elements of any situation should be regarded as parts of a system'. In other words, we find it useful as scholarly practitioners to assume that all component parts relate with each other forming a complex whole. We find it useful to assume that all parts connect somehow in ways to be discovered through action and study.

The dynamic approach rule challenges us to be concerned with multiple energising or motive forces. At the minimum, this requires data to be collected and analysed at multiple levels of social analysis. As we consider the issues implicated in a particular change, we discipline ourselves to describe separate components and to assert how they might be influencing each other. No matter which level we enter – individual, group, inter-group, organisational or inter-organisational – we work to notice and hypothesise about connections across the boundaries of these levels.'

Lewin's field theory

Neumann (2012) summarises field theory in the following manner:

'Applying field theory in organisational change and consulting requires an acceptance of its central premise that people and their surroundings and conditions depend closely on each other. In Lewin's words: "To understand or to predict behaviour, the person and his environment must be considered as one constellation of interdependent factors".

(1946, p. 338)

Thus, the notion of field refers to: (a) all aspects of individuals in relationship with their surroundings and conditions; (b) that apparently influence the behaviours and developments of concern; (c) at a particular point in time.

Lewin's field theory rule states that "analysis starts with the situation as a whole". By gaining an overview as early as possible, we intend to broaden the perspective from which we as scholarly practitioners engage with the general characteristics of the challenge or opportunity facing our organisational clients. Lewin highlighted the importance of characterising the atmosphere (e.g. emotional tone or climate) and the amount of freedom existing in the situation.

Such an overall perspective counteracts the pull to repeat the same unsuccessful attempts at change and development. Field theory leads us to conclude that such a pull to repetition comes from forces within the field. As outsiders we may be prone to believe that we won't succumb. Thus, after starting with the total situation, our analysis needs to focus on more specific variables that might be at play. We aim to represent everything in the field (i.e. people and their environment) that helps or hinders movement towards the goals for change and development.

Neumann (2012) adds that a specific criterion for objectivity when using field theory can improve the quality of organisational change practice. Lewin asserts that we should aim to represent the field "correctly as it exists for the individual in question at a particular time" (1946, p. 338). Even when working with collective phenomenon, this discipline for analysis remains. We need to avoid offering predetermined solutions or getting caught in the same field of forces as our clients. Instead, scholarly practitioners take the time and effort to study the idiosyncrasies of each total situation and make a representation of the forces being experienced by clients. From that analysis, we discuss working hypotheses with our clients to assist them in changing their field (i.e. their behaviour and related surroundings and conditions). We may also be able to cooperate with them on experiments in moving towards their change goals'.

Lewin's contemporaneity rule

Neumann (2012) summarises contemporaneity rule as follows:

> 'As the basis of action, contemporaneity points to concentrating on elements of the current situation that motivate or otherwise influence people and their environment and thus shape change. Lewin asserted that: "Only conditions in the present can explain experience and behaviour in the present".
>
> (Gold, 1992, p.70)

Therefore, we concern ourselves primarily with systematic causes and not historical-geographical ones. The nature of the conditions of change means that effects can only be produced by that which is concrete, something that exists within the same time-period (Lewin, 1936, pg. 32) of the situation being addressed.

In drawing a representation of a situation therefore: "We take account only of what is contemporary"; that is, existing at the same time or during the same time-period, while we accept the "necessity of excluding events which roughly speaking belong to past and future time" (Lewin, 1992b, pp. 34–35). The purpose of such a diagnosis, for scholarly practitioners of organisational development and change, is to explain or predict change in a certain situation. We do this by linking the change with the inter-connected, concrete "conditions of the field at that time" (Lewin, 1992a, p. 211).

In designing interventions for change and development within the particular situation, the contemporaneity rule helps us understand the underlying causality in action research. By setting up "tests of the present" it becomes possible to discern those concrete elements within the time and field that may be influencing people in their environment. Lewin clearly states that the "total field includes time perspective at a given time" (1992a, p. 207), by which he includes psychological past and psychological future. He differentiates the actual past and future from that which exists in the present. For example, goals can exist in the present, but their actual content cannot because they have not yet been realised. Crucially, the power of expectation – Lewin terms this "subjective probability" – can be very important as an influence on behaviour in the present. Expectations tend to be "affected by perception on the one hand and memory on the other" (1992b, p. 208).

Many staff members at the Tavistock Institute would consider that transference from the past needs to be recognised as an element of the present. This psychoanalytic provision cannot be credited to Lewin, even though he insisted that systemic causality "does not imply a neglect or underestimation of historical problems" (Lewin, 1936, p. 32). By definition, transference means consciously or unconsciously repeating elements of the past in the present. Such enactments can emerge from individuals, within a collective and/or evolve into a mutually constructed dynamic. Three common approaches for intervening are: (1) bringing the transference from the past to awareness in the present; (2) testing the degree to which the past is "alive in the present"; and (3) experimenting in the present by intentionally acting differently from the past. Such a practice rooted in the scholarship of psychoanalytic tradition resonates with the contemporaneity rule by treating the transference as something concrete exerting influence in the current situation'.

Lewin's constructive method rule

Neumann (2012) summarises constructive method rule as follows:

'Lewin's constructive method rule prioritises the creation of concepts, however intangible, that seem necessary for explanation (Gold, 1992, P. 70). At minimum, we aim for thick, rich descriptions of the total situation as it is being experienced by the people involved. The overall purpose or objective of the consultancy, guides the inquiry, as do the resource limitations negotiated for the project. In order for the conceptualisation to be useful, it must represent psychological "processes not as single isolated facts but in their mutual dependence as expressions of a concrete situation" involving definite people in a definite condition (Lewin, 1936, p. 2).

The more the conceptualisation shows how "the different facts in an individual's environment are related to the individual" (Lewin, 1936, pp. 12–13) the more client system members feel understood and able to explore together how to make use of the concepts. At minimum, such a conceptualisation helps clients and consultants search for an understanding of the total situation. Practically and somewhat unexpectedly, it also provides a reframed goal to guide actions for change and development. Instead of struggling, for example, to convince each other to aim for change in a preferred way, stakeholders find a joint goal that is wider or deeper in how it helps connect their differences towards something mutual'.

Countervailing force fields

Summarising Lewin, we assert that viewing organisations as (i) systems of countervailing force fields that serve to support or resist change, (ii) identifying the change agent's role as helping to 'unfreeze' stabilising forces and (iii) identifying gatekeepers as high leverage players who exert influence to move the system are but three concepts that have been pivotal to planned change theory. Despite the passage of time, Lewin's theoretical and practical concepts are remarkably contemporary. From these ideas, change theory has evolved considerably, a pattern that Lewin, ever the practical theorist, would most definitely appreciate.

The characteristics of action research

An action research model for evaluation and consultancy practice is described by Cohen and Manion (1989, p. 344):

> *Essentially as an on the spot procedure designed to deal with a concrete problem located in an immediate situation. This means that step-by-step process is constantly monitored (ideally, that is) over varying periods of time and by a variety of mechanisms (questionnaires, diaries, interviews, and case studies, for example) so that ensuing feedback may be translated into modifications, adjustments, directional changes, redefinitions, as necessary, so as to bring about lasting benefit to the on-going process itself.*

The legacy of Lewin's work, though contested (e.g. McTaggart, 1996, p. 248), is powerful in the steps of action research set out by Kemmis and McTaggart (1992, p. 2):

> *In practice, the process begins with a general idea that improvement or change is desirable. In deciding just where to begin in making improvements one decides on a field of action ... where the battle (not the whole war) should be fought. It is a*

decision on where it is possible to have an impact. The general idea prompts a 're-connaissance' of the circumstances of the field, and fact-finding about them. Having decided on the field and made a preliminary reconnaissance, the action researcher decides on a general plan of action. Breaking the general plan down into achievable steps, the action researcher settles on the first action step. Before taking this first step the action researcher becomes more circumspect and devises a way of monitoring the effects of the first action step. When it is possible to maintain fact-finding by monitoring the action, the first step is taken. As the step is implemented, new data start coming in and the effect of the action can be described and evaluated. The general plan is then revised in the light of the new information about the field of action and the second action step can be planned along with appropriate monitoring procedures. The second step is then implemented, monitored and evaluated; and the spiral of action, monitoring, evaluation and re-planning continues.

McKernan (1991, p. 17) suggests that Lewin's model of action research is a series of spirals, each of which incorporates a cycle of analysis, reconnaissance, reconceptualisation of the problem, planning of the intervention, implementation of the plan and evaluation of the effectiveness of the intervention.

Rappaport (1970, p. 499) states that action research differs from other social science approaches in the 'immediacy of the researcher's involvement in the action process'. Cummings and Worley (2001, pp. 24–27) suggest that action research involves 'a cyclical process of diagnosis-change-research-diagnosis-change-research'. The results of diagnosis produce ideas for changes; the changes are introduced into the same system, and their effects are noted through further research and diagnosis. Zuber-Skerritt (1992) differentiates action research approaches, traditional social science and natural science approaches to research in the following ways:

1 Action research is intended to make a practical difference to participants (note the intentional avoidance of the term 'subject'), with advancement of the theoretical field or discipline serving as a second goal.
2 Action research is participative and collaborative, empowering and involving participants in the research process and demystifying the 'researcher' as a white-coated academic, instead fostering a partnership approach to achieve the research goals.
3 Action research regards as valid the views of each participant, with participants asked to reflect continuously on their situations and to explore as many avenues for action as possible.

Peters and Robinson (1984) found the following shared features in their analysis of the writings of 11 action researchers: (a) problem focus, (b) action orientation, (c) cyclical process and (d) collaboration/participation.

For Susman and Evered (1978), the essential characteristics of action research are as follows: (a) future-oriented, (b) collaborative, (c) contributing to system development, (d) diagnostic and (e) situational. Others (e.g. Argyris, 1983; Stebbins and Snow, 1982) specify the phases in action research in greater detail and cover what Shani and Bushe (1987, p. 5) in their view of relevant literature term four 'key emergent processes': (1) the emerging socio-task system, (2) the co-inquiry process, (3) the integration process and (4) the experimentation process. Action research always involves two goals: to solve a problem and to contribute to science.

Two further elements are:

1 Those involved – the researcher and the organisation – should learn from each other and develop their knowledge and skills.
2 The understanding developed is holistic, and the researcher must focus on the totality of the problem.

Action research requires cooperation between the researcher and the organisation, feedback to the parties involved and continuous adjustment to new information and new events as performed in this research. Action research is a way of both researching and stimulating social action in organisations. It involves the researcher in working with members of organisations to create change in response to concerns that matter to them (rather than simply studying them or participating with them). In parallel, it requires a commitment to developing either a contribution to basic knowledge or a theoretical insight, about the situation. The insight may be brought into the public domain in the form of a general observation or used by the members of the organisation.

The purposes of action research

1 Contributes to the theory and knowledge base to enhance practice
2 Supports the professional development of practitioners
3 Builds a collegial networking system
4 Helps practitioners identify problems and seek solutions systematically
5 Can be used at all levels and in all areas of education
6 General research skills needed to:
    i Design research
    ii Develop instruments
    iii Select subjects (if necessary)
    iv Collect data
    v Analyse data

Goals

1 Overall goal should be to solve a problem
2 Include collaboration

3 Professional development
4 Enhance professional practice

From the above, action research is clearly both a process and an approach to working on organisational problems. Although consultants are not usually employed as researchers, we will show that the application of an action research methodology increases the ability for the consultant to form collaborative relationships with the client system. We will show not only how action research differs from consultancy practice but also how it can enhance a consultant's capacity to make a diagnosis and form collaborative relationships with the client system.

Using the action research model for organisational interventions

The action research model is a practical tool for ensuring that planned changes in organisations lead to real improvements. In the first step, the consultant conducts preliminary research; here, 'consultant' usually refers to an outsider, but the change agent for an organisational development project can be either an external or an internal consultant. In the case of an external change agent, some of this preliminary research might amount to a marketing study in order to find clients, but it also would include the casual and formal gathering of information that occurs during the initial meetings between client and consultant. For internal consultants, preliminary research occurs during the period of trust-building required to obtain managerial commitment to the change process.

During this initial period, the consultant learns about the organisation's problems and opportunities and informs the client about the methods and anticipated benefits of the action research process. The preliminary research terminates with the potential client's decision about whether to engage the consultant's services for the change effort. If the potential client does not accept the consultant's offer, the intervention stops. If the client says 'yes', the atmosphere setting phase begins. During the atmosphere setting phase, the organisation and the consultant become familiar with each other; and the action research is designed by the client and by the change agent, who acts as a consultant process expert.

After the atmosphere setting and design phases, members of the organisation and the consultant cooperate to collect data about the organisation and its interface with its environment. These data can take many different forms. For example, in a comprehensive organisational development project the consultant team could collect data about employee satisfaction, supervisory practices, job design, productivity (efficiency), performance (output), and customer satisfaction with the services or products.

Next, the data are communicated to the members of the organisation. Often, the data feedback will take place in team-building sessions. This allows the organisation's members to view the organisation's problems and opportunities objectively. Ideally, the data feedback would lead to concrete identification of problems and their analysis.

Using the data feedback, members of the organisation plan actions to solve problems and maximise the organisation's opportunities. Finally, the organisation implements the recommended actions.

The action steps are intended to improve the functioning of the organisation; however, there is no guarantee that plans will accomplish their intended purposes. Organisations' social and physical environments probably will change; today's solutions are not necessarily adequate responses to tomorrow's challenges. Therefore, the next step of the action research process is to evaluate the effects of the intervention, particularly to determine how well the intervention worked and whether future changes are advisable.

The action research model is a closed loop system; that is, after the evaluation, the next step is to recycle through the process. The action research intervention then begins again with a contracting phase to determine whether the client wants to continue through another full cycle of the process. Presumably, if the process is worthwhile (returning greater benefits than its material and non-material costs), the organisation would want to repeat the process. Clearly, action research is not a 'quick fix' or a 'patch up' for ailing organisations. Instead, action research is an ongoing process of renewal for organisations that wish to optimise their task and sentient systems.

Summary

The key aspects of action research are diagnosis, data gathering, and feedback to the client group, data discussion and work by the client group, action planning and action. The sequence is cyclical with the focus on new or advanced problems as the client group learns to work more effectively together.

Action research is concerned with both the generation of scientific knowledge and its usefulness in solving practical problems, bridging the gap between theory and practice. Collective participation bridges the gap between social research and social action. It is not enough to explain things; one also must change them.

Changing human systems cannot be controlled as in traditional research methods. Human systems can only be understood and changed by involving members of the system in the inquiry process itself. The first step in the action research spiral is fact-finding and diagnostic thinking. Shifts in understanding come from dismantling existing mind-sets and overcoming defence mechanisms and inertia.

Action research involves experimentation with transformative action. To understand or predict behaviour, the person and his environment must be considered as one constellation of interdependent factors. The 'field' refers to all aspects of individuals in relationship with their surroundings and conditions that apparently influence behaviours and developments of concern at a point in time.

The role of action researchers is to create the conditions for democratic dialogue among participants. Action learning involves engagement with real problems rather than with fabrications, and is both scientifically rigorous in confronting the problem and critically subjective through people learning-in-action. Large group interventions are designed to engage representatives of an entire system, whether it be an organisation or a community, in thinking through and planning change. Action research is an emergent inquiry process in which applied behavioural science knowledge is integrated with existing organisational knowledge and applied to solve real organisational problems.

Exercise

1 How would you design an intervention to a large complex global organisation to address issues of leadership?
2 Why is co-design important and relevant?
3 What might be the consequences of 'off-the-shelf' designs?
4 What are the advantages and disadvantages of collaborative design?
5 Why is data-gathering and analysis prior to an intervention so important?
6 What could be learned about an organisational system as one 'crosses the boundary'?

Chapter 6

Evaluation of systems psychodynamics activities

Approaches and challenges

Dione (Sanji) Hills

Introduction

There is a growing call for organisational development interventions to be effectively evaluated. Evaluation of an intervention can serve different purposes: it can provide regular opportunities to review the work and adapt this to changing circumstances. It can provide feedback to those who commissioned the work, and it can contribute to building an 'evidence base' on what works well, and less well, in organisational development practice.

However, to those new to the field, the terms and language used in evaluation can be confusing. In consultancy activities, the term evaluation may be used to describe the process of reviewing an activity to see how it is going, and whether anything needs to change. However, more widely, the term evaluation also refers to activities undertaken by evaluation practitioners, who draw on a large body of theory and practice, specialist journals, associations and websites. Somewhere between the two, the term can also be used to describe an activity built into or added to an organisational development intervention, which provides the opportunity to review and learn from what is going on, that uses resources drawn from the professional evaluator's 'toolkit' to provide good data and analysis to support this activity.

In this chapter, to make a distinction between these meanings, the first of these is referred to as 'reflective practice' or simply 'reviewing' ongoing work. The second is called 'full scale', 'independent' or 'external' evaluation, and third, either self- or 'embedded' evaluation. The differences between these three are not hard and fast: professional evaluators may work inside an organisation or provide support to those undertaking evaluation of their own work. There is also a close relationship between evaluative thinking and reflective practice, which is discussed later in this chapter.

In this chapter, some basic principles of evaluation are described, together with a description of some of the different approaches and terms that you are likely to come across in the evaluation literature. The next chapter describes some of the more practical points that need to be considered in planning, undertaking or commissioning someone else to undertake, an evaluation of a consultancy intervention. Although neither chapter goes into great depth about

DOI: 10.4324/9781003368663-10

individual evaluation approaches and research methods often used in evaluation, they do provide signposts to where more information about these can be found. A key theme running through both chapters is the importance of evaluation activities being compatible with, and ideally supporting, the intervention itself.

Other themes run through and form the structure for the rest of this chapter:

1 Lack of prior evaluation in the organisational development and group relations fields and why this might be the case
2 Different types of evaluation and how evaluation differs from research
3 The importance of planning and key factors to consider when planning an evaluation
4 Ensuring compatibility between the evaluation and the activity being evaluated
5 Conducting an evaluation and the usefulness of 'consultancy' skills when doing this
6 How to ensure that evaluation findings are used

The chapter draws on the experience of evaluation undertaken by Tavistock Institute consultants and evaluators. At the Institute, the relationship between evaluation and consultancy is a close one, with evaluation activities building on the strong 'action research' tradition at the Institute, as well as incorporating elements of reflective practice and systems thinking. A systems psychodynamics perspective helps evaluators think about the dynamics of entering and working with a 'system'. Consultants and evaluators can reflect on ways in which dynamics within the evaluation process might be reflecting dynamics within the project, programme, training or organisational development activity that is being evaluated.

Many issues can emerge while undertaking an evaluation, especially when the evaluation is of a complex project or programme, as many organisational development interventions are. The chapter also includes thoughts and guidance provided by other evaluators working in the organisational development field, and several examples of evaluations in which, although well designed and often undertaken by experienced evaluators, things went awry. These examples are taken from the book *Evaluation Failures* (Hutchinson, 2018), which provides 22 accounts from experienced evaluators, organisational development evaluations that went wrong and what they learned from this.

Lack of evaluation in organisational development field

Although there is a rich and extensive literature on the theory and practice of organisational development activities, the amount of research and evaluation that has been undertaken in this field is quite limited. Published accounts will often provide rich detail on the issues being addressed, the actions that were taken, and some account of what changes took place because of the intervention. However, in 'evaluation' and 'research' terms, these would be described as case studies rather than full-scale evaluations. The difference between a case study and an evaluation is that the former is usually a description of an intervention, but without the kind of detailed data collection and analysis that is required by a full-scale evaluation. In an evaluation, it will be important to find ways to demonstrate that the intervention was causally related (responsible for) to the 'outcomes' identified, and to review how these related to the original aims for the intervention.

A number of writers have expressed a concern at the lack of more rigorous research and evaluation in the organisational development field, arguing that this has led to a lack of robust evidence about 'what works' in organisational development practice, or systematic testing of the theoretical basis for this work. There is a rising demand for 'evidence-based' practice in many different fields, reflected, for example, in the establishment of a number of 'What Works' centres in the UK to review evidence in various policy areas (https://www.gov.uk/guidance/what-works-network).

The other writers have expressed concern that consultants are not doing enough to review their own work systematically or provide feedback to clients on its effectiveness. Both of the above concerns are raised in the following quote from Waclawski and Church (2008):

> An evaluation of the success of the OD effort should always be undertaken. Often this requires collecting additional data regarding the impact of the intervention in the light of the deliverables that were agreed on in the contracting phase, as well as brainstorming about process improvements for future OD efforts. Clearly this is easier said than done. One of the truly unfortunate situations in many OD efforts over the past thirty years, and one that has damaged the reputation of the field somewhat as well, has been the lack of significant attention to evaluating the success or failure of an OD process. As many researchers and OD scholars have noted (Golembiewski and Sun, 1990; Porras and Robertson, 1992; Woodman and Wayne, 1985), there is a real need in the field for the consistent application of evaluation strategies to the entire consulting cycle.

Evaluation and research

There are debates in the field about whether evaluation is a sub-discipline of 'research', or whether it is a separate discipline, which uses social science research methods (Rogers, 2014). What the activity is called is less important than an understanding of ways in which evaluation activities can differ from research commissioned for other purposes and how this may influence some of the dynamics involved.

In terms of purpose, as already noted, evaluation can be used to generate general knowledge (and evidence) about an area of activity, or it can be used to support learning and reflection on activities as these are taking place. Evaluation may also be undertaken because funders or clients require this in order to show that the resources have been used appropriately (accountability) or may be used to demonstrate that the activity should be continued after initial funding comes to an end (sustainability) or could be introduced elsewhere (often referred to as replication). Having a clear picture of *why* an evaluation is being undertaken helps ensure that the right questions are asked, and the right approach and methods are used. These three topics – purpose, questions and methods – are explored later in this chapter and in the next.

Unlike many research projects, an evaluation *always* starts with an intervention that is seeking to bring about change. This intervention may be a project or programme, or an organisational development activity that has a specific set of aims, or a training activity, which is seeking to enhance individual skills or knowledge. Where there is an intervention, there will also be a client or specific audience who have either asked for the evaluation or are interested in its outcome. A research project, on the other hand, usually starts from an identified gap in knowledge, or with theory that needs to be tested, and has the aim of producing 'generalisable' knowledge, often for generic audiences, such as academics, or practitioners working in a particular field. Evaluations can also generate useful knowledge, but this may be secondary to the primary task of providing feedback to a client or audience on how an intervention is working.

Barker et al. (1995) highlight this 'utilisation' aspect of evaluation, noting that this is usually undertaken to assist decision-making, rather than add to an existing body of theoretical knowledge. Weiss (1972) points out that evaluations usually take place in a complex of 'action sets', rather than in a more controlled academic research environment (Weiss, 1972).

Unlike many research studies, evaluation quite often has consequences for those involved in the intervention being studied. Jobs and livelihoods, as well as reputations, may hang on evaluation findings. For this reason, they can arouse anxiety. Evaluators may also find themselves under pressure or notice attempts to control the kind of data they collect, how this will be analysed and what findings are produced (and how these are reported). To paraphrase Barker et al. (1995), evaluation can be a sensitive activity that takes place in a socio-political and organisational context.

When things go wrong: Programme managers in a multi-site programme evaluation vigorously rejected extensive evidence (drawn from interviews, a survey and case studies) that local staff wanted to have greater contact and communication with the central team. This masked the concern from the central team that they did not have the capacity to provide this level of communication with sites. When presented with more contextual information and suggestions of how this challenge could be addressed without a major investment of resources, the evidence was (reluctantly) accepted.

Hutchinson, K., (2018) *Evaluation Failures*, Chapter 20

Another aspect of evaluation that makes it different from (most) research is that it includes something referred to as 'evaluative thinking'. Evaluation seeks not only to generate knowledge and evidence, but also to derive 'meaning' or learning from this. The word 'value' is at the heart of 'evaluation'. Vo et al. (2018) describe this aspect of evaluation 'the ascription of merit, worth, significance, importance' to an intervention. In other words, undertaking evaluation involves making a judgement. Is the intervention working well? Or not? Is it producing the results and benefits anticipated? This, too, can arouse anxiety in those who are at the 'receiving end' of the evaluation activities (sometimes referred to as the 'evaluands').

The 'evaluative thinking' aspect of evaluation is also the element that ties it closely to the idea of reflective practice. Evaluators themselves need to be self-reflective and alert to what is going on in the project or programme in which they are working, and how their own activities might be influencing this. Their activities may also, as Carol Weiss (2013) notes, support reflective practice in the organisation and individuals with whom they are working. Evaluators can enable ...

Program people {to} reflect on their practice, think critically, and ask questions about why the program operates as it does. They learn something of the evaluative cast of mind—the sceptical questioning point of view, the perspective of the reflective practitioner.

(pp. 323–327)

Reasons for the lack of evaluation of organisational development

There are several reasons why there is a lack of evaluation of organisational development activities, one of which being the sensitive and political nature of the evaluation task. However, there are also practical difficulties that can make the task challenging. These include the difficulty in articulating, and measuring, outcomes, a lack of resources, and concern that the evaluation will interfere with the intervention itself.

The challenge of articulating and measuring outcomes: Organisational development interventions, particularly those that are systems psychodynamically oriented, usually begin with the identification of an issue or problem. A consultant (internal or external) may be brought in because there is a problem (such as high levels of staff turnover, low levels of productivity or conflict between different groups in an organisation). At this stage, it may not be clear what kind of intervention the consultants will put in place, or even exactly what will be the outcome (except in quite broad terms). It may turn out, following the diagnostic phase, that the problem is not quite what was initially thought, which means that outcomes from any intervention might also be different to those initially expected (see Chapter 11 on entry and contracting; going beneath the presenting problem).

In this context, it can be useful to view both an organisation in receipt of an organisational development intervention and the organisational development activities themselves, as 'complex systems'. The behaviour of complex systems is often unpredictable and is never totally 'static' – change may fluctuate considerably over time and across different sites.

Measurement of change is much easier if the intervention has a set of SMART goals or objectives.

SMART objectives are

- Specific (simple, sensible, significant)
- Measurable (meaningful, motivating)
- Achievable (agreed, attainable)
- Relevant (reasonable, realistic and resourced, results-based)
- Time-bound (time-based, time-limited, time/cost-limited, timely, time-sensitive)

(Doran, 1981)

In practice, it may be quite hard to identify a set of SMART goals early in an organisational development intervention. Fortunately, evaluators have several tools that can help overcome this difficulty, which are described later in this chapter, including system and theory of change mapping. There are also many validated 'scales' that have been developed specifically for assessing relatively abstract concepts like 'wellbeing' or 'empowerment'.

Lack of resources: In many organisational development interventions, there are resources only for the intervention itself, not for additional activities such as evaluation, particularly if this requires additional data collection and analysis. Consultancy clients may not be persuaded that an evaluation will add value to the intervention and be unwilling to provide additional funding for this. The resources required include not only money – for the extra time and effort involved – but also specific skills and expertise. This includes an understanding of evaluation, social research and statistical expertise in the design and analysis of qualitative and quantitative data, and often other skills, such as IT expertise for developing an online survey or a database to capture data.

Consultants *may* have some or all these skills and may also need to involve others with appropriate skills. There are various ways of doing this. There may be others in the consultancy firm, or the client organisation, who have these skills, or it may be necessary to bring in an external evaluator. Involving someone internally can strengthen an 'embedded' evaluation and work well where the primary aim is one of learning, accountability, or provide justification for continuation of the work. An external evaluator can also be very helpful in supporting this kind of evaluation too, but engaging external evaluation support becomes increasingly important where the primary aim is the generation of knowledge, and particularly when seeking to demonstrate the effectiveness of a particular action so that this can be replicated elsewhere.

This is because to produce generalisable conclusions from an evaluation requires research methods that can be heavy on resources and require quite specific expertise. If the findings are to be useful to a wider audience, they will need to be made available through an appropriate channel: usually via a peer-reviewed journal, book chapter or specialist website. Turning an evaluation report into a journal article or book chapter requires time and resources, for example, ensuring the findings are 'situated' in a larger body of research and theory. Publication also requires the careful 'anonymising' of the information to ensure that readers are unable to identify the organisation or individuals who provided data. Finally, organisational development clients themselves may also be reluctant to have the inner workings of their organisation on public display, either because of general concerns about confidentiality or for reasons of commercial sensitivity.

Concern about interfering with the intervention. One of the key concerns in a cross-boundary management development programme and the Leicester conference evaluation (Hills, 2018) was that the presence of the evaluators would get in the way of the dynamics of the intervention itself. In the Leicester conference example, although there was some evidence that participants and particularly staff felt conscious of the presence of the evaluators and may have changed their behaviour in response to this, overall, their response was positive. Having a researcher present supported the learning aims of the conference.

Undertaking evaluation in a sensitive environment

The Leicester conference is a two-week immersive learning experience for those wishing to understand organisational and group dynamics in depth, particularly from a systems psychodynamics perspective. The conference establishes a 'temporary organisation' in which staff help participants to make sense of and draw learning from their experiences. The Tavistock Institute has been running the conference for over 60 years but had not undertaken an evaluation of the event, in part because of concern that introducing evaluation might interfere with the process and dynamics of the conference itself.

In 2012, an evaluation was undertaken by two consultant researchers from the Institute who also had experience of the group relations approach to learning, although they were not part of the staff running the event. To ensure the evaluation fitted in with the values and aims of the conference, plans were discussed with both the directors of the conference and the staff group. Out of this consultation, it was ascertained that an evaluation would both provide feedback on the event and generate an account of the conference that would be useful for a wider audience.

Three evaluation questions were settled on:

- What key learning and insights are generated by the Leicester conference (2012)?
- Which aspects or elements of the conference contribute most to this learning?
- How did participants make use of this learning on their return to their 'back home' work?

The evaluation was designed to minimise interference in the conference dynamics. Researcher presence was limited to two days when they were available in the dining room during breaks for anyone who wished to be interviewed, and observation of a small number of events on these two days. Throughout the evaluation, regular discussions were held with the directors and staff to ensure that time and space boundaries around the conference activities were respected and maintained. Participants were informed in advance that the research was taking place and assured about the confidentiality of any data collected and that participation in research activities was purely voluntary.

The data generated included:

- Responses from three online surveys: sent electronically to participants before, immediately after and 9 months after the completion of the conference
- Interviews with staff and participants part way through and towards the end of the conference
- Observation of two large group events and one staff meeting

Most people responded positively to the inclusion of this research element, feeling that this supported, rather than undermined, the overall learning aims of the conference. Many participants and staff volunteered to be interviewed during the two days that the evaluators attended the conference. Response to the first two surveys was good but rather low on the follow-up survey.

The findings from the evaluation indicated that participants and staff rated the learning that they had gained from the conference highly, particularly in key areas such as authority, leadership and group dynamics. Many also felt that they were now more comfortable with dealing with difficult emotional situations, and several reported on ways in which they hoped this learning would be relevant when they returned to work.

Unfortunately, the low response on the follow-up survey meant that it was difficult to assess the longer term impact of the conference, although those who did respond gave examples of ways in which they were now approaching their work — and particularly their approach to leadership – differently. Although many were able to note ways in which different activities contributing to their learning, overall, most felt that it was the whole event, including the length of the conference, and the fact it was residential, that had been central to this.

A report on the findings was sent to the conference directors, and a presentation was also made to a conference attended by many involved in psychodynamic organisational development and group relations activities. An article on the research was also published in a peer-reviewed journal with a similar audience (https://www.tavinstitute.org/wp-content/uploads/2018/12/Dione-Hills-OPUS-V18-N2-2018-Final-PDF-1Oct18.pdf).

Reducing the 'interference' of evaluation activities is much easier if the evaluation activities are compatible with, and supportive of, an organisational development intervention. This is one reason why many writers in the field favour an 'embedded' or self-evaluation approach, in which the evaluation is seen as specifically supporting the intervention itself. Hodges (2017), for example, summed up some key reasons why, despite the difficulties, consultants might work at agreeing an evaluation process with their clients. She describes evaluation as a joint process between the consultant and the client that needs to be incorporated into the contract agreed during the contracting phase and running throughout the consultancy cycle. This should include:

1 Task issues (what was done)
2 Process issues (how it was done)
3 People issues (what individual impacts were there)

Including these three aspects enables the evaluation to support the organisational development intervention, by helping to identify major areas of concern for remedial action, giving a barometer of opinion at various times and enabling the situation in different departments, functions, locations and teams to be compared.

For Burke and Noumair (2015), evaluation allows the consultant and client to return to the original objectives of the engagement, to be specific about what outcomes were expected and to find out if they have been achieved. The results of an evaluation can facilitate planning for the next steps of the change, identify any barriers to implementing change that needs to be addressed, help to understand aspects of the change that did or did not work as anticipated, and enable the consultants to learn from the experience and apply the lessons to future work.

However, all of this requires considerable skill, both on the part of the consultant and, if engaged, any external evaluator involved, who needs to have a basic understanding of what it is that the consultant is trying to do. It also requires the evaluator to have good interpersonal skills. Some of these are summed up in the list of evaluator skills required, in lists put together by Block (2000), Cheung-Judge and Holbeche (2011), Cummings and Worley (2009) and Huffington et al. (1997) and summarised by Cameron and Green (2015).

Evaluator skills

1 Ability to show how evaluation is a key aspect in the whole change process
2 Capacity for analysis
3 Ability to co-design, implement and monitor evaluation methods and metrics
4 Financial acumen to evaluate costs and benefits of interventions
5 Assessing the success of the interventions across a range of appropriate measures and agreement on the need for further action or exit
6 Being involved at a personal level
7 Be open to the idea that all feedback is data
8 Skills and leadership for project management
9 Ensuring different stakeholder groups have clarity about the objectives and whether they have been achieved

Similar lists of capabilities have been developed by professional evaluation associations, such as the UK Evaluation Society, United Nations Evaluation Group, and by international organisations involved in the field of evaluation (https://www.evaluation.org.uk/ http://www.uneval.org/).

Different types of evaluation

Navigating the evaluation world can be confusing at first. One of the reasons for this is the fact that the discipline of evaluation has been influenced by different academic disciplines and evolved slightly differently in different sectors. This has led to variations in terminology, which can be particularly confusing for those coming to the practice from the outside. For example, different terms are used when considering what aspect of an intervention the evaluation is focusing on, at what point the evaluation is being undertaken, and to the overall approach taken to its design.

Process, outcome and impact evaluation

These terms refer to the **focus** (and to some extent, purpose) of an evaluation.

Process evaluation is one in which the focus is on how an intervention is being delivered. This can be particularly useful if the main aim is to learn what is working best in terms of delivering an intervention, for example, in looking into which training activities have been most successful in recruiting participants, or what events have produced the most positive response from those involved. This can be particularly helpful when regular findings are fed back to those putting the intervention in place as it provides the opportunity to bring about changes if things are not going as anticipated. This kind of evaluation is sometimes called '**formative**' evaluation because it contributes to the 'formation' or development of the project or intervention. Information (Process data) may come from documents, interviews and observations, as well as purely quantitative data such as the number of people taking part in an activity, or the number of times it takes place.

Evaluation questions in process evaluations often take the form of questions such as 'Did we do what we planned to do?' or 'Did we reach who we planned to reach?'

Impact or outcome evaluations are evaluations that are primarily concerned with how far the intervention was successful in achieving its aims, and sometimes also how much of an impact it has had (how far staff retention or absenteeism has improved, or business has improved). A key aim of this kind of evaluation may involve 'proving' that any outcomes were indeed the result of the intervention (rather than just being random change or influenced by other factors). For this reason, this kind of evaluation is particularly useful to contributing to the 'evidence base' for interventions of a similar kind but may also be important where the central purpose is accountability, sustainability or replication. This kind of evaluation often requires quantitative data, and the question of causality (see below) is particularly important.

Evaluation questions in outcome evaluations may take the form of 'Was our intervention successful (did it work)' or the more nuanced 'What worked well for whom and where?'

Economic or value-for-money evaluations are in some respects a particular type of outcome evaluation, in which the primary focus is on the question of how much the intervention cost and whether this investment brought about the anticipated (financial or otherwise) benefits. Economic evaluation draws on methods from the field of economics, usually with a strong focus on those aspects of the intervention, which can be expressed in financial terms. (Staff time, turnover or absenteeism, changes in production or sales.) There are different economic evaluation approaches (e.g. cost benefit, value for money, social return on investment), and including this element in an evaluation does require specialised input.

Evaluation questions in an economic evaluation typically ask something like 'Was it worth the investment?' or possibly 'How did the intervention affect the business' "bottom line"?'

In practice, many evaluations look at both process and outcomes and may also include an economic element. It will often be hard to understand why a particular outcome came about unless something is known about the activities that were put in place to bring about change, and hard to talk about how a programme or intervention is being delivered without saying something about what changes are taking place as a result.

Ex-anti, ex-post and post-implementation evaluation

These terms refer to the timing or **stage** at which an evaluation is undertaken.

An **ex-anti evaluation** takes place at an early stage in the planning of an intervention, usually to make a prior assessment of the value or viability of taking action. In some sectors, an ex-anti evaluation is called **appraisal** as it overlaps with 'appraising' the viability and cost of the intervention – and its likely value for money.

There is also another 'early' activity that is sometimes carried out, which is called an **evaluability assessment**. The purpose of this is to assess whether an evaluation would be useful and viable. This helps both in deciding about whether to undertake an evaluation, and in the design of an evaluation that is practical and useful, given any constraints in the situation. It covers:

1 The purpose (and utility) of carrying out an evaluation
2 The availability of data
3 The feasibility of undertaking the evaluation in practical terms

Ex-post or post-implementation evaluations are evaluations that are carried out once a project or programme is being fully implemented, and in some cases, not until the implementation has (almost) come to an end (e.g. undertaking a review of staff attitudes after a consultancy activity has come to an end). Another term sometimes used is **summative evaluation**, which involves an assessment towards the end of an intervention, usually with a strong focus on outcomes or impacts.

Carrying out an evaluation after the main activity has ceased can be difficult as opportunities to collect useful data have been lost, and the evaluator will have to rely on whatever data they can find, and the memories of those involved. It is advisable to start planning and undertaking an evaluation from the early stages of an intervention to enable data collection opportunities to be identified and made use of.

Evaluation approach

It has already been noted that it is important that an evaluation approach is appropriate to – and compatible with – the organisational development intervention itself. There are some key areas in which evaluation approaches differ from one another. These include:

1 Data and analysis used
2 How causality is approached and demonstrated

3 How far participants are engaged in the evaluation process
4 Whether they use or adopt an action research approach

Data and analysis used: Evaluation, it has been noted, makes use of research methods usually drawn from the social sciences, including related fields such as psychology or health sciences. A distinction is often made between **quantitative** and **qualitative data**: these require different expertise in their design and analysis and have different strengths and weaknesses when used in an evaluation. There is more information about these two different types of data in the next chapter.

Decisions about what kind of data to collect depend on several factors: what evaluation approach is being used, what is most acceptable to the audience of the evaluation, and how feasible it is to collect it (given the resources available or any local constraints in place). Working this out is an important part of undertaking an 'evaluability assessment' mentioned earlier. However, what kind of data clients, and other key stakeholders will accept as being 'valid' may also play an important part.

When things go wrong: An evaluation of a programme was being undertaken in a high-stakes public policy environment. 'Difficult' findings were challenged because they were based on qualitative rather than quantitative data, with the situation becoming more high profile when 'challenging' findings receiving media coverage.

> To them (the committee receiving the report) numbers constituted 'real' data and qualitative information was nothing more than anecdotes and opinions. At times, our conversations felt like we were speaking two different languages. We had different views of data evidence and evaluation methodologies.
> Hutchinson, K., (2018) *Evaluation Failures*, Chapter 7

How causality is addressed: It is quite possible to undertake an evaluation (particularly for accountability purposes) that provides a description of what happened, and what changes took place. However, people (e.g. the client) may ask whether the evaluation 'proves' that the changes resulted from the intervention, or whether something else took place (such as a change in management, upturn in the market or just the passage of time), which resulted in the recorded impacts. This raises the question of attribution or causality – providing proof that (a) caused or resulted in (b). There are two broad approaches to addressing this: experimental designs and theory-based approaches.

Experimental designs. These are widely seen as providing one of the most robust ways of 'proving' that an intervention caused an outcome, sometimes referred to as the 'gold standard' although this is increasingly being challenged.

Experimental designs are widely used in health research and increasingly in the generation of 'robust' evidence-based practice in a wide range of fields. In an experimental design, one group of people (or part of an organisation) receive the planned intervention, while another does not (possibly receiving another set of activities) and a comparison is made between the 'outcomes' for each of these. If the 'active' group shows a statistically stronger outcome than the 'comparison' or 'control' group, then this is seen as 'proving' that the intervention was effective.

While this design appears to be very straightforward and sensible, this is usually quite difficult to use in an organisational development setting, and particularly in an embedded evaluation. It requires a high level of 'control' over the whole intervention, ensuring that the activities are applied evenly over time, and control over the selection of who can take part, to ensure that the intervention only reaches those for whom it is intended, and not those who are in the comparison or control group.

When things go wrong:

An evaluation adopting a semi-experimental design compared one group of participants who received new (financial) resources with another who did not. The evaluation approach aligned well with an initial logic model but failed to show any significant difference in outcome between the two groups. Exploring why, the evaluator realised that they had failed to identify that the intervention was just one part of a larger system (they had placed the **boundary** in the wrong place); that there were important system-level interconnections between all recipients whether in receipt of the new resources or not; and that those not receiving new resources were receiving other kinds of support (other than the specific benefits being assessed).

Hutchinson, K., (2018), *Evaluation Failures*, Chapter 19

Experimental designs also depend heavily on quantitative data and will require expert input to ensure appropriate sample sizes, design good data collection instruments and carry out an appropriate statistical analysis. It is also important to identify whether there are any other important differences between the two groups that account for a different outcome, for example one group willingly signed up for a particular activity, or were sent to take part, while the others didn't or weren't. In the 'pure' form, this is addressed by assigning people randomly to one group or the other – but this is rarely possible in an organisational development intervention. An experimental design also works less well where the wider context has a strong influence on these activities and how people respond, and has little to say about the 'processes of putting the activities in place' – since it is assumed that these have followed the original plan or protocol used in the intervention.

Theory-based evaluation: To get around many of these difficulties, since the 1990s another broad category of evaluation design has emerged, broadly called 'theory-based evaluation'. These involve drawing up and testing a theory about the intervention concerning what change it is hoped to bring about and for which parts of the organisation. This approach is interested not only in the outcomes, but what might have led to these, including whether it worked the same way for everyone, and in every situation, and what contribution, if any, broader factors made to this success or lack of success.

There are different types of theory-based evaluation, including '**theory of change**', **realist evaluation** (Pawson, 1997, 2013) and **contribution analysis** (Mayne, J. 2008). There is more information about drawing up a theory of change in the next chapter. Realist evaluation is specifically concerned with what were the *mechanisms* of change, and how these might be different in different situations or contexts (e.g. an experiential approach to training might be effective with one group of staff, while another group might want more background information about why a particular skill is required). Contribution analysis is useful for developing, and testing, an account of why a particular intervention contributed to change – for example, how new training activities *contributed* to enabling staff adjust to a restructuring of a department, when put in place alongside other forms of support, such as changes in management input and support from the personnel department.

Evaluation approaches use both qualitative and quantitative data and can potentially be used in either an external or embedded evaluation. There are many sources of information on how to do these although an experienced evaluator can be useful in providing support. For example, running a 'theory of change' workshop with stakeholders is often easier when facilitated by someone external to the organisation and the organisational development intervention.

There are now several sophisticated analytic methods that have been added to the evaluation 'toolkit' designed to provide greater (statistical) robustness to evaluation designs that have previously relied heavily on qualitative data. Two of these are **qualitative comparative analysis** (QCA) (Marshall, G., 1998) and **process tracing** (Collier, 2011), and their underlying theory of causality is closer to theory-based than experimental evaluation approaches. Although very promising, these do require considerable expertise and can be quite resource-intensive to use.

Involvement of participants in evaluation activities: There are evaluation approaches (e.g. participative, empowerment, democratic evaluation) in which participants in the activities or who are the 'target' of a change intervention take an active role in the evaluation itself. In addition to providing data, these may help to identify evaluation questions, help in selection and design of data collection instruments, and be actively involved in the collection of data (e.g. as interviewers) and making sense of the findings and what these mean going forward. These evaluation methods are particularly appropriate for interventions, which themselves have a participative or empowerment aim. They can be helpful for introducing people to evaluation and 'evaluative thinking' and in reflecting on any evaluation findings. A participative element could be included in any of the other evaluation approaches mentioned, but will be less appropriate in an experimental design, where 'control' over all aspects of the intervention, data collection and analysis, often by an external evaluator, is particularly important.

Including an action research element: Action research involves having repeated cycles of activity and assessment of these in terms of their outcomes and any learning arising that can contribute to the next cycle. An important part of the Tavistock Institute's evaluation activities from the early days, an action research approach was seen as a good way to build in a strong formative or learning element. In this evaluation approach, the evaluators (internal or external) work closely with those putting the intervention in place, to identify what data is required at each stage, collect this and feed this back regularly to support thinking about the next step of the work.

This approach is very compatible with an embedded evaluation in an organisational development consultancy, as described in some of the literature, undertaken by the organisational development consultants themselves, with or without the support of an external evaluator. This can also be undertaken in a very participative way, engaging people at different levels in the organisation actively in both the collection of data and making sense of the findings.

More recently, Quinn Patton (Patton, 2010) has formalised a few elements in this 'action research' evaluation approach under the name of **developmental evaluation**. This is seen to be particularly appropriate in the evaluation of innovative projects and programmes in which the action – and outcomes – is emergent. He also ties the basic principles of this design closely into the principles of complex adaptive systems. It is an approach that is seen as very supportive of the intervention itself, building in learning and reflection at various stages – so much so, that some have seen this approach as being more like consultation than evaluation.

Mixed-method evaluation: Many evaluations use a combination of the above approaches or aspects of these. For example, if an experimental design (having a comparison or control group) is seen as desirable, this can be strengthened by undertaking some initial theory of change or system mapping and ensuring that elements of a process evaluation are also included. Some evaluations include aspects of realist, participative or developmental evaluation approaches without implementing the full approach. Reading about these methods may help you to think more clearly about the theory that underpins the interventions, what 'mechanisms' are involved and how to engage people in an organisation more actively in the design of the evaluation.

Summary

There are growing calls for more evaluation of organisational development activities. This is partly because of a demand for a stronger evidence base for consultancy practice, and partly because evaluation is seen as a way in which consultancy activities themselves can be strengthened. Both are very desirable, but they have different implications for evaluation, in terms of its purpose, the questions it addresses and the best methods and approaches to use. X

The first aim – generating knowledge about consultancy activities – may require approaches and methods, as well as the skills, time and resources that are beyond the scope of the consultancy itself and the consultants involved.

The second evaluation for the purpose of reflection and learning can be particularly useful when incorporated as part of a consultancy intervention and appropriate for 'embedded' or 'self'-evaluation – undertaken by the consultant, with or without input from an experienced evaluator.

There is a wide range of evaluation approaches, methods and tools available that are suitable for the evaluation of consultancy activities. Some of these theory-based, participative or action research–based approaches can be particularly helpful in supporting a systems psychodynamics–oriented consultancy and will generally be quite comfortable for a consultant working in this mode to adopt. Experimental methods may be possible, and may be requested by clients, but are more likely to require adapting the intervention to enable the evaluation to take place.

Whatever evaluation approach is adopted, this will involve both some research and evaluation skill, as well as some consultancy skills, to ensure that the system in which they are being used and the way the evaluation is implemented supports rather than interferes with the intervention. The evaluator or consultant will need to be able to respond sensitively to internal dynamics and power dimensions in the organisation in which the intervention is taking place. The evaluator should also provide feedback in appropriate ways, following these up, if they are part of the contract and with support in putting recommendations in place.

Questions

1 What reasons have been given for the lack of evaluation of organisational development interventions?
2 What are the challenges in undertaking evaluation of organisational development interventions?

3 In what ways can evaluation be useful when undertaking an organisational development intervention, and support the intervention itself?
4 When can evaluation be undertaken by the consultants themselves, and when is it useful to bring in external expertise?
5 What are some of the different kinds of evaluation, and in what circumstances are these most useful?

Chapter 7

Planning and conducting an organisational development evaluation

Dione (Sanji) Hills

In the previous chapter, some general points were made relating to the purpose of evaluation and different approaches that might be used. This chapter is about the 'nuts and bolts' of planning and conducting an evaluation. This includes some thoughts on who should carry out an evaluation of an organisational development intervention, and when and how to commission an external evaluator, and some general principles to bear in mind when presenting findings. Like the previous chapter, there are some useful examples included indicating what can happen if general points about good practice suggested are not followed carefully!

Planning

The centrality of planning to the success of an evaluation cannot be overstressed. It can, however, be rushed or overlooked, particularly if evaluation is something of an afterthought, or 'tagged on' at the end of a project or programme.

Guidance on how to plan an evaluation is widely available, with particularly useful resources being the UK Government guide to policy evaluation – 'the Magenta book' (H. M. Treasury, 2020) and the Better Evaluation Rainbow Framework (https://www.betterevaluation.org/). The second of these identifies 8 distinct 'tasks' when undertaking an evaluation: manage, define, frame, describe, understand causes, synthesise, report and support use.

All such guides emphasise the importance to starting to think about evaluation from an early stage. This is particularly important when seeking to embed the evaluation in an organisational development consultation, as outlined by Nicholas (1979):

1 It provides the opportunity to get baseline measures, to pilot test instruments and to refine the design before the consultation begins.
2 Evaluation procedures that are integrated into consultation from the beginning become a natural part of the intervention and are much less disruptive.
3 The persons who are to use the evaluation information can be identified early.
4 Consequently, evaluation criteria and methods can be selected to fit their informational interests and needs.

DOI: 10.4324/9781003368663-11

Starting the evaluation early can also allow the intervention itself to be designed in ways that make it easier to evaluate. This is particularly important if an experimental evaluation design (see previous chapter) is being used, as this would require a comparison or control group: that is sites or individuals not affected by the intervention. In the previous section, the idea of undertaking an evaluability assessment is also mentioned – this can help in making decisions both about whether to undertake an evaluation, and in the design of an evaluation that is practical and useful, given any constraints in the situation.

There are three factors to be born in mind when designing an evaluation. Stern (2012) calls this the 'design triangle'. This includes:

1   The purpose of the evaluation
2   The 'system' or intervention being evaluated
3   The evaluation designs available

Each of these is discussed below.

The purpose of the evaluation

In the previous chapter, different reasons for undertaking an evaluation were mentioned. These included knowledge creation (or contributing to the 'evidence base' for organisational development interventions), learning, accountability, sustainability and replication. Quinn Patton (1997, 2010) in his 'utilisation-focused evaluation' framework recommends the identification of specific decisions that will be taken as a result of the evaluation and by whom, which helps to ensure that the evaluation findings and data will be useful in supporting these decisions. This can be particularly helpful when undertaking an evaluation alongside an organisational development intervention, enabling data collection and reporting to be synchronised with key decisions being taken in the planning and delivery of the intervention itself.

Being clear about purpose helps in identifying what will be the focus of the evaluation, which, in turn, helps in the choice of appropriate evaluation questions, and then the best way to answer these.

The focus of evaluation and evaluation questions

A key step in planning the evaluation is to identify a set of evaluation questions around which the data collection and analysis will be framed. The questions are framed partly around the overall aims of the intervention and partly by the aspect of the intervention that the evaluation will focus on.

In the previous chapter, a distinction was made between a 'process' and 'outcome' evaluation. The literature on organisational development evaluation tends to emphasise the first of these, in part because these support the aims of learning and reflection and are very well suited to an embedded evaluation.

Process evaluation may look at whether the activities were put in place as planned, whether the right people took part (in sufficient numbers) and what people felt about the activities. From a systems psychodynamics point of view, it may be particularly useful to focus on the relationship between the consultant and the consultee, as is recommended by Czander (1993), following his criticism that one of the most serious deficiencies in management consultancy is the failure to evaluate consultancy. Schwartz (1958), Lippitt (1959), Lippitt et al. (1958) make a similar point and suggest the following questions that might be posed in relation to the consultant-consultee relationship:

1 Did the consultant form a sound inter-personal relationship with the client?
2 Did the consultant pay attention to the nature of the dependency relationship that might evolve in the client?
3 Did the consultant focus on and think clearly about the problem?
4 Did the consultant respect the client?
5 Did the consultant appropriately achieve influence in the organisation?
6 Did the consultant communicate clearly to the client that the skills the consultant possessed related to the client's needs or the problem at hand?
7 Did the consultee fully understand the nature of the consultant's role and contribution? All consultants differ about how they see the problem and how to intervene. The style in which a consultant intervenes must be communicated clearly so that the client does not have a set of expectations that cannot be realised.
8 Did the consultant express a willingness to have his/her services evaluated?

While these questions might be of considerable interest to the consultant themselves – and to other consultants wanting to understand the consultation process better – clients are likely to be more interested to hear about results – whether the aims of the intervention have been achieved, in other words, an **outcome or impact evaluation.** Gallessich (1982) gives a list of useful impact questions that an organisational development evaluation might address:

1 The degree to which the desired goals are reached
2 The factors that contribute to both positive and negative outcomes
3 Interim feedback about how an intervention is progressing
4 The cost/benefit ratio of interventions
5 The consultant's overall effectiveness in the various stages and processes of consultation, such as contracting and diagnosis

Gallessich's fourth point draws attention to another 'type' of evaluation: **value-for-money or economic evaluation** that was briefly discussed in the previous chapter. This kind of evaluation usually requires specialist input.

The system

To design an evaluation, it is important to be clear about **what** it is that is being evaluated. In an organisational development intervention, there are three important elements to be aware of:

1 the organisation (or part of the organisation) in which change is sought
2 the actions that are being taken to bring about change
3 The wider context in which this is happening.

These may all be considered as one system, separate or interlocking parts of a system. One of the challenges in planning an evaluation is knowing where to place a 'boundary' around this: is the focus of the evaluation the whole organisation, the organisational development intervention or just one part of this intervention (e.g. training provided to one group of staff). In the Leicester conference example (Hills, 2018), we looked at the 'whole system' in terms of how it created learning outcomes, although we were also interested to find out how particular parts of the system (different activities, the role of staff) contributed to the whole. Although we included both participants and staff in the evaluation, the evaluation could have focused on just one or another of these groups for more detailed investigation.

An important task for evaluators is to clarify which aspects of an intervention are the focus of the evaluation. The outcomes for the consultation enable the clients, consultants and evaluators to relate the activities taking place to the outcomes and help set a boundary around what will be evaluated.

Theory of change and logic maps: These are now being widely used in the evaluation world and involve drawing up a diagram or map of the intervention that includes the issue or problem being addressed, the actions being taken to address these, their immediate, longer term and ultimate outcomes.

Key elements in a theory of change map, see Rogers, P. (2014, also see DIY Toolkit for examples, 2020).

Context: the issue addressed plus any contextual factors, which might affect the outcome of the intervention (including what issues are addressed)

1 *Input*: what actions were planned? What resources were used?
2 *Outputs*: what happened, what actions were delivered, how often, to how many? To which group of clients? What immediate response there was to the actions taken?
3 *Outcomes*: what intermediate- or short- and medium-term changes took place?
4 *Impacts*: what longer term outcomes? – particularly in terms of achievement of initial objectives

In addition to identifying key steps in the process of implementing an intervention, a theory of change map also explores the assumptions underpinning each step: why do people think that this input will lead to this output, and what conditions need to be in place in order for this output to be achieved (e.g. assumptions might be made that staff will be allowed to attend an activity during work hours or be willing to attend something outside of their normal work hours). Assumptions can also be useful for identifying more detailed evaluation questions. For example, following the identification of the assumption above, the evaluation may want to find out to what extent did staff and managers support the activities put in place? Or 'did the activity reach those for whom it was intended, and in sufficient numbers to bring about change?'

Another important element in drawing up a theory of change map is knowing what is taking place in the wider context (such as the rest of the organisation, change in key members of staff or improvement or downturn in the market) that might impact on the success of the organisational development intervention.

Ideally, such a map is drawn up with the help of those immediately involved through running one or more workshops. The process of drawing up the map is as (or more) important than the output, and the process of drawing up a map can also be helpful in supporting the organisational development intervention itself. It can help to identify issues, clarify plans and provide the opportunity for negotiation between different stakeholders about the interventions and its likely outcome. Leaving out key stakeholders can lead to difficulties later in the evaluation.

When things go wrong

An evaluation was undertaken of a communication and outreach plan designed to increase understanding and take up of services of a government department. An initial diagnosis and theory of change map identified that trust – between the public and public servants – was a key issue, and the evaluation design took this as a central focus. Unfortunately, the staff involved in the delivery of the programme were not kept sufficiently informed of this change in focus. The methodology was subject to closer and closer scrutiny before the whole evaluation was called to an abrupt halt.

Hutchinson, K., (2018) *Evaluation Failures*, Chapter 8

The initial theory of change map, however, can only be as good as the information currently available, in which there are usually many 'unknowns'. It is a map of what is in people's minds when initially putting in place the intervention. Revising this regularly helps build in any new information coming forward, or changes that are made to the activities, to ensure that this remains relevant to the current situation. It is important to do this in consultation with those involved.

Kirkpatrick (1994, 1996) **framework** (Kurt, 2016): Theory of change maps share several features with the Kirkpatrick framework, which has been used in the evaluation of training activities for many years. This sets out four different levels of impact from the training intervention and can provide a great way of thinking through what kind of data is required.

1 *Level 1*: The reaction of the study to the training activities is like the outputs in theory of change.
2 *Level 2*: learning (increase in knowledge of capability) is like short-term outcomes in theory of change.
3 *Level 3*: Extent of behaviour and capability improvement is like intermediate and longer term outcomes.
4 *Level 4*: Effects on the business environment resulting from the trainees' performance are like impacts in theory of change.

Level 1 and 2 data can usually be derived from simple feedback sheets or discussions at the time of training, while Levels 3 and 4 require data that can be quite difficult to collect. This experience from the Leicester conference evaluation is typical – that is, few people returning a survey sent out nine months after the conference, which sought to explore the longer term impacts of conference attendance.

An evaluation of a management development initiative

This training and development initiative was designed to provide support for 40 middle managers in a local health authority in their general learning and development, with a particular focus on learning around the issue of cross-boundary working. Managers increasingly required to work across professional and departmental boundaries, partly because of structural changes taking place and partly because of developments in the wider policy environment and more generally, in order to create a more 'joined-up' service for patients.

The intervention involved three Large Community Change Conferences and six Action Learning Sets (ALSs). The ALS met monthly for half a day over 12 months, providing opportunities for managers and clinicians to discuss and learn from their experiences of working at the 'coal-face', focusing on the following themes:

• Manner and style of communication systems with colleagues and staff
• Managing the complexity of cross-boundary working in relationships with and between individuals, teams, professions, organisations and sectors

- Moving towards a shared vision in a constantly changing complex organisational environment
- Creating smooth transfer of patients across services
- Increasing understanding of negotiating/managing change across professional boundaries

An evaluation was undertaken alongside the intervention by two researchers from the consultants' own organisation, but who were not directly involved in the intervention itself. It addressed several **evaluation questions** including the following:

- Did participants gain valuable learning experiences from the ALSs?
- Were participants able to put into practice the lesson they take from the ALSs and transfer these lessons into actual action?
- What impact has the initiative had on the wider function of the Health Economy, such as new cross-boundary working activities developed, new alliances been instigated, or wider changes in the way the Health Economy runs its operations?

The evaluation design was broadly underpinned by the four levels of the **Kirkpatrick (1983) framework**:

- *Level 1*: the effectiveness as perceived by the trainee (reaction)
- *Level 2*: measured evaluation of learning (learning)
- *Level 3*: observed performance (behaviour)
- *Level 4*: business impact (results)

A key consideration was the need to consider the sensitivities inherent in the relationship between the evaluators and the members of the Action Learning Sets (ALSs). This was addressed by conducting a **formative evaluation** with a **participative** approach. In order to achieve shared ownership of the evaluation process, early active involvement of the ALS participants was sought in the design of the evaluation, utilising a subgroup of ALS representatives acting as a liaison point with the evaluators, which continued its collaboration in the process throughout the evaluation period.

The data used in the evaluation were primarily **qualitative** and focused on two main domains:

1 Gathering views and information from the actual participants in the programme and

2 Exploring the wider organisational context to understand the impact of the initiative on the wider organisation through the eyes of people who did not attend the initiative.

Specific data collection methods included the following:

- Focus groups with ALS participants during and after completion of the programme
- Critical incident technique
- Interviews with:
  - People who could not attend the programme or withdrew
  - Senior managers in key positions in the organisation
  - The two consultants who facilitated the action learning groups
- Documentary analysis

Interview and focus groups were tape-recorded and analysed from transcriptions of these discussions. The findings suggest that the intervention was well received by participants and were an effective means of developing general managerial competence, particularly in planning, decision-making and people management skills. The programme also provided a significant fit between the development needs of the managers participating in the programme and the needs of the wider organisation in which they worked. The evaluation also helped to identify problematic issues including barriers to wider learning within the organisation. The structures within the organisation were characterised by many managers as insular 'silo' cultures, and this created barriers to the aims and benefits of the programme being effectively communicated across the organisation, which resulted in some managers disengaging from the programme at various stages. (The time commitment required was also given as another reason for dropping out of the programme.)

Systems maps: Another set of tools, which are now being used in evaluation, are systems maps. These are particularly useful in complex settings where it may be hard to see how different factors are inter-related or influencing one another. They are also very useful in providing information about the wider context in which the intervention is taking place (Figure 7.1).

Rather than focusing on the project or programme, a systems map looks at the broader picture and all the factors that contribute to the way things are currently, or which could lead to change in the future. There are several ways of doing this, some of which involve the use of software, which allows for experimentation – increasing or decreasing various factors in the map to see what difference this makes to the particular area of interest. (For example, levels of pay, training or manager support could be moved up or down to see how each of these impacts on staff behaviour or turnover.) There are also less technology-dependent ways of getting a broad picture of the context – drawing a rich picture is one such method (Oakden, 2014).

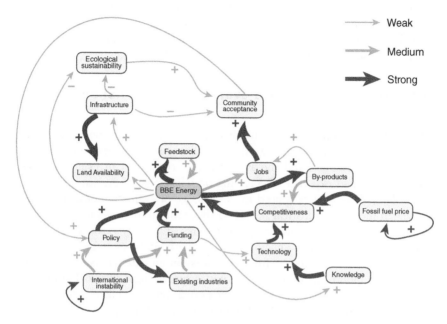

Figure 7.1 An Example of a System Map. From Penn AS, Knight CJK, Lloyd DJB, Avitabile D, Kok K, Schiller F, et al. (2013). Participatory Development and Analysis of a Fuzzy Cognitive Map of the Establishment of a Bio-Based Economy in the Humber Region. *PLoS One* 8(11): e78319. https://doi.org/10.1371/journal.pone.0078319 © 2013 Penn et al.

Like theory of change maps, systems maps should be drawn up in consultation with key stakeholders, as these are the main source of data. It is also the process of drawing up the map that is as useful as the outcome: a systems map (particularly a complex one) drawn up without proper consultation may be of little use.

When things go wrong

An evaluator proudly produced a system map of healthcare intervention to demonstrate to the steering group the complexity of the issue – and its wider environment. The map was met with stunned silence, and someone later commented 'Maybe systems maps are a better investigative tool than a communications tool'. As well as learning how important it is to involve key stakeholders in drawing up a system map, the evaluator also felt that drawing up a rich picture might have been more helpful for identifying issues such as conflicts, emotions and politics.

Hutchinson, K., (2018) *Evaluation Failures*, Chapter 11

Once drawn up, both theory of change maps and systems maps can be helpful when talking to people about the evaluation and in identifying the data needed and how this will be collected. They can also help in shaping the analysis and be used to frame or illustrate a report of the findings.

In-house or out-of-house evaluation (internal or external)

Some of the decisions to be taken when designing an evaluation will be determined by what resources are available. The resources required cover not only financial resources and the availability of consultant or evaluator time, but also skills and expertise. Depending on what kind of evaluation is being undertaken, there may be a need for knowledge of evaluation design and use of research methods, statistical skills and the ability to use relevant technology (online survey tools, statistical or qualitative research analysis software).

Where the evaluation is an 'embedded' activity, undertaken by the consultants themselves, it may be useful to commission an external evaluator or researcher to support the evaluation activities, providing additional skills and experience. Clients may prefer to have the evaluation undertaken entirely by an external evaluator: this has both advantages and disadvantages.

Using an external evaluator	Undertaking the evaluation using internal resources
Advantages	
• Outside the organisation, and able to provide a 'fresh' perspective	• Are 'inside' and familiar with the organisation, its culture and context
• (Perceived) independence and credibility (which may have traction with people outside of the programme, e.g. funders)	• Ensures that evaluation activities are fully 'embedded' in the organisation.
• Difficult to manipulate as independent	• Can act as champions to advocates, change agents
• May possess certain evaluation/ research skills and knowledge that the internal may not have	• Will remain with a project and thus invested in the results, increasing the potential of learning from the evaluation findings being used
Disadvantages	
• Not knowing the full story	• Being used or manipulated
• No or little follow through as they leave the organisation at the end of the evaluation	• Perceived lack of objectivity by being part of and identified with the system
• Can be more costly	• No follow-through if they are not party to action. Can be time-consuming – internal involves staff time that may draw on limited resources
• Take knowledge away	

If an **external evaluation** is to be commissioned, then several points will need to be clarified early on. For example, it will be important to be clear as to whether the evaluator is going to be selected, and contracted, by the organisational development client, or by the consultant, and whether the cost of this will be separate from or part of their overall consultancy budget.

Once this is clarified, then a specification will need to be drawn up and, ideally, a few evaluators invited to apply for the contract. In some cases, this might be quite broad, specifying mainly the kind of experience or skill required from the potential evaluator. In the case of a systems psychodynamically oriented consultancy project, for example, it will be particularly important to ensure that the evaluator has some understanding of the nature of this kind of work and that the evaluation is designed in a way that will support, rather than cut across, the dynamics of the organisational development intervention. There may also be sensitivity around providing too much information, prior to contracting an evaluation, concerning the organisation, the issues being addressed or the aims of the organisational development intervention. However, the more information provided, the easier it will be for an evaluator to come up with a suitable evaluation design.

Points to cover in a typical evaluation 'terms of reference'

- Information about the project or programme to be evaluated
- Why an evaluation is required: that is, whether this is required to support learning within the intervention, or to focus gathering data on impact for accountability, sustainability or replication purposes.
- Any expectations about the kind of evaluation required (e.g. is an experimental or highly quantitative evaluation approach, or a value-for-money element)
- Timescale for the project and/or its evaluation
- Reporting requirements
- Experience or skills required
- Anticipated costs
- Details about the contracting process (e.g. timescale, criteria for assessing proposals, who to contact for further information)

Conducting the evaluation

Designing an evaluation requires some knowledge of evaluation theory and methods. Putting the evaluation in place also requires skills in navigating organisational dynamics in a sensitive and intelligent way. In other words, good evaluation requires consultancy skills, as well as research skills.

Initial stages

Even in the planning stages of an evaluation, understanding who should be involved or consulted about this and doing this appropriately require both skill and an understanding of the 'system' in which the organisational development consultancy is taking place.

In an embedded evaluation, this may be easier: an external evaluator will often have to ask many questions and read a lot of documentation before fully understanding what is going on, and may still lack insight into particular organisational culture or any power dynamics taking place. This is why, if an external evaluator is involved, it will usually be useful to have an initial 'scoping phase' during which they can familiarise themselves with the organisation and the organisational development intervention, either revising or coming up with a more detailed evaluation plan based on their greater understanding of the situation.

Being on the boundary: Evaluation usually takes place on the boundary of a system – the evaluator being neither fully 'outside' nor fully 'inside' the system. Different evaluation approaches require different positions: an experimental approach is generally best undertaken from a relatively 'outside' and 'objective' position (which is why it is difficult to do as part of an 'embedded' evaluation). Participative and action research approaches require building a close relationship with those inside the system.

Whether fully 'embedded' and 'engaged', or external and objective, evaluative thinking, as noted earlier, requires adopting a questioning frame of mind that challenges assumptions, often bringing to light data and information that might not be welcomed by everyone inside the system. The very process of 'throwing light on' and questioning things can sometimes be experienced as uncomfortable, and evaluation findings can often be challenged or resisted.

Particularly in the early stages, when stepping 'over the boundary' into the system, it is particularly important for those undertaking an evaluation to consult widely and be fully transparent about what they were doing. This helps ensure that the evaluation doesn't present any 'nasty surprises' and gives people an opportunity to voice their concerns. Beyond this, it will be up to the evaluator to 'read' signals (red flags) coming from the system that the evaluation is causing concern or upset. If people are expressing concern or upset about the evaluation, this may provide some useful 'data' about where the intervention itself has problems that need to be addressed.

When things go wrong

An evaluation was asked for to provide training to local farm co-ops across multiple countries. However, key staff – including country-level evaluators – appeared reluctant to be involved in or failed to attend planning meetings. In spite of this and the frequent turnover of key staff, the evaluation continued and a final report was presented to the programme management. This was returned covered in mark ups and requests for change: apparently, innocuous findings were challenged angrily and proposals that had been discussed and agreed with local participants, strongly rejected. It later turned out that the programme had been running for several years with similar problems having been identified in at least two previous evaluations that the evaluator had not been told about.

Hutchinson, K., (2018) *Evaluation Failures*, Chapter 21

Collecting and analysing data

In the last chapter, two broad categories of data were mentioned: qualitative and quantitative. In practice,

Quantitative data may be derived from surveys and questionnaires, which have been specially designed, or from information collected within the organisation itself, such as staff numbers and financial data. It may come from elsewhere, such as population data sets or national surveys (e.g. the national census or annual crime and attitude surveys). Quantitative data is seen by some as having more validity and robustness than qualitative data, particularly as it can be subjected to statistical analysis.

One type of quantitative data is the validated scale. This is a scale that has been rigorously tested and validated in earlier research that can be used for assessing changes in areas that might otherwise seem quite difficult to measure (validated scales for 'wellbeing' and 'empowerment' were mentioned earlier).

Qualitative data can be taken from a wide range of sources, including documents (such as minutes of meetings), interviews and open-ended questions in surveys, focus group discussions and observation. It is particularly good for conveying the 'feel and sense' of what is going on and helpful for capturing information about things that hadn't previously been anticipated, or 'negative' outcomes (which may not have been part of the initial evaluation design). Qualitative data (together with photographs and videos) can provide quotes from participants, case studies and illustrations that add colour and interest when feeding back findings. Although some people feel that that qualitative data lacks the rigour of quantitative data, in practice it requires a similarly high level of skill and rigour in its design and analysis and can be undertaken using specially designed software tools.

Whatever kind of data is going to be collected, it will be important to identify in the early stages of planning how feasible it is to collect this, ideally testing the instruments to be used either through consulting with those who will be asked to provide data (take part in interviews, focus groups or respond to surveys) or piloting these with a small group of participants. Care should be taken about any administrative data being used, to ensure this comes from a valid source, has been robustly collected and is fit for purpose. Another consideration is whether the data is available, or people willing to share it (commercial and confidentiality issues can come into play here).

When things go wrong

An evaluation was undertaken of a programme supporting small enterprises in South Africa to build up the local black economy. Information from the programme was to be verified using procurement and financial data from the larger corporations involved (buying services from the local enterprises). Despite early assurances, few corporations were willing to supply this information, giving commercial sensitivity and practical difficulties as their reasons. Combined with severe difficulties in collecting other programme information (including a major computer crash and loss of key data), the evaluation findings were severely limited.

Hutchinson, K., (2018) *Evaluation Failures*, Chapter 16

Evaluation data, whether qualitative or quantitative, is only as good – or bad – as the instruments used to collect it. A badly designed survey, interview topic guide or observation template can mean that the data collected is inaccurate, biased or unusable. Who is involved or where the data is collected is also important. Those collecting the data need to have the time, resources and skills to do this accurately and impartially.

Data collection also involves engagement with people who may be uncomfortable with the idea of an evaluation taking place. People can often resist the idea that there is someone 'overlooking' their work and questioning how effective this is. As well as ensuring that those providing data are representative of the overall picture, they also need to be reasonably well-informed, and willing to be honest in talking about their experience or views. They may, for example, be worried about saying something about which others would disapprove or have something to gain by putting across a particular view. Data may be promised, but not forthcoming, or may turn out to be unreliable or unusable.

Evaluators have a number of 'tools' at their disposal to help them overcome these difficulties. These are included in the good practice and ethical guidance, which governs the disciplines of evaluation and social research (for more information, see https://www.evaluation.org.uk/professional-development/good-practice-guideline/).

These require steps to be taken to ensure that activities are not harmful in any way and that participants give 'informed consent' before being asked to provide data and are given assurances of confidentiality. Research data is also governed by laws covering data protection, which requires the evaluator to ensure that data is kept in a safe and secure place. When reporting evaluation findings, steps need to be taken to avoid revealing the identity (implicitly or explicitly) of informants, unless specific consent has been given for this.

Analysis: However good the data, this can quickly be undermined by faulty or inappropriate analysis. There are very different skills required for qualitative and quantitative data. The first of these requires at least some level of statistical skill, even when quite simple 'descriptive' statistics (totals and averages or means) are required. Marked variations on the outcomes may be masked by an 'average' or total, which indicate that parts of the organisation responded quite differently to the intervention. Qualitative data requires transparency in how this has been analysed, which shows exactly how a conclusion was drawn from the data available.

Type I and Type II errors

There are two kinds of error that can be made in drawing conclusions: in Type I, an intervention is shown to have been successful, but really, it was not. In Type II, the intervention is shown to have been unsuccessful when it produced positive results. Both errors can be damaging to further decision-making.

Define Type I and Type II errors

Null hypothesis: In a statistical test, the hypothesis that there is no significant difference between specified populations, any observed difference being due to chance.

Alternative hypothesis: The hypothesis contrary to the null hypothesis. It is usually taken to be that the observations are not due to chance, that is are the result of a real effect (with some amount of chance variation superposed).

Consider Aesop's Fable about Peter and the wolf:

> *A boy has the job of protecting a flock of sheep from wolves. If a wolf comes, he is to ring a bell and cry out "wolf", so that the men from the village will come with their guns. After a few days with no wolf, the boy is getting bored, so he pretends that a wolf is attacking.* The **null hypothesis** is that there is no wolf; the **alternative hypothesis** is that there is a wolf

The men come running and praise the boy even when they find no wolf, believing his story of the wolf having run off. **A type 1 or false positive error** has occurred

The boy enjoys the attention, so repeats the trick. This time he is not praised. The men do not believe that there was a wolf. When a wolf really does attack and the boy rings his bell and cries "wolf", the men do not come, thinking that he is playing the trick again. The wolf takes one of the fattest sheep. **A type 2 or false negative error** has occurred

Type I error (false positive): Incorrectly rejecting null hypothesis, for example villagers believing the boy when there was no wolf

Type II error (false negative): Incorrectly accepting the null hypothesis, for example villagers not believing the boy when there actually was a wolf

Providing feedback

A first principle in good evaluation, it was suggested earlier, is that it is useful. This means that the results of the evaluation – its findings – need to be shared with those who can make use of it.

Feedback can take many forms. A long evaluation report, which provides both findings and information about the research methods and analysis from which these are derived, may not be helpful for those who want to make decisions, but can be very important for other purposes, particularly if the aim is 'knowledge' generation and publication. However, for an internal audience and clients, a short report, presentation and meeting are likely to be much more useful. This may take the form of a 'validation' event at which the findings are presented, and feedback obtained as to whether these make sense and what implications they have for further action. Verbal reporting is particularly important if there are 'difficult messages' to be communicated (i.e. that things didn't go well or produce the anticipated change).

Outline of an evaluation report

A good evaluation report covers the following points:

- An executive summary containing a condensed version of the most important aspects of the evaluation (see previous point)

- A summary of the evaluation's focus with a discussion of the purpose, objectives and questions used to direct the evaluation
- A summary of the evaluation plan
- A discussion of the findings of the evaluation, with complete statistical and case study analysis
- A discussion of the evaluation's conclusions and recommendations
- Any additional information required, such as terminology, details of who was involved in the evaluation, etc. in an appendix.

Taken from https://www.betterevaluation.org/en/evaluation-options/final_reports

Delivering findings

(In relation to delivering findings, see Levinson, 2002).
   According to Levinson (1994),

> An ethical consultant must answer such questions, report what he or she has learned in a manner that can be understood and recommend steps for change. These recommendations can be the basis for discussion within the organization and for evolving a plan of change that is in keeping with the organization's capacities and competence. All this requires a formal, comprehensive diagnostic process … and solid psychological skill.
>
> (pp. 51–52)

At this stage, it is also important to be clear what role the evaluator is expected to take. If they have been brought in specifically to undertake the evaluation, then presenting findings, perhaps with some recommendations, will represent the end of their assignment. If the consultant is being evaluated, should they also be supporting the implementation of the recommendations?

Mission creep: There can be two kinds of 'mission creep' in evaluation that can take those involved outside the boundary of their role and their original contract and budget. An evaluator may be so interested in the findings that they are itching to be part of developing and implementing recommendations. Alternatively, there may be pressure on an evaluator to tell the client how to solve their problem and help to put the solution in place, even if the original contract did not indicate this. Either of these can undermine the organisation's own capacity to think through the problem for themselves and put in place a solution. It also puts the evaluator at risk of being blamed if things go seriously wrong. The evaluator needs to know when to hand over their findings and conclusions to others. The consultant needs to fully engage others when implementing the findings and recommendations.

Conclusion

Good planning is essential to successful evaluation. This requires thinking carefully about why the evaluation is needed (its purpose), what exactly it is that is to be evaluated (the system) and what kind of evaluation approach is required (evaluation methods and approaches). There are a range of different evaluation approaches and different sources of data that can be used, some of which are described in the previous chapter. In an organisational development intervention, particular care needs to be taken to ensure that the evaluation approach is broadly compatible with the intervention itself, and ideally, proper consultation has been conducted during the planning process and throughout the delivery of the evaluation. This is particularly helpful in ensuring that those involved understand the reasons for undertaking an evaluation, its overall approach and what will be required of themselves. Reassurance about the safety of data and confidentiality will be particularly important. This will help create a framework and culture within which participants are more willing to cooperate with the evaluation, and in which the findings can be received, discussed and acted upon.

Questions

- What needs to be considered when planning an evaluation?
- What is the difference between a theory of change map and a systems map?
- In what way is a theory of change map similar, or different to Kirkpatrick's evaluation framework?
- What are the main differences between qualitative and quantitative data, and in what circumstances is each most useful, and why?
- What is the difference between a Type I and a Type II error – can you think of examples from your own work?
- Name three things that can go wrong when planning and undertaking an evaluation?
- What needs to be considered when giving feeding back on the findings of an evaluation?

Chapter 8

Varieties of action research

David Lawlor and Mannie Sher

The action research paradigm

de Guerre (2002) quotes Reason and Bradbury (2008) when they suggest that it is premature to define action research, and they suggest it is '... a participatory, democratic process concerned with developing practical knowing in the pursuit of worthwhile human purposes, grounded in a participatory worldview that is currently emerging (Reason and Bradbury, 2008, p. 1)'. Indeed, to try and further define action research would be stifle its development (van Beinum et al., 1996). It is not going too far to suggest that action research is a radical enough departure from traditional academic forms of scholarship to take on some of the characteristics of a new social science paradigm. There are many variants of action research. Gloster (2000) outlines the socio-ecological systems action research model developed by Fred Emery (1981, reprinted in Trist, 1997). He differentiates between action research (ar) that improves the practical affairs of a particular social system and Action Research (AR) that in addition contributes to social scientific knowledge. To describe socio-ecological AR, following Peirce (1878), Emery demonstrated that the type of logical inference required to generate concepts, and hypotheses about their connections, was based primarily on the logic of abduction:

> *Peirce demonstrated that there were three forms of logical inference and not just the two, deduction and induction, that were generally supposed. He distinguished between induction as a form of statistical generalization and abduction (retroduction) as a form of inference that yielded 'reasonable ex post-facto hypotheses'. He showed (1878)....that it was only by this ability to arrive at 'reasonable hypotheses' that we could advance scientific knowledge.*
>
> (Emery and Emery, 1997, p. 1)

In this model, inquiry begins with a surprising phenomenon or a problematic situation. In the case of action research conducted through the two-stage model (Emery, 1999), it is often a new demand or opportunity that creates the need for inquiry. Such AR often begins as 'ar' with a pragmatic real-world situation rather than the hypothetical pursuit of theory (de Guerre, 2002).

Below, we describe the multiplicities of action research.

DOI: 10.4324/9781003368663-12

Varieties of action research

Reason and McArdle (2005) describe the varieties of Action Research:

Organisational change and work research: This approach draws on a variety of forms of information gathering and feedback to organisation members, leading to problem-solving dialogue. This tradition is well represented in publications such as Toulmin and Gustavsen (1996), Greenwood and Levin (1998), and Coghlan and Brannick (2004).

Cooperative inquiry: A cooperative inquiry group consists of people who share a common concern for developing understanding and practice in a specific personal, professional or social arena. All are co-researchers, whose thinking and decision-making contribute to generating ideas, designing and managing the project, and drawing conclusions from the experience; they are also co-subjects, participating in the activity, which is being researched. Cooperative inquiry groups cycle between and integrate four forms of knowing – experiential, presentational, propositional and practical (Heron, 1996; Heron and Reason, 2001).

Action science and action inquiry: These related disciplines offer methods for inquiring into and developing congruence between purposes, theories and frames, behaviour and impact in the world. These practices can be applied at individual, small group and organisational levels. Their overall aim is to bring inquiry and action together in more and more moments of everyday life, to see inquiry as a 'way of life' (Argyris et al., 1985; Friedman, 2001; McKay and Marshall, 2001, Torbert, 2001).

Learning history: It is a process of recording the lived experience of those in an action research or learning situation. Researchers work collaboratively with those involved to agree the scope and focus of the history, identify key questions, gather information through an iterative reflective interview process, distil this information into a form which the organisation or community can 'hear' and facilitate dialogue with organisation members to explore the accuracy, implications and practical outcomes that the work suggests (Roth and Kleiner, 1998).

Action learning: For Revans (1998), the founder of action learning, action learning involves engagement with real problems rather than with fabrications; action learning is both scientifically rigorous in confronting the problem and critically subjective through managers learning in action. While its practice is demonstrated through many different approaches, two core elements are consistently in evidence: participants work on real organisational problems that do not appear to have clear solutions, and participants meet on equal terms to report to one another and to discuss their problems and progress (O'Neil and Marsick, 2007). Action learning has traditionally been directed towards enabling professionals to learn and develop through engaging in reflecting on their experience as they seek to solve real-life problems in their own organisational settings. As such, it is a powerful organisational development approach (Rigg,

2006). As a form of research that seeks to generate knowledge beyond the direct experience of its participants, action learning has not received a great deal of attention. In recent years, there have been explorations of action learning's philosophical grounds (Coghlan and Coughlan, 2010; Pedler and Burgoyne, 2008), and, from a research perspective, on research accessible through empirical engagement in practice and in collaboration with those who seek to resolve problems.

Appreciative inquiry: Practitioners of appreciative inquiry argue that the extent that action research maintains a problem-oriented view of the world diminishes peoples' capacity to produce innovative theory capable of inspiring the imagination, commitment and passionate dialogue required for the consensual re-ordering of social conduct. Devoting attention to what is positive about organisations and communities enables us to understand what gives them life and how we might sustain and enhance that life-giving potential. Appreciative inquiry begins with the 'unconditional positive question' that guides inquiry agendas and focuses attention towards the most life-giving, life-sustaining aspects of organisational existence (Ludema et al., 2001). Appreciative inquiry aims at large system change through an appreciative focus on what already works in a system, rather than what is deficient (Ludema and Fry, 2008). It utilises a cycle of appreciative inquiry that is sometimes expressed as the 4 'D's (Discovery, Dream, Design, Delivery/Destiny) or alternatively the 4 'I's (Initiate, Inquire, Imagine and Innovate) (Reed, 2007; Watkins and Mohr, 2001). Appreciative inquiry is often misunderstood and perceived to be a simple process of focusing on the positive. As Bushe (2010) argues, appreciative inquiry did not begin its life as an intervention technique. Rather, it began as a research method for making grounded theory-building more generative. Accordingly, Bushe argues that it is a deeper and richer process than a change technique and has an underlying capacity to leverage the generative capacity of metaphors and conversation to facilitate transformational action. Appreciative inquiry has become a prolific way of engaging in organisation development (e.g. Yaeger et al., 2005).

Whole systems inquiry: Large group interventions or processes are events designed to engage representatives of an entire system, whether it be an organisation or a community, in thinking through and planning change (Bunker and Alban, 1997). What distinguishes large group interventions is that the process is managed to allow all participants an opportunity to engage actively in the planning (Martin, 2001). Rather than aim at a single outcome, in dialogue conference design (Gustavsen, 2001, 2003) and whole systems designs (Pratt et al., 1999), the role of the researchers and consultants is to create the conditions for democratic dialogue among participants. A feature of the newer forms of organisational development is the large group type of intervention (Bunker and Alban, 1997). These large group interventions have different names, such as whole-community inquiry conferences, search conferences, future search, open space, real-time strategic change and others (Holman et al., 2007; Purser and

Griffin, 2008), but they have in common the notion of bringing the whole system into the room and engaging in conversation about present realities and how to create new future realities. While large group interventions have their origins in traditional organisational development (Beckhard, 1967), they have flourished as 'dialogic organisational development' insofar as they provide the setting for multiple perspectives to be shared and developed into new agreement. Such large group processes are integrally linked to action research (Martin, 2001).

Participative action research: Usually used to refer to action research strategies emerging from the liberationist ideas of Paulo Freire (1970) and others in countries of the political 'South', participatory action research (PAR) is explicitly political, aiming to restore to oppressed peoples the ability to create knowledge and practice in their own interests and as such has a double objective. One aim is to produce knowledge and action directly useful to a group of people, another, to empower people at a deeper level through the process of constructing and using their own knowledge so they 'see through' the ways in which the establishment monopolises the production and use of knowledge for their own benefit. PAR practitioners emphasise emergent processes of collaboration and dialogue that empower, motivate, increase self-esteem and develop community solidarity (Borda and Rahman, 1991; Selener, 1997).

Cooperative inquiry: Heron and Reason (2008, p. 366) define cooperative inquiry 'in which the participants work together in an inquiry group as co-researchers and co-subjects'. The participants research a topic through their own experience of it in order to understand their world, make sense of their life, develop new and creative ways of looking at things, and learn how to act to change things they might want to change and find out how to do things better.

Developmental action inquiry: Developmental action inquiry is an expression of action science. Torbert (2004) adds the developmental dynamic of learning to inquire-in-action. As leaders progress through adulthood, they develop new 'action-logics' by progressing through stages of emotional and intellectual development. Developmental theory offers an understanding of leaders' transformations through a series of stages, thus gaining insight into their own action-logics as they work to transform their organisations (Fisher et al., 2000).

Sustaining the results: To sustain the results of utilising an action research methodology, it is important to be clear about the purpose of action research as a consultative intervention. Action research should contribute to the theory and knowledge base of the system to enhance the primary task of the organisation. It should help organisational members identify problems and seek solutions systematically. In action research, the goals are more focused on problem-solving and the enhancement of organisational functioning. It is important for the action researcher and consultant to understand action research methodologies through designing research, developing instruments, selecting subjects, and collecting and analysing data.

The overall goals of action research should be to solve a problem, include collaboration, develop the organisation and enhance the capacity of members of the organisation to take up their roles. Action research also requires passion about the issues and ability and desire to change and improve the system. Action research methodology requires answers to the following:

1 Have we a written statement that gives the project focus?
2 Have we defined the variables?
3 Have we developed questions for examination?
4 Can we describe the intervention or innovation?
5 Can we describe the action research group?
6 Can we describe the negotiations that need to happen?
7 Have we developed a timeline?
8 Have we developed a statement of resources?
9 Have we developed data collection ideas?
10 Are we able to put an action plan into action?

Argyris et al. (1985) summarise Lewin's action research (AR) concept:

1 AR involves change experiments on real issues in social systems and seeks to aid the client system.
2 AR involves iterative cycles of identifying a problem, planning, acting and evaluating.
3 The intended change in an action research project typically involves re-education, a term that refers to changing patterns of thinking, and actions that are presently well established in individuals and groups. Effective re-education depends on participation by clients in diagnosis, fact-finding and free choice to engage in new kinds of action.
4 AR challenges the status quo, involves the widest possible participation, which is congruent with the aims of effective re-education.
5 AR is intended to contribute simultaneously to basic knowledge in social science and to social action in everyday life. High standards for developing theory and empirically testing propositions organised by theory should not be sacrificed nor should sight be lost of its relation to practice.

Action research and organisational development: Action research has several roots (Greenwood and Levin, 2007; Reason and Bradbury, 2008), and among them is organisational development. The work of Lewin (1946 a, b, c, 1947 a, b, c, d, 1948, 1951) and the organisational development tradition grew out of the T-group and NTL Institute in the USA; socio-technical systems theory grew out of the work of the Tavistock Institute in the UK and 'workplace democracy' in Scandinavia were major roots of action research in the Northern Hemisphere (Bradbury et al., 2008; Pasmore, 2001). Nevertheless, there were important roots and strands of action research existing outside of the organisational development tradition. The consciousness-raising work of Freire (1970) and the Marxist-based liberation movements in the Southern Hemisphere, frequently referred to as emancipatory or participatory action research, feminist approaches to research, epistemological notions of praxis and the hermeneutic school of philosophy associated with Habermas, are important strands and expressions of action research, which did not grow out of the organisational development tradition (Reason and Bradbury, 2008).

The two fundamental differences between the action research tradition within organisational development and the emancipatory action research tradition lie in the purpose and location of the research. The organisation development tradition of action research occurs within organisations and aims to help organisations change and at the same time to generate knowledge. The emancipatory action research tradition tends to be in rural and urban communities and aims to empower the participants to take control of some aspect of their own environment, which frequently pits the less economically powerful against the more powerful. Indeed, organisational development action research may be criticised by the emancipatory tradition as supporting the capitalist status quo and not being radical enough. While organisation development and action research are closely interlinked, each has an existence independent of the other.

Organisation development and action research then and now: According to Coghlan (2011), the action research model that developed in organisational development between the 1960s and 1990s was a consistent one and was captured in several important publications (Burnes, 2007; Clarke, 1972; Coch and French, 1948; Cunningham, 1993; Foster, 1972; French and Bell, 1999; Frohman et al., 1976; Pasmore and Friedlander, 1982; Shani and Pasmore, 1985; Shepard and Katzell, 1960).

This action research model is captured by the following definition that expresses both traditions:

> *Action research may be defined as an emergent inquiry process in which applied behavioural science knowledge is integrated with existing organisational knowledge and applied to solve real organisational problems. It is simultaneously concerned with bringing about change in organisations, in developing self-help competencies in organisational members and in adding to scientific knowledge. Finally, it is an evolving process that is undertaken in a spirit of collaboration and co-inquiry.*
>
> *(Shani and Pasmore, 1985: 439)*

One of the most clear and practical accounts of the relationship between organisational development and action research is found in Frohman et al. (1976), a seminal article capturing the essence of how organisational development and action research complemented each other and differed from each other at this time. The authors describe how action research used with organisational development is based on collaboration between the behavioural-scientist-researcher and the client where they collaborate on exploring problems and generating valid data on the problem (the research activity), and jointly in examining the data to understand the problem. They then develop action plans to address the problems and implement them. They evaluate the outcomes of the actions, both intended and unintended. This evaluation may then lead to further cycles of diagnosis, action planning and action. Cyclical-sequential phases may be identified that capture the movements of collaboration from initial scouting to evaluation. Frohman et al. (1976) note that these activities may serve also to generate new behavioural science knowledge, which is fed into the depository of information for other behavioural scientists as general laws, types of problems or the process of consultant-client collaboration, thus addressing issues beyond the specific case.

The organisational development and action research model was distinctive because it followed a cyclical process of consciously and deliberately (a) diagnosing the situation, (b) planning action, (c) taking action, (d) evaluating the action, leading to further diagnosing, planning and so on. Both approaches were collaborative insofar as the consultant and facilitator, and the members of the system participated actively in the cyclical process. This action research approach to organisation development was powerful. It engaged people as participants in seeking ideas, planning, taking actions, reviewing outcomes and learning what worked and did not work, and why. This approach was in stark contrast with programmed approaches that mandated following pre-designed steps and which tended not to be open to alteration. These latter approaches assumed that the system should adopt the entire package as designed. Action research and organisation development, on the other hand, assumed that each system is unique and that a change process must be designed with that uniqueness in mind and adapted in the light of ongoing experience and emergent learning.

A case study

A consulting team conducted an assessment process in an UK police constabulary to address the aftermath of a difficult Job Evaluation and Pay Review; to improve collaborative working relationships across the Force and its partner organisations and re-build trust; and to deliver increased leadership competency, including internal coaching and mentoring capability to the constabulary's leadership teams.

Implementation of an action research and action learning programme involved working together with stakeholders and leaders at several levels throughout the constabulary. The action-oriented intervention assumed that everyone participating in it would be the 'client' of the programme and would be fully engaged in all phases of the work. Collective accountability was the key.

The approach pivoted on the formation of a series of integrated work-focused action learning modular events, designed to bring about a rapid positive shift in effective working together across the Force. The consulting team worked collaboratively with the constabulary's Chief Officers' Group, the organisational development group, the trades union and other key groups that developed along the way. Some of the aspects of the action research lent themselves to immediate implementation; others were aligned with other 'business-as-usual' organisational initiatives.

The views of the consulting team were that the constabulary was ONE organisation with a strong identity and a powerful culture. The constabulary had previously been led by a commanding Chief Constable who was said to have managed the organisation in a patriarchal and autocratic way, which generated a high degree of dependency, low sense of autonomy and independent thinking among the officers and staff, including the senior teams. At the same time, however, the sense of security and certainty was also high in the Force and people spoke about the previous chief with admiration and nostalgia.

Upon his retirement, he was replaced by a new Chief with a dramatically different leadership style, which threw the organisation into a state of chaos, failed dependency and even abandonment.

The prevailing experience in the Force was of being impacted by a poorly conducted Job Evaluation exercise. The organisation seemed to be split in terms of its perceived life cycle of 'before' and 'after' this Job Evaluation process, and in terms of its human processes between the 'good' and the 'bad' and 'victims' and 'villains' – those who were and those who were not involved in the Job Evaluation activity. The story told was very powerful without discrepancies in its telling.

After the team's first visit, the picture of the organisation changed into forward-looking attitudes and a wish to move away from the mistrust and sense of injury that had prevailed at the time the current Chief Constable took up this post. The hope in the organisation of the new Chief Constable's leadership was about the potential of the middle ground and re-integration.

This training and development programme for the constabulary involved consulting and coaching senior personnel to extend their action learning and organisational development leadership and management skills in their work within the constabulary.

The outcomes of the organisational development and change initiative included the following:

- A sharply integrated cadre of constabulary senior leaders and managers were coached to help the different parts of the constabulary achieve the overall strategy of becoming a top-performing Force in four years.

- All constabulary personnel of the initiative (between 90 and 100) improved their individual and collaborative team leadership capability and commitment throughout the constabulary.
- All participants and their teams and action learning groups developed high levels of trust and confidence within the Force.
- The organisational development and change initiative led to:
  - Enhanced culture change in the Force
  - Improved 'whole systems' change
  - Greater cross-organisational collaboration
  - Reduced silo-behaviour
  - Inspired reputation of the Force
  - Improved performance on all policing indicators

The organisational development and change initiative and training programme based on action research and action learning principles was made up of two phases:

I   Phase I involved carrying out a diagnostic assessment of the learning needs of the constabulary to assess individuals' interest and capability to take up leadership and management roles for enhancing organisational development and change in the Force.

II Phase II consisted of a training programme for senior personnel to deepen their understanding of organisational dynamics of policing with which they were working. The organisational development programme paid particular attention to leaders' and managers' abilities to help their teams deepen their understanding and their skill in (a) resolving organisational problems and (b) implementing the Force's strategic objectives, and (c) improving collaborative work across the Force.

The organisational development programme combined the contributions of personnel with ideas and experiences of the Tavistock Institute's 'action learning' and 'whole systems' approaches towards organisational development and change. The programmes added value to the constabulary's existing capability and addressed the challenges of collaboration, innovation and transformation in the Force. The action learning approach, by also focusing on 'beneath-the-surface' dynamic processes in the Force and in consultancy processes themselves – in individuals and in groups – helped senior staff and their teams to identify and utilise these processes to reach deeper levels of understanding and increased effectiveness in their organisational development work.

The 'action learning' and 'whole systems' approaches enabled the constabulary senior groups to improve their engagement with other parts of the Force, build confidence and trust in Forces' management and helped middle and lower ranking managers to affirm their leadership capability and commitment. Personnel increased their capability in working with the senior management groups that combined practical leadership and organisational development theories put into practice.

Phase I diagnostic assessment

The purpose of the diagnostic phase was to assess the learning needs and outline a development programme for the constabulary for tackling individual, team and organisational leadership issues. The diagnostic phase provided a first level of clarity in answering the question:

> Which specific elements in the organisational development and change and training programmes are needed to improve the leadership and management capacity of the Constabulary's personnel?

Focus of activity

Members of the senior management teams and representatives of the lower ranks were interviewed by the consultants to develop an outline organisational development and training programme. Findings were presented to meetings of the Force leadership and other representatives. At these meetings, senior officers began working on an agreed organisational change and learning development strategy.

The consultants helped senior staff identify and construct strategies for working with their teams. The aim was to develop their organisational transformational strategies for moving the Force forward within the change agenda frameworks. Another aim was to begin to put those strategies into effect.

After full understanding was gained of the constabulary's personnel learning needs, work on Phase II was started.

Phase II building an organisational change and training programme

Building an organisational change and training programme to assist the constabulary's personnel in their work using 'action learning' and 'whole systems' methodologies consisted of: (i) understanding and working in Action Learning Sets, (ii) understanding 'working through', and (iii) designing and running whole-community inquiry conferences.

(i) Action learning

The rationale for following an action learning methodology was based on the principles of an educational process whereby participants in small groups, called Action Learning Sets, study their own actions and experiences in order to improve performance. Action learning powerfully enabled each person to reflect on and review the action they had taken and the learning points arising, which guided future action and improved performance. The method was in contrast with traditional teaching methods that focus on the presentation of knowledge and skills by experts. Action learning focuses on research into action taken, and knowledge emerges as a result that leads to improvement of skills and performance.

Action learning involves awareness of gaps in relevant knowledge and an openness to explore areas of ignorance with suitable questions and help from other people in similar positions. Action learning is a well-established approach to the education of leaders. It puts the person-in-role, group and organisational issues before syllabus, so following the principle of 'theory follows the action'. Action learning strongly supports learning in the workplace, where learning lends itself to working on real problems, for example improving productivity or morale, rather than constructing a balance sheet. Powerful learning comes from people learning 'with and from others'; hence, many action learning programmes put the 'Action Learning Set' at the heart of the process.

(ii) 'Working through'

The need for 'working through' occurred because of intense feelings that threatened relationships (inter-personal, inter-group, inter-organisational, international) that had developed between people and groups of people across the workforce and the management, which included rejection, damage, hurt and loss, shame and guilt.

'Working through' happened because the feelings were traced and accepted, whatever their cause, and faced one by one, over and over again, to the point at which they were sufficiently weakened to lose their effect. This 'working through' towards resolution happened, through relationships that were characterised by verbal expression, that is talking, dialogue, discussion, conversation, debate and argument.

(iii) Whole-community inquiry methodology

Whole-community inquiry methodology sought to change the understanding of how organisational continuity and change occurred through intensive processes of joint inquiry among diverse participants from the

Force. The focus shifted from the design of outcomes to the design of and participation in inquiry processes. Whole-community inquiry methodology did not investigate static sets of facts to find simple causal connections. Rather, it was an active ongoing process of re-creating work-based situations, making fresh sense between police officers and civilian colleagues of how they got to be where they were and how they could move on, thus re-making the situations they were continuously constructing together.

Aims

- The aim of using of 'action learning' and 'whole systems' approaches (Action Learning Sets, whole-community conferences, role consultations) was to enhance business-specific and cross-organisational efficiencies across the Force with which senior Force personnel were working.
- Successful 'action learning' and 'whole systems' strategies relied on the integration and coordination of organisation-wide interventions by senior governing bodies, for example Chief Officers' Command Teams, organisational development groups, or similar, within the Force.

Practice

Throughout the period of the organisational development and training programmes, each participant established and consulted to their teams and participated in the Force's 'whole systems' change programme involving whole-community conferences, Action Learning Sets and role consultations.

The consultants assisted the cohort of 100 personnel to establish Action Learning Sets and 'whole systems' programmes as part of their organisational development work within the Force. They tutored the constabulary personnel in whole-community conferences involving events of between 100 and 200 people that led to the formation of Action Learning Sets with which personnel worked for between 12 and 18 months. All Action Learning Sets had as their themes some aspect of the Force's overall strategy of becoming a top-performing Force, such as the 'One-Team Strategy'; People Programme; Process Review; Private Security Industry and Role of Uniform Patrol; Citizen's Charter and Shared Services. The 100 personnel managed their work in their Action Learning Sets and the 'whole systems' programmes throughout the period of the programmes.

Post-programme continuation

After completion of the organisational development and training programme, the constabulary personnel continued consulting to their teams. The senior staff had access to the consultants for individual or group advice and consultation on their ongoing work as change consultants.

The transition from then to now

At the same time, there was a growing unease that positivist science was not altogether useful to the world of practice. Susman and Evered (1978) argued that the conditions from which people learn in everyday life are better explored through a range of philosophical viewpoints: Aristotelian praxis, hermeneutics, existentialism, pragmatism, process philosophies and phenomenology. They proposed that action research provides a corrective to the deficiencies of positivist science by being future-oriented, collaborative, implying system development, generating theory that is grounded in action, agnostic and situational. Schon (1995) contrasted how researchers can view practice from the high ground, where they can study issues from a distance, for example, because they are not organisational members or because their data are based on pre-constructed surveys or interviews. Or they can be immersed in 'swampy lowlands' where problems are messy and confusing and incapable of a technical solution, because they are either organisational members, whose actions influence the reality they see, or are outsiders who are contracted to influence what they see. He concluded that unimportant issues may be studied from the high ground according to predetermined standards and rigour, while the critically important ones, such as how to generate the changes in practice we wish to see, can only be confronted by being immersed in the 'swampy lowlands'. In his view, work in the 'swampy lowlands' involves a new scholarship, which requires a new epistemology.

Action research and its relationship to systems psychodynamics

Susan Long (1997, 1999) perhaps presents the most integrated description of action research and its relationship to systems psychodynamics:

> *Social systems are dynamic and changing and a research method that studies not only the current state of an organisation, but also its ongoing dynamics, conscious and unconscious, is required. The process of knowing about the system is itself part of the social system. People continuously use their knowledge and the process of 'coming to know' in order to make decisions and to act. The action researcher can aid organisation members to develop knowledge in a systematic and thoughtful way. The alternative is to go about knowing in a practical, fragmented or biased manner,*

as may occur, for example, when knowledge is regarded as the prerogative of a particular person or group within the system, such as 'management' or 'the union'. This fragmentation is often the result of unconscious splitting and projection, which requires interpretation within the research.

(Long, 1999, p. 263)

Using a systems psychodynamics theory to understand action research processes allows us to pay attention to the dynamic process that the researcher or consultant is subject to. The attention to the changing relations that the consultant has with the organisation constitutes valuable data. The experience of the consultant is created by the system and its culture. All these experiences can be studied by examining the transference, countertransference and the social defence systems that come into play once the consultant begins to probe the system's 'ways of doing things'. Susan Long helpfully shows how a team of researchers or consultants can also use their own process to study the reflected dynamics that often occur. A team of consultants can often act out or reflect the unconscious dynamics of the organisation. The team's reflection on their experiences is very valuable data on the organisational difficulties or impasse that they may be experiencing. Long suggests the following capacities are required by an action researcher:

1 Making judgements when limited data are available
2 Following through on decisions when peer pressure is exerted to prevent this
3 Recognising the validity of others' points of view
4 Consulting others and listening to them
5 Taking up authority and exercising it responsibly
6 Knowing when one should have confidence in one's decisions, intuitions or knowledge and knowing one's limitations

Long says 'many of these qualities emerge from wide experience and from self-development where assumptions, thinking, reflection and action are challenged and one has to face one's own emotional realities' (p. 266). We suggest that such developmental opportunities are afforded by personal psychotherapy or attendance at group relations conferences. A combination of the two would be ideal.

Integrating research – dynamic consultancy: a Tavistock institute approach

The action research model is a basic model underlying most organisational development and consultancy activity. Action research is especially well suited for planned change programmes. Action research is a method for learning and doing – learning about the dynamics of organisational change and doing or implementing change efforts. In relation to consultancy practice, Heller et al. (2005) argue that the human resource area frequently fails to draw on relevant social science knowledge or theory and may therefore produce sub-optimal

results for clients (Sorge and Witteloostuijn, 2004). To overcome this problem, they suggest that consultancy incorporates an appropriate dynamic search
methodology. The approaches are: firstly, Research Action and its cousin Action
Research and secondly, group relations theory and practice. The outcome of a
process that uses one or both methodologies can be called Research Dynamic
Consultancy. The term Research Action has been applied to situations that
require systematic knowledge gathering before adequate solutions can be con-
fidently recommended. The term Action Research is appropriate where reliable
knowledge, often supported by a model or theory, is already available (Heller,
2004). Group relations theory and practice can fall into either category. While
it has already established a substantial body of knowledge and experience, there
are areas of application, for instance, in conflict resolution, where the knowledge
and experience base is thin and needs to be strengthened.

Action research and consultancy – research action

There are important differences between action-oriented research methodologies. The term Research Action is now applied to projects for which little or
no knowledge is currently available. It is therefore important to start with a
systematic learning procedure. The research phase must produce what Argyris
(1993) calls 'actionable knowledge' before a change process can meaningfully be
engaged. Although the term Research Action was not used at the time, it accurately describes most of the early work of the Tavistock Institute, for instance,
Bridger (1990), Curl (1947) and Bing (1947). Research Action also *describes* the
important action and policy-oriented work of Kurt Lewin (1947), which, at
the time, he called Action Research. However, in the 1990s the term Action
Research was increasingly associated with action and organisational change and
minimised or even avoided the preliminary knowledge acquisition stage (see
the new Sage Journal: 'Action Research' Vols I & 2). We now use the term
Action Research when an adequate body of knowledge and experience is already available, perhaps supported by a model tested in previous projects. The
socio-technical model is an obvious example (Cherns, 1976; Emery, 1993; Passmore, 1995). When change is advocated without previous or currently available
knowledge, we prefer other terms like Change Agency or simply Organisational
Change (Attwood et al., 2003; Schein and Bennis, 1965). We accept that some
learning takes place in monitored change situations and this is a very important
additional input to understanding and to the sense-making process, but it is
rarely an adequate substitute for pre-change available knowledge.

Research Action and Action Research share three attributes (Heller
et al., 2004):

1 A joint main objective is the utilisation of valid existing knowledge, but
   Research Action is additionally concerned with facilitating discovery of
   new knowledge.

2 The benefit of the acquired knowledge accrues to the client in the first place, but diffusion to others including consultants and the knowledge-producing community is important.
3 Evidence that something useful has been achieved and that the process leads to changes that are *effective* in the circumstances is validated through the action process itself (this can be called action validation).

Consultancy is also concerned with change as an objective or an outcome. On its own, the term consultancy covers a confusingly wide range of methods and rarely incorporates a systematic acquisition or use of validated knowledge (Clark and Fincham, 2002; Collins, 2000; Kanter, 1983; Sadler, 1998; Werr and Stiernbeg, 2003). The unsatisfactory nature of this variety of approaches trading under the term 'consultancy' is well illustrated by Clark and Fincham (2002). It begins with a piece by Edgar Schein who notes how confusing the concept of consultation is and speculates on how to reduce this confusion (p. 21). He starts by objecting to the subtitle of the book, 'Management Advice Industry'. Schein says that 'giving advice in the arena of human problems is generally one of the quickest paths to failure as a consultant'. He then describes the psychodynamics of providing a helping relationship, which includes working with the client until a satisfactory outcome is reached. However, most consultancies finish with advice, usually in a written document, and leave the implementation to the client. The client may of course hire a consultant to implement the diagnosis and advice. Furthermore, a substantial area of consultancy is in the form of 'packages' for training (Sturdy, 2002). Other packages concentrate on productivity improvement like Total Quality Management (Karen Legge, 2002). Then, there are consultants that derive their inspiration from case examples they have collected themselves (Kanter, 1983; Pettigrew, 1973). Some consultants develop a line of working that elevates them to the status of 'gurus', for instance, Rosabeth Kanter, Peter Senge, Steven Covey and Michael Hammer. Gerlach (1996) tells us that Bill Clinton sought advice from Anthony Robbins who wrote a number of best-selling books on motivation. Consultants and management gurus are often accused of basing their technique on fads and buzzwords like: 'let's get the big picture', or 'my approach is a paradigm shift' (Collins, 2000).

The question is whether the advice or the helping hand given by traditional consultants in the human resource area is based on actionable knowledge. By actionable knowledge is meant valid information derived, for instance, from research action or action research described above or group relations theory and practice described below. While there are some exceptions, for instance Chris Argyris, Edgar Schein or work based on Total Quality Management (TQM), the evidence reviewed suggests that the bulk of traditional consulting operates from a very tenuous knowledge base. This conclusion is supported by Aired Kieser (2002) who reviews the literature on knowledge transfer. He challenges the widespread view 'that knowledge that is of relevance to management practice travels rather easily ... to consultants who process it in order to increase its applicability, and then pass it on in the form of transferable practices to business organisations'. (p. 206). In contrast to this assumption, he finds that there are substantial barriers between knowledge creation, consultancies and business organisations.

Integrating group relations theory and practice into action research

Research action and action research and group relations theory and practice are central to the Tavistock Institute's mission, which is to advance the social sciences through involvement in practical human problems and concerns. Experience shows that action-oriented social scientists are best placed to gain access to critical aspects of the functioning of social systems. In group relations work, they take on a professional role in which they are helping these systems to tackle real issues of development and change. Action research, research action and group relations practice are problem-centred, not discipline-centred. They are anchored in values and practices that offer ways of examining and understanding how people get caught up in unconscious processes. In this way, they can learn to exercise their own authority. There is a relationship between Tavistock group relations theory and practice and the experiential study of group and organisational processes operating at individual, group, organisation, community and society levels. Group relations methodologies and conceptual frameworks rest upon two distinctive bodies of knowledge: psychodynamic and psychoanalytic theory and general systems theory. These are commonly known as the Tavistock systems psychodynamics approach. The objective is to value and help people gain greater influence over their environment.

It is important to emphasise the responsibility that action-oriented consultants take in their professional relationships for the consequences of their interventions in the client system. Research action and action research and group relations consultancy adhere to liberal democratic values. The group relations contribution to action-oriented research and organisational consulting is the recognition that individuals and groups develop mechanisms to give meaning to their existence and to defend themselves from fear and uncertainty. These defences are often unconscious and deeply rooted and threatened by change, and consequently, it is an important aspect of the research-dynamic consultant's role to serve as a container during the 'working through' of change, to tackle not only the overt problem, but also the underlying difficulties.

Additionally, Tavistock research-dynamic consultancy practice acknowledges the importance of countertransference in worker-client relationships: that is to say, the consultant's feelings may provide significant evidence about underlying feelings within the client system. Staff, who are professionally involved with the client system, directly influence the types of theoretical constructs they generate. Their models for understanding organisations need to be communicable to client groups and need to take account of sources of resistance to change. Research conducted from other roles would tend to generate other types of models (Clark and Fincham, 2002; Collins, 2000; Kanter, 1983; Werr and Stiernbeg, 2003).

Therefore, integrating a group relations methodology into an action research methodology gives a deeper and richer picture of the dynamic processes within the client system, thereby enabling the consultant to make more well thought-out interventions, such as applied group relations experiential learning.

Summary

Action learning involves engagement with real problems rather than with theory, is both scientifically rigorous in confronting the problems and is critically subjective in the working-through with managers learning-in-action.

Appreciative inquiry argues that the extent that action research maintains a problem-oriented view of the world and diminishes peoples' capacity to produce innovative theory capable of inspiring the imagination, commitment and passionate dialogue required for the consensual re-ordering of social conduct. Appreciative inquiry begins with the 'unconditional positive question' that guides inquiry agendas and focuses attention toward the most life-giving, life-sustaining aspects of organisational existence.

Whole systems inquiry is designed to engage representatives of an entire system, whether it be an organisation or a community, in thinking through and planning change. In whole system designs, the role of the researchers is to create the conditions for democratic dialogue among participants for multiple perspectives to be shared and developed into new agreement.

Cooperative inquiry involves participants working together in an inquiry group as co-researchers and co-subjects. The participants research a topic through their own experience of it to understand their world, make sense of their life, develop new and creative ways of looking at things, and learn how to act to change things they might want to change and find out how to do things better.

Developmental action inquiry adds the developmental dynamic of learning to inquire-in-action. Leaders as they progress through adulthood develop new 'action-logics' by progressing through stages of emotional and intellectual development. Developmental theory offers an understanding of leaders' transformations through a series of stages, thus gaining insight into their own action-logics as they work to transform their organisations.

Group relations is based on over 70 years of theory, research, and practice. Group relations is an applied discipline that integrates open-systems theory and psychodynamic perspectives as a lens through which to view human behaviours in groups.

Exercise

1 What distinguishes action research from regular research?
2 Why are action research and organisational development close bed-fellows?
3 What are the core elements of Lewin's field theory?
4 Name and discuss three research methodologies that have their roots in action research.

Part III

Leadership and whole systems

Part III comprises five chapters on social ecology, complexity, leadership, social dreaming and digitalisation, artificial intelligence and virtual working.

Chapter 9 introduces the concept of organisational ecology – the field created by several organisations whose inter-relations comprise a system at the level of a field or domain. The overall domain is the object of inquiry and is characterised by environments of increasing complexity, at an increasing rate, and is more interdependent. Like socio-technical systems, social ecology involves wider social systems than the single organisation. The environment is conceived as an extended social field with a causal texture, which affects the behaviour of all systems within it. Social ecology is an open systems view of internal and external dialogues between organisations and their environments. Environments have causal textures and take on lives of their own, which no organisation can fully control or predict. The 'turbulent field' signifies the contextual interdependencies of organisations in rapidly changing environments. Causal textures studies environmental types and analyses how organisations in their environments intersect. In this chapter, Camilla Child contributes a piece on Developing NHS Citizen: a large-scale engagement intervention: a story of boundary control.

Chapter 10 on complexity theory helps move beyond the limitations of earlier versions of systems theory. The central concept of complexity theory is that of non-linear dynamics, viz. systems spontaneously reorganise towards states of greater heterogeneity and complexity, achieving a steady state at a level where they could still do work. The chapter describes how complexity theory improves systems psychodynamics through studying non-linear behaviour, importing energy through network interactions, and co-production to increase fitness function of the group. Eliat Aram presents a case of an orchestra as a complex system that illustrates how complexity theory combines with systems psychodynamics theory by grasping complex behaviour and assumptions about plans, connections, fitness functions and population dynamics of individuals and groups.

Chapter 11 covers the systems psychodynamics of leadership with contributions from Eliat Aram, Anton Obholzer and Jonathan Gosling. They focus in different ways on the dynamics of behaviour in systems; Eliat Aram writes

DOI: 10.4324/9781003368663-13

an illuminating essay on 'Love and Leadership: what's love got to do with it?' Anton Obholzer raises issues of leadership and authority and how they link with the development of the individual leader's inner world as a baby, based on its experience of being 'contained' by its primary carer. Jonathan Gosling challenges the idea of leadership and change and argues for leadership that conserves the status quo and, most appropriately, adjusts and repositions to better meet constantly evolving challenges. The chapter urges the reader to think about better designed and better managed boundaries, reminding us that the task of leadership is located on the boundary between the organisation and its external environment. By standing at the boundary, monitoring the organisations' primary task, leaders create a controllable environment in which the organisations activities are organised and coordinated to respond to change. The chapter concludes that the systems psychodynamics lens addresses the undercurrents of organisational life through inter-personal communication, group processes, social defences and the organisation-in-the-mind.

Chapter 12 deals with social dreaming, pioneered and developed by Gordon Lawrence and Paddy Daniel in 1982 as a method of social inquiry to address the unthought and unconscious dimensions of the social world. Social dreaming also links the post-Freudian and post-Kleinian developments in conceptualising the nature and function of the dream. Using free association, thoughts contained in dreams can be expanded, and through amplification, thoughts in the dream can be related to phenomena beyond the individual to the culture of an organisation, community or society. Social dreaming can be used for developing social as distinct from personal meaning. Social dreaming assumes that dreaming is not just for individuals, but forms part of a larger context in which we live. Social dreaming accesses the associative unconscious – the network of ideas, signs and symbols collectively held by an interacting culture; not available in its entirety to any one person, only accessible through collaborative dialogue.

Susan Long contributes a piece on anticipating the use of social dreaming in helping groups, organisations and societies to discover the anticipations of their members as part of a research and risk assessment strategy. The importance of social dreaming, Susan Long writes, is that it is a method that combines the vagaries of the unconscious with reflective practices about workplace roles and problems. In this chapter, David Armstrong writes on the *Authority of the Dream* in memory of Gordon Lawrence. Two illustrations of social dreaming are presented to suggest that the terms 'authority of the dream' and 'leadership of the dream' correspond to developments of thinking about unconscious processes that are associated primarily with the work of Wilfred Bion and Gordon Lawrence. They both regard social dreaming as a form of sustained thinking, generated pre-verbally on and from emotional experience. Social dreaming is a generative process that articulates, works through and seeks to resolve internal conflicts in individuals and the social dreaming matrix that can then be deployed to life and relationships in the outside world.

Chapter 13 deals with three important changes to the world of work over the past 30 years – the impact of digitalisation, artificial intelligence (AI) and virtual working. Olya Khaleelee contributes to this chapter with a piece on how current societal issues, such as climate change, political correctness, the impact of COVID and the effects of AI and robotics, affect organisations and organisational culture currently and in the future, and on the skills needed for organisational consultancy.

This chapter describes the Fourth Industrial Revolution and its blurring of boundaries between the physical, digital and biological worlds. The Fourth Industrial Revolution is a complex environment of integrated and interactive cyber and physical worlds that sustains hyper-connectivity, hyper-convergence and hyper-intelligence, technologically and socially. The Fourth Industrial Revolution represents a new stage in the organisation and control of the industrial value chain when coupled with machine learning and artificial intelligence. The systems psychodynamics models of open systems theories, psychoanalysis, and complexity and socio-technical concepts of boundaries, authority, role and tasks will be as relevant as ever and applicable. The chapter ends asserting that systems psychodynamics models will continue to promote user participation in systems design and in the politics of labour conditions, and labour-management conflicts through improved workplace democratisation.

Chapter 9

Socio-ecological

Working with large complex collaborative partnerships (whole systems)

David Lawlor and Mannie Sher with Camilla Child

The application of socio-ecological methods

Khalsa and Passmore (1993), in writing about the contributions of Eric Trist, argue that just as socio-technical systems was a term coined by Trist and his colleagues that developed into a robust body of theory and practice in individual organisations, so too has social ecology been a forerunner of ecologically rooted theory and practice in socio-organisational domains. They describe the development of the socio-ecological theory and practice. Trist (1977) introduced a concept of organisational ecology. He said this referred to the organisational field created by several organisations, whose inter-relations compose a system at the level of the field as a whole. The overall field becomes the object of inquiry, not the single organisation as related to its organisation set. He pointed out the emergence of organisational ecology from earlier organisation theory that can be traced and illustrated from empirical studies. He related organisational ecology to the task of institution-building in a world in which the environment had become exceedingly complex and more interdependent. Trist characterised it as a field in organisational studies concerned with complex change processes that affect multiple aspects of multiple organisations, called domains.

Like socio-technical systems, the development of social ecology had its beginnings in projects undertaken by the Tavistock Institute, during the 1960s, involving wider social systems than single organisations, and they had a future orientation with a much longer time horizon than earlier projects (Emery and Trist, 1973; Trist and Murray, 1997, p. 32).

Turbulent fields

Trist and his colleagues observed that *'the environmental contexts in which organisations exist are themselves changing, at an increasing rate, and towards increasing complexity'* (Emery and Trist, 1965, p. 21), requiring an advancement of the understanding of the systemic implications of these changes. Emery and Trist first explicated these implications in a paper entitled 'The Causal Texture of Organizational Environments' (1965), which began their journey into social ecology. The brilliance of the

DOI: 10.4324/9781003368663-14

piece was twofold: first, it recognised the nature of internal and external dialogues between the organisation and its environment – that environments have causal textures. Second, it postulated that environments were taking on lives of their own, which no organisation could hope to fully control or even predict.

Emery and Trist posited a new, increasingly prevalent organisational environment called the 'turbulent field', which can be distinguished from three other causal textures (termed 'placid-randomised', 'placid-clustered' and 'disturbed-reactive') by the significance to the organisation of the contextual interdependencies in its rapidly changing environment. The socio-ecological approach is based in an open-systems view of an organisation's strategic situation, where the core unit of analysis is the shared field of inter-organisational action (Lewin, 1952). According to Emery and Trist (1965), causal textures theory (CTT) as a part of the social ecology school that studies environmental types helps to analyse how a system such as an organisation and its environment (composed of forces, factors, actors and interactions) intersect. The actors with whom a central actor interacts are in its more immediate 'transactional' environment, which can involve actors in several industries. These interactions in the transactional environment are in turn situated in a broader 'contextual environment', made up of factors, which the central actor cannot influence. Several interacting organisations, their shared environments and the connexions that link them jointly constitute a 'field'.

Emery and Trist (1965) demonstrated that the environment has a distinct set of 'lawful' relations. CTT uses the symbol L to denote links within an organisation, within the environment and between them. It uses the symbol 1 to represent the organisation, and the symbol 2 to represent the environment. Consequently, the two-way links between an organisation and its environment involve transactional relations: planning (inside-out) L12 relations, and learning (outside-in) L21 relations.

Links within an organisation are L11; those within the environment are L22 (Emery and Trist, 1965; Selsky, et al., 2007). Organisations act in relation to the environment, and are influenced by the environment, through L12, L21 relations. In CTT, the L22 distinguishes the transactional and contextual environments from each other (Ramírez and Selsky, 2014). Emery and Trist, 1965) proposed four causal textures of the environment, distinguished by the salience, complexity and uncertainty of L22 links for the organisations in the field.

1   The placid-randomised environment refers to the simplest form of organisational environment in which resources, goals and values are distributed randomly and remain unchanging. Inputs, such as resources, goals and values, are distributed at a constant pace or frequency. The organisational environment survives without much knowledge or direction on the part of its members. Adaptability and cope-ability (Motamedi, 1977) are low in the placid-randomised environment. In a 'placid-randomised' (Type I) causal texture, resources, goals and noxiants are randomly distributed in the field. This corresponds to 'perfect market' conditions.

2 The placid, clustered environment refers to the semi-complex form of organisational environment in which resources, goals and values are unchanging and located in clusters. Examples of clusters include segmented markets, vendors and products. In a placid-clustered environment, the organisation's survival is linked to its ability to connect the right specialised knowledge, processes and technologies with their corresponding cluster. Placid-clustered environments need to develop multiple specialised competencies for each cluster. In a 'placid-clustered' (Type II) causal texture, resources, goals and/or noxiants are located in advantageous positions, corresponding to conditions of imperfect competition, with market failure.

3 The disturbed, reactive environment refers to scenarios in which multiple social systems dominate the same environments. In disturbed, reactive environments, the social systems are dependent on one another. The survival of systems in disturbed, reactive environments depends on the system's knowledge of other system's reactive behaviour, as well as their resources, values and goals. In a 'disturbed-reactive' (Type III) causal texture, the structure of the field corresponds to an oligopoly with similar organisations in competition. 'Game-based' strategies are used; rapid decision-making to take an advantage over other actors sharing the same field is characteristic of a causal texture where L11, L21 and L12 are the most salient connections.

4 The turbulent field environment refers to chaotic scenarios in which there are no clear cause-and-effect relationships between the organisational system and its environment. There are constant external fluctuations and uncertainties. An organisation's survival in a turbulent field environment is dependent upon the organisation's knowledge of the changing environment and its ability to endure sustained emotional stress. Surviving turbulent field environments requires high amounts of adaptability and cope-ability. In a 'turbulent' causal texture (Type IV), the whole common shared ground is in motion; L22 connections become uncertain and changing. Distinctions between L12–L21 and L22 begin to break down. There is no survival for systems acting alone; collaborative strategies among dissimilar organisations in a field are necessary.

McCann and Selsky (1984) highlighted that the experience of turbulence is subjective. Ramirez and Selsky (2014) suggest that the distinctive contribution of the social ecology school is to

> '... examine unpredictable uncertainty as (i) a contextual-level phenomenon, produced in a field of tightly coupled interactions which can produce unexpected bifurcations ... and field-level unintended consequences; and (ii) as a distinguishing property of a distinct "texture" of the environment'.
>
> 'The dynamic properties arise not simply from the interaction of the component organisations but also from the field itself—the 'ground' is in motion'.
>
> Emery and Trist (1965, p. 26)

Emery and Trist noted that in order to survive under such conditions, organisations would need to develop greater 'requisite variety' (Ashby, 1960), flexibility and alliances with others.

From the socio-ecological tradition (Trist, Emery, and Murray, 1997), notions exist that can be directly applicable to inter-organisational relations and power dynamics within, across and among referent organisations. A broader organisational theory, like that provided in the Tavistock Institute's socio-ecological perspective Trist et al. (1997), helps when working as a consultant with inter-organisational relations. Trist's notion of inter-organisational domain focuses on 'field-related organisational populations'. 'An organisational population becomes field-related when it engages with a set of problems, or a societal problem area, which constitutes a domain of concern for its members' (Trist, 1983, p. 269). Emery and Trist's (1965) seminal contribution to systems thinking was to characterise the environments of systems, consistent with important assumptions concerning human behaviour (e.g. purposefulness, ideal-seeking) and consistent with 'the early recognition by Ashby (1956) that if living systems are to be treated as open systems, we must be able to characterise their environments' (Emery, 1969, p. 9). They questioned von Bertalanffy's description of an open system as too limited for human organisations because 'it neglected to deal with processes in the environment that are, themselves, among the determining conditions of organisation–environment changes'. This led Emery and Trist to add an additional concept – 'the causal texture of the environment' (Jackson, 1992, p. 65).

For a comprehensive overview of open systems, the history and relationship between open socio-technical systems thinking and the human relations movement with relevance to 'Large Group Methods', see Merrelyn Emery's (2022) reworking of her earlier paper on the 'Evolution of Open Systems Theory', https://www.socialsciencethatactuallyworks.com/_files/ugd/d59011_3214407c6aad4b628b8b3c90cfb55f7b.pdf.

NHS Citizen – working with unconscious processes and boundaries in a whole systems intervention

By Camilla Child

Introduction

This study outlines the work (2013–2015) by four organisations (The Tavistock Institute, Involve, The Democratic Society and Public-i) commissioned by NHS England to establish a digital and face-to-face participatory system of engagement and dialogue between the Board of NHS England and members of the public. Our work together and with

NHS England and citizens led to the creation of NHS Citizen, an entity that still exists today. NHS Citizen in the form originally envisaged achieved partial success, and this is an account of it and some of the challenges we faced together as a partnership. Although the design was emergent, Board members anticipated an annual process whereby citizens and the Board of NHS England would meet in an Assembly to discuss issues identified by citizens as important to them.

NHS England is responsible for commissioning and coordinating healthcare spending in England, the National Health Service (NHS). There was potential conflict between the Board and the political system in Whitehall.

The aims for NHS Citizen, as it was to become, were bold. It was to 'build citizen voice and influence throughout the NHS commissioning system, so that citizens hold the NHS to account, driving improvements in quality and outcomes' (NHS Commissioning Board, 2012). Another intention was also to 'hold up a mirror to the Board' (Field note with NHS England Board Member, 2013) and 'ensure that those most marginalised members of the public were able to participate in conversations about health which affected them'. The work was to be co-designed with the general public, not just those who are active in health policy debates, but those who do not normally engage in the healthcare decision-making.

As it evolved over the course of the funding, NHS Citizen took the shape of a series of inter-related phases and work programmes. At the heart of it, lay a co-production approach with a one-year design phase, when the team worked with individuals and stakeholder groups across the country using mixed media, followed by implementation.

The phases of work consisted of (i) a *Discover* phase, which sought to identify conversations, which were already taking place among citizens; (ii) a *Gather* phase, where people could upload their chosen topic onto a digital platform and hold discussions about it with others; (iii) following phases (i) and (ii), this phase involved a Citizen's Jury selecting five topics, which were to go through to a national *Assembly Meeting*. This brought together the full NHS England Board and 250 citizens in a day of discussions around the selected issues. These sessions were live streamed, with live Twitter conversations and online discussions for broader participation. They were fully accessible for people with disabilities.

The NHS Citizen model, as it emerged, was cyclical, based on an action research model. It is depicted in Figure 9.1 and was developed during the co-design workshops. Figure 9.1 does not indicate that following the Assembly Meeting, it was expected that the data generated would be taken back into NHS England, and any developments would be reported on during the following cycle and next Assembly Meeting.

Figure 9.1 NHS Citizen Model.

Two cycles of NHS Citizen in the format described were carried out between 2013 and 2015. Several issues were brought to the table, which were bubbling under NHS attention. For example, during the first meeting, transgender issues and the status of mental health funding were brought to the Assembly. Following the Assembly Meeting in 2015, the programme was delivered as a public engagement exercise. While in some senses it was seen as good practice that NHS England should deliver on the public participation intentions itself, as our own work was ended at this point, we experienced some frustration and sadness of a job that was only partially completed.

The fact that NHS Citizen did not attract further funding was due to the commitment of the Board failing to deliver on agendas over which it only had limited control. Large-scale public meetings were also seen to be expensive. In the analysis below, the focus is on the challenges of boundary control when introducing a large system intervention into NHS England.

The role of the Tavistock Institute team

There was widespread recognition that holding conversations, which were open, honest and on equal terms, would require an acknowledgement of the power differential between the different parties, and a change in behaviour to facilitate this. The NHS was built on the foundations of a culture of clinical experts and passive recipients of medical services (patients). There is now a shift towards health coaching, but this is not articulated within NHS England. We saw it through behaviours around decision-making and priority-building, which were low on the agenda, 'maybe the fourth or fifth item to do, so by then decisions are already well on the way' (senior NHS England manager).

While in NHS Citizen the main interactions between public citizens were with the Board of NHS England, it was clear that this new kind of openness and listening would need to permeate throughout NHS England to embed a strong culture of public participation. A culture change stream was therefore developed to support the Board and extended beyond this to the senior management tiers within NHS England. Underpinning our approach to culture change was the practice of systems psychodynamics and socio-technical systems.

The work of Isabel Menzies Lyth (1960) was useful, suggesting as it does that organisational defences are created to defend against and contain the complex and difficult feelings that are engendered through work. These defences are created at an unconscious level and serve to diffuse responsibility from the individual to the system, so helping the individual to function. Analysis of our early interviews and meetings resonated with this, as we encountered the anxiety of several Board members and senior leaders in working with citizens. Senior leaders had multiple and complex agendas and defended against change of organisational practices. They had difficulty finding information, meetings were difficult to set up, and they were caught in a culture of busy-ness.

In a socio-technical systems framework, the technical/task aspects of work (what needs to be done? and how work must be organised?) need to dovetail with the social aspects of work (e.g. inter-personal dynamics, the feelings people had about NHS Citizen, the symbols and behaviours which are represented by choices of venues – conference hall vs community hall). Our concern was that the design of a successful public participation system would need to focus as much on the feelings people held about power, their place in the system and how decisions are made and not solely on the technical side of constructing a fit-for-purpose model.

Our work with the system

In our contacts with different sub-system members and the system as a whole, we used concepts drawn from our practice, that is working systemically, with a concern for the underlying unconscious processes, which would support or inhibit change. We worked at the boundaries between sub-systems to help us understand the power relations between them. Making sense of the system itself was problematic – we were interested in the Board, senior management of NHS England, the wider NHS England and citizens. So where were we to start and end in such an expansive system? Staff were also citizens, citizens fractured into competing groups, and the Board was supported by practical policy makers who were drawn into complex discussions they did not feel was their business, and so on. Our intention was to work with the inter-relation and interconnections of the constituent parts and how they were relating to the system as a whole. But aside from the large Assembly Meeting, in the main, the sub-systems did not often meet each other, despite attempts to introduce staff to sessions with citizens (it was generally not possible the other way around, itself a dynamic). The result was often conflict or avoidance – a fight/flight dynamic. We often had to address issues of power and how different groups interacted with others often in the abstract. Most had a sense of both their power and powerlessness in making decisions, so coming together to work differently – or even thinking about the 'other' – was often laden with frustration and even conflict. Citizens were often the most marginal and seldom heard, Board and senior leaders were aware of their power in the distribution of resources, but they found the voices of the more marginal members of society disquieting.

Our aim therefore was to work with the senior leadership in the first instance, to explore why public participation was currently relatively weak, and to identify where changes could take place. We set up new spaces for workshops and used meetings that were pre-existent so as not to make too many additional demands on their time. It included working directly with Board members, preparing them for encounters with citizens, for example by working on listening hard to what citizens were saying, rather than what they expected them to say. We focused on helping members of the Board to understand their role as containers of anxiety and distress rather than experiencing encounters as solely an attack. We had to choose our language carefully given most people in the system had little experience of working with unconscious processes. The experiences could be difficult for them, especially in public and they experienced meetings even with us, as an attack on their authority. Seeing the point of view of the 'other' in such circumstances and moving to discussion rather than a binary 'you said', 'we said' was often laboured.

Equally, our hypothesis from our early encounters was that both senior leaders and citizens alike would benefit from the Board demonstrating their commitment to the agenda. To this end, three Board members held conversations with diverse audiences whereby they were explicitly encouraged to question and debate with each other on related issues, rather than hold a line. As the work progressed, we designed and facilitated workshops with senior leaders within NHS England, which explored the underlying culture of the organisation, their understanding of citizen engagement and the experiences they had around their own power. These conversations generated intense feelings of anger and sadness. We were invited to join a task-and-finish group to develop a clear plan of action for embedding the approach to good patient and public participation in the direct commissioning of primary care and specialised services.

Opportunities were provided by NHS Citizen to explore the dynamics of change and make them apparent in small- and large-scale events and in the different team meetings. Competition emerged between the teams, for example around the body of theories, which underpinned the project and how we worked with them. Our methods and thinking were not broadly shared across the partnership. We seemed to spend as much time working with these aspects with our partners as we did trying to gain entry into the Board and the organisation more generally. Our hypothesis was that this was an envious attack, based on rivalry and competition and power, based on which partner had the 'best' ideas and who was closest to the power structure within NHS England. This mostly felt weighty, with our interpretations about anxiety or hatred and the defences that these brought up, often rejected. Indeed, it seemed at times that we, as Tavistock consultants, held the projections of anxiety for the whole system, while the partners 'got on with the job' of working with the technical, task aspects. Our collective difficulty was bringing these two aspects together; it reflected the difficulties in the system into which we were intervening. In fact, in many instances, we noted the mirroring which took place, in frenetic activity and demanding impossible deadlines of each other. This was experienced with fury and compliance within the partnership as within NHS England.

Boundary control

NHS Citizen had a complicated relationship with power – expressed in competition about who NHS Citizen belonged to and what were its limits. There were competing views about all of this and therefore who controlled or managed the boundary function (Miller and Rice, 1967). For the NHS England Board members who conceived the idea of a public participation model, NHS Citizen belonged clearly to citizens. These Board members located NHS Citizen firmly with the people, suggesting even in the early days that it might be considered as a social movement. While this latter statement is contentious in itself – can a social movement be initiated and funded by an organisation? – they took their position from the NHS Constitution, the first statement of which is 'The NHS belongs to the people'. These Board members were relaxed about the boundary and were confident that NHS Citizen could be sanctioned by citizens from outside the boundary, and staff from within, mediated by the partnership, including the internal public voice team, the technology and held by the Board. The generally confident perspective of the Board member trio was in contrast with the CEO of NHS England and several of the Executives on the Board, that is the Directors of NHS England whose primary concern was to deliver on the now published business plan and control scarce resources. Equally, some members of the Board found the Assembly Meetings when they were in discussion with up to 250 citizens on issues they were not always expert on, a real challenge. Over the course of the two-year funded project, this regulatory function of the boundary was never sufficiently agreed, and the partnership often found itself caught in disputes between citizens and NHS England and its Board, receiving either approbation or anger.

Approbation came in the form of approval of a method that centred on co-production of attempts at inclusivity, and keeping the agenda broad in the face of opposition. Anger came in the form of accusations of duplication of efforts made by other organisations, of lack of clarity of purpose, of cost, of sub-optimal technology supporting the 'Gather' phase, of opening the scope too broadly. While there was some truth in all of these, we, the consultants, took these also as expressions of deep anxiety about an intervention that had at its heart a deeply destabilising outcome. However exhausting, we were keen to absorb the projections, and looked to them as data to help us understand further the dynamics of the intervention and what we would learn from them.

There were further challenges around the boundaries of our work as a Tavistock team. Ostensibly, we were working with the Board of NHS England and citizens to hold meaningful, open, non-hostile conversations in a public space. In reality, raising issues with the Board was a complex bureaucratic process; that is, producing briefing papers and involving external agencies on, for example, transgender issues, the status of mental health resourcing, made communication and exchange extremely complex and problematic.

The space in which we were working could seem vast and without containment. In these moments, mobilising staff for whom NHS Citizen was a peripheral concern was difficult. NHS Citizen had been presented by the Board as an exciting opportunity for citizens (including NHS England staff in their multiple roles) to bring forward issues that were of concern to them for public debate. Commitment was high among many interested citizens who actively participated in the different activities. It was more complicated for NHS England Board members and particularly staff whose role was to deliver on the business plan, as well as being encouraged by NHS Citizen partners to keep acting from their citizen role as well as their staff role inside the organisation. We were sometimes told in discussions with NHS England Staff that this could cause internal conflict: staff found it difficult to take up these two roles simultaneously as the positions they may have had to take as gatekeepers of resources might have been in opposition to their 'citizen' perspective. We noted, that in effect, these people were mobilised as key defenders against change, with increasingly ambivalent Board members unwilling to take up their authority to ensure papers were received in a way that they felt they could respond properly. The work of Tavistock Institute consultants was in part to support the leadership in letting go to see what emerged. However, the leadership found the anxiety of not controlling the direction of travel with an end result in sight, intolerable. Indeed, it is the view of one of the initiating Board members that NHS Citizen was showing signs of doing the job that it was hoped for, which was to create an NHS, which truly belonged to the people, who could share the decision-making around NHS priorities and bring to the fore issues, which were often marginal. The view was that NHS Citizen no longer operates in the way intended as it posed a great challenge to the status quo.

Conclusion

The inter-systemic nature of NHS Citizen – that of citizens outside the NHS England meeting, those within the organisation at a contested boundary – sheds light on the difficulties that the introduction of broad-ranging public dialogue interventions with a social justice basis can bring. The defences against change that were mobilised – often unconsciously, as we were aware – were almost impossible to counter. Despite this, NHS Citizen achieved some success insofar as a complex system was co-designed, and there was dialogue between the power elite and citizens who seldom had a voice, through the process of Assembly Meetings.

Domains

Based on field observations during action research engagements in Europe and North America, Trist (1973, p. 98) advocated, 'domain-based, problem-oriented research', which was 'field-determined' (i.e. not determined by abstract academic interests) and 'generic' (i.e. not focused on a single instance of a problem or on a single organisation). Trist observed that the large-scale problems that were festering or accelerating in Western societies were multidisciplinary, multi-organisational and messy. They cut across the purposes of single organisations and public institutions, such that, with careful analysis, one might identify missing institutions and create innovating organisations between micro (single organisation)- and macro (organisation of the state)-scales of society to cope with such problems. These field observations led Trist (1977) to describe the behaviour of organisations in shared environments in ecological (but not Darwinian) terms. He developed the notion of the inter-organisational domain, which is:

> . . . *concerned with field-related organisational populations. An organisational population becomes field-related when it engages with a set of problems, or societal problem area, which constitutes a domain of common concern for its members. The set of organisations is then 'directively correlated' . . . with the problem area.*
>
> (Trist, 1983, p. 270)

Domains form when actors come to new appreciations of a large-scale problem and realise they share these appreciations (Vickers, 1965). A figure-ground reversal (Trist, 1977) in perspective on the problem is key to appreciating the importance of focusing on the domain development. 'Figures' are specific organisations and events that rise and fall in the domain over time, whereas the problematic issue and shared ideals and values constitute the common 'ground'. The reversal of perspective to focus on the common ground is important for many reasons. For instance, it enables a shift in stakeholder models from a 'hub and-spoke' approach focused on a dominant organisation and its various claimants, to an 'ecological' approach focused on a shared issue and those interested in it Frooman (1999). The reversal also enables the theory to account for the fact that the issue is likely to evolve due to figural events, that is due to the actions of organisations associated with the domain and due to exogenous influences (Trist, 1983). The reversal also fixes the domain and not a specific organisation in it, as the focal unit for action research. In open systems theory, a domain is conceived as a 'functional social system' in an environment (Trist, 1983, p. 270). Its constituent elements are not the organisations themselves, but the relations between and among organisations and other social actors that give shape to the domain. The interests may be identical, pluralistically diverse, or polarised. The relations between and among the domain actors have a network, not a hierarchical character, based on socio-ecological, not bureaucratic design principles (Trist, 1977).

The socio-ecological designs principles promote self-regulation of the domain and its relations, rather than top-down or outside control. Because the domain concept is concerned with building collective adaptive capacity for action to deal with issues produced by turbulence, a key concern is how domains develop. Domain development takes a resource mobilisation perspective in which collective strategies are formed among the members of the organisational population. Through collective strategies managed by referent organisations, domain stakeholders attempt to influence the course of the shared issue. The relationships among stakeholders, issue and context are recognised as co-evolutionary and emergent, and these relationships shape the domain over time.

Neumann (2010) suggests that researchers and consultants need theories that give them confident working hypotheses for (a) arguing in favour of including so-called external stakeholders, (b) defining the inter-organisational domain more broadly and (c) applying the notion of 'primary task' courageously to the organisational development and change intervention strategies. From the socio-technical tradition (Trist and Murray, 1993), we can expand how 'primary task' can be used, and from the socio-ecological tradition, we can find concepts for analysing and intervening in non-linear workflows. From the socio-ecological tradition (Trist et al., 1997) notions exist that can be directly applicable to inter-organisational relations and power dynamics within, across and among referent organisations.

The environment is conceived as an 'extended social field with a causal texture, which affects the behaviour of all systems within it' (M. Emery, 1997, pg. 8). Firstly, we see the environment of the primary work group within the organisation consisting of other work groups. Secondly, the environment is the field of other organisations and influences that create interdependencies for the 'focal' organisation; and the environment is the wider context of organisations, influences, and forces, which multi-organisational systems interact with.

Turbulence

Turbulence is both an objective condition of a field and a condition that is relative to the adaptive capacity that an actor perceives that it has or can mobilise in that field (McCann and Selsky, 1984). Decision-making when in this texture is challenging because the sources of disturbances and problems in the field cannot be pinned down, and thus paths to solving it are unclear. It is not unusual for individuals and organisations to respond to turbulence in maladaptive ways (Emery, 1977), such as by dissociating from the realities of their world, or by polarising their world into 'ins' and 'outs'. Collective maladaptive responses can manifest in a variety of ways, such as volatility in the ground rules governing competition in an industry, emergent public-policy issues (e.g. homelessness; gaps in health insurance), social problems (violent crime in schools; road rage), or degradations in the natural environment (ozone depletion; mudslides and floods due to deforestation).

Collaborative endeavours among the systems inhabiting the same field are posited as the actively adaptive means of coping with turbulence. Collaboration is grounded in the ideal-seeking capacities of human beings (Emery, 1977). Ideals are not to be reached (as are goals and objectives) or enacted directly (as are values). Instead, shared ideals (e.g. nurturance, humanity) can give meaning to ambiguous and complex situations (Emery and Trist, 1965, 1973) and are advocated as guides to active-adaptive behaviour. They help actors to make choices among different value-based behaviours, which they think might help to repair the effects of turbulence. Shared ideals are discovered through task-oriented work in democratically managed forums, such as search conferences.

The resource mobilisation perspective connects the domain concept to sociological concepts of community structure, power and social movements, and to recent strategy concepts of business ecosystems (Moore, 1996); Hawken, 1993) and value constellations (Normann and Ramirez, 1993). Methodologically, active-adaptive planning (Emery, 1977; Baburoglu, 1992), search conferences (M. Emery and Purser, 1996), participative design workshops (M. Emery, 1999), referent organisations (Trist, 1983), and action learning methods (Wright and Morley, 1989) have been developed to give voice to active adaptation in dealing with turbulence. When applied to domains, they enable (1) common ground to be forged among stakeholders, based on an articulation of the system principle and an appreciation of the extended field; and (2) concrete strategies and action plans to be developed and implemented to cope with the problematic issue. The system-in-environment is the essential construct in the socio-ecological model. The environment is real, consequential and able to be acted on. The third track of the theory identifies the inter-organisational domain as the locus of active adaptation for a relevant class of systemic issues. The methods and techniques for active adaptation are normatively grounded in democratic participation and rationalisation of conflict.

The socio-ecological perspective and inter-organisational relations approaches

As we have seen, the socio-ecological perspective is a school in organisation studies whose origins lie in the work of Fred Emery, Merelyn Emery, Eric Trist and others on the relations between systems and environments (Emery (1999, 2000); Selsky et al. (2007); Ramirez et al., 2014). The socio-ecological perspective has an analysis on the important class of systems, namely, inter-organisational fields, and their constituent parts, namely, complex organisations and their transactions with their environments.

According to socio-ecology, a set of systems (for our purposes, organisations), the transactions among them and their relevant environments constitute a social field. Social ecology holds that field-level (rather than organisation-level) interventions are required to address the contextual disturbances, which erupt in social fields. But the structuring of such fields tends to be weak and ad hoc (Trist, 1977); McCann, 1983), so an important question is, what is the principle, or basis, for the design of large-scale fields? Echoing Emery (1969) and Barton and Selsky (2000), we inquire as to how social ecology might inform the design thinking needed for the regulation of inter-organisational fields.

The salient characteristics of the turbulent environment are rapid change, uncertainty as a function of the complex and unpredictable changes in the task, social and geopolitical environment, and unprecedented levels of interdependence and complexity caused by an extremely dense population of organisations pursuing independent, short-term goals (Emery and Trist, 1973; Trist, 1981). Issues emerging under conditions of rapid change are muddled together (Schon

1971) and seldom arise as solitary problems with single causes. As the rate of change has accelerated, the issues confronting organisations have emerged as 'indivisible' problems (Aldrich, 1976) or 'messes' (Ackoff, 1974; Ackoff and Emery, 1972). Contemporary issues and social problems are now so complex and interdependent that they tax, and often exceed, the response capacity of individual firms and single sectors working on their own (Miles, 1980).

The inter-organisational relations approach (Aldrich and Whetten, 1981) to issues of management derives from a resource-dependence framework, which presumes that organisations enter relationships to secure needed resources and to reduce uncertainty. Inter-organisational relations approaches are consistent with organisational theorists' contentions that organisations faced with uncertain external environments engage in strategies such as coalescing, co-opting or cooperating to mitigate the uncertainty (Thompson, 1967) and manage the interdependence (Pfeffer and Salancik, 1978). Inter-organisational relations approaches are many and varied and range from loosely structured business networks and corporate political action committees (Maitland and Park, 1985) to tightly structured organisations such as business roundtables and self-regulatory organisations (Lad, 1985).

Burke and Biggart (1997) on writing about inter-organisational relations suggest the following that the body of work is large but can be divided into two distinct literatures: (1) macro-environmental studies of the political and competitive aspects of relations between and among organisations, and (2) micro-studies of the process by which organised groups relate to each other and the factors that are likely to lead to a successful collaboration. They suggest that although organisation sets and inter-organisational fields are still important conceptual categories, recent conceptualisations are of the organisational network. Network analysis differs from organisational set and industry analysis in seeking not only to identify the relationships among organisations, but also to examine the character and structure of those relationships.

The systems psychodynamics perspective

From the systems psychodynamics perspective, inter-group relations is a useful conceptual framework for considering inter-organisational networks and relationships. In the creation of collaborative alliances, organisations are attempting simultaneously to manage competition and their shared overlapping interests. The work of group relations theorists (Rice, 1969) can contribute to the identification of phenomena that may help to overcome this challenge. For instance, Burke and Biggart (1997) argue that organisation members' perceptions of other organisations and their members can be expected to exert a strong influence on their abilities to exploit opportunities and resources offered by those organisations. Although perceptions of members of other organisations may be inevitable, at least in initial stages of contact, the experience of 'outsider-ness' can be either potentially threatening and undermining, or potentially enhancing and thus valuable. Perceptions of outsiders can thus influence the viability of any collaboration endeavour by two organisations. Therefore, from a socio-ecological perspective organisational success may lie with how well an organisation is linked with other firms in their environment. Its performance may be linked to its position in a network of relations. The network may be the best source of information rather than individual organisations. It is important to remember that organisations enter alliances either to accomplish a goal that cannot be achieved alone or to share costs. Successful inter-organisational relations are the result of well-managed processes that are negotiated through predictable stages.

System domain defences

Bain (1998) points out that while Menzies (1960) wrote of the hospital, or the nursing system within the hospital, as though it contained the social defence system, the system of defences was actually operating in a much wider arena – an arena akin to what Eric Trist (1981) has called a 'domain'. In this case, the 'domain' would be described as all those many institutions with a similar primary task to the hospital, and what is described as a 'system domain'. What is being hypothesised is that organisations with a similar primary task, which together constitute a 'system domain' as described, are likely to have similar social defences against anxiety. Part of the difficulty in modifying the social defences within an institution, in Menzies case a hospital, is because they are an expression of system domain fabric and are not 'stand-alone' institutions. By 'system domain fabric' is meant that which is shared across the institutions that comprise the system domain. Besides a similar primary task, this may include:

1 Roles, organisation structure and authority systems
2 Policies and procedures, information systems and accountabilities
3 Professional training
4 Funding arrangements
5 Technology and technical systems
6 Representational systems, for example trades union, professional associations
7 Knowledge base
8 Organisational culture and 'system domain in the mind'
9 Capacities and psychological characteristics of the people employed
10 Environment – political, social, economic, physical, etc.

Bain (1998) argues that if Menzies had been successful in introducing changes within the nursing system in the hospital, it is likely that the changes would have been washed away over time due to the nursing system being part of a wider system domain of defences. The social defences Menzies described were widespread in UK hospitals at the time. When people move from one local institution within a system domain to another, in this case from hospital to hospital, they carry with them their 'system-domain-in-the-mind' to the new institution, which is likely to include the current system domain defences. Unless there are concurrent shifts in significant domain fabric factors, such as authority systems, policies and procedures, professional training, and system domain culture, changes in a local institution are likely to be eroded over time. The more positive aspect of this is that where local change has been successful the people involved become the carriers for these ideas into other institutions. The concept of the 'system-domain-in-the-mind' is a development of Pierre Turquet's original concept of the 'institution-in-the-mind' (Lawrence, 1986). This indeed is the fate of many action research and consultancy projects, including a number that Bain had carried out. He points out that as a consultant working with an institution, which forms part of a systems domain; it is tempting to view the institution as a 'stand-alone' and not take fully into account the wider system domain defence system. There, in fact, may be no proper recognisable 'client' because of the nature of the system domain.

The concept of 'system domain defences' with its focus on institutions with a similar primary task is to be distinguished from Gilmore and Krantz's concept of 'domain-based defensive processes'. In their article, Gilmore and Krantz (1990) explored how the social defences of 'managerialism' and the cult of the 'charismatic leader' operated to split leadership and management within many kinds of organisation in the USA. Their concept of 'domain' is much wider than the 'systems domain' described by Bain. Indeed, their 'domain' is more akin to a regional 'global domain', as the social defences they have uncovered operate in other societies, for example Australia and the UK.

Organisational learning and system domain defences

Bain (1998) applies the concept of organisational learning to consultancy work, which considers system domain defences. He hypothesised that during action research and consultancy projects that initiate organisational change, there is a co-evolution of 'organisational container' and 'contained'. This co-evolution of 'organisational container' and 'contained' is to do with growth of capacity, and this growth is inseparable from the co-evolution of 'organisational container' and 'contained'.

Bion's (1970) concept of 'container' and 'contained' provides a bridging link between individual learning and organisational learning. While individual learning is a constituent of organisational learning, the two are distinct concepts, and Bain sees organisational learning as something different from the summation of individual learning within an organisation. A shift in focus is required akin to Bion's shift from observing individuals in a group to observing phenomena that arise at the level of the group. In this case, organisational learning arises at the level of the organisation. Organisations consciously construct space for common reflection on activities, which allow for a developing awareness of the 'whole', that is the organisation, and its interconnected parts. As awareness of the social defences against anxiety develops, in other words people become conscious of them rather than remaining unconscious, other ways of exploring and modifying this anxiety become possible, so the maladaptive aspects of the social defences change. Bain says that there are certain essential features of these 'learning spaces' that are the same in each of the three projects he worked on:

The agenda for the work of these learning spaces was largely derived from the members of the organisation themselves working on the task of the program.

1   The learning space was not filled up by the CEO or equivalent.
2   The groups came to accept silence at appropriate times rather than filling in the silence with talk.
3   The learning spaces allowed for a stronger connectedness to develop between individuals and organisation.
4   The resistances to change emerge in the relationship of project members to the consultants, which can then be explored in these learning spaces. Working on perceptions of this relationship, the transference, helps to deepen insight into work processes, and decrease the power of damaging projective systems, which thereby modifies the social defences against anxiety. The process increases the project team and organisation's capacities for discerning and managing reality Bain (1982).
5   As the social defences against anxiety are modified or changed, the organisation concurrently develops a capacity to learn and develop.

Bain has an interesting way of describing the organisations that lack learning space, or reflective space, which allows for organisational awareness, as 'asleep' to their own behaviour. The organisation may appear to be awake and responsive, but in fact is acting in a repetitive way without thought or reflection. This 'pre-learning' organisation is characterised by mainly individualised nodes of organisational awareness, which are frequently highly differentiated from each other and to a large extent role-dependent.

Changing the 'container' for organisational experience and developing a container for organisational awareness, together with reflection on what is 'contained', bring these nodes of organisational awareness together with a potential for creating new thoughts and different actions.

Consultancy of the kind that is being alluded to tend to wake the organisation from its sleep, and part of the consultancy is to create space for developing organisational awareness. Bain offers a more general hypothesis that the 'power' of system domain fabric, and the system domain defences generated to prevent localised change occurring and being sustained during an organisational change project is a function of the level of authority within the local system. The extent to which system domain factors lie within the authority system, or influence, should assist members of the organisation to achieve change. The concept of system domain defences is located between the concept of social defences at the level of the local institution, as evidenced by Menzies' study of the nursing system of a hospital, and the concept of 'domain defences' identified by Gilmore and Krantz.

Bain articulates five factors that he considers were significant in which organisational learning was taking place in his action research consultancy:

1 Primary task
2 Project ownership
3 Leadership, authority and roles
4 Individual, group and organisational interdependence
5 Reflection and learning spaces

All three organisations during the action research or consultancy projects developed a level of organisational awareness that was not present before. This level of organisational awareness was the result of the co-evolution of 'organisational container' and 'contained'.

Summary

One of the key insights of the systems approach has been the realisation that the network is a pattern that is common to all life. Wherever we see life, we see networks.
(Capra, 2002)

A main problem in the study of organisational change is that the environmental contexts in which organisations exist are themselves changing, at an increasing rate and towards increasing complexity. This point, in itself, scarcely needs labouring. Nevertheless, characteristics of organisational environments demand consideration for their own sake if there is to be an advancement of understanding in the behavioural sciences of a great deal that is taking place under the impact of technological change, especially at the present time.
(Emery and Trist, 1965)

Extended social fields may be inter-personal and intra-organisational, organisational or multi-organisational. Environments have causal textures. As we noted above, Emery and Trist (1965) identified four textures: placid-randomised, placid-clustered, disturbed-reactive and the turbulent field. Each texture is associated with a suggested adaptive response: tactics, strategy, competitive operations, and collaborative endeavours, respectively. The causal texture of a field conditions the relations among the local actors who inhabit the same field. Because systems and environments co-evolve, the causal texture of these fields is an emergent property of the whole (system plus environment). The whole is produced by the interactions of systems inhabiting the same extended field plus the effects of external forces acting on those systems. The intended and unintended consequences of an organisation's actions intersect and trigger unpredictable changes in the environment that they share. The shared environment itself becomes highly unstable and affects all actors within it – and may also reverberate outside it (Emery and Trist) (1965). In this way, the turbulent texture displaces the disturbed-reactive texture.

An organisation's survival in a turbulent field environment is dependent upon the organisation's knowledge of the changing environment and its ability to endure sustained emotional stress and high amounts of variety, flexibility, alliances with others, adaptability and cope-ability. Social ecology examines unpredictable uncertainty as a contextual-level phenomenon produced in a field of tightly coupled interactions, which can produce unexpected bifurcations and field-level unintended consequences. Socio-ecology applies directly to inter-organisational relations and power dynamics within, across and among referent organisations that helps when working with inter-organisational relations that focus on a set of problems, or a societal problem area, which constitutes a domain of concern for its members. If living systems are to be treated as open systems, we must be able to define and characterise their environments. Domain-based, problem-oriented research is multidisciplinary, multi-organisational and messy.

Domains are groups of organisations that are concerned with large-scale problem areas and who share their appreciations and focus on domain development. In open systems theory, a domain is conceived as a 'functional social system' in an environment in which the constituent elements are not the organisations themselves, but the relations between and among organisations that give shape to the domain – a network, not a hierarchy. Turbulence is an objective condition of a field and a condition that is relative to the adaptive capacity of the field actors. Socio-ecological design principles promote self-regulation of the domain and its relations, rather than top-down or relying on outside control, building collective adaptive capacity for action to deal with issues produced by turbulence. Sources of disturbances and problems in the field cannot be pinned down; thus, paths to solving it are unclear, often leading individuals and organisations to respond to turbulence in maladaptive ways. Collaborative endeavours among the systems inhabiting the same field are posited as the actively adaptive means of coping with turbulence, grounded in the ideal-seeking capacities of human beings. Shared ideals are discovered through democratically managed forums, such as search conferences.

Exercise

1 Map your organisation and its network of inter-organisational relations.
2 How would you describe the emotional field of this network?
3 Where do you see the tensions?
4 How does the hierarchy of your organisation respond to network working and influences?
5 How would you rate your organisation's adaptive or maladaptive capacities towards its environment?

Chapter 10

Complexity theory

David Lawlor and Mannie Sher with Eliat Aram

Bringing complexity and systems psychodynamics theories together to improve consultancy practice

Jackson (2006) made the point that experiences immediately prior, during and after the Second World War led the pioneers of applied systems thinking to conclude that important changes had to be made to the traditional scientific method if it was to be effective in tackling the real-world problems they were interested in. They advocated, under labels such as operational research, systems analysis and systems engineering, methodologies that were more holistic and interdisciplinary, and put client and user objectives first. The 'hard systems' methodologies developed were, and still are, efficient at tackling a particular range of problem situations. However, as society continued to become more complex, turbulent and heterogeneous, problem situations arose, which proved difficult to tame using even these methodologies. Fortunately, the systems community responded with new approaches, methodologies and models, better designed for the circumstances of the modern era. System dynamics, organisational cybernetics, complexity theory, soft systems thinking, emancipatory systems thinking and postmodern systems methods were developed. This advance in the competence of systems thinking and practice led to a new kind of problem: How can we understand the strengths and weaknesses of these different systems approaches and use them creatively, in combination? Complexity theory has the potential to invigorate systems psychodynamics thinking in ways that move beyond the limitations of earlier versions of systems theory (Aram, 2012, 2015a, 2015b, 1015c, 2016). Stacey (2001) points out that the central systemic concept in the Tavistock approach is that of the open system (von Bertalanffy, 1950), while the central systemic concept in the complexity perspective is that of non-linear dynamics.

Stacey quotes an early reference to self-organising made by Emery and Trist (1960):

> *such systems may spontaneously reorganise towards states of greater heterogeneity and complexity, and they achieve a 'steady state' at a level where they can still do*

DOI: 10.4324/9781003368663-15

work. Enterprises grow by processes of internal elaboration and manage to achieve a steady state while doing work, i.e. achieve a quasi-stationary equilibrium in which the enterprise as whole remains constant, with a continuous throughput, despite a considerable range of external changes.

(Emery and Trist, 1960, p. 85)

Anderson (1999) on complexity states that the aim is to increase our conceptual tools and improve the analytic possibilities of systems psychodynamics through four key elements:

1 Complex organisations exhibit surprising non-linear behaviour. Complexity theory provides conceptual tools that enable new approaches to analysing and understanding non-linear interactions within and between organisations.
2 Complex organisations have 'agents with schemata': individuals, groups or coalitions of groups whose behaviour is determined by a cognitive structure, a plan, over time, given their perception of the environment.
3 Self-organising networks are sustained by importing energy: individuals or groups that are partially connected to one another so that the behaviour of an individual or group depends on the behaviour of a sub-set of all the people in the system.
4 Co-evolution to the edge of chaos: people and groups co-produce or co-evolve, each agent adapting to its environment by aiming to increase a payoff or fitness function over time (Holland and Miller, 1991). Everyone's payoff function depends on choices that other agents make so that each agent's adaptations – mapping their behaviour to their objectives – are constantly shifting (Leventhal, 1997).

The system evolution based on the recombination means that complex adaptive systems adapt over time through the entry, exits and transformation of agents. New constellations of people and groups may be formed by recombining elements of previously successful agents. Linkages between agents may evolve over time, shifting the pattern of interconnections, the strength of each connection and its sign and functional form.

Since the emergence of the open systems view of organisations in the 1960s, complexity theory has been a central construct in the lexicon of organisational development consultants (Aram and Noble, 1998, 1999). Open systems are open because they exchange resources with the environment; they are systems because they consist of interconnected components that work together. A complex system is made up of many parts that have many interactions (Simon, 1996). A complex organisation is a set of interdependent parts which together make up a whole that is interdependent with some larger environment (Thompson, 1967).

The move from defining organisations primarily as structural entities to more comprehensive analyses of the relationships between organisations and their environments is an important development for consultants. With respect to organisations, complexity equates with several activities or subsystems within the organisation, along with three dimensions:

1 Vertical complexity, referring to the number of levels in an organisational hierarchy
2 Horizontal complexity, referring to the number of job titles or departments across an organisation
3 Spatial complexity, referring to the number of geographical locations. With respect to environments, complexity is equated with several different items, activities, suppliers and customers that must be related to simultaneously by the organisation (Scott, 1992, p. 230)

The relationship between systems thinking and complexity thinking and how both are combined represents a genuinely new way of simplifying the complex and of encoding natural systems into formal systems. Instead of making nonlinear systems compliant and manageable by reducing them to a set of causal variables with a degree of error built in, complex adaptive systems typically show how complex outcomes flow from simple schemata and depend on the way the agents are interconnected. Rather than assuming that aggregate outcomes represent a homeostatic equilibrium, they show how such outcomes evolve from the efforts of agents in complex interconnections to achieve higher fitness.

Complexity theory combined with systems psychodynamics theory makes it possible to grasp complex behaviour by varying assumptions about the plans, connections, fitness functions or population dynamics that characterise the individuals or groups without abstracting away their interdependencies and non-linear interactions. Jackson (2020) describes Snowden's Cynefin (Snowden, D.J., Boone, M.E., 2007) complexity framework as a 'sense-making' device, which can help people arrive at a shared understanding of the complexities they face and how to respond to them.

Cynefin identifies four 'domains', having different characteristics, which demand different responses from decision-makers. 'Simple' domains exhibit linear cause-and-effect relationships, which are easily identifiable and lead to predictable outcomes. Decision-makers can employ best practice or simple methods to achieve good results. In 'complicated' domains, cause-and-effect relationships can be identified but are often separated in time and space and linked in chains that are difficult to understand. Experts can be called in who can help understand the behaviour of the system of interest using approaches such as system dynamics. In 'complex' domains, there are so many agents and relationships that it is impossible to trace the interactions and predict their outcomes. The innumerable cause and effect and linking together of a chain series or concatenations do, however, produce emergent patterns of behaviour that can be discerned in retrospect. In Jackson's (2020) view, a weakness of Cynefin is its failure to recognise the value of soft systems approaches in the complex domain.

Complexity theory

There is no single unified theory of complexity, but several theories arising from various natural sciences study complex systems, such as biology, chemistry, computer simulation, evolution, mathematics and physics. This includes the work undertaken over the past four decades by scientists associated with the Santa Fe Institute (SFI) in New Mexico, USA. Kauffman (1993, 1995, 2000); Holland (1995, 1998); Waldrop (1992); Murray Gell-Mann (1994) worked on complex adaptive systems (CAS). Peter Allen (1998); Goodwin (1995); Webster

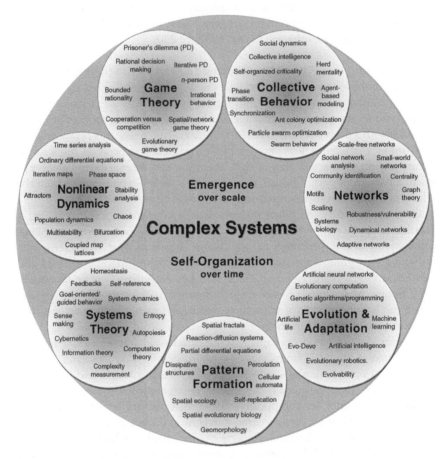

Figure 10.1 Visual, organisational map of complex systems broken into seven subgroups. Created by Hiroki Sayama, D.Sc., Collective Dynamics of Complex Systems (CoCo) Research Group at Binghamton University, State University of New York, 2010, https://commons.wikimedia.org/wiki/File:Complex_systems_organizational_map.jpg. This file is licensed under the Creative Commons Attribution-Share Alike 3.0 Unported licence.

and Goodwin (1996) worked on cooperation. Axelrod (1990, 1997); Axelrod and Cohen (2000); Prigogine and Stengers (1985); Nicolis and Prigogine (1989); Prigogine (1990); Gregoire Nicolis (1994) worked on dissipative structures; Varela and Maturana (1992); Niklaus Luhman (1990) and Mingers (1995) worked on autopoiesis; and Gleick (1987) worked on chaos theory (Figure 10.1).

From chaos theory to complex adaptive system

Working from mathematical chaos has revealed patterns that were previously considered random:

1 The patterns are paradoxical
2 Non-linear systems develop unpredictable forms of behaviour when they operate far from equilibrium
3 Butterfly effect (local action has global impact)

Prigogine defined dissipative structures in thermodynamics systems, for which he won the Nobel Prize in Chemistry in 1977, as non-linear systems developing unpredictable forms of behaviour when they operate far from equilibrium. In 1997, he wrote *The End of Certainty* where he departs from determinism (Einstein, Newton, Schrodinger) (quantum physics; the thought cat experiment) saying that determinism loses its explanatory power in the face of irreversibility and instability; that is, a ball at the top of the hill is in an unstable situation. Murray Gell-Mann, a Nobel prize–winning physicist from the Santa Fe Institute in Mexico ('Adventures in the Simple and the Complex'), takes his title from Arthur Sze, a Chinese American poet: *The world of the quark has everything to do with a jaguar circling in the night.*

Goodwin, a biologist, wrote about how a healthy heartbeat is paradoxical, both stable and unstable at the same time. Ideas from these new sciences were taken into theorising about organisations and management during the 1990s. His proposition was that theory of connections equalled non-linear connections.

Chaos theory

With the dynamic of mathematical chaos, we have ideas of bifurcation points, the strange attractor and a state of non-equilibrium. The idea of non-linearity leads to paradox: stable and unstable; predictable and unpredictable, at the same time. With the developing capacity to compute difficult mathematical equations, it has become possible to investigate formula containing both positive and negative feedback. Mathematical chaos reveals patterns in phenomena previously thought to be random. The patterns are paradoxically regular and irregular, stable and unstable. Chaos theory (Gleick, 1987) demonstrates that even simple nonlinear equations, for example, as used to describe weather systems can display uncertain, complex behaviour that makes anything beyond short-term prediction impossible. However, the 'chaos' that ensues is not chaos in the everyday meaning of the word. Chaos theory also reveals that, between order and complete disorder, a hidden order can appear. In this middle ground, behaviour never repeats itself but is drawn to 'strange attractors', which seem to set limits to what is possible. In these circumstances, patterns can be recognised, and it becomes possible to predict the overall shape of what can happen. In meteorology, physics, and chemistry, the behaviour of systems can indeed sometimes be modelled on the basis of a small number of variables with fixed interactions. In social and ecological systems with huge numbers of elements (people in a city, species in a forest), with different and evolving characteristics, and impacted by numerous internal and external changes, it is much more difficult to discern the influence of strange attractors.

Dissipative structures

Chaos performs the important task of amplifying small changes, or fluctuations, in the environment, causing the instability necessary to shatter an existing behaviour pattern and make way for a different one. Systems may pass through states of instability and reach critical points where they may spontaneously self-organise to produce a different structure or behaviour that cannot be predicted from a knowledge of the previous state. This more complex structure is called a dissipative structure because it takes energy to sustain the system in that new mode.

What if?

If we live at the edge of chaos, our lives can be characterised by a state of paradoxical existence. This implies that order and chaos, planning and emergence, predictability and unpredictability are all always occurring at the same time.

Complex adaptive systems

The term 'complex adaptive systems' describes the loosely organised academic field that has grown up around the study of systems. Complexity science is not a single theory. It encompasses more than one theoretical framework and is interdisciplinary, seeking answers to fundamental questions about living, adaptable, changeable systems. The study of complex adaptive systems focuses on complex, emergent and macroscopic properties of systems (Holland, 2006). Complex adaptive systems focus on top-level properties and features like complexity, self-similarity, emergence and self-organisation. In complex adaptive systems, the agents and the system are adaptive and the system is self-similar with high levels of resilience in the face of agitation. Other important properties are adaptation (or homeostasis), communication, cooperation, specialisation, spatial and temporal organisation and reproduction. They can be found at all levels:

cells specialise, adapt and reproduce themselves just like larger organisms do. Communication and cooperation take place on all levels, from the agent to the system level.

Writers on complexity have used the term 'complex adaptive systems' to denote a system in which a perfect understanding of the individual parts does not automatically convey a perfect understanding of the behaviour of the whole system (Miller and Page, 2007). The study of complex adaptive systems is essentially interdisciplinary and blends insights from the natural and social sciences to develop system-level models and insights that allow for heterogeneity, referring to differences across the units being studied; phase transition (or phase change) describing transitions, for example, between solid, liquid and gaseous states of matter, during which certain properties of the medium change, often discontinuously, as a result of changes in external conditions, such as temperature or pressure; emergent behaviour (Auerbach, 2016), the phenomenon whereby larger entities arise through interactions among smaller or simpler entities, such that the larger entities exhibit properties the smaller/ simpler entities do not exhibit. Complex adaptive systems are complex when they are composed of many components, which may interact with each other. In many cases, it is useful to represent such a system as a network where the nodes represent the components and the links their interactions. Examples of complex systems are the earth's global climate, organisms, the human brain and the immune system, the cell and the developing embryo, social and economic organisations, like cities, markets, governments, industries, ecosystems, social networks, power grids, animal swarms, traffic flows, social colonies, a living cell and ultimately the entire universe. Human social group-based endeavours, such as political parties, communities, organisations, war and terrorist networks are also considered complex adaptive systems. The internet and cyberspace composed, collaborated and managed by a complex mix of human and computer interactions, is also regarded as a complex adaptive system.

Self-organisation

Complex adaptive systems can be hierarchical, but more often exhibit aspects of self-organisation. This means that their evolution cannot be traced back to simple explanations of cause and effect. Self-organising is the ongoing joint action of communication in the living present as continual interaction between humans who are all forming intentions, choosing and acting in relation to one another as they go about their daily life, but no one can step outside an interaction to arrange it or design it. Patterns form and structures emerge without a master plan or a blueprint: Simple basic rules can create a complex phenomenon with infinite possibilities – which are both recognisable and different at the same time (self-similar). Ant colonies, city neighbourhoods, artificial intelligence, distributed networks in the human brain all are able to assemble and transform themselves without any master planner calling the shots.

The genes in a developing embryo organise themselves in one way to make a liver cell,
and in another way to make a muscle cell.

(Waldrop, 1992, p. 12)

Complex adaptive systems are unpredictable in that agents interact locally, and it is in this local interaction that global patterns emerge without any global blueprint, design or programme. The systems evolve in an intrinsically unpredictable manner into an undetermined future. They are interdependent, with local action at one scale having unpredictable consequences at all scales through complex relationships over time. The systems co-create their future. Paradoxical processes and interactions, taking the form of both positive and negative feedback, can, broadly speaking, display three dynamics: stable to the point of rigidity; unstable to the point of disintegration; and, paradoxically, patterns that are both stable and unstable simultaneously.

Capacity for learning

Double loop learning (Argyris and Schon, 1978) showed that 'species evolve for better survival in a changing environment and so do corporations and industries' (Waldrop, 1992, p. 11).

Competition and conflict emerge, and the evolution of the system is driven by agents
who are trying to exploit each other, but the game can go on only if neither side succeeds
completely or for long in that exploitation.

(Stacey, 1996b, p. 340)

When the agents in a complex adaptive system differ from each other, the system displays the capacity to transform itself. It is only at a critical level of diversity that a system can produce novelty (Allen, 1998a, 1998b). Such systems are adaptive in that they do not simply respond to events but evolve or learn. Each agent is guided by its own schema, or rules of behaviour, and also by schema shared with other agents. Interpreted in the organisation literature, single-loop learning occurs when schema remain unchanged, while double-loop learning involves changes in current schema, so producing more fundamental changes of kind (Argyris and Schon, 1978).

Self-organising process

A complex adaptive system is capable of self-organising, that is producing emergent novelty when it operates in the dynamic at the edge of chaos. This capacity consists of iterative non-linear interactions. These interactions are heterogeneous and hence take on a life of their own which means they are characterised by transformative rather than formative causality.

The complex responsive processes perspective

Stacey spent years in the corporate planning functions of commercial enterprises and his driving questions were why leaders, policymakers and managers in all organisations are so bad at forecasting the consequences of their actions and why, given the frequently surprising and often unwanted consequences of their actions, they carry on with strategic planning processes. If they do not accomplish what they anticipate through their plans, then what is it that they are doing to accomplish what they accomplish? These questions made it natural for Stacey to respond to the emerging complexity sciences. During the first systemic phase of his work, he applied first chaos theory and then the models of complex adaptive systems to organisations and management, arguing that organisations are complex adaptive systems and that the patterns in the actions of organisations, which are their strategies, emerge unpredictably in self-organising processes. Leaders, policymakers and managers are bad at forecasting because it is impossible to predict the consequences of actions, a conclusion supported by the complexity sciences. Management is not the rational, analytical decision-making it is made out to be, but a fundamentally political process. To integrate mainstream management theories within the notion of organisations as complex adaptive systems, Stacey offers a contingency theory of organisations in which the appropriate forms of decision-making and control depend upon the nature of the change situations that are faced.

The second phase of Stacey's work reflects his collaboration with Doug Griffin and Patricia Shaw. This phase drops the application of complex adaptive systems to organisations, arguing that it is invalid to simply apply the natural sciences to human action. Instead, the complexity sciences are regarded as a source domain for analogies, and when these analogies are transferred to the domain of human action, they need to be interpreted in a manner that takes full account of the attributes of human agents, namely, that they are conscious, self-conscious, emotional, often spontaneous, often thoughtful and reflective beings who have some degree of choice over what they do. Human agents are basically interdependent, they respond to each other, and their choices and intentions play into each other producing unpredictable, emergent patterns over time. To signal the move from the domain of the natural sciences to the domain of human action, Stacey and colleagues refer to these processes as complex responsive processes of relating. These responsive processes take the form of:

1 Communication understood as conversation (George Herbert Mead)
2 Patterns of power relations, which take the form, drawing on Norbert Elias, of the dynamics of inclusion-exclusion and identity
3 Ideology as a combination of values and norms, drawing on the work of Hans Joas, William James and John Dewey; and evaluative choices

It is in these local responsive processes that there emerge population-wide patterns of activity, culture and habits. Organisational life is thought of as the game people are invested in and organising processes are understood to be the ordinary politics of everyday life.

Stacey and his colleagues (Griffin, 2002, Stacey, 2000, 2001, 2003a, 2003b) use Mead's (1934) conceptual framework in making sense of phenomena emerging in organisational settings. They make a distinction between an individual and the social system. They do not consider individuals as autonomous of their environment; that is, they cannot form goals and action plans without at the same time being influenced by their environment. Following Mead (1934), the theory of complex responsive processes theory describes individual and organisational identities as self-organising processes of relating and expressing little variation. The theory discards the notion of a system and embraces a process view of individuals and organisations. In contrast to what they refer to as the rationalist and formative causes of human action, they depict a causal framework to which they refer to as transformative teleology. In *Changing Conversations in Organisations – A Complexity Approach to Change*, Patricia Shaw (2002) describes the practice of complexity thinking in organisational consultancy and a critique of systems theory. Her central theme is 'How do we go about changing complex organisations?' If we believe the best metaphor for organisations today is not the machine, nor even the metaphor of the living system, but an open-ended drama (because humans have choices that are limited by the choices of others, the paradox of being free and not free at the same time).

What are the implications for leaders and our practice as consultants? What if we accept the new thinking about chaos, complexity and self-organising systems in which uncertainty, diversity, paradox, plurality, emergence, politics and interdependence all play an important part? How does change take place and how can it be fostered? Shaw advocates a discipline that focuses attention on the emergence, out of a web of conflicting choices, between people in communicative processes in which meaning is always being constructed and negotiated. We make the choice but do not know what will come of it. Shaw does not suggest throwing out all our disciplines. She argues that different motivations, intentions and activity are emerging socially and being experienced individually through the self-organising patterning of these processes. She reorients us towards some of our existing disciplines, and she produces a different answer to what might be going on when we study processes via our traditional disciplines. The essence of her process is conversation and herself. The core of her practice is 'ordinary conversations' that may start with a few people and gradually spread in a self-organising, almost 'subversive' way that changes how people see things and generates energy and innovation. A new awareness or consciousness emerges from conversations and that brings about change. It is like a 'virus' spreading through the organisation.

Complex responsive processes and systems thinking

The perspective of complex responsive processes is a move away from thinking about organisations as systems to thinking about organisations as inter-related processes. The complex responsive processes perspective conceives of change in terms of spontaneous novelty in individual responses in the present moment, which is potentially amplified in subsequent public interaction and private role play into individual and organisational transformation. The complex responsive processes perspective implies that change does not result from someone first intending an intervention and then 'letting' this change emerge from the inter-action between the parts of a system. Rather, everybody is acting intentionally, on an ongoing basis; thereby change is seen as emerging from the interplay of intentions, possibly into shifts in population-wide tendencies to act in particular ways. In this way, interaction enables and constrains further interaction, result-ing in re-emergence and emergence of familiar and of new patterns of behaviour.

The reality of experience

Human interaction is inherently and inevitably local. This is because values, ideologies and strategies, and so on, are not stored anywhere but perpetually constructed in the public interaction and silent conversations of individuals. Whatever the global themes one might want to articulate for an organisation or a society, they have reality only insofar they are expressed in local situations in the living present (Griffin, 2002, p. 170). The main implication of the com-plex responsive processes perspective is in its goal to refocus attention to what people in organisations 'are already, and always have been, doing'. The 'whole' of interest should be one's own, direct experience of 'relating and managing in relationship with others' (Stacey, 2000, p. 412).

Complex systems are not 'designed' in great detail. They are made up of inter-acting agents, whose interactions create emergent properties, qualities and pat-terns of behaviour. It is the actions of individual agents and the immense variety of those actions that constantly influence and create emergent macro-patterns or structures. In turn, the macro-structure of a complex ecosystem influences individual entities, and the evolutionary process moves constantly between micro-behaviours and emergent structures, each influencing and recreating each other.

The complexity approach to managing is one of fostering, of creating en-abling conditions, of recognising that excessive control and intervention can be counterproductive. When enabling conditions permit an organisation to explore its space of possibilities, the organisation can take risks and try new ideas. Risk-taking is meant to help find new solutions, alternative ways to do business, to keep evolving through established connectivities while establishing new ways of connecting (Mitleton-Kelly, 2000).

Critical systems thinking and complexity

Critical systems thinkers such as Jackson (2019) have put forward the idea that the labels such as 'tame' and 'wicked' are used to describe two quite different types of problem. Tame problems have causes that are easy to understand, and they can be solved based on prior experience or simple analytical methods. Wicked problems feature high levels of both systemic and people complexity. Systemic complexity relates to the interdependency of problems, which makes it impossible to solve them in isolation, and to environmental turbulence, which means solutions are out-of-date before they are implemented. People complexity refers to the pluralism of stakeholder perspectives, which invariably surround social and organisational issues and the different evaluations and conflicts that occur as a result. Wicked problems must be managed using critical systems thinking. Critical systems thinking embraces and builds upon those complexity theory and systems thinking approaches that are based on solid research and have proven the most valuable in improving problem situations in the face of complexity. Critical systems thinking advocates using different systems approaches in combination to navigate the multi-dimensional complexity posed by wicked problems. It provides a comprehensive evaluation of outcomes and suggests what needs doing next to ensure continuous improvement.

Jackson (2020) distinguishes what many authors regard as the key features of 'complexity'. Some concentrate on the complexity they see as existing in the world – on 'ontological complexity'. Others highlight 'cognitive complexity' – the complexity they see arising from the different interpretations of the world held by observers. Others recognise the added difficulties flowing from the interactions between 'ontological' and 'cognitive' complexity. Jackson (2020) suggests how things might have been different had the 'critical systems thinking' (CST) view of complexity been employed and a 'critical systems practice' (CSP) approach adopted in preparing for a possible pandemic and responding to it.

Jackson's view is that in systems thinking and complexity theory, two different reactions to the hyper-complexity are found in the modern world. He cites an understanding using Morin's (2005) distinction between 'restricted complexity' and 'general complexity'. According to Morin, it is essential to understand that we are confronted by a case of 'general complexity'. General complexity produces what Rittel and Webber (1981) call 'wicked problems', which are intractable for decision-makers:

> The planner who works with open systems is caught up in the ambiguity of their causal webs. Moreover, his would-be solutions are confounded by a still further set of dilemmas posed by the growing pluralism of the contemporary publics, whose valuation of his proposals are judged against an array of different and contradicting scales.
>
> (p. 99)

General complexity resists universal truth. All attempts to model it are partial, and therefore, the fundamental problem of general complexity 'is epistemological, cognitive, paradigmatic' (Morin, 2005), concerned with the ways we seek to understand and manage complexity. Jackson (2020) summarises five systemic perspectives that have demonstrated a capacity to provide significant insight into complex problem situations and appear to cover the ground – 'machine', 'organism, 'cultural/political', 'societal/environmental' and 'inter-relationships'. He suggests that using them enables us to make suggestions about where failings are occurring and how things can be improved:

1 *Machine*: is there an agreed goal, are the necessary parts well connected together to achieve the goal, and are the necessary components to hand or easily obtainable? The machine is judged on whether it demonstrates efficacy (is well organised to achieve its purpose) and efficiency (does so with minimum use of resources).

2 *Organism*: is the system viable, are the sub-systems functioning well, with their own autonomy but still serving the whole, and is the whole adaptive to the environment, resilient in the face of shocks, and capable of learning? The organism is judged on whether its semi-autonomous parts are well coordinated and controlled, and whether the system is anti-fragile (Taleb, 2013), in the face of its turbulent environment.

3 *Cultural/political*: is there agreement that the system is doing the right things (effectiveness), has this been subject to challenge (not emerged from groupthink), and are there processes for dealing with conflict? This systemic perspective is not used as an exemplar. Rather, it alerts practitioners to look out for a variety of cultural and political factors that may require attention in the problem situation.

4 *Societal/environmental*: Have the interests of all stakeholders (including those of the marginalised and future generations) been considered, and have sustainability and environmental issues received sufficient attention? This systemic perspective is used to identify neglected stakeholders, discrimination, and inequality, and to argue that interventions should take into account the situation of the disadvantaged and the consequences for the environment.

5 *Interrelationships*: Can we identify chains of mutual causality in the problem situation and leverage points for bringing about change? The issues identified by the other systemic perspectives will, of course, be interrelated. Although general complexity forestalls mathematical modelling of these interrelationships, it may occasionally be possible to identify important linkages which offer leverage points for achieving improvement and/or suggest unintended consequences that might follow from proposed actions.

The different systemic perspectives provide breadth and depth to the exploration of the problem situation. Each reveals new matters worthy of attention and may provide a different explanation as to why the issues of concern have arisen. They will often provide conflicting information and explanations, and this is particularly helpful in gaining a full appreciation of the complexity involved and in supporting informed decision-making. Once the complexity of the problem situation has been untangled in this way, appropriate systems methodologies can be chosen to address the most pressing aspects of complexity.

Case illustration

The orchestra as a complex system

Eliat Aram

An orchestra has poetic qualities for describing the nature of a complex system. Eliat from the Tavistock Institute, worked with Dr Rune Rønning of AFF Norway with one such organisation.

The organisation (orchestra) had sought consultation assistance in its development. The development effort was to consider the special character of work in an orchestra. The role of the consultants was to identify such characteristics, to identify organisational risks and challenges emerging from them, to point to interventions that may be effective in preventing problems and to assist in carrying out and evaluating such interventions.

The consultants produced a 'working note', which included our understanding of the organisation as a whole, within its environment; described the particular characteristics of its task and work processes and ended with recommendations for further interventions. All based on extensive interviews with around 50% of the orchestra's employees – musicians of all the instrument groups, as well as management and administration.

The organisation as a whole:

The orchestra is a foundation, which was set up in the 18th century. Its income is 85% state-sponsored and 15% tickets and other sales. It consists of various committees – including management, programme, orchestra, environment and conditions, and board.

The organising (or primary) task of the orchestra is to make music.

This breaks down to arranging and performing concerts, but also to making recordings. Both musicians and administration/management work together towards carrying out this task.

To give concerts and to carry out the artistic programme, the orchestra practices up to 25 hours together per week; not more than five hours a day. In addition, individual musicians practise on their own.

The organisation needs to ensure a viable framework for making music to survive. This includes securing continued funding from the State and from sponsors, developing an attractive programme, marketing and selling the orchestra to the general public as well as supporting the performance of the task of making music through suitable logistics, securing a suitable physical environment and providing resources such as instruments and musical scores. Both musicians and administration work towards carrying out this task; more implicitly for the musicians and more explicitly for management.

Thus, it is not sufficient for the organisation's survival that the concerts and recordings are of high musical quality; the organisation also must create what could be called an image – a brand; 'a mythology of quality and value', in its environment to survive. This includes working with youth and participating in education, etc.

A complex adaptive system has a few core characteristics:

- it is self-organising; it has coherence and structure, but there is no blueprint
- its structure is both emergent and unpredictable, as well as patterned and coherent at the same time
- the formal and informal systems are inter-dependent, and power plays determine the shifting patterns of relationships and authority
- it is paradoxical and essentially fractal – so infinitely created and recreated

These are observable through the following paradoxical dynamics:

Temporary vs long-lasting:

Music is an art of the moment; it is created in the now, always afresh. Therefore, the output of an orchestra is ephemeral; music performed happens in the 'now', and it is 'consumed' as it is produced – no corrections are possible. Thus, for the individual musicians, errors and mistakes that happen in the 'now' of the concerts are final and can never be corrected. This means that task performance for the musicians is characterised by a high level of exposure and risk. As one musician put it: *the concern for performance and even performance anxiety is always there*. Thus, anxiety and the potential for shameful failure are likely consequences of task performance, but there are also potentially great rewards when concerts are successful.

Individual vs group

For each musician, playing music is an embodied and emotional individual task and the consequence is that the boundary between professional and personal identity becomes blurred. A mistake is thus not simply a professional mistake, but potentially a personal catastrophe in terms of compromised identity. Thus, conditions that increase the risk of mistakes may lead to high levels of frustration.

Leadership vs followership

However, playing in an orchestra also requires what one might call: '*The art of followership*' – coordinating with others and generally working together, including submitting oneself to the conductor's authority. The conductor's influence thus constitutes an important dependency relationship in the performance of the task. Hierarchy, as an important aspect of orchestral life, stands in fascinating tension with the interdependencies of co-creating music.

The now of concerts is also the time when the musicians are free to do what they want if they feel differently to the conductor … so some rebellious behaviour is also possible during concerts -*management (head) vs musicians (body)*.

Task performance is characterised by a high level of interdependency and by close physical proximity to colleagues. The musicians emphasise that the task requires extreme concentration over long periods of time. This makes the working conditions particularly significant, as adverse conditions may impair the capacity for concentration.

The musicians are unequivocal in stating that their task and role is the most important and most demanding in the organisation, and that 'management *is here for us*'.

Many musicians do not think the administration share this view. They said: '*the administration see themselves as the head and the musicians as the body – and they do not respect the body. They see action as emanating from the head – not from the body*'.

Management/administration vs musicians' relationships:

Creating and playing music and the work of ensembles and orchestras is often idealised and romanticised in professional settings and in society generally. The practice, the endless rehearsals, the working around the clock, the bodily tensions, the muscle aches, the injuries, the risk of hearing loss contradict this image; often, this is made light of by jokes or flippant remarks, and results in the musicians feeling that their complaints are ignored. They do not always feel recognised, appreciated or cared for.

On the other hand, administrative staff feel squeezed between many committees with managerial and leadership responsibilities, which are seen by the committees as far more important and critical than the tasks/jobs the management/administrators are fulfilling. Management/administrators are aware of the musicians' hardship and problems but can be prevented from making changes due to external factors. So, they too report not feeling recognised or appreciated occasionally.

The musicians and administration agree that the primary task of the orchestra is to make music. The problem is in the operationalising the task (Stacey et al. (2000) describe that as complex responsive processes of relating).

Linked to the above is the theme of the particularities of playing instruments:

The characteristics and peculiarities of different instruments become significant in relation to the management of the organisation. They effect coordination, playing together, positioning, sound-level stresses, other physical hazards (spittle falling from bells of brass onto clarinetists and oboists), need for practice and for rest after concerts, need for adjustment of musical scores, even (in the case of the harp and the timpani) the micro-structures of the orchestra – all these constitute what we might call the 'anatomy of the orchestra' – and should not be neglected. Generalised management discourse, however, grasps these particularities with difficulty.

Management's lack of fully expressed empathy with the musicians' situation may thus be mediated and sustained through a dominant management discourse. The complexity and systems psychodynamics discourse however offers a nuanced way of understanding the system.

Dealing with criticism

Given the risk of professional and personal identities becoming blurred, confronting individual musicians with playing out of time/tune may be experienced as a personal insult rather than a professional comment made by a group leader or a supportive colleague.

More broadly, it seemed to us that no structures/systems exist for dealing with the conflicts, which may emerge from such occurrences. One consequence is the absence of a clear 'quality system', or system for development/improvement in place in an organisation, which lives off high quality. This is left to the discretion and self-discipline of individual musicians.

Another consequence of the collective reluctance to provide an effective system of 'peer assessment' serves as a defence against the anxiety and shame associated with the effect of exposure as an inadequate musician, but leads, paradoxically, to higher risk of precisely that happening. Thus, the defence becomes self-reinforcing.

Linking these two themes of no clear quality system and peer assessment is what we call the overt versus the hidden structure of the orchestra. In this process, the formal communication in the orchestra during rehearsals is restricted to the line of conductor – principals – musicians. This 'line' provides, according to some interviewees, 'a calming structure'.

The hidden structure we observe occurs when musicians 'play with' other musicians, that is to say: they modulate their own playing and co-ordinate it with others: cellos at one time, woodwinds at other times and so on. This hidden structure can keep the orchestra going even when the conductor 'loses it'.

> *Thinking of the orchestral organisation as **an organisation of nested systems** we assume that a problem in one group or part of the orchestra – is a fractal of the wider organisation, and hence would show up in similar yet different ways in other parts. This insight helps members of the organisation to engage in different ways so as to shift patterns and continue to grow and adapt towards fulfilling their primary task and thrive – not just survive.*

Summary

Complexity is looking at interacting elements and asking how they form patterns and how the patterns unfold. It's important to point out that the patterns may never be finished. They're open-ended. In standard science this hits some things that most scientists have a negative reaction to. Science doesn't like perpetual novelty.

(Arthur, 1999)

Of interest to consultants is the work of Ralph Stacey and colleagues at the Complexity and Management Centre, University of Hertfordshire. Stacey (Griffin, 2002; Luoma, 2007; Stacey et al., 2000; Stacey, 2000, 2001, 2003a, 2003b) claims that there are two potentially problematic underlying assumptions in systems thinking:

1 Individuals have the capability to choose their goals and actions by stepping outside the system of which they are a part. In other words, individual behaviour is determined by the intentions they choose without the influence of others. Their thinking and behaviour are not constrained by their

environment. Stacey (2001) refers to this causal framework as the 'rational-ist teleology'.

2 It is meaningful to discuss social institutions as systems where the sys-temic structures lie – or are thought to lie – 'outside' the interactions they produce. In other words, an individual is a victim of their mental models, which determine how they react to their environments. Stacey (2001) refers to this causal framework as the 'formative teleology'.

The first assumption holds that individuals are free to choose whether they con-form or change their systemic structures. The latter assumption, on the other hand, holds that individuals are objects in the systems they are a part of – the structures determine how they behave. Thus, the two assumptions above are in contradiction with each other. According to Stacey (2001), this conflict is relaxed in systems thinking by assuming that individuals are both subject to influence of a system and free from it. Stacey (2001) and Griffin (2002) refer to this as the 'both ... and' structure inherent in systems thinking in which the rationalist and formative cause are kept apart, although it is not clear how this distinction should be made or how the distinction is formed to begin with. Stacey (2001) also recognises systems thinking is not just one unified theory. It is rather an umbrella term for a variety 'methods, tools, and principles, all look-ing at the interrelatedness of forces' (Senge et al., 1994, p. 89). Systems are 'per-ceived whole[s] whose elements continually affect each other and where there is no single right answer to the question, "what is the system?"' (ibid., p. 90).

Luoma et al. (2011) make the following points in relation to complex re-sponsive processes; they state that systems thinking literature assumes that the concept of a system is useful in management and organisational research. Sta-cey and his collaborators, however, have questioned this. Stacey (2001) makes the point that the Tavistock approach is that of the open system (von Berta-lanffy, 1968), while the central systemic in the complexity perspective is that of non-linear dynamics. The emphasis in the Tavistock work is on the regulatory function at the permeable boundary rather than on the spontaneously reorgan-ising capacity of the system. Stacey et al. have presented the theory of complex responsive processes (CRP), as an alternative to systems thinking. Luoma argues that systems thinking and the CRP perspective are complementary. The CRP illuminates many of the micro-behavioural, local interaction and creativity-related organisational phenomena, while the systems perspective is useful for other purposes. The insights of CRP should and could be incorporated, not switched, with the systems perspective. The systems intelligence perspective, proposed by Hämäläinen and Saarinen (2008), provides a framework to accom-plish that. By integrating systems thinking and the CRP model, they hope to provide a platform from which it is possible to appreciate the relative merits of the two apparently conflicting strands of thought.

See: https://www.academia.edu/3308421/Acting_with_systems_intelligence_integrating_complex_responsive_processes_with_the_systems_perspective

Zhu (2007) argues for 'pragmatic sensibility' and for appreciating systems as 'a dynamic web of the tensions, reciprocities and transformations between various aspects of organisational life, each differentiated from and connected with, depending upon and affecting, each other' (Zhu, 2007, p. 460). Zhu (2007, p. 459) supports many of Stacey's ideas, but criticises his focus on processes and lack of consideration of any kind of organisational structure. He advocates linking pragmatism to Stacey's ideas so that leaders/managers can translate this theory into practical guidance for action. Stacey (2012) recommends that leaders/managers should use existing tools and techniques, but in a reflexive way, exercising practical judgement, and accepting that they cannot fully control how these tools and techniques will work out in a specific, real-world situation.

Experiencing the system in order to know it

C. West Churchman (1979), one of the pioneers of systems thinking, acknowledged that the reality of a system, in general, is neither 'out there', nor is it solely in the mind of an individual pondering what the system is. They are rather contexts within which some outcomes are experienced and within which individuals strive to influence what those emerging outcomes are. Thus, the above critique concerns only a narrow interpretation of systems thinking since no one theory of systems thinking exists. Stacey's and his colleagues' critique is relevant because it points to how the 'systems language' is conceptually limited to discussing human interaction in terms of entities, systems' boundaries and so on. The language is limited in its capability to explain how entities and systems originally have emerged. Reality is far richer than any systemic description of it. It is to be noted that while systems, their components and their interconnections are identified, action is already taking place. While we can, to some extent, inquire what a system seems to be, it is already continually being constructed. It seems that Stacey's and his colleagues' critique on systems thinking stems from the recognition of the importance of paying attention to the direct experience within perceived wholes and not limiting oneself to merely observing and re-designing them.

Exercise

1 How would you apply ideas about complex adaptive systems to your organisation?
2 Describe a consultancy project from a complexity perspective.
3 What are the difficulties/opportunities of applying complexity theory in your work?
4 How does systems psychodynamics complement complexity theory?
5 Do you think there is room for basic assumption theory (Bion) of projective identification influencing individual behaviour within a system, and complexity theory's 'intentionality', 'self-organising' and 'emergence'?

Chapter 11

The systems psychodynamics view of leadership

David Lawlor and Mannie Sher with Eliat Aram,
Anton Obholzer and Jonathan Gosling

Introduction

The systems psychodynamics approach to leadership focuses on the dynamics of human behaviour, and the idea that if we study what affects behaviour, we can understand how people and systems function and why they react the way they do. Thus, an important function of the leader is to facilitate the process of having people gain insight and identify their own needs and patterns of emotional reactions to other people. The key components to this approach are as follows: leaders are more effective when they have an insight into their own psychological makeup, or act in certain ways, and in turn use that information to be better leaders and followers (Abraham, 2013; Cilliers, 2005; Czander, 1993; Krantz, 2006).

Case illustration

'In space, no one can hear you scream'
    At the top, loneliness is like living in a vacuum...
    Wanting to learn more about her leadership style, Cynthia, a Director of HR services in an NHS Trust for ten years, tells her coach how her role has changed recently, not always for the better. Now she is surrounded by protocols and timetables, demands and gatekeepers. The air has de-oxygenated the further she has moved from the ground. She feels people prefer her to stay away for fear that the changes she wishes to introduce will affect their work and their relationships, even their jobs. Cynthia says she notices how people avoid her or tell her things they think she wants to hear, and how relationships with colleagues have changed from collegial to hierarchical. 'Authority' changes everything, she says; she is acutely aware how counterdevelopmental this is, and she worries. To be sure, as Cynthia moved up the ranks to reach the Director role, she skilfully managed the tensions between the organisational demands for innovation, and HR personnel's need for stability and continuity and

DOI: 10.4324/9781003368663-16

the 'containment' they provided for the Trust's 8,000 employees. Nevertheless, the pressures to know how to respond to the latest round of downsizing and re-organisations, and to have answers to problems, deal with unpredictable events, and the lack of powers to resolve them, make her feel very alone and sometimes burdened and frightened. She recognises she is at the epicentre of multiple and competing stakeholders – the Trust's board, executive directors, departmental managers, patients, workers and communities served by the Trust.

In a session, Cynthia says she worries about the subtle changes in her judgement of her direct reports. Before her appointment to the Director role, she held her colleagues in high regard. She was fulsome in her praise of their team spiritedness, willingness to respond to sudden crises and their commitment to the humane principles of their profession in an increasingly impersonal healthcare system. She has noticed a gradual loss of confidence in them and an increasing sense of disappointment. 'Is it my style of leadership? The role? Is it their behaviour and attitude? Is it "the system"? or "is it me?"', she asks. Cynthia feels troubled, she cannot get comfortable; she feels more isolated, tired and lonely. A lot of the time she feels she is floating in space with only the barest connection with the Trust. Cynthia talks to her coach about how different hospital functions activate different identifications among the HR staff – some strongly identify with specific departments and consultants and others with specific patient groups like children (paediatrics), mental ill people, or the elderly, while she, Cynthia, must take an organisation-wide view and implement government-imposed budgetary cuts. Each cut makes her feel as though she is betraying the Trust's patients, her HR staff and her own principles and values.

Cynthia's coach listens and prods gently with questions, comments and summations and other helpful lines of inquiry, empathically commenting on Cynthia's feelings, even asking after her dreams. Conversations are sometimes focused; sometimes, they follow unintentional avenues, shedding light, opening challenges and inviting new perspectives. The conversations are geared to developing new thinking, not necessarily searching for solutions. They sometimes focus on organisational challenges or theory, on inter-personal relations, role relationships and personal idiosyncrasies; at other times, they focus on Cynthia's mood, why some behaviours get repeated, seemingly unconsciously, and others are avoided; feelings and emotions are discussed, helping to distinguish those that stem from the role and those that stem from her as a person. Frustration and anger are two emotions, she says, that interfere with having a clear head, her common sense and an ability to maintain her humanity and her values. At the end of each session, Cynthia usually feels a sense of relief and thinks more clearly about the issues and the feelings they generate. The coach has no axe to grind; he is on Cynthia's side, working in her interest, allowing her to discover different leadership capabilities within herself to adapt to the changes that need to be made to protect, to provide and be fair towards all sections of the total Trust system – general hospitals, specialist hospitals, primary care and other segments of the Trust. The coaching helps Cynthia to strengthen her leadership role, and her sense of self by helping her to investigate unexpected sources of her feelings that had lain dormant for years.

Between coaching sessions, Cynthia tests her new discoveries and monitors responses and reactions to them. She discusses the changes with her coach, and they move on to deeper layers of understanding and to ever-widening circles of dialogue and insight. Cynthia also raises her frustrations about the coaching – the slow pace, struggling with a new idea that she is not yet ready to assimilate; the unexpected memories that get evoked, the constant trial and error and the emphasis on self-discovery that avoids creating unnecessary dependency on her coach. The coaching encourages meta-levels of thinking that are associated with the complexities of Cynthia's position and the intricate web of relationships of her roles inside and outside the Trust.

The executive coaching serves as a support for Cynthia; it is constructive for her as a person; for clarifying roles; for improving performance of the Trust system, and it is a space where the 'scream' of the CEO is heard by the sympathetic presence of 'another'.

Managing internal and external boundaries

When boundaries are poorly designed and managed, they can cause a great amount of stress and anxiety (Hirschhorn, 1993; Obholzer, 1994; Rice, 1963, 1965). The task of leadership must therefore be located on the boundary between the organisation and the external environment (Rice, 1963). Thus, at the boundary, the leader integrates the mission with the means for accomplishing it, weaving the means and ends to articulate a mission, which can realistically be achieved (Krantz and Gilmore, 1990). Organisational leadership relates means and ends and has both a strategic and operational perspective. By standing at the boundary, leaders create a more controllable environment in which the activities within the boundary are organised and can be coordinated to respond to changes (Hirschhorn, 1993). Obholzer (1994) added that leadership is also directly related to the pursuit of the organisation's aims and primary task. It is through monitoring the primary task that the leader can avoid abuse of power, maintain on-task leadership and minimise the occurrence and spread of basic assumption activity in the organisation (Obholzer, 1994). The relationship between the leader and followers will depend on the extent of the leader's capacity to manage the relationships between the internal and external environments in such a way that it enables the followers to perform their primary task (Rice, 1963).

Furthermore, Rice (1963) reported that a task of leadership is to manage relationships with other sub-systems and with the whole. Lapierre (1991) provided a definition of leadership derived from the works of Erikson (1958, 1993), Zaleznik and Kets de Vries (1975, 1991), Zaleznik (1977, 1989, 1990), Kernberg (1979), Kets de Vries (1980, 1984, 1989, 1991), Levinson (1982), and Kets de Vries and Miller (1984, 1985). Their view is that leadership is the result of the personal predispositions, qualities and attributes of the individual occupying positions of authority. Leadership is defined as the part of executive action directly attributed to the person exercising authority, and more specifically to the projection of deep-seated elements of their personality (Lapierre, 1991). It is impossible to separate the leader from the person – leaders must bring their person (themselves) to the role and invest their role with their own affects (Hirschhorn, 1993; Lapierre, 1991).

De Vries and Cheak (2014) maintain that the psychodynamic approach provides another lens to the study of organisational dynamics. It addresses the undercurrents of organisational life through issues such as:

1   Inter-personal communication
2   Group processes
3   Social defences
4   Organisation-wide neurosis

The psychodynamic approach focuses on:

1   Personal insight on the part of the leader and follower
2   Creating reflective practitioners
3   In-depth and systemic investigation of a single person, group, event or community

It emphasises the relationship between leader and follower by focusing on the underlying drivers of each and what accounts for the type of relationship between them. Ideally, leaders will eventually internalise the ability to learn, work and reflect with the psychological realm in mind, and in doing so improve their organisational relationships and team performance.

Below, we have three eminent practitioners in the field of systems psychodynamics writing on the current issues facing organisations and leadership, viz. Eliat Aram, Anton Obholzer and Jonathan Gosling.

Working with leadership

Love and leadership – what's love got to do with it?

By Eliat Aram

Love is the fuel that drives us

This is my thinking that love is the fuel that drives us. That love at work – of our work, of our colleagues, of clients – is so powerful a feeling that we fear owning it and expressing it. When we are too scared of the intensity of loving feelings, we make mistakes, stop contact and build walls; we develop processes and structures that hide our intense emotional world; we develop bureaucracies to defend against our passions and desires; and we complicate things to defend against the primitive, raw nature of love. But if love is such a gratifying experience, why do we try to avoid it then, why are we so afraid and of what?

1st thought: fear of love

For many years, I have avoided the question of love at work because I thought it was an inappropriate concept for organisational context – too cheesy, too passionate, too sexual, too feminine, too spontaneous, too 'young' and too unprofessional. The fear of owning our feelings of love drives the worst behaviours in organisations including corruption, blaming, bullying and harassment.

2nd thought: fear of love, dependency and accountability

'Institutions' and 'organisations' are often treated with suspicion and contempt. We often hear consultants, and others talk about their withdrawal from institutional life and working independently because they 'do not trust the organisation' or are 'fed up with the institutional dynamics' or 'feel disappointed with the system'? What do we mean by the expression 'to be institutionalised?'

These are all ideas, which indicate we have split ourselves from our contribution to what we have created and instead reified our creation by distancing ourselves from it and removing our accountability for the result.

3rd thought: the ethics of love; servitude and spirit

In our work, systems psychodynamics is often felt as hardship. Why would I suggest that love has anything to do with work? What's to love?

We are often caught by the politics at work, stress, burnout, working too hard, not earning enough, not recognised, not liking colleagues and not feeling liked. In consultancy, we often feel we are the garbage bin of the organisation's negativity and conflicts, becoming our clients' bad objects. Yet most of us love to work, to come to a workplace and to engage in our task of working. What purpose does this serve and why do we struggle to express love at work?

In working, we engage in the eternal work of creation through ordinary practice. We don't find it easy to talk about our work in terms of love perhaps because love is meant to be an extraordinary experience whereas work is mundane, humdrum, especially if the primary task of our work is defined as doing something for someone else. When engaging together in the task of creation and servitude, there is also the recognition of dependency on others, sometimes of hierarchical relations – yet there is no servant without a master, no teacher without students, no customer without a provider – and that recognition, when being the boss does not necessarily mean you are in control, when we are 'in' love we feel the fullness as well as the emptiness of it, we might get scared. To stay in [the] love we need to work through our dependencies.

4th thought: 'the soul is partly in eternity and partly in time'.

Plato called love the child of fullness and emptiness. We love Love, as Plato in his Symposium elaborates in the conversation between Socrates and Diotima, and we have high hopes and expectations that love will make us complete even if past experience has shown us that love can be painful and disturbing. There is something self-renewing in love; love can renew its virginity in a bath of forgetfulness. Love itself is eternally young, and the progress we make may simply be to re-enter it freely time and time again, in spite of our suspicions, in spite of our past experience of being devastated or pained by it, to always draw to the darkness and hollowness that are mysteriously necessary in love.

There is celebration of friendship and intimacy in ancient books, but no talk about how to make relationships work. The emphasis is on what love does to the soul. Does it bring broader vision? Does it initiate the soul in some way? Does it carry the lover away from earth to an awareness of divine things?

I have also learnt in reading about love that Platonic love is not love without sex; it is love that finds in the body and in human relationship a route towards eternity. Ficino (1492) says concisely in his book *Convivium* (his response to the Symposium) that 'the soul is partly in eternity and partly in time'.

Love is complex and paradoxical – it is the ordinary experienced as extraordinary, and vice versa – the miracle of love expressed and experienced as daily ups and downs, even routines. It is in our daily servitude that we find humbled divinity; it is when we are in awe with someone that we find his or her realness. Freud says that love always involves transference – having feelings in the present that derive from early family relationships. Mother, father, brother, sister are always implicated in love as an invisible but influential presence. When love stirs, he says, deeper fantasies are evoked into action. We can of course read Freud in a reductionist way to see present love simply as an evocation of old love, or we can read Freud as inviting us to consider how love makes the soul fertile with memories and images. Freud reminds us that love ushers in a whole community of people. Freud's principle is that love sparks imagination into extraordinary activity. 'Being in love' is like being 'in imagination'.

Robert Burton in his self-help book of the 17th century 'The Anatomy of Melancholy' says that the only cure for the melancholic sickness of love is to enter it in abandon. In modern writing, romantic love is criticised as an illusion to be careful of, we need to distrust, keep our wits about us and be careful not to be led astray. Thomas Moore suggests that maybe we need to be cured BY love of the attachment to life without fantasy; maybe one function of love, he ponders, is to cure us of an anaemic imagination, a life emptied of romantic attachment and abandoned to reason.

We think we know what love is, but love leans towards the mysterious dark niches of the soul's underworld. Its fulfilment is death. Love takes us to the edge of what we know and what we have experienced. Love keeps the soul on track of its fate. Love is very important to the soul. There is no way towards love except through the discovery of human intimacy and community – one feeds the other. It may help us in times of trouble, to remember that love is not only about relationship; it is also an affair of the soul. Disappointments in love, even betrayals and losses, serve the soul at the very moment they seem to be tragedies. The soul is partly in time and partly in eternity. We might remember the part that resides in eternity when we despair over the part that is in life.

5th Thought: compassionate leaders as good lovers

At the Leicester conference of 2007, I exposed my anxiety and vulnerability twice in my opening address. One was forgetting to introduce two of my elderly colleagues, and the other was to call the 'opening' the 'closing' plenary. These two significant and embarrassing moments of exposure in that opening plenary were also useful. I exposed my vulnerability in making mistakes, embarrassed myself. I was ashamed, what an opening for the conference. With the help of my colleagues, I found compassion for my shame – as the conference unfolded, members and staff explored the nature of competence and incompetence in the conference and the tension between ability and disability, and how these were linked to competence and creativity. The question of how we look after each other, questioning mindfulness and citizenship was pronounced through a member in a wheelchair and an experience of the fire alarm going off early one morning, leaving that member exposed in her vulnerability and in need of others' support, which failed to arrive.

6th Thought: fear of freedom

In thinking differently about leadership, we need to think differently about organisations and ourselves within them. If organisations are social constructs, then they carry different symbolic resonances for everyone within them. Individual experiences of organisations are shaped by the nature of the work, by relationships between people and groups engaged in the work and by the nature of individual desires and emotions. Our understanding of organisations is made up of different sets of pre-conceptions, assumptions and myths. When we think about organisations through this lens, we are then bound to examine our own accountability in creating those organisations within which we operate. They are not separate to us. We have the authority over that, which we complain about or feel the victim of.

Freedom

Authority is the embodied experience, which is often exciting and frightening at the same time, which sometimes can be a spiritual experience, and which often is non-verbal or hard to articulate – the experience we have when we are able to make sense of a role we have taken up or found ourselves in; when meaning emerges; when we have a sense that we are authors of our own actions and freedom.

Leadership on the boundary

The work of leadership in contemporary organisations involves working on the boundary. Khan (2001) notes the traditional hierarchical structure routinely managed anxiety through the provision of predictability and certainty (Hirschhorn (1990). In previous times, hierarchical systems, in conjunction with support from leaders, coworkers, and mentors, offered a reasonable base of security that felt trustworthy and stable to organisational members. In a world characterised by fewer and weaker boundaries, organisational hierarchies offer less security. Leaders and mentors are often in the position of knowing as little as or less about daily operations than do their subordinates and mentees (Hirschhorn (1990); Kram (1996). No longer can individuals count on others to provide rules, goals, clear promotional ladders and protection. Khan (2001) suggests we need to conceptualise other structures that help manage people's experiences of anxiety in this very permeable and potentially boundary less world. He argues that the concept of the holding environment is a useful one. The holding environment concept was developed by British psychoanalyst D. W. Winnicott (1965) to describe the nature of effective caregiving relationships between mothers and infants. Winnicott's insight was that 'good-enough mothering' involves physically holding infants, whose subsequent experiences of feeling safely encompassed enable the initiation and movement of developmental processes.

Khan points out that a holding environment is not easy to put in place and is even more difficult in the digital environment that has been created by the COVID pandemic. Group, inter-group, and organisational contexts and dynamics may prove too difficult. Although people also desire support, they also retreat from disturbing emotions and difficult situations, where they may experience an anxiety against which they have defended.

Leadership and authority issues nowadays

By Anton Obholzer

'At an early stage I had accepted the "bon mot" which lays down that there are three impossible problems: educating, healing and governing' – Sigmund Freud. How right he was!

This paper is about governing as it was then called – nowadays, it is leadership and authority. Over the past century, the field was manageable to a degree and the foundations of the discipline more or less agreed, though there were many different versions and languages in their expression and application. Given the socio-political climate of the past century, the human development and its anthropological enquiries, one might expect a substantial input from that sector. And yet a search of the psychoanalytic literature with an eye on authority and leadership issues gives a surprisingly meagre trawl: some Freud (1921), no Klein, the expected Bion, Jaques, Menzies Lyth and Money Kyrle (see Bion, 1961, 1962a, 1967, 1977, 1980, 1984; Jaques, 1948, 1951, 1953, 1965; Menzies-Lyth, 1979, 1983, 1990; Money Kyrle, 1978), but little else. Hinshelwood (1989) in his dictionary of Kleinian thought makes no mention thereof.

The Tavistock Institute of Human Relations' writings add the riches of the Leicester Conferences and of some consultancy (see Lawrence, 1977; Miller and Rice, 1967). So do some other psychoanalytically oriented consultants. The above picture is, however, misleading, for it leaves out a wealth of ideas that I believe are essential to an understanding of authority and leadership issues by addressing them under the umbrella of different terms and concepts, for example, the development of the inner world, identity, containment.

In my view, it is not possible to have a view of authority issues without that view considering the development of the individual's inner world; with the latter concept then goes the issue of the inter-relatedness of the various 'inner world' inhabitants and thus, by implication, matters of authority, both internal and external. To grasp the basic assumptions about authority and leadership as held in the 20th century, it is necessary to spell out the thinking behind the philosophy as it was applied (and to an extent is still so).

It would be fanciful to say that the individual is born with a genetically determined attitude to authority – but not that fanciful. There has been a school of thought that certain chromosomal abnormalities lead to an increased tendency to violence, and thus presumably to a certain attitude to authority. Be that as it may, there is no dispute about the fact that the baby comes into the world with a certain genetic/intrauterine disposition to the world, and that it is this disposition that provides the baseline for the interaction between the baby and its world.

The baby/mother interaction leads by processes of projective and introjective identification to the creation of an inner world in the baby, based on its experience of being 'contained' by the mother. The Bion (1967) concept of container and contained are crucial at this stage of development.

Bion likens the process of 'containment' to the early interactions of a baby and mother. The baby experiences a state of distress or ill being while not being clear what the problem is – merely the fact that there is a problem. The mother recognises that the baby has a problem without being clear what it is – she does, however, by and large have a greater capacity to embark on the process of dealing with the problem and working towards a joint resolution of the difficulty. In this model, the mother is the container, the distress the contained. This model, in my view, has a key application in understanding organisations. Other versions of the above model might be a container that does not have the capacity to contain, and even one that acts as an 'echo chamber' aggravating the problem.

How 'containing' the style of the leader and how given to blaming others when things go wrong (paranoid/schizoid position) versus acknowledging one's or one's institution's contribution towards the trouble one is in (depressive position) depends to a very large degree on the individual's capacity to maintain a relatively mature stance as opposed to falling into a defensive/paranoid one, and this capacity is based on early experiences and their later reworking as the life cycle progresses.

The underlying assumption of this aspect of psychoanalytic theory is that you cannot 'contain', in Bion's sense, the inevitable disturbances associated with an authority-cum-leadership role, unless you yourself have not only been 'contained' in your own development, but also that you have identified with your 'container' and by a process of introjective identification made the process a part of your inner life. This facility is then available to you as a psychic tool when you are called on, in turn, to act as a container as part of your authority and leadership role.

It is assumed that the nature and style, possibly the gender flavour of this function, will be affected by your personal experiences as you build up this capacity within yourself, but it is not assumed that it will take the form of a concrete one-to-one link.

Freud's views on authority were very much linked with male-female stereotypes – a hundred years on these stereotypes have been replaced with expertise in the states of mind, which might arise in one as one gets to function under the pressure arising from institutional roles.

It is interesting to note that the essential feature of this idea of containment is 'good enough' communication. Winnicott (1971) describing this process spoke of 'the nursing couple' and the activity they were engaged in as 'primary maternal preoccupation'. Bion called it 'containment' and 'reverie'. They all have in common intense connectedness and communication at a face-to-face level. It is perhaps worth keeping this in mind when we consider the complex 'communication cascades' and other clichés that we are presented with in large organisations nowadays.

The entire emphasis of the container/contained process is on the capacity to listen, to take in and to react in response. In child development, not listening gives the child a picture of the world of being on her/his own, and of there being no supporting resources, which might be drawn on. A container that is so full of anxiety that it is not capable of taking in and metabolising the child's anxiety, and instead spills its own anxiety into the child, is equally ineffective as a psychological growth medium for the child.

The above describes non-listening, non-communicating exchanges, which of course not only happen in mother/child relationships, but also happen endemically in institutions and in the workplace, where not being heard or understood is a complaint of management and workers alike. It would be going too far to say that unless a manager has had a good experience of containment as an infant, he/she cannot develop an effective managerial style – it is, however, quite reasonable to ascertain that the capacity to communicate easily comes more naturally to some than to others, and that whatever the training and however good the institutional system, such differences will show. And the manager's capacity to 'contain' institutional issues depends not only on the above-mentioned developmental experiences, but also on the present-day situation of the manager in their organisation. Some organisations and their structures are clearly more supportive and containing of managers than others, and this is likely to show by an effect on the entire organisation.

Bick (1987), a Kleinian psychoanalyst at the Institute of Psychoanalysis in London, and founder of the child psychotherapy training unit at the Tavistock Clinic, London, was the first to introduce infant observation as a key training component in the training of therapists. She also introduced the concept of the skin as a psychic boundary of the individual and spoke of the development of the individual personality from a two-dimensional to a three-dimensional format. These concepts, vital to the development of the inner world, are of course essential in later life organisational roles, for without concepts of boundary and therefore of role definition, it would be hard to manage any effective institutional participation.

I believe that there are also forerunners to one's capacity to operate and deal with various types of management structures in early life. R.S. Britton has written about what he calls the 'Oedipal situation' and how these early experiences influence individuals' later capacity or incapacity to relate to social structures. Whether the organisation one finds oneself in later life has a flat or a pyramidal structure, and how one lives within such a system, has its counterparts in early life, because pyramidal structures have as their psychic forerunner child/parent(s)/family structures, whereas flatter structures presumably draw on one's relationship with siblings, increasingly with step-siblings in reconstituted families, and certainly in peer group relationships. Jealousy, essentially a three-person emotion, and envy, a two-person one, are seldom written about as applied to institutional function, as opposed to in personal life, yet it must be obvious to any observer of institutional life that envious attacks on colleagues are an everyday phenomenon and that the 'bite' of envy, the spoiling attack, can extract a heavy price when it comes to institutional functioning.

Klein (1959) described the paranoid/schizoid position with the accompanying process of projective identification as an early, normal, at times lifesaving psychological process. With time, the individual moves along the developmental spectrum to the depressive position, but never to the extent of having 'achieved' any position once and for all.

In the paranoid/schizoid position, the state of mind is essentially one of splitting and projective identification. The fault lies elsewhere – clearly so – blamelessness and righteousness rest with oneself. Negative elements of self are seen, often with crystal clarity, in others by a process of projective identification. The downsides of this mechanism of functioning are as follows. First, because of the forceful evacuation of one's own 'blame', one is at risk of harvesting an emotional ricochet effect and seeing others blame and persecute one. More important is the issue that if all blame lies outside of oneself, then one does not have to change oneself – all change needs to happen 'out there'; hence, learning from experience is very difficult, if not impossible. With this state of mind, be it managerial or institutional, it is not hard to see that any organisation suffused with this state is seriously risking its future.

The depressive position is more integrated. There is more reflection and less blame, and the emphasis is on the contribution one makes oneself towards the position one finds oneself in. In my view, Klein's concepts are very useful in understanding the nature of the functioning – the state of mind – of the organisation, how it views its difficulties and what routes it follows to address its difficulties.

It remained, however, to Bion to postulate a link between individual inner-world phenomena and group phenomena of a primitive nature – what he called basic assumption groups. He differentiates between work groups, which are task-oriented, and basic assumption groups, which are fundamentally off-task and in the grip of unconscious group processes. Bion describes a process he calls valency, and though he himself does not make the above-mentioned link, it is there by implication, for valency is about the individual's personal vulnerability to one or other of the basic assumption group processes which Bion describes. Valency is thus a linking concept between personal 'inner world' make-up and particular personal susceptibility to a group process, and a 'destruction of work' one at that.

On leadership

As mentioned previously, the concept of leadership as such has hardly occupied psychoanalysts at all, and thus features only marginally in the psychoanalytic literature. But it would be a mistake to draw the conclusion from this that psychoanalysis has no contribution to make to a discussion of leadership qualities and issues. Viewed from a psychoanalytic perspective, the concept of envy, so important in clinical work, is equally important in looking at leadership issues. It is a key quality of leadership that the leader encourages and brings to fruition the productive qualities of staff in the organisation.

Such positive qualities in others are of course the qualities that risk stirring up envy in the leader. The resultant envy, while not often causing overt envious attacks on the members concerned, nevertheless often takes the form of blocking, bureaucratic, non-facilitating responses to creative ideas that at heart are envious attacks by the leader on the creativity of the followers.

The leader's capacity to recognise and contain such envious feelings, and the capacity to desist from envious attacks and facilitating creativity instead, is a most important quality, for it is after all the capacity of an organisation to foster its members' creativity that is more important than any other quality in ensuring its ongoing functioning and ultimate survival.

The leader therefore needs to have the capacity to recognise that others, perhaps many others, are 'better' than him or her, and to continue to create the climate for such qualities to flourish. The effective leader thus shows his or her qualities by encouraging others to 'overtake' him or her in a creative sense, while retaining the capacity to manage the organisation as a nourishing matrix.

A further aspect of the leader mismanaging institutional development on account of envy is a withholding of approval for the enviable achievements arrived at by members of the organisation. Such behaviour has the effect of stealing the acknowledgement due to good achievement and is a form of envious attack on creativity.

The reverse side of envy also holds true, namely that the leader needs to conduct him or herself in such a way as to minimise the envy created in others. As Joseph (1993) makes clear in her paper on envy, a little envy can act as a stimulant, a 'nudge' in the direction of emulation. More than that elicits destructive attacks on the leader, and thus on the overall well-being of the organisation.

The leader's capacity to bear the institutional 'transference' appropriate to the role, without being carried away by it, is from a psychoanalytic perspective an equally important capacity. By this, I mean that the leader needs to be aware of the projections that he/she has to carry on behalf of the membership, and be aware of the risks to the leader, and thus to the institution, of such processes. The story of Holofernes in the Apocrypha is an excellent example of the risks involved. The entire tale is made up of an idealisation of Holofernes and his leadership – hubris abounds. When Judith appears with Holofernes' severed head, his entire army takes flight. As Freud says (1921), it was as if all Holofernes' men themselves had lost their heads and fled, and so of course it was, as the entire 'head' element of all his troops had been projected into Holofernes. No doubt, while it

lasted, Holofernes felt omnipotent, but the effect on his cause was ultimately catastrophic.

The leader therefore needs to be aware not only that aspects of the institutional whole are being projected into him/her, but also must consider
what they are and the risks to all concerned in the institution.

A further effect of this process is the risk of charismatic leadership
leading to a 'successor vacuum', a process contributed to, not only by
the above-mentioned group projective processes, but also by envious attacks on successors. The Sultans of Istanbul, on taking over the Sultanate,
would have all the rival princes put to death – in subtler ways, this process still takes place in many a poorly managed organisation.

The authority of the leader is thus not exclusive and, in exercising the
authority arising from the role, the leader should not reduce the authority
of others; sharing in the risks of the joint work enterprise is also a process
that makes for a more depressive position in institutional functioning.

The above summary of the accepted thinking in a large sector of the
leadership/authority field just about got away with that way of going
ahead with one's business. It needs to be acknowledged that there have
been and still are other approaches in the field mostly in the business
school and philosophy sectors of the work. But the major sector and its
principles is rooted in the approach described above.

The problem nowadays is that this approach no longer works and that
there is now an urgent need to 'mend one's ways' or else drown. How
has this come about? While the above-described approach more or less
worked in unaltered society, the whole global environmental climate has
changed. There are still some star dinosaurs of managerial thinking that
continue to peddle the traditional snake oil, but it is clear to most in the
field that it no longer serves its purpose.

Leaders of old based themselves on idealisation, narcissism and hubris.
It worked because few followers or employees ran the risk of calling it 'as
it is'. The story of the emperors' new clothes or the fate of Enron, Parmalat
and others reveals only too clearly what happens if the truth is revealed.

There was a time when leaders were in possession of facts and resources
that only they controlled, and this gave them immense power in the
organisation. Furthermore, they surrounded themselves with a cohort of
dependents whose position hung entirely on the 'goodwill' of the leader.
Any 'calling' of the facts then led either to riots and revolution or else an
attempt to bridge the process of transition from tyrant to democracy. The
problem was and is that any potential acceptable replacement leaders will
have been 'dealt with' by assassination, imprisonment or other means so
there were no agreed acceptable candidates to take over.

In politics, the technique for dealing with this dilemma is for the leader to be 'hospitalised', thus alive but absent and might return at any moment to act out revenge at treachery. Note how long Salazar, Franco and Stalin, for example, lay in hospitalised 'coma' states till it was relatively safe to acknowledge their 'passing on' (death). The 'coma' period was used to work at finding an acceptable transition.

The Leadership/Authority climate nowadays has completely changed with the arrival of electronic communication in which every kind of news is available at the same time as it reaches the leader and his/her authority base. The source of their power is thus chopped off at the knees and it is there for all the public or the employees to see.

Estate agents sometimes get it right. The latest ads read 'It is not an estate agent you need – It's a partner in property'. The same applies in the Leadership field. It is not a narcissist, the omnipotent singleton leader you need – you need a 'partner in leadership'.

How is this to be achieved? By openness as a state of mind in the entire organisation – not only in the executive dining room. By allowing followership an important role – including the followership sometimes taking leadership roles and for leaders to experience its reality of followership in the organisation. A day spent in servicing the toilets or reception might be a lot more useful in understanding and leading the organisation than an in-depth report from a global consulting firm.

But more important than this is the inevitable shift from a pyramid structure of leadership to a flatter one in which leadership is a group event even though the chairing of such an event is important to avoid the risk of 'basic assumption' group behaviour as detailed elsewhere in this book.

It has also in the past and still in the present been a practice to form a collusive management cabal, for example, in the appointment of remuneration committees or of all male management executives. While lip service is nowadays fulsomely expressed in the move for change, the existing group members fight tooth and nail to retain their present privileges.

It is interesting to note that while after the Second World War the Allied Powers insisted on much more 'open' management systems in Germany, they did not apply the same 'medicine' to their own industries.

Looking ahead, it is inevitable that a more open approach to management and leadership will 'chip away' at some of the more noxious leadership and management practices, but resistance to change in 'the establishment' is strong and empty promises of change need to be seen for what they are.

The time has come for the attitude of 'something needs to be done' without spelling out what and by whom and when is over. Central to keeping up the momentum of change for the present century is what can I do, in whatever role I am in, to put my shoulder to the wheel of change?

Grint (2020) wrote that the COVID-19 pandemic that swept through the world in late 2019 through 2022 and beyond provides a test not just for all societies and their leadership, but for leadership theory. In a world turned upside down, when many conventions are disposed of, it became clear that things will not return to the status quo ante any time soon, if ever. Grint went on to suggest we might reconsider the way governments and their leaders act against the frame of societal problems, originally established by Rittell and Webber in 1973. Grint suggested that all three modes of decision-making (leadership, management and command) are necessary because of the complex and complicated nature of the problem and concluded that while command is appropriate for certain times and issues, it also poses long-term threats, especially if the context is ignored.

According to Grint (2020), the arrival of COVID-19 has turned the world upside down for many of us, and when it stabilises, it will not be exactly as it was, though what it might look like is not determined by events unfolding before us. The pandemic has exposed the limits of market-based economic and health systems but also threatens to engulf even the most egalitarian societies. And in times of crisis, it appears that many of us seek out charismatic leaders or authoritarians, who can, allegedly, defeat the virus just by remaining positive or simply by denying the evidence, confusing as that is.

Grint (2020) makes a persuasive case that if leadership is partly about making people face up to unfortunate truths – and it surely is – then we need leadership that embodies this, at the same time as we manage the research and resources to keep the systems going. Of course, we also need commanders when and where necessary, but all these decision modes need to be contextualised and deployed carefully. And we need to be especially wary of commanders who seek to persuade us that 'the situation' – which they cannot reveal for fear of frightening us further – is so dire that they need to continue the state of emergency, 'for our own safety'. Otherwise, as Winston Smith persuades himself in Orwell's *1984*, he was previously an enemy of the people, but now he does, after all, 'love Big Brother'.

We can see that the managerial paradigm for modern organisations will need to change because of the recent COVID-19 disruptions and the widespread adoption of digital technology. Managers will increasingly lead hybrid teams with people working remotely from different locations. This will require new leadership approaches and styles that effectively support individuals to achieve/exceed organisational goals. It is time to revisit management and leadership theories to redefine organisational management perspectives and future management research areas. The importance of paying attention to under the surface dynamics will be ever more important but inevitably more taxing via digital technology. The technology while very helpful in communicating facts and figures poses real problems in paying attention to human dynamics and emotion.

Leadership in change: denial, salvation and adaptation

By Jonathan Gosling

Change is not so special

Societies have often faced extremes of anxiety – there is nothing unprecedented about the sudden onset of life-threatening, systems-shaking shocks from invasion, colonisation, famine and plague. Societies also live with profoundly corrosive illnesses affecting huge numbers of people (around 400,000 people die of malaria every year, many are much-loved children under 5).

Organisations are not so different. Although leaders are often lauded for an ability to create change, this is mostly hyperbole: disruptive change is inherent in our natural environment because of global heating and in our economies because global financial markets demand increasing returns on capital, achievable only by constant innovation and intense exploitation. Writing in 1844, Marx and Engels (1844) foresaw the effects on society and its institutions:

> The bourgeoisie cannot exist without constantly revolutionizing the instruments of production, and with them the relations of production, and with them all the relations of society ...... Constant revolutionizing of production, uninterrupted disturbance of all social relations, everlasting uncertainty and agitation, distinguish the bourgeois epoch from all earlier ones ....

In the face of this relentless onslaught of change, no wonder that often people want leaders who will resist; conserve the status quo or – most appropriately – adjust and re-position to better meet constantly evolving challenges. Sometimes 'adjustment' upsets vested interests and established privileges; sometimes, it intensifies existing inequalities. In either case, it can be hard-fought and contentious, so it certainly feels as if leadership is important on all sides.

This is one reason that organisational change programmes are so often described as if they have a clear beginning, middle and end (metaphorically described as 'unfreeze-change-refreeze' (Lewin, 1947)). The myth of a settled state just the other side of a meltdown is meant to be reassuring and follows the narrative form of an action movie, which lays out the inevitability of conflict rising to a crisis before a denouement and closing settlement. In reality, organisational life is more plural and complex – less like an action movie than a soap opera, with multiple plotlines, deferred climaxes and no end in sight! But theories of change are not meant to describe what is happening; rather, they provide a sense of continuity and reassurance. A narrative of change that is linear, progressive and time-limited is one way of containing the incipient anxiety that might erupt as organised relations are 'unfrozen'.

So, to conclude this section, the work of leadership is as much concerned with continuity as with change.

Leadership in anxiety-provoking circumstances

Facing challenges to the status quo, some leaders tend towards 'more of the same', deepening their commitment to existing ways of organising. They act according to virtues that are admired and valued in that culture, even amidst the collapse of conditions in which these virtues are effective. To take a simple example, an organisational culture may admire and promote the knowledge and courage required for exploring wild countryside and oceans in search of minerals or oil. But these become irrelevant when satellites and drones can do the job more accurately, quickly and economically. The basis of legitimate authority, once self-evident, shifts from explorers to geeks.

Similarly, health systems institutionalise expertise and status in certain ways, subtly and without explicitly intending to do so, embedding inequalities along professional, gender and ethnic lines. Change tends to be slow, though pandemics, budgets and innovation are among the forces that shove and squeeze the status quo to adapt.

On the whole, societies find resilience to existential crises if they already have a diversity of organising modes and cultures. Organising modes include, *inter alia*, authority exercised vertically, such as through leadership, management and coercion, and horizontally, such as in collaboration, peer-pressure and self-authority (Alvesson and Blom, 2019). Diverse organising cultures include a mix of hierarchies, collectives, enterprising individuals and critics who analyse and make suggestions from the side-lines.

Nonetheless, even in the most pluralistic and resilient societies, uncertainty about immanent infection, invasion, famine and collapse prompts emotional responses. Some of these tend to open-heartedness and unselfishness, but others undermine the ability to trust others, tolerate differences, recognise new realities, reassess values and change behaviours. Leadership can easily promote these less-helpful responses, as if the work that people require of their leaders is to deny the reality of the situation or to save them from it. With care and thoughtfulness, a third kind of leadership may emerge: leadership of adaptation. These three may be summarised as follows:

Leadership of denial, can be intentional, but many unconscious acts demonstrate (and represent for followers) a deep-seated wish for it 'not to be so'.

(a) Denying that there is a problem. In the COVID-19 pandemic of 2020, President Trump denied its potency. The Chief Medical Officer of Scotland unconsciously acted-out denial when she drove miles to visit a holiday home on the same day that she announced the lockdown.

(b) Admit there is a problem but hijack the anger and grief and project it towards hatred and despair (Eisenstein, 2020). Hence, the proliferation of conspiracy theories is usually associated with right-wing political movements mobilising typical leadership tactics of visionary simplification, charismatic aesthetics, adolescent machismo, and threatened or actual violence.

(c) Despair is less tangibly 'led' but is expressed in widespread depression.

Leadership of salvation – Many people are motivated to take up leadership because they hope to rescue the situation (or at least their colleagues). The desire for salvation is manifest in the way we invest hope in instant vaccines, colonising space, imagined technologies and the miraculous effects of mindfulness and prayer.

Leadership of salvation is likely to have a religious or apocalyptic character because its energy derives from the intuition that there is another reality, less complex and dirty than this, just behind a veil of misunderstanding and ignorance. It can also make use of professional mystique – the scientists have it in hand, the algorithms will give us warning, the economists have a model. One tangible source of salvation from COVID-19-angst is the physical exercise guru Joe Wicks, followed online by millions in the UK, and I imagine there are equivalents in every country. The psychological wellness is undeniable: not all salvation is delusional (at least in the short term).

Leadership of adaptation is diverse and sometimes hardly recognisable as leadership. It may be found in countercultural experiments, in some protest and some policing, and often persistent and undemonstrative in the sustaining institutions of society (schools, churches, professions etc.). It helps us reconcile with the situation, measure the appreciation of risks, grieve when we suffer loss, weigh discretion when our options seem narrowed, and choose pragmatic and courageous change.

In an influential paper on 'deep adaptation' to the possibility of societal collapse, Jem Bendel (2018) outlines '4 Rs', which constitute a neat summary of the kinds of work to which leaders could contribute:

1 Resilience, through stewardship of psychological, cultural, natural and material resources
2 Relinquish habits and possessions that can no longer be sustained
3 Restore trust, confidence, shared values and other social goods

4 Reconcile with those who we have fallen out with, in recognition of our interdependence and that life is much enhanced by amity and good will

With this job description, leadership of adaptation is likely to be distributed through the community, much of it 'close-up and personal'. But we can also look to political, media and business leaders to light the way in this regard. At the time of writing New Zealand premier Jacinda Ardern is a positive example, Boris Johnson sadly not so. For an analysis of his failings in this regard, see Tomkins (2020) 'Where is Boris Johnson? When and why it matters that leaders show up in a crisis' in Leadership'.

In practice, the leadership of denial, salvation and adaptation are seldom so clearly separated. The urge to deny a problem exists alongside a wish to be saved from it. Even leaders committed to adaptation find themselves called on to offer reassurances and hope of salvation. So what we might call 'the politics of adaptation' involves a complex of conscious and unconscious dynamics, often contradictory – akin to thoughts such as 'I know death is unavoidable and I want to be saved from it'.

But sometimes it really is that clear-cut. There are prominent leaders today – as everyday – who unashamedly act out the impulses of denial and the fantasy of salvation with no perceptible capacity to lead the work of adaptation. It is incumbent on theorists of 'change and continuity' to call it out, and also to ensure our leadership education and development is attuned to the work of adaptation. This crisis is just the beginning – we should prepare!

Adapted from a blog originally published in *Leadership for the Greater Good: Reflections on the 2020 Pandemic*, published by the International Leadership Association (www.ila-net.org)

Summary

When boundaries are poorly designed and managed, they cause a great amount of stress and anxiety.

The task of leadership is located on the boundary between the organisation and the external environment. At the boundary, the leader integrates the mission with the means for accomplishing it, weaving the means and ends to articulate realistic achievement of the mission. Organisational leadership relates means and ends and has both a strategic and operational perspective. By standing at the boundary, leaders create a controllable environment in which the activities within the boundary are organised and can be coordinated to respond to changes.

Leadership relates to the pursuit of the organisation's aims and primary task. By monitoring the primary task, leadership avoids abuse of power, maintains on-task leadership and minimises the occurrence and spread of basic assumption activity in the organisation. The relationship between leaders and followers depends on the leader's capacity to manage the relationships between the internal and external environments so that followers can perform their primary task. The task of leadership is to manage relationships with other sub-systems and with the whole.

Leadership is the result of the personal predispositions, qualities and attributes of the individual occupying positions of authority. Leadership is defined as the part of executive action directly attributed to the person exercising authority, and more specifically to the projection of deep-seated elements of their personality. It is impossible to separate the leader from the person – leaders bring their person (themselves) to the role and invest their role with their own affects. Recognising and dealing with one's own feelings can be anxiety-provoking. The exercise of leadership can activate or re-activate primitive fantasies that lie at the core of cognitive and motivational activity.

Systems psychodynamics approaches to leadership focus on the dynamics of human behaviour, which are often the most difficult to understand because people are complex, unique and paradoxical beings with a mix of drivers, and decision-making and interaction patterns. Applying systems psychodynamics concepts to organisational life contributes to our understanding of the vicissitudes of leadership. Through accepting and exploring the hidden undercurrents of human behaviour, we can begin to understand organisational life in all its complexities. The systems psychodynamics lens addresses the undercurrents of organisational life through inter-personal communication; group processes; social defences and the organisation-in-the-mind. The systems psychodynamics approach focuses on personal insight on the part of the leader and follower; creates reflective practitioners; and focuses on in-depth and systemic investigation of a single person, group, event, community or network. It emphasises the relationship between leader and follower by focusing on the underlying drivers of each and what accounts for the type of relationship between them. Leaders internalise the ability to learn, work and reflect within the psychological realm to improve their organisational relationships and team performance.

Exercise

1 What 'valency' do you think you have (personal characteristics) that get mobilised by groups when you are in a leadership role?
2 Describe the extent to which this 'valency' is on-task or off-task.
3 What is your view on your leadership valency as 'preserving' or 'changing' the status quo?
4 Describe a situation from your leadership role where you had to contain the anxieties of your team/organisation
5 What feelings were evoked in you?

Chapter 12

Social dreaming

David Lawlor and Mannie Sher With Susan Long and David Armstrong

Background

Armstrong (2019) describes social dreaming, as pioneered and developed by Gordon Lawrence and his colleagues, is, to put simply, a practice of sharing and working with dreams within a social space. Since the first experiment, launched by Gordon Lawrence and Paddy Daniel at the Tavistock Clinic in 1982, while practice has continued to evolve and develop, there have been a small number of constants, which may be taken as guiding principles that serve to define the field and its boundaries. These concern respectively the parameters of task, process, setting, management and leadership.

From the outset, the setting in which social dreaming takes place was called a 'matrix', not a 'group'. Suggested initially by Paddy Daniel, Gordon Lawrence was later to write how 'we thought that to call it a "social dreaming group" would elicit the dynamics and transferences familiar to us in group relations settings and might cut across and intrude into the work of transacting dreams and exploring the multiple 'dreams in association'. In short, our fantasy or working hypothesis was that dreams would speak with dreams: breeding, growing and developing new thoughts and new thinking, beyond either the more subjective focus of individual therapy (what does the dream mean for me?) or the more group-centred focus of group relations events (what does the dream mean for the group?)' (Lawrence, 2011, unpublished).

Social dreaming is a pioneering methodology that addresses the unthought and unconscious dimensions of the social world. Social dreaming makes possible the examination of the social unconscious, which comes into existence when people come together and relate to each other through their individual dreams on the basis that dreams reflect the unconscious (Westen, 1999). A new view of dreaming was developed by focusing on thoughts and knowledge in the dream. Using free association, a thought contained in a dream could be expanded, and through amplification, the thoughts in the dream can be related to phenomena beyond the individual – the culture of an organisation, community or society.

The meaning contained in dreams emerges through the shared efforts by the participants. Dreaming is usually perceived as an individual activity and

DOI: 10.4324/9781003368663-17

preoccupation, but it is a process that can be used for developing social, as distinct from personal, meaning. Biblical dreams, for instance, are usually interpreted as prophetic references to events in society.

Social dreaming sheds light on social and organisational shadows

Social dreaming assumes that we dream not just for ourselves, but as part of the larger context in which we live. This perspective regards dreams as more than the private possession of the dreamer, but as also relevant to social reality. Society is grappling with a greater sense of uncertainty and challenge after a year of COVID-19; elections in two of the world's largest democracies, galloping climate change and the restructuring of organisations in the economic downturn and the resulting dislocation and disorder in society. The theory of social dreaming considers that dreams tell us about the nature of our organisations and the national, cultural and social contexts in which we work. The matrix provides a different kind of container for the dream than that used conventionally and shifts the focus from the dreamer to the dream itself, thus allowing the possibility of an exploration of these wider contexts and their meanings. Social dreaming incorporates dreams, metaphors and myths to help us gain a deeper understanding of what is left obscure in our work, organisations, communities and societies.

The primary task of social dreaming is to associate with one's own and participants' dreams, which are made available to the matrix (group) to make links and find connections between private thought and social meaning. It is not necessary to bring a dream to take part. No previous experience or knowledge is necessary – people attend who wish to better understand the deeper dynamics of the self in relation to their social environments.

> *The task of social dreaming is to transform thinking through exploring dreams, using the methods of free association, amplification, and systemic thinking, so as to make links and find connections in the discovery of new thinking and thoughts.*
> *(Lawrence, 2004)*

A social dreaming matrix is a social science research-based practice that evolved out of the Tavistock tradition of working with groups. Participants in the consultant-facilitated events bring and share their overnight dreams into a group space to make wider associations with the current socio-political environment. In the process, they evolve new meaning and sense by making connections between their dreams (private thoughts) and the social context. Essentially, it is a transformative process of thoughts in the realm of the unconscious into new social meaning.

Social dreaming involves an interest in phenomenological aspects; the use of 'unbounded space', in which participants are free to come and go as they choose; a philosophy of working with a 'transient social dreaming population' (the matrix takes place regardless of how many/few individuals turn up); and a focus on participatory, action research approaches. Spaces for social dreaming are 'temporary and no single dream provides a definite statement, an answer to questions; it is the democratic sharing of a multitude of dreams that offers multiple insights into social phenomena. Social dreaming can be considered as the ultimate form of the democratic ideal' (Sher, 2019).

What are the aims and objectives of social dreaming?

The context of a social dreaming matrix, that is the frame in which the dreams are explored, is twofold: the matrix makes links with ongoing events and activities in the world on any given day such as the migration crisis, US presidential elections, Brexit, war in Ukraine, global warming. The social context informs the matrix events in their work towards:

1 The engagement of a wider public in the question of the social unconscious and in the processes of co-creating new thought in the 'here and now'
2 Drawing comparisons between dreams as memory and dreams as the surfacing of unprocessed thought or raw archival material and creating possibilities for the new
3 Experimenting with new ways of engaging with dream material, in keeping with Tavistock tradition and the ethos of action research.

Methodological considerations

When a dream is voiced in a social dreaming matrix, it becomes an object to be owned by all present, able to be freely associated with, to become an object that can be mentally played with by all the participants. It is important that the matrix is aware of this and recognises that social dreaming is not intended as a therapeutic analysis of dreams. Instead, dreams will be opened to provide broader reflections on societal hierarchies, anxieties and conditions.

Consultant/facilitator considerations

The facilitator role is to ensure the primary task is upheld and to hold/contain the work of the group, ensuring that dreamers are steered away from more personal interpretations of dreams. In practical terms, an example of how the facilitator might do this is to reframe and redirect a participant; so in response to a dreamer asking, 'What does the dream say about me?' the facilitator refocuses: 'what does the dream say about society?' (Sher, 2013). Facilitators will be experienced in working experientially with groups; vulnerable people and working with and supporting diversity.

Information/consent considerations

Each session will be clearly framed by the lead facilitator with opening state-ments inviting participants to share their dreams and make associations (rather than interpretations) between their dream imagery and the social context of the group.

Reflections from each of the social dreaming matrices will be made avail-able for further comment and association to build on the work of the group and subsequent groups. Examples of how these reflections will be shared and anonymised can be found on the Tent City Social Dreaming blog (https://socialdreamingeventstentcityuniversity.wordpress.com/); in short, reflections will focus on the dream imagery and stories, with consideration of how these link to external events, for example the Tavistock Institute archive project (http://tihr-archive.tavinstitute.org/the-archive/)

By framing the event, providing context and anonymising dream data, we ensure the event tackles ethical issues appropriately. In practical terms, this will be facilitated through information provided at the start and end of the group; a dedicated member of staff who makes sure that all participants have received all the relevant information; and an invitation for participants to contribute to ongoing discussions arising on the blog.

Interventions: social dreaming

While consulting to the board of a Rural Development Authority, an offer to host a social dreaming matrix was eagerly accepted because the board of 9 members felt stuck; their discussions were circular; and there was more disagreement in the board than willingness to resolve issues. Indeed, some issues seemed to be insurmountable – the decline of village life as the young abandon the countryside and as the lives of rural dwell-ers become more distracted, transient, isolated and lonely. The board, made up mostly of city dwellers, seemed to be 'carrying something' that did not belong to it, which they could not understand. Lethargy and low morale characterised its mood.

A social dreaming matrix lasts about 45 minutes, in which the par-ticipants share night dreams as a way of finding possible connections between the board's overt work task for which it is responsible, the pres-ence of concealed thoughts, beliefs, ideas and feelings, which may conflict with the board's task and the surrounding social and stakeholder context. The matrix is followed by a 15- to 20-minute review of the matrix to discuss the participants' experiences in it, what was 'released' by it, what was learned and how the learning could help the board get on with its business.

During the review, a participant, Allan, remarks excitedly what a wonderful matrix that was. He said he had had a visceral reaction to the dreams that were presented because, in his view, they pointed to what the board was neglecting – listening to the views of the people in the rural communities. By focusing primarily on 'development and change', the board, it seemed to him, had 'sold its soul', had lost its way. Allan pointed to the relevance of two dreams in the matrix – the first one where the dreamer is in a car sitting in the back seat. The driver of the car is dead; the dreamer jumps out of the car and tries to take control, but he cannot reach the controls in time. Meanwhile, other cars are whizzing by. In the second dream, the dreamer is trying to take control of a bus while sitting upstairs.

Another member of the board, Berenice, reminds the board of their current social context, viz. that the country has just gone through a referendum that voted to take the country out of the EU, giving expression to feelings of disaffection of being controlled by others and lacking control over themselves and their lives. The result of the referendum had been a shock to many people, and Berenice says that she thinks control is an illusion and that we as a board should not delude ourselves about the level of control we have over the Rural Development Authority. We, the board, she continued, still have difficulty seeing a clear direction and knowing what to do. The board members think about this for a while and the possible connection to the dreams. After a moment, Colin, who represents business associations in the development authority, says that perhaps the board does not see the situation in the same way as its constituent members and therefore more research work must be done. Perhaps, Colin suggests, that like the dreams, there are issues that our constituents are grappling with that we do not see; we do not understand how our decisions may impact on them. Many businesses and farmers are dogged by illness, absence and death, and these life events affect the commitments of this rural community – life (like the cars in the dream) is passing them by while they struggle with the viability of their enterprises. These factors include the younger generation who choose to leave the rural life instead of succeeding their parents. It is all very well for the board to encourage new businesses, but what if there are too few people to run them? Our efforts at sustainability are undermined at the first hurdle. The board had introduced new ideas for self-sustaining energy supplies, but meetings with members of the community were poorly attended, and it was difficult to raise enthusiasm for the project.

John reminded the board during the Review of the dream in which the dreamer described being chased by Nazis while he was taking the rubbish out, doing two things at once – dodging the soldiers while dragging the rubbish. The dreamer had thought it was not so bad for the rubbish not to be collected for one week, but if it went uncollected for longer, he would be overwhelmed by the rubbish. On the other hand, John went on, 'rubbish' has a social element – creating hills of rubbish that blight the land elsewhere. The discussion went on to associate 'Nazis' with 'nasties', and the board referred to its role of managing change in the Rural Development Authority to prevent the 'nasties' from coming out. Another member of the board, Peter, shared an association that he had been travelling on a train with his back towards the direction of travel and it did not bother him, but it does bother him that the board may be facing the wrong direction; that the 'rubbish', that is the difficult feelings in the board that keep it stuck, may be suppressed while they focus so centrally on planning and management, without thinking about the consequences for the communities. It seemed clear, Peter said, that the dreams directly link to the realities of the board's experiences; they are not illusions; we should not regard our dreams as a waste of time or 'rubbish'. We must deal with our 'rubbish', not shift it elsewhere. Our communities are withdrawing from our projects, and they do not agree to participate in them. The board would have to reconsider how it relates to and intervenes in the rural communities. We have become the 'nasties' for them, and the communities want to have the 'rubbish' board removed.

Emily said she felt sad that we cannot work well together with the communities. How can we help the communities connect well to the outside world without disrupting traditional attitudes and ways of relating? Perhaps, Allan said, we should stop regarding the community leaders as 'nasties', which we do because of their conservative views, which we have regarded as 'rubbish' and engage more constructively with them by asking what they would like for themselves, by respecting their views and way of life?

The board is disturbed by Allan's comments and questions, and it falls into a reflective silence. His questions seem to have uncorked critical thoughts about itself and the board's conduct in relation to the communities they serve. The board turned to a discussion about how it is carrying out its role without fully considering the emotional and sentient needs of the communities it purports to lead. Fundamental questions are raised about the arrogance of the board and its belief that it knows what is best for others, a position that actually precludes listening well to the views of the communities, being in 'driving' or 'delivery' mode before fully grasping the core issues of identity, history, tradition and dynamics of rural communities who in their own ways over generations have developed strategies for coping with change.

The board felt chastened; the dreams of the board had revealed an elitist streak, believing that the communities they were helping simply did not know what was good for them; it led to the board 'flogging a dead horse'. The board concluded that it had got itself sucked into a bog; its good intentions had not really been authorised by the people on whose behalf they were making decisions. The board agreed it had adopted a task that did not in fact belong to it. There was no way the communities were going to allow the board to control them. Ideas about control that had developed in the board were illusory. The most painful piece of learning was that the system of communities had to fail for the communities themselves to become mobilised – movement just had to grow from within. The more the board pushed, the more it stimulated resistance and the more it was kept in an antagonistic relationship to the communities. The board needed to learn to 'invite' rather than 'tell'. By standing back somewhat, the board would be helping the communities 'own' their needs. By 'standing back', the board 'contains' the communities and it 'contains' its own anxieties to 'do things'. The board had learned that it had to be watchful about what it is invited into because of the unseen community dynamics and their ways of doing things.

Comment

This case is a good example of the mutual projective and introjective dynamic processes between the board and the communities they represent and on whose behalf they work. These dynamics are commonly found in all representational systems, and inter-group processes and consultants need to pay attention to and work with them; otherwise, the dynamic can be disruptive and potentially undermine the task and render the board ineffective, as this board felt.

Social dreaming: anticipations of the future

By Susan Long

Social dreaming is a method that has helped groups, organisations and societies to uncover their shared concerns. It gives a portal into the inner lives of participants. As a way of working, it was first created by Gordon Lawrence in the 1980s although he had been using the knowledge given by dreams long before that in his group relations work. I was lucky enough to be a participant in one of his study groups at Leicester in 1979 where members' dreams were recounted and aided in understanding the group's dynamics.

The method grew as Lawrence discovered that dreams belong to a collective social realm and are not simply the property of the individual who has the dream experience. Following Bion's (1967) idea that thoughts are part of the infinite unconscious while requiring thinkers to express and develop them, he used the social dreaming matrix to, as it were, to capture dreams to enable matrix members to associate with them and make connections between them (Lawrence, 1998, 2003, 2005, 2007, 2010). This is no ordinary group process. The matrix has participant members and a host or hosts. The structure is such that the participants and hosts do not face each other or sit in rows but sit in a format – Lawrence preferred a snowflake pattern that encourages an inner reflective stance. The dreams are spoken, and associations and connections are made. The hosts hold the boundaries of time and encourage the reflective task, themselves making connections when appropriate. When the matrix is worked by all and is working well, there is a deeply reflective, almost reverential space; not empty of emotion as in quiet meditation, the often-intense feeling aroused by the dreams is held in and between participants. Matrices are often followed by reflective discussions that work on sense-making and may be applied in a variety of ways depending on their context.

Having been part of social dreaming matrices since 1992, I have come to see it as one vehicle for accessing the associative unconscious – that network of ideas, signs and symbols collectively held by an interacting culture, not available in its entirety to any one person, only accessible through collaborative dialogue (Long and Harney, 2013). Hence, there is the need for groups, organisations and societies to bring forward such content for creative progression.

But humans are anticipatory beings (Rosen, 1985, 2010; Poli, 2017) meaning they have internal ideas and models for anticipating the future and have behaviours compatible with these. Moreover, the organisations within which they live hold anticipations alongside memories and current pre-occupations in their associative unconscious (Long and Harney 2016). Dreams can give an indication of unconscious anticipations and of the culture that 'calls forward' the dreams of its members. It is rare that an organisation will pause ongoing activities to allow members to reflect on their work and far rarer for its members to find the space to pay attention to the dreams called forward. If we can allow spaces in our organisations to attend to our dreams and their anticipations, there is much to be learned that can inform thinking about the future.

Can we think of an organisation or even a society having a history, a current expression and an anticipation of a future built into its very structures and its culture? Just as it can be argued that political ideologies become built into institutions and political structures so that different groups become subjugate to others (see for example, Habermas, 1971; Zizek, 1989), so too it can be argued that ideologies and ideas in the culture have within them expectations and anticipations of the future: some that we might consider as ethical, creative and progressive; some as destructive, divisive and regressive.

The anticipatory nature of dreams is an actualisation of the unconscious anticipations of dreamers. Following Grotstein's (2000) lead, we have the idea that such anticipations are called forth by an internal audience who require the dream as an indication of a disturbance or problem. In a system such as an organisation, the problem may be found in the latent associative unconscious of the system. It is 'as if' the system calls forth the dreams in order to understand itself and its potential. Because dreams come to individual members, their social meanings for the system can only be discerned through a process of sharing, associating and making connections to the experiences of members within the system and its context. Social dreaming as a process aids in the discovery of such system anticipations.

One social dreaming matrix began with 'not a dream, but someone calling out my name'. The matrix was part of a writing retreat where participants gathered to progress a piece of their own writing with the help of some educational workshops, individual supervision sessions, and peer support and sharing. The participants came to the retreat for different reasons: some to progress academic essays, articles or books; others to write novels or poetry. Living, writing, eating and sleeping under the same roof quickly built a community.

The first workshop on day 1 emphasised the need to understand, discover and move into the role of author, and participants began the process of authorising each other in this role. It was as if this first night-time revelation of name calling was echoing the call into authorship or the call into the community that was emerging. The dreamer was unsure about the nature of the call. Was it a dream or not? For the dreamer, the boundary between the unconscious in the dream and reality was blurred; an experience of exposed liminality found in those moments between sleep and wakefulness; a timeless uncanny moment where distinctions between past, present and an anticipated future are not made (Fenichel, 2019). Did it bring the events of the day together with the anticipated future movement into a new role, into the present in the form of the call? At a communal level did it symbolise calling each into the role of author?

Dreams about the workplace are common. They may be dreams about fear of losing one's job; performance anxieties or fears about interpersonal relations, and all these may be experienced directly or tangentially through metaphor. But often the dreams are about tasks that have to be undertaken or problems that have to be solved. When a work team or organisation is able to use social dreaming methods to surface these dreams, new ways of working may be discovered. They may, for example, indicate that roles need attention or tasks need changing.

A team of hospital staff shared their dreams in a social dreaming matrix. Two dreams caught their attention.

The first was of a flock of birds that were confused. They were flying south rather than north. The flock leader looked injured and had lost a sense of direction and other birds simply flew off in a different direction. One swooped over the dreamer almost hitting them. The dreamer associated that she felt the flock was flying into the cold.

The second dream was of a woman undressing in public. It seemed natural to everyone around until she turned into a hairy creature from the waist up. People were then horrified and fled, rushing away so that they were trampling each other.

The associations with these dreams culminated in concern about the team leader – a woman who worked long hours but who found difficulty in delegating work to others because of what the team saw as her perfectionism. They felt their leader was confused about the direction the team should go in limiting or not, their specialisation. An association with the second dream was of a gorgon – a mythical creature whose stare could turn the viewer into stone. In the Dream Reflection Dialogue following the matrix, the team talked of their fears of facing the team leader with their concerns about her working hours and her concerns about delegating. They felt this would be seen as criticism and that she would not be able to contain her hurt feelings: she would feel trampled. They also expressed the wish not to injure her.

The dialogue opened a discussion about the future of the team and the need to re-design some roles. It allowed the team leader to open the discussion about their future ways of working. She admitted her perfectionist leanings but was able to hear the needs of other members to take on more responsibilities. The dreams of these team members were a starting point for re-visioning the future. It was as if the associative unconscious of the team called forth the dreams to avoid an anticipated unwanted future.

The future of the method of social dreaming in groups and organisations may be to discover the anticipations of their members as part of a research and risk assessment strategy. The importance of the method is that it combines the vagaries of the unconscious with reflective practices about workplace roles and problems. The future contains uncertainties, as well as repetition.

A portion of this piece is repeated, with permission, from Long, S. (2019). Dreaming a culture. Socio-Analysis, 21, 59–70.

The Authority of the Dream

David Armstrong

Paper presented at 'The Dreaming Consultant': In Memory of W. Gordon Lawrence, Israel, 11–12 December 2014

It is characteristic of innovators, as of their innovations, that they can make you re-think or re-question what you have hitherto taken for granted; ways of thinking and working that may extend beyond the boundaries of the innovation itself.

So, with Gordon Lawrence's innovations in and with social dreaming, one of its signal contributions in and to my experience has been how it has extended the ways I have found myself thinking about dreams and dreaming in a variety of practical contexts that lie somewhere between psychoanalysis and social dreaming 'proper'.

I want to start by sharing two particular experiences falling within this in-between space, what they seemed to generate and then circle back to social dreaming 'proper', linking both to post-Freudian and post-Kleinian developments in conceptualising the nature and function of the dream. I will suggest that these developments have significant implications for how we can understand and make use of social dreaming, its gains and, on occasion, its losses.

The experiences I want to share came out of one or other of two practices familiar, I imagine, to most of this audience: role consultation and group relations.

A dream remembered

In a paper written for the annual symposium of ISPSO in 2000, so not that long since I had first begun working with Gordon Lawrence, I had described a dream offered unexpectedly by a client a year or so in from a series of role consultations (Armstrong, 2005). I cannot recall now whether this was the first time that this or any other client had shared a dream in the course of a Role Consultation, though I suspect it was. And certainly, this was not something that hitherto I would have prompted or invited.

My client was the head of a large training college for young (and some older) adults in a deprived and disadvantaged inner city area. At the time I first started working with her, she had just taken over as Principal and was preoccupied with needing, as she saw it, to breathe new life into an institution, which in some respects appeared rather closed, embattled and under-managed. At the coal face, in the interactions between students and staff, there was exciting work being done, as good as she had seen anywhere else. But these interactions appeared privatised, uncoordinated, fragmented and fragmentary learning encounters. Staff and students inhabited, as it were, a series of dislocated boxes. There was little sense of corporate accountability, lax financial management and a certain lack of direction. At the same time and within a year, the college would be facing the challenge of a government-initiated transition to self-governing status and must stand or fall on its own in a much leaner environment.

For the first two years I worked with her, the main themes of the consultancy concerned my client's thoughts and plans for renewal. A highly imaginative and resourceful woman, she quickly moved to recruit a new governing body and to establish a network of political links with actual and potential stakeholders and other strategic allies from the local community, which was itself committed to 'regeneration'. Simultaneously, she began to evolve a highly original approach to setting in place a new organisational structure, while constantly maintaining a visible presence throughout the college as a strong and inspirational leader. New staff were recruited into senior positions, new posts created, new curricular initiatives introduced. There was a bolder mission statement, a sharper curriculum focus, new student and staff charters, and a clear sense of direction and purpose.

First Dream

Half-way through the third year, I became aware, as did she, of a sea change in her feelings. She was beginning to wonder about the future and being tempted with new opportunities elsewhere. On occasion, she appeared almost depressed, preoccupied with the tensions and differences she was feeling between those who still for her represented the old guard and the newcomers. Yet, all the evidence was that the place was flourishing. Opportunities for a new building were in the offing, exam results were encouraging, and the college was establishing something of a reputation, both locally and nationally.

I felt, a little dimly, that she was wrestling with things to do with her own relatedness to the college and vice versa. The 'sea change' in **her** was perhaps a reflection of and a response to a sea change in the college. There was also a parallel between this dynamic and the dynamic around her relation to her own daughter, who was on the threshold of puberty; a parallel she would sometimes bring into sessions as a kind of commentary or counterpart to her organisational experience.

Approaching her fourth year, towards the end of one session, she suddenly recalled a striking dream from some time back. In the dream, she had taken a baby, wrapped in a blanket, from a brick in a wall which she had dislodged, and she had to fly with the baby on a plane to Israel. All through the flight, the baby remained covered in the blanket. But when she had landed and unwrapped the blanket, the baby was not there: it had 'evaporated'.

I took this dream, as did my client (or rather we didn't so much take it, as at once sensed it) as having been recalled and offered, here and now, as a commentary from her unconscious on the situation my client was in, organisationally (also through the link to her daughter, familial) and which we were trying to understand.

From this perspective, the dream appeared to have an immediate transparency as a realisation of my client's current experience and dilemma as Principal. The blanketed baby, taken from a brick in the wall she had dislodged, could stand for the 'baby' she had given to the college from the gap in the wall opened by her appointment as Principal. (In the early days of the consultancy, she had described the college as a 'fortified castle' inhabited by 'robber barons', a kind of internal mafia). Israel was the land of promise the baby would inherit. So, what of the 'evaporated baby'? This image could give expression to a reality she both sensed and had resisted: that the baby she had both made and found, to borrow Winnicott's phrase, the image of the college she had formed and given life to, was no longer **hers,** to be shaped or moulded or cared for by her. It had rather, in a graphic phrase she used, 'disappeared into the ether'.

This linked to and in turn helped to generate a transformation in how she began to conceive of the task she and her senior colleagues were now faced with. She was later to frame this as requiring a shift from **intention** to **attention,** from care to support, from minding to mindfulness and formation to 'engagement', a term she herself drew on and offered.

The recalled dream, you could say, was released by her to release her. In so releasing her and drawing on her own formulation, it changed the terms of her engagement with the college, as its head.

Recently, I happened to come across a passage in Bion's autobiographical novel, 'A Memoir of the Future', in which PA, who represents the psychoanalytic voice, comments apropos a certain moment in human development, how 'the good mother, of whatever sex ultimately qualifies to be vulnerable to loss. The product becomes capable of independent existence…' (Bion 1991, p 353). One might think of the dream as both emerging from and giving a transformative meaning to such a qualification.

When I first had occasion to describe this dream, I had been preoccupied with questions around the meaning or meanings attached to emotional experience in an organisational setting and the consultant's role of probing this world collaboratively with his or her client. What I may have, if not exactly missed, at least not have adequately understood or emphasised has to do with what might be termed the epistemological status of the dream itself, its mode of knowing, what I want provisionally to refer to as its peculiar creative authority, as a mental event and in real time.

Before expanding further on this, though, I want briefly to touch on a second, later experience, this time within a more specifically group context.

Second Dream

The dream as leader

Two years ago, I took part in a Group Relations Conference in Lithuania, jointly sponsored by the University of Vilnius and the Tavistock Institute and directed by Eliat Aram. I was assigned to consult to one of the Small Study Groups, scheduled after the first day immediately following an early morning large group. For the first two days, staff had experienced something of a struggle in both the small and the large groups in bringing a more unconscious undertow to life. There was a sense, partly triggered by previous experiences in these conferences, of something hidden, echoing from a past social and historical memory. (Both many of the staff and a fair proportion of the members had been part of such previous experience).

Then, on the third day, I think maybe for the first time in the Large Study Group, a member who was from the same Small Study Group (SSG) that I was working with, shared, almost it had seemed without further comment, a dream he had had of two nests, in one of which there was a dead chicken, in the other a dead stork (bringer of babies). In the subsequent SSG, following a somewhat desultory series of exchanges between the men, one of the women turned to the dreamer to say how affected she had been by this dream and what it had evoked in her: the memory of stories told by her grandmother of experiences during the War, living near the German border, foraging for food; how she had fallen into a relationship with a Belgian prisoner of war, who had left, the war over, and whom she could never again find. 'Could I have done what she did; would I have had her courage?' Suddenly the group seemed suffused by memory, their own or that of their parents or grandparents, each of which touched on themes of a lost courage (a play perhaps on the image of the dead chicken in the nest), of death and of the struggle to bring something or keep something alive, which seemed to refer both to the personal and group present and to the historical and societal past.

It was as if the dream, without interpretation or any attempt to probe its more personal meaning for the dreamer, had once again, but now in a group context, served to release something, the block of and on the 'hidden' with its particular emotional register. In this way to move things on.

In the closing plenary discussion of the Conference, after what had seemed a rather endless and narcissistic preoccupation with leadership, I found myself saying that the most striking example of leadership that I had witnessed during the conference was not the leadership of the person but the leadership of the dream, elicited but not willed, spoken but not exactly self-authored, that seems to touch, at least at times, on the authority of the unconscious, as it speaks from and to our contextual embeddedness, more exactly perhaps our relatedness to that embeddedness.

Thinking about dreams

I want to suggest that these ways of talking, of 'the authority of the dream' in my first example, the 'leadership of the dream' in my second, are more than just neat or playful turns of phrase; that they correspond to and follow from developments in ways of thinking about and conceptualising unconscious mental processes and the nature and function of dreams and dreaming that have arisen out of what might be termed the 'epistemological turn' in psychoanalysis, associated primarily with the work of Wilfred Bion. In turn, I suggest, this reconceptualisation, or at least some aspects of it, is fundamental to both the understanding and the practice of social dreaming, like necessary, if not sufficient conditions.

Gordon Lawrence was himself aware of this link, and in his paper of 2003, *Social Dreaming as Sustained Thinking*, he charts much the same course (Lawrence 2003). As in some of his later writing, though, Gordon's extensive universe of reference at times threatens to overwhelm the reader, as if he or she were having to chase and track down too many hares (something similar to the way in which in a matrix the mushrooming of associations can sometimes threaten to drown out or 'cage', as a member of a recent London matrix put it, the dreams themselves).

Here, I want to stay closer to a particular account of the psychoanalytic turn I am referring to, as presented in Donald Meltzer's book *Dream Life: Psychoanalytical Theory and Technique*, first published 30 years ago, so, more or less coincident with Gordon's early explorations (Meltzer, 1984).

Dreams as thinking

For Meltzer, as for Bion, dreaming is conceived as a form of thinking, generated pre-verbally, working on and from emotional experience. The dream is seen as (and is felt by the dreamer as) a life event, a 'mode of real experience of life', not simply a working over in sleep of the experiences of waking life, as for Freud; nor simply a continuation during sleep of the unconscious phantasies accompanying waking life, as for Klein. As Bion was to put it, in the *Key to A Memoir of the Future*,

> I find it useful to treat 'happenings' as being as real when the dreamer is in that state of mind as the 'happenings' which are experienced by the person who is supposedly awake and has 'all his wits about him'.
>
> (Bion, 1991, p. 606)

In contrast to both Freud and Klein, Meltzer outlines an account of the dream, as he experiences it in analytic work, as generative, that is as directed at spelling out, working through and resolving, or seeking to resolve, emotional problems and conflicts presented and apprehended internally within the inner world. It is in this sense that dreaming becomes a form of unconscious thinking (like play in small children), linking back to Freud's early definition of thought as 'experimental action, experiments designed to solve problems and conflicts without needing recourse to action in the outside world'.

'Dream life', he says,

> can be viewed as a place to which we can go in our sleep, when we can turn our attention fully to this internal world. The creative process of dreaming generates the meaning that can then be deployed to life and relationships in the outside world.
>
> (Meltzer, op cit., p. 46)

On this account, the work of the dream is no longer to be thought of so much in terms of Freud's four categories (displacement, condensation, symbol formation and secondary revision) or seen as means of disguise, representing the 'trickiness of the dreamer vis a vis the dream censor', where it is as if the mechanism of the dream, its manifest content, seeks to destroy meaning rather than to generate it. Rather, the dream is seen as working on principles analogous to 'poetic diction' (Sharpe, 1937), through simile, metaphor, alliteration, onomatopoeia, ambiguity, where obscurity of meaning is not necessarily to be identified with the cryptic or the hidden; and the analyst's role may be less to do with interpreting as with understanding, trying to dream and read the dream with the dreamer.

There are respects, it seems to me, in which the two dreams I started with can each be taken, in different ways, as bearing on and exemplifying much, if not all, of Meltzer's account. Both share the sense of a mental function at work, responding to a certain emotional undertow elicited in the dreamer (depression/deadness) and shaping it into something that, metaphorically, begins to look rather like what Gordon Lawrence was fond of calling a 'working hypothesis': this is what is happening here, and this is why. The difference between them is perhaps that the first dream contains its own solution, carries its own creative authority. The second invites the solution, from the group; invites them, implicitly as it were, 'to dream and read the dream with the dreamer'. This is its form of leadership. Meltzer calls this process (reading the dream with the dreamer) 'formulation', a collaborative teasing out of meaning in contrast to 'interpretation', which he reserves for working at the significance of the dream in relation to the transference.

The dream in social space

Where both dreams, however, depart from Meltzer's account is in what I referred to earlier as their 'contextual embeddedness'. Meltzer came from a very classical Kleinian tradition, profoundly influencing both his thinking and his practice. Throughout his writing, including *Dream Life...* primacy is invariably accorded to the internal world, of objects and part objects in dynamic and constantly shifting relation. The movement of meaning in his account of psychic life is always from internal to external. As if the furniture of the external world can only, as it were, borrow and not generate meaning.

For those of us, however, working in social and organisational contexts (Shmuel Erlich's 'marketplace'), the movement of finding and making meaning is as much bi- as uni-directional. Inner and outer shape or echo each other is something akin to a dialectical process, as in my client's dream of the flight to Israel, which simultaneously draws on and counterposes the two worlds of her experience, private and public, weaving the link between them in a way which adds meaning to each.

In both the psychoanalytic and the socioanalytic fields, the point of origin, what sets the dream thought going, is emotional experience, sensed pre-verbally. But in the latter, this point of origin is not to be taken as simply subsumed/located within the individual. Rather, it is diffused, as it were, across a social space. Correspondingly, one might say, the dream elicited within a social or organisational context is speaking both from and to that space, however personal or individual the features of its imagery or narrative. As the dream of the two nests, whatever the individual resonance of its imagery may have been spoke from and to the space of just this 'conference' in just this social and historical setting, representatively.

In a wonderfully illuminating book by the American philosopher and psychoanalyst Jonathan Lear (2006), Lear tells the story of the native American tribe of Crow Indians (the Crow Nation) faced with the imminent end of their way of life and of the dreams brought back to the tribe by their last and future Great Chief sent out as a boy in a familiar tribal ritual to plead for the Great Spirit to grant a dream, at a time when the Nation was at something of an historical impasse (Lear, 2006).

The Crows habitually sought and used dreams (for them visitations from a Great Spirit) to gain insight into the future, to determine whether circumstances were auspicious in relation to their wishes and intentions, to know where a hunt could be found, or a battle successfully joined. 'What is striking (though)', Lear says,

> about the young (future chief's) dream, and the interpretation the tribe gave to it, is that it was used not merely to predict a future event; it was used by the tribe to struggle with the intelligibility of events that lay at the horizon of their ability to understand.
>
> (Lear, op cit., p. 66)

Differentiating from Freud's early account of dreams as wish fulfilments and citing Freud's later acknowledgement of the possibility that a dream might be a manifestation and representation of anxiety, Lear reads the young man's dreams as an

> integral part of a process by which the tribe metabolised its shared anxiety, conceptualised not as specifically located in this or that person but as diffused throughout the tribe. It is the tribe, or perhaps even more accurately, a way of life that is anxious, though it cannot yet say what it is anxious about. (The young future chief) picked up these inchoate anxieties and turned them into dreamlike form. He dreamt on behalf of the tribe and the dream transformed these anxious concerns into narrative form. The elders of the tribe were then able to take the dream narrative and turn it into an articulate conscious thought about the challenges that the tribe would be facing.
>
> (Lear, op cit., p. 77)

On this account, so consonant in some ways with Gordon's conceptualisation of social dreaming, the dream can be seen as an imaginative resource, a capacity that, Lear claims, 'might help us to respond better to the world's challenges than we would be able to do without it'.

It is this capacity, I believe, that Gordon was both to rediscover and to reframe in the practice of social dreaming. At the same time, though, I think Lear's account, read alongside the two examples from which I started, may serve to bring into sharper relief the conditions on which the realisation of such a capacity may depend. I want to suggest 3 such conditions, each of which concerns what may be termed the location of a matrix in social space. These are:

1 the felt presence of a shared context, which has
2 emotional salience for its members
3 is in the process of becoming, that is uncertain, not fully known.

That these are necessary (if not sufficient) conditions follows I think from the conceptualisation of dream thought or dream thinking I outlined earlier: in particular, its dependence on an emotional undertow, able to be contained enough to elicit a mode of representation, but the meaning of which remains to be found and made (another way, incidentally, of accounting for the enigmatic quality of dream imagery). If a shared context is not sensed or felt, or if it lacks emotional salience, or if it somehow evades ambiguity or uncertainty, there is too little for the dream to work on. Nor any guarantee that if, nonetheless, a dream **is** shared it has any specific social reference.

I do not think that these are just abstract considerations. I think they relate to and may throw light on those occasions when, for example, a matrix gets flooded with dream material in a way that seems undigested, or when the rate and complexity of associations or amplifications threatens to drown out the dreams themselves. It is as if, on such occasions, a shared context has not been fully felt or engaged with emotionally, or, alternatively, is being evaded, dreams or associative material then being used rather to evacuate or disperse than to generate meaning (a process not unfamiliar also within psychoanalysis (Segal, 1991).

Gordon, himself, was always insistent, dogmatically at times, on the importance of not addressing or attending to group processes within a matrix, which he saw as compromising the focus on what might be termed the 'dream-in-itself' or 'dreaming as a mode of being'. But, of course, this does not mean either that the matrix or the dream material itself can altogether escape such intrusion, the attack on 'linking'.

Third Dream (or is it the fourth?)

The argument is more complex than I am making it sound, both linked to but also differentiated from Gordon Lawrence's thinking, and ranges across a variety of frames: therapeutic, group and societal. What I want to pick up from it here relates to Fromm's discussion of a dream by a young woman in treatment, brought and reported to the Community Meeting of a residential therapeutic community ,which she had recently entered.

In this dream, which she had hesitated to tell, questioning whether it was appropriate, it was as if she were anticipating, foreseeing a potential community trauma in which a particular patient, whom she didn't at first name fell or jumped from the third-floor landing:

> I was awakened by this loud crash. I was terrified. I thought for sure that X had fallen or jumped from the third-floor landing. I ran to the door to get help, but I was afraid to open it. I stood there and prayed for a few seconds. I remember I was sweating. Then I opened the door. It was a member of the night staff who had dropped something. I was so relieved.

The telling of this dream and in the presence of the dream patient, who was in reality in a quasi-suicidal state (hence the dreamer's reservation in the telling), was to initiate what Fromm calls a 'vital dialogue', in which others were able to acknowledge something of their own fear and shock in the face of regressive behaviour, and contrary to the dreamer's fears, the real patient was able both to recognise and own her impact **on** the other and feel herself in turn as recognised **by** the other.

Recounting this episode, Fromm goes on to say:

> I am suggesting here..., 1) that dreaming this dream, which might be thought of as an anticipatory trauma dream, was an act of citizenship, 2) that the dream depicts an act of citizenship, 3) that the telling of the dream **is** an act of citizenship and 4) that it calls Ms X (the dream patient) and others back to the (role of citizenship).

I think that this shift, from simply seeing the dream and its telling as a 'window into' to seeing it as an 'act of' unconscious citizenship, is central to the idea of the authority of the dream as I am trying to understand it.

From this perspective, one might say social dreaming, as conceived by Gordon, is a way of putting this potential function to work, testing it out, questioning it within and across different contextual settings. In this sense, a mode of Action Research, but in which and to which as it were, unconscious thinking holds the key, is itself the research instrument.

Whether Gordon would have seen social dreaming in just this way is an open question. Particularly in his later writing, Gordon's preoccupation becomes increasingly with a kind of generic function to do with the generation of thought and thinking, as it were the process side of social dreaming, rather than its object or the context in which it is set. Hence his latest formulation of purpose, occasionally now at risk of becoming something of a ritual, reads, 'to transform thinking through exploring dreams by the methods of free association, amplification and systemic thinking, so as to make links, find connections and to discover new thinking and new thoughts'. Here, the context is either taken for granted or is elided, to simply become the context of a community of dreamers or of people dreaming together. In my experience, this can give rise to a curiously disembodied feeling, where the accompanying mantra of 'our focus is on the dream not the dreamer' risks robbing the material of its psychic energy, the sense of the dream as a 'real happening' in 'real time', something that comes across, by contrast, with a compelling urgency in the conjoint workshops, Israeli and Palestinian, described by Hanna Biran in 'The Dreaming Soldier' (Biran (2007).

No dream can be fully abstracted from the dreamer any more than a poem can be fully abstracted from the poet. What lies behind the mantra 'dream not dreamer' is the wish to avoid any temptation to read the dream in terms of its more personal meaning. But if one thinks rather of that aspect of a dream as a 'window into unconscious citizenship', it is surely and nonetheless a window from an individual vantage point or position. In this respect, one might think of the matrix as an aggregate of such vantage points, rooted in individual experience, seen as elements or fractals of the 'context-in-the-mind'. The work of finding and making social meaning then becomes the tracing of what emerges from the succession of dream and dream, with their associative undertow. Indeed, it is precisely this that distinguishes social dreaming from each of the examples I have previously cited.

What then happens to the idea of the authority of the dream within a matrix, when sharing and working with dreams and dreaming becomes the manifest work task of a particular, socially bounded aggregate, gathered together (Work task (W) in Bion's terms)?

I am not sure how to answer this question. And perhaps the purpose of this paper is simply to ask it. Or maybe to invite us to keep on asking it, matrix by matrix, without just taking it for granted or leaving it aside. Perhaps one should think of authority as an emergent property: those moments when a dream or a dream sequence, as in the dream of the two nests, moves things on, or, as in my client's dream of the flight to Israel, answers a dilemma; changing the ways in which we have come to frame the contexts in which we live and work.

It is this mutative aspect of dreaming, I am wanting to suggest, in which authority is to be found, out of the unconscious processing of social experience and not just its acknowledgement; the place in the mind, as Yeats was to put it years ago, where 'responsibilities begin'.

Summary

The dream is always, at some level, an invitation to expand individual and social consciousness (Hollis, 2021). The eye sees a thing more clearly in dreams than with the imagination being awake (Edward MacCurdy) on Leonardo da Vinci (2002). Social dreaming assumes that we dream not just for ourselves, but as part of the larger context in which we live. The theory of social dreaming considers that dreams tell us about the nature of our organisations and the national, cultural and social contexts in which we work. The matrix provides a different kind of container for the dream than that used conventionally and shifts the focus from the dreamer to the dream itself, thus allowing the possibility of an exploration of wider contexts and their meanings. Social dreaming dreams are temporary, and no single dream provides a definite statement, a final answer to questions; it is the democratic sharing of a multitude of dreams that offers multiple insights into social phenomena. Social dreaming can be considered as the ultimate form of the democratic ideal. Dreams belong to a collective social realm and are not simply the property of the individual who has the dream experience. Social dreaming accesses the associative unconscious – that network of ideas, signs and symbols collectively held by an interacting culture; not available in its entirety to any one person, only accessible through collaborative dialogue.

Exercise

1 Consider the ease or difficulty with which you attribute relevance or value to dreams.
2 Discuss your dreams' relevance/values.
3 Are your dreams connected to emotions and feelings?
4 'The Dream is always, at some level, an invitation to expand consciousness' (James Hollis). How would you expand this idea to encompass social consciousness?
5 How would you apply social dreaming to the life of an organisation?

Chapter 13

Systems psychodynamics and the impact of digitalisation, AI and virtual working on the eco-system

David Lawlor and Mannie Sher with Olya Khaleelee

The Fourth Industrial Revolution

How can systems psychodynamics help us understand work in the contemporary world? The current period is described as the Fourth Industrial Revolution, a way of describing the blurring of boundaries between the physical, digital, and biological worlds. The era of the Fourth Industrial Revolution is a complex environment in which the cyber world and the physical world are integrated and interact. In order to successfully implement and be sustainable, the Fourth Industrial Revolution of hyper-connectivity, hyper-convergence and hyper-intelligence recognises the importance of both the technological aspects (that implemented digitalisation) and the social aspects. Both are important. Socio-technical systems (STS) theory describes complex interactions between the environmental aspects of human, mechanical and biological systems. Contemporary STS is a fusion of advances in artificial intelligence (AI), robotics, the Internet of Things (IoT), 3D printing, genetic engineering, quantum computing and other technologies. According to the World Economic Forum Global Risks Report (2017),

> the Fourth Industrial Revolution has the potential to raise income levels and improve the quality of life for all people. But today, the economic benefits of the Fourth Industrial Revolution are becoming more concentrated among a small group. This revolution is about more than technology – it is an opportunity to unite global communities, to build sustainable economies, to adapt and modernize governance models, to reduce material and social inequalities, and to commit to values-based leadership of emerging technologies.

The Fourth Industrial Revolution, climate change and systems psychodynamics

Ison (2017) argues that it is now accepted that humans are changing the climate of the Earth and this is the most compelling among a long litany of reasons as to why, collectively, he says, we have to change our ways of thinking and acting. Most people now recognise that we have to be capable of adapting quickly as new

DOI: 10.4324/9781003368663-18

and uncertain circumstances emerge: this capability will need to exist at personal, group, community, regional, national and international levels, all at the same time. Perhaps one of the greatest challenges facing the planet and the Fourth Industrial Revolution is climate change. It is now evident that climate change has and is having an impact on how we think and behave in relation to our environment and the impact we as a species are having on it. But climate change denial is a feature of the climate debate. From a psychological point of view, Le Feuvre (2012) makes the case that climate change denial can be seen in various ways and a psychodynamic view has much to contribute. In his paper, he looks at denial from a descriptive and psychodynamic perspective. Freud's (1923) views about denial are summarised. The views of John Steiner (1993) are of particular importance as they offer a differentiation between turning a blind eye and omnipotence.

Psychoanalyst Sally Weintrobe (2016, 2020, 2021), in an interview in the New Statesman with India Bourke (2022), claims that insights are devastatingly relevant to today's political world. As she explains in her book, *Psychological Roots of the Climate Crisis* (2021), we are all caught up in an ongoing conflict between the caring and uncaring sides of our psyches. When a rigid, narcissistically entitled mind-set prevails, people can exhibit exceptionalist behaviours, which, in turn, she argues, are responsible for environmental destruction across the globe. Such an exception mentality means that people see themselves in idealised terms and believe they are not subject to the normal limits of law or morality. Individuals who present themselves as 'exceptions' feel entitled to rearrange unpalatable realities to better suit their interests – think of the former US president Donald Trump's cries of 'fake news' about the small crowds at his inauguration. *'The "exception" … cuts ties to reality'*, Weintrobe says,

> It might set a target, but it doesn't have to reach it. It can say 'we are the best in the world', but it doesn't have to back that up with facts. Reality and facts present limits to the exception's scope and the exception doesn't like its freedom to be curtailed.

Weintrobe fears. *'Exceptionalism means you don't have to take responsibility for consequences'.* As a defence mechanism, denial protects us from various anxieties. The anxieties aroused by climate change are discussed from a descriptive and psychodynamic perspective noting the unconscious processes described by the psychoanalyst Harold Searles (1972).

Within psychology and psychoanalysis, there has been much denial of the psychological importance of the natural environment. Some psychoanalytic and other relevant views of the psychological significance of the natural environment are discussed. In many ways climate change denial may thus be seen as a defence against feelings of vulnerability and dependence. Le Feuvre (2012) points out that accepting the reality of climate change means accepting dependence on the natural environment. This is a difficult thing to accept when we have had so much experience of power over nature and may not feel a close relationship with it. Climate change can evoke depressive position feelings of loss, sadness and guilt. This emotional depression connects with the despair that Joanna Macy discusses: 'Confronted with widespread suffering and threats of global disaster, responses of anguish, fear, anger, grief and even guilt are normal' (Macy, 1995).

Searles (1972) implies that the ecologically deteriorated, technological world lends itself to a more paranoid schizoid perspective. 'The proliferation of technology, with its marvellously complex integration and its seemingly omnipotent dominion over nature, provides us with an increasingly alluring object upon which to project our non-human strivings for omnipotence' (p. 368) while at the same time the 'animal-nature based components of our selves become impoverished' (p. 368). This conflict between animal and technological selves, seen as either good or bad in this paranoid schizoid thinking, can then get projected onto external reality: 'the war in external reality between the beleaguered remnants of ecologically balanced nature and man's technology' (p. 368). There can thus be an omnipotent defence against the vulnerability of nature, both inner and outer:

> At an unconscious level we powerfully identify with what we perceive as omnipotent and immortal technology, as a defence against intolerable feelings of insignificance, of deprivation, of guilt, of fear of death and so on.
>
> (p. 370)

Le Feuvre (2012) argues that there is a need for an ecopsychoanalysis (a psychoanalysis that incorporates the psychological significance of the natural environment), made more urgent by climate change. It is crucial that politically, culturally and individually, we are able to understand and contain the anxieties that are evoked by climate change; trying to minimise the potential for denial of reality and to maximise the chances of a realistic response.

Le Feuvre (2012) quotes Harold Searles:

> The environmental crisis embraces, and with rapidly increasing intensity, threatens our whole planet. If so staggering a problem is to be met, the efforts of scientists of all clearly relevant disciplines will surely be required. It seems to me that we psychoanalysts, with our interest in the unconscious processes which so powerfully influence man's behaviour, should provide our fellow men with some enlightenment in this common struggle.
>
> (1972, p. 361)

Hoggett and Nestor (2021) question the definition and application of the primary task, is it merely for the survival of an organisation and system or should it also be linked to purpose and values (Reed and Armstrong, 1988)? Hoggett and Nestor argue that the fossil fuel energy industries are destructive by creating the instruments for destroying the planet. Ecological thinking knows that people, all living organisms and the non-human world are deeply embedded in interdependent relationships and that the interconnection between living and non-living systems is a fundamental reality, which cannot be denied (Capra, 1996; Lovelock, 2000). Psychoanalysis proposes that the problems of ecological disasters originate in human aggression and hostility to the idea of dependence (on our ecological systems) and likens this hostility to an attack on the Kleinian 'good breast'. Psychoanalysis and the psychosocial approach bring individual human experience into the realm of the shared social fabric of human systems, which can help us understand the social defences and unconscious processes at play in the earth's destruction. Global warming is the symptom of this 'disease' that needs to be 'cured'. The 'body' of humankind becomes the 'body' of the planet so that illness is interwoven and necessarily shared by human and non-human. James Lovelock considered the world as Gaia, a living entity. He has suggested that the planet is 'ill' in this way (Lovelock, 2005). Weintrobe's own contribution deals with the central psychosocial concern of socially and psychologically produced anxiety in relation to climate change denial. Hoggett (2019) discusses 'perverse thinking' and how virtual realities become confabulated with actual reality and converted into meaningless targets by governments who need to believe in a simulated reality in order to psychically and politically survive.

We can see Bion's Basic Assumptions at play, the ever-flowing breast, dependency, the denial of attack on the breast for its largesse, and the realisation that it does not originate in the self. Our omnipotent phantasies show up on a regular basis with the idea that climate change will be solved by a technological fix. Biblical (faith) supporting the illusion that climate is a reward/punishment for bad/good behaviour, is a regression to magical thinking. This illusion is a defence against helplessness, which is connected to basic assumption pairing that someone or an institution, will come up with a solution.

Built into basic assumption dynamics is that the hope of a solution will never be realised because the dawn of reality is more painful. The notion that the work group is the real solution to the dilemma, but that means connecting to reality, for example stop buying things, flying, endless growth is not seen to be realistic activity.

Is Extinction Rebellion the basic assumption fight or a work group? We see the use of projection of fight by the rest of us onto Extinction Rebellion so that they carry all the social anxiety about the catastrophe we are in, while the rest of us continue to go shopping, drive our cars and fly on holiday and form of splitting, whereas in the Bible, which could be seen as an expression of the social unconscious, we are encouraged to lead lives that are balanced. It would seem by the force of splitting and projection we are alienated from the natural order and balance.

The Fourth Industrial Revolution is changing how we live, work and communicate. It's reshaping government, education, healthcare and commerce, and almost every aspect of life. In the future, it can also change the things we value and the way we value them. The global pandemic has underlined the technological revolution. Industry 4.0 is used interchangeably with the Fourth Industrial Revolution and represents a new stage in the organisation and control of the industrial value chain. Industry 4.0 (2021), especially when coupled with machine learning and artificial intelligence, will substantially change conditions for workers: it is argued that many jobs will disappear while we will gain a lot of new jobs, and many repetitive tasks will shift from manual labour to automation. It will have a big impact.

	First Industrial Revolution	Second Industrial Revolution	Third Industrial Revolution	Fourth Industrial Revolution	Fifth Industrial Revolution
	Mechanisation	Electrification	Automation and globalisation	Digitalisation	Personalisation
Time Period	Occurred during the 18th and 19th centuries, mainly in Europe and North America	From the late 1800s to the start of the First World War	The digital revolution occurred around the 1980s	Start of the 21st century	Second decade of the 21st century
Technology	Steam engines replacing horse power and human power	Production of steel, electricity and combustion engines	Computers, digitalisation and the internet	AI, robotics, IoT, blockchain and crypto	Innovation purpose and inclusivity
The social	Introduction of mechanical production facilities driven by water and steam power	Division of labour and mass production, enabled by electricity	Automation of production through electronic and IT systems	Robotics, artificial intelligence, augmented reality, virtual reality	Deep, multi-level cooperation between people and machines. Consciousness

As the Fourth Industrial Revolution unfolds, companies are seeking to harness new and emerging technologies to reach higher levels of efficiency of production and consumption, expand into new markets, and compete on new products for a global consumer base composed increasingly of digital actors. Yet in order to harness the transformative potential of the Fourth Industrial Revolution, business leaders across all industries and regions will increasingly be called upon to formulate a comprehensive workforce strategy ready to meet the challenges of this new era of accelerating change and innovation.

The table above shows the sequence of the five industrial revolutions. You will see how each revolution sets the scene for the next one. Note also the time period of each revolution.

According to Zarka et al. (2019), new digital technologies are changing the way organisations are designed and work is done. Companies that have seized this opportunity are finding that they can speed up innovation, enhance collaboration across boundaries and enable greater commitment and creativity. This totally new approach for digitally enabled collaboration doesn't stop at the edge of an organisation's boundary but extends beyond it in space and time. They refer to these new ways of organising as 'braids' – an intertwined network of contributors with different capabilities, not controlled or managed by a formal hierarchy, who work together to invent ways to accomplish a common purpose in line with organisation's mission and strategy. Braids allow significant advantages over traditional, hierarchical, mechanistic and bounded ways of organising. These include access to knowledge and capabilities that are key to achieving breakthrough levels of performance; improved coordination among individuals and groups performing interdependent tasks; increased organisational agility; enhanced knowledge-processing as experts contribute more directly to the most important technical and strategic decisions; and greater motivation, as people team together to leverage their capabilities to innovate and accelerate performance. Learning from the trailblazing experimentation of companies like Airbus, Procter & Gamble, Red Hat and Dassault Systèmes, they outline how to approach designing braided organisations for a variety of purposes, such as enhancing open innovation or enabling greater supply chain adaptability in order to respond to changing customer demands. In the past, human limitations have restricted the ways companies to organise for growth. They argue that today, there's no excuse for allowing the organisational chart as it's currently drawn to constrain possibilities for improved performance and innovation.

The ideas and practices that make up systems psychodynamics are opens system theory (inputs, conversion and outputs), psychoanalysis (e.g. projection and projective identification), the BART model (boundaries, authority, role and task) and socio-technical systems (joint optimisation, autonomous workgroups) and socio-ecology (inter-organisational collaboration, turbulence). The work of Tavistock researchers and consultants from its inception to today shows that these concepts are as relevant now as they ever were.

Virtual teams

Since the COVID pandemic working in virtual teams and the use of the internet to conduct work meetings has grown astronomically. Bergiel et al. (2008) findings indicate that the main advantages of virtual teams are flexibility, having access to larger talent pools and networks, gaining local expertise and reduction of travel time and costs. Disadvantages show risk of misinterpretations, challenging to build trust and team feeling, lack of transparency and information sharing. Considerations related to communication methods and tools, best practices such as regular team meetings, people and communication skills, but also trust was considered to be more critical in virtual teams than in traditional teams.

Törmänen (2017) suggests that one should start with team-building exercises and if possible conduct those in physical events to initiate building of relationships within the team. First meetings and impressions tend to have a strong impact on the direction the team will take. He goes on to recommend the following strategies:

> … emphasising psychologically safe as part of team culture; continuously improve relational development, and enhance building of trust, since trust is a vital part of well-functioning team. Törmänen recommends awareness of virtual team's unique considerations, limits and possibilities. In virtual teams, build a knowledge-sharing culture and have appropriate tools and methods in place to enable this. Roles, responsibilities, norms and work habits should be well-structured and commonly agreed. It is important to acknowledge that not everyone is psychologically suited for virtual teams. It is important to have communication, IT and people skills and acknowledge cultural differences when building teams. One should bear in mind the advantages and disadvantages of virtual teams when planning work. Not all projects will suit virtual working.

Ken Eason (2011) reminds us that the introduction of technology into the workplace has always been associated with disruption. With the introduction of smartphones and social media, our lives are now intertwined by the use of these technologies. The study of socio-technical systems encompasses the sociological, psychological and technological factors in the interaction between human beings and technology. Eason (2011) argues that virtual organisations, in which the technology mediates the interactions in the social system, are an emergent form of socio-technical system. He questions whether socio-technical concepts are appropriate for emergent forms of virtual social community and concludes that many socio-technical characteristics are also likely to be found in these forms of organisation and concludes with a plea that we go beyond the design of technical systems to support virtual organisations and, in the tradition of socio-technical systems research, concern ourselves with the joint design of the social and technical components of virtual organisations. For Eason, the elements of the socio-technical conceptual structure have continuing significance in an age of virtual organisation. Eason contends that there can be no doubt that the movement towards virtual organisations is creating forms of socio-technical systems that have new characteristics. The fact that the technology takes on a pivotal role as the mediator of communications in a social system whose members may only know one another through the technology means that these are organisations unlike others we have known. The most important lesson is that socio-technical systems design is not just about the design of the technical system; it must be about the joint design of both the technical and the social system.

Value chain

Value chain management encompasses the planning and management of all activities involved in sourcing and procurement, conversion and all logistics management activities. Importantly, it also includes coordination and collaboration with channel partners, which can be suppliers, intermediaries, third-party service providers and customers. In essence, value chain management integrates value and demand management within and across organisations. Value chain management is an integrating function with primary responsibility for linking major organisational functions and organisational processes within and across organisations into a cohesive and high-performing business model. It includes all the logistics management activities noted above, as well as manufacturing and service operations, and it drives coordination of processes and activities with and across marketing, sales, product and service design, and finance and information technology.

Collaboration in an integrated value chain that is based on the concept of the 'total system' usually leads to better utilisation of information flow, significant reductions in demand amplification without substantial expenditure, separating out the flow of stand-alone passing-on-orders mode from inventory-controlled feedback systems as they are passed up the chain. A good inventory control system is one with revalue options that have shorter lead times. Demand and fixed ordering costs are small relative to holding costs – the primary objective is to achieve steady-state behaviour in the value chain – a challenge that is difficult to achieve because of individual and group human dynamic elements, especially those that emerge when people coalesce into different large groups or entities.

Fluctuations of production and inventory levels, the so-called 'bullwhip effect', are typical of multi-level material replenishment processes with significant lead times and fluctuating demands. In the client's value chains, the 'bullwhip effect' was observed in simulation of analytical models to result from a combination of classical local ordering policies that sustained or even amplified this effect. Local procurement policies such as an inventory-based policy of the base-stock type, or an order-based policy, combined with local feedback loops reinforced the oscillations and generated instability. However, smoother production and inventory levels were observed under a mean demand-driven policy in which the partner enterprises did not directly influence each other. By responding to integrated or averaged demand evolutions in parallel, global consistency in production and assembly was achieved.

In an example of value chain behaviour from the British National Health Service, a Tavistock Institute-initiated Action Learning Set undertook to intervene in a complex organisational change initiative involving four organisations with common boundaries that they believed needed to be made more permeable in order to facilitate the smooth transfer of patients across services. The Set investigated and mapped existing transfer processes and their obstacles, alternating this with reflections on the nature of the barriers they were encountering. Once a draft was completed, they contacted all the actors identified in the transfer process map and explored with them the reasons why bottlenecks occurred and why patient transfer was problematic. Positions on the map where forces and interests had been identified and intersected and which prevented a smooth transfer of patients were marked with 'cockroaches', a very powerful image that helped to capture the imagination of everyone involved. Discussions were henceforth framed as attempts at eliminating the 'cockroaches', that is to identify practical ways to remove obstacles to smooth patient transfer. By mapping the territory, the Action Learning Set had, in fact, changed it. The reflective exploration activity allowed the Set to build the necessary relationships and support and what followed was a change process and new procedures for patient transfer, mitigating the 'bullwhip effect' in the health service supply chain. Most importantly, once news of the Set's activity started circulating through the organisations, the Set members were contacted by local directors who invited them to present their work at higher level meetings. This constituted both an acknowledgement and an endorsement of their work and their bottom-up empowerment strategy, as well as a further source of influence for the Set in support of their activity (Nicolini et al., 2004).

Organisation and organisational culture

By Olya Khaleelee

Three current societal issues will affect organisations and organisational culture in future: climate change and the culture of Political Correctness (PC); the impact of COVID on employment and work practices; and the effect of AI and robotics on man-machine systems. In turn, these will impact on the skills needed for organisational consultancy.

Climate change and the PC culture

Individuals, groups, organisations and societies have inevitably always had to manage anxieties and challenges, which relate to survival. Fifty years ago, the main societal anxiety was about the possibility of nuclear war. Most recently, it has been climate change that has created the greatest anxiety about annihilation. This anxiety influences the products of organisations that wish to operate in a more sustainable, ethical, ecologically sound way. Organisations are additionally affected by the PC, woke and cancel cultures that increasingly inhibit open discussion for fear of giving offence. This inhibition will impact on the content of boardroom discussions, as well as on how the consultant takes up the role. There is already a need for heightened sensitivity and awareness to individual and group interpretations of consultant interventions, and the increasing dominance of this culture is having an impact on the capacity of clients openly and fully to debate important organisational and ethical issues.

The effect of the pandemic

The impact of COVID-19 is that unemployment levels are changing dramatically, higher rates of poverty, especially children, reliance on foodbanks, a continuing widening of the gap between rich and poor, bringing more mental illness, higher suicide rates and the threat of social unrest. Society over the next few years will look rather different to the full employment society that existed prior to the onset of the pandemic.

Changing work patterns will impact on the usage of office space and how often employees work in the office or from home. In the USA, the impact of coronavirus, as well as high city taxes, has led to an exodus from city to countryside (Kelly, 2019). The same is true of the UK, with more of a focus on work/life balance (Jones, 2020).

In view of the contraction of the economy, firms may well be keen to cut the costs of office space, may downsize, may decide to work virtually on a permanent basis or may adopt a hybrid policy of part-time home working and part-time face-to-face working, with hot-desking as the norm rather than the exception. One way of thinking about this is that society is in a major transitional process, the outcome of which is not clear. For organisations that are growing, particularly those originating from family businesses, there is also the issue of cultural and country differences and how those are to be managed. Connectedness between employees, therefore, will alter, which may impact on their sense of status, on levels of creativity and on the social cohesion of the workforce as a whole. How to maintain this cohesion could be a real challenge.

The boundary between home and work will be more blurred. Karam Filfilan (2020) reports that:

> A survey of 2,000 workers by 02 and YouGov found that nearly half (45 per cent) expected to work more flexibly after lockdown is lifted, with a third expecting to work from home three days a week and 81 per cent wanting at least one remote working day.

The article goes on to describe how the lockdown has shifted people's expectations of work, with the focus more on the employee as an individual as the biggest cultural outcome. In turn, employee wellbeing and mental health support have become as important as profit and productivity. He quotes Lloyds Banking Group as an example, where 45,000 employees have shifted to remote working implementing a focus on mental health.

> The bank has provided employees with 24/7 access to counselling, set up an online centre advising colleagues on how to deal with the pandemic, offered workshops on yoga, virtual choirs and wellbeing activities, and sent office equipment to help homeworkers settle into a new way of working.

For an organisation to be successful under these circumstances requires a change in expectations regarding attitudes towards work and building on the trust, empathy and personal connections that have been made with employees during the lockdown.

For organisational consultants, this presents a more complex picture of the system to be held in the mind, a system that will have a more fluid presentation and will have an effect on employee perceptions of 'one of us' and 'not one of us', of 'inside' and 'outside', of 'belonging' or 'not belonging', of where authority is perceived to reside and of where the boundaries are located.

The impact of AI and robotics

Embracing digital technologies with AI is having a significant impact. The effects of AI will compound the problem and will impact on government support of populations, initially the more unskilled. Some aspects of the care sector can already be carried out by machines, including the provision of companionship for older people, as well as technical skills. Later, aspects of professional life will also be carried out via AI. It is likely that the effects of AI will impact on the mental health of the working population, especially men, who have traditionally relied on work to sustain their personal identity. This will add to growth in the counselling/coaching/therapy business, especially online, funded by the employing organisation to maintain wellbeing of employees.

AI and robotics have generated a mixed response. Much robot development has already taken place in the automobile industry, particularly in the USA. While previously many manufacturers have had to send jobs offshore because they could not compete with low-cost foreign labour, robotic automation now allows manufacturing to compete by creating more jobs in robotics and associated fields.

Programming, engineering, end-effector design, operators, data analysts, robot manufacturing and systems integration are all needed. People are needed to help service the machines. Robots allow manufacturers to lower costs and bring jobs back to the home country, resulting in more jobs for workers. Robots also protect workers from having to do repetitive, mundane, and dangerous tasks that could negatively impact on their ability to work ('Why Robotic Automation Is the Future in Manufacturing', 2019).

Upon the publication of a report on 'Automation and the Future of Work' by the Business, Energy and Industrial Strategy (BEIS) Committee, the Chair, Rachel Reeves, said:

> *The Government should come forward with a UK Robot and AI Strategy to support businesses and workers as they manage the transition to a more automated world of work. This new strategy must seek to get the right support in place, on issues such as skills, investment and training, to ensure that all parts of the UK share in the jobs and growth benefits offered by automation.*
>
> (Business, Energy and Industrial Strategy Committee, 2019)

According to the parliamentary report, the UK has just 85 robots per 100,000 workers, putting it in 23rd place in the league table of worldwide robot density. There is some debate as to whether the UK needs more robots as it is essentially a service economy. On the other hand, it lags behind other more manufacturing focused nations in productivity. Robotics could rectify this longstanding problem (Baxter, 2019). Furthermore, the effects of COVID, the US/China trade war and the loss of inter-country trust may lead to more manufacturing being relocated back to the UK. This will impact on the need to train more skilled workers in digital competence. What happens to the unskilled, or those others who do not have the capacity to adapt to a digital world?

Another issue has arisen through the Black Lives Matter (BLM) movement, which has highlighted the relative lack of investment in BLM enterprises. The killing of George Floyd has generated much discussion about the systemic inequalities that exist across sectors including government, business and banking. Costa (2020) reports on two BLM entrepreneurs who are breaking this mould and harnessing AI within their organisations in different ways. She describes how Jason Pinto, co-founder of Pace, uses AI to pioneer 'dynamic pricing … by algorithmically matching supply and demand on a daily and even hourly basis'. This greatly reduces waste and inefficiency in the retail market, hotel, airline and car rental businesses by analysing fluctuations in customer demand to instantly adjust prices faster than a human being could.

The second entrepreneur described by Costa is Paris Petgrave, founder of *We Love Work*, who 'provides companies with anonymised employee data from real-time culture audits to predict team performance and fit. It also helps companies assess culture and values fit during the recruitment process as part of a longer-term diversity and inclusion strategy'. The aim is to recruit staff whose values are unconsciously aligned to those of the organisation to maximise organisational effectiveness.

Research by the CIPD describes the effects of increasing AI as twofold ('Are Robots Stealing Our Jobs?' 2018). Firstly, because machines can work fast and up to 24 hours a day, there is increasing pressure on pace. This is both positive and less positive because although more efficient, AI can increase stress on humans, which in turn can impact on their mental health.

The second effect is that increased AI also provides an opportunity to stand back and reflect. Therefore, we might expect that organisations of the future will focus on strategy even more than operational capacity. This in turn will mean that organisational consultants may well need a better understanding of the whole business system including strategic elements, and how structure and culture, including human processes, fit with it.

According to this podcast above, robotics has also had an impact on how far technology can be trusted, given that it is programmed by humans. Issues raised included the unconscious biases built into technology, for example voice recognition, and so far, some difficulty in incorporating diversity of thought, experience, articulation and so on.

A recent article (Blakely, 2020) emphasises this work capacity of robots. Professor Cooper, director of the Materials Innovation Factory at the University of Liverpool, said in the article that one thing robots cannot do is frame a hypothesis, so 'we're not making ourselves redundant – yet'.

This is just as well, given the potentially malignant effects of AI, such as the development of 'deepfakes', which can use AI to create fake videos. Technically AI, in learning what someone's face looks like at any angle or with any expression, or what someone's voice sounds like, can create an entire deepfake ecosystem, particularly in porn. Schick (2020) describes how it is used to 'out' and intimidate those who speak out of turn or put forward an unacceptable view within other professions. 'Now that AI can be used to hijack our identity and create audio-visual clips in which we say and do things we never actually did, it represents a significant threat to our civil liberties and rights to privacy'.

A further issue will be social isolation. The lockdown of 2020 has had a major impact on mental health and home working. Home working, while perhaps positive from the perspective of work/life balance, can also lead to isolation from colleagues and from the experience of physically working together, especially for the approximately 2.5 million under 65s who live alone (Clark, 2019).

As Durkheim said, the whole is more than the sum of the parts (Emile Durkheim, 2020). Can that be sustained if some workers are physically present and others are not? Can those not physically present be held in the mind, or will they be split off and temporarily forgotten? What impact will this have for organisational social defence mechanisms, for what gets projected into whom, and for authority relations? And how will organisational consultants work with these issues?

Universal Basic Income (UBI)

The impact of AI is that government policy regarding Universal Basic Income (UBI) in the UK will need to be fleshed out. This is already being trialled in Finland, Canada, Spain and other countries. The largest trial has been in Kenya where the charity GiveDirectly is making payments to more than 20,000 people spread out across 245 rural villages (Samuel, 2020). The results of pilot studies demonstrated increases in wellbeing and in motivation to invest in small business, especially in African countries. Thus, UBI and AI will develop mutual synergy over the next decades, especially in developing countries.

Together AI and UBI they may well foster the setting up of new organisations, technical innovation and expansion in organisational life. State-of-the-art technology will be an important feature, indicating a need to increase investment in technology solutions so that homeworkers do not have to suffer outdated solutions with confusing interfaces. New forms of organisation and structure are developing to meet the 'new normal'. Resource organisations already exist, for example, helping companies develop work hubs strategically located nearer to a team and its customers. Designing such venues would offer a technology-enabled space where workers can network together and interact with other hubs using virtual tools. This would satisfy the need for human interaction and provide a less crowded and therefore potentially less infectious space where people can congregate for key business events and meetings.

Such innovations raise the question of the best organisational structure, culture and processes to fit with long-term business strategies for growth and will likely be the dominant preoccupation for the future.

It was Neumann, Miller and Holti, writing with great prescience in 1999, who said:

> Consultants need to develop a portfolio of consultancy methods that enable them to address not only cultural changes (e.g. attitudinal and change) but also structural changes (e.g. organisational design). Today, most clients who hire organisational consultants do so to complement technological and strategic changes anticipated or already undertaken. OD practitioners need to increase their ability to understand and work with change managers, and their consultants, who see the world predominantly through technological and economic eyes.

Twenty years later, this prediction is even more true, but in a world that is more fluid, more unpredictable and more anxious than ever before in our lifetimes.

The impact of the pandemic on organisations

Stephen Sinofsky (2021), a former senior Microsoft executive, writes in an essay titled, 'Creating the Future of Work', what will the world of work look like following the pandemic, what will our post-pandemic future be like? In relation to work, three main possibilities are currently being described:

1 Continuing to work from home (WFH)
2 A hybrid mode in which we spend some time in the office but also two or three days WFH
3 A return to commuting to the office

Sinofsky suggest that if these are the only options under consideration, then there is a serious underestimation of the industrial significance of the pandemic. *Of course*, the nature of work will have been changed by what has happened. But what is more significant, he contends, is that the shock will also reshape the nature of the businesses in which most of us work. The problem is that most of the people who run large organisations and corporations haven't understood that as yet. Sinofsky's background is that he was president of Microsoft's Windows division for three years. Before that, he was responsible for the development of Windows, Internet Explorer, Outlook.com and SkyDrive. He's now on the board of Andreessen Horowitz, a major Silicon Valley venture capital firm. He writes on his blog, Learning by Shipping. His argument is that the organisational impact of the pandemic will be profoundly disruptive for companies, but not in the way we might expect. He points out that many organisations have been surprised by the way technology has enabled them not only to keep functioning, but in many cases to thrive. He thinks that organisations have not yet realised that surviving the lockdowns by using technology indicates that their pre-pandemic ways of doing things need comprehensive re-examination. Disruption, Sinovsky writes,

> is not linear or predictable and, most importantly, when it is happening, no one knows it. The one thing we know is entities being disrupted claim to be doing the new thing everyone is talking about, but they are doing it the old way.

Worse still, he says, companies have an inbuilt tendency

> to view disruption as a single variable – Amazon has a website, so therefore Walmart needs one. But Amazon had warehouses, custom software, its own last-mile shipping, and on and on. Disruption is never one variable, but a wholesale revisiting of all the variables.

That's why the debate over remote work vs hybrid vs back to the office is only part of the picture. It's interesting and it matters to employees, but it's not where the focus should be. Many employees have been changed by the trauma of the pandemic, but corporate leaders have not yet. They may not have thought through what happens to workers, when technology creates a new, disruptive way of doing things. Managers who insist that all employees return to the office once vaccination has worked its magic may therefore be in for a surprising discovery; that they and their managerial hierarchies are the incumbents who are threatened by the pandemic's disruption. Or, as Sinofsky puts it: 'The idea that everything stays the same, except for a few changes around the edges causes every incumbent to lose in the face of step-function change'.

We think that here we can see that the pandemic is likely to have an impact on the socio-technical systems in organisations. It could be argued that the move to online and digital working, which was greatly accelerated by the pandemic, is now forcing organisations into having to redesign their organisations and how they authorise and empower staff. If they are able to use participative design methodologies, then they are likely to be successful but those organisations who wish to return to the status quo of pre-pandemic conditions will probably have significant problems.

Summary

Conditions for workers will be changed; many jobs will disappear; new jobs will be gained; repetitive tasks will shift from manual labour to automation. Companies are harnessing new and emerging technologies to reach higher levels of efficiency of production and consumption, expanding into new markets, and competing on new products for a global consumer base composed increasingly of digital citizens. Business leaders will be called upon to formulate comprehensive workforce strategies to meet the challenges of this new era of accelerating change and innovation. The systems psychodynamics model of opens system theory, psychoanalysis, and the BART model of boundaries, authority, role and task is still relevant and applicable. The focus of STS includes user participation in systems design and recognises the politics of labour conditions and labour-management conflicts through improved workplace democratisation. The design and introduction of computing systems in new settings best illustrates computer-based information systems: information systems development and adoption efforts. It involves participation of end users in the design, introduction and integration of system features and workflow to make system-based work more satisfying and rewarding. Key terms are user involvement, participatory design, user satisfaction, human relations and workplace democracy. The steady advancement of digital technology enables global connection and integration across populations and organisations that has catalysed fundamental change in societal norms, behaviours and expectations, for example the integration of social media into the lives of populations everywhere, easy access to and expectations of transparency of information, and the impact of the internet on awareness and expectations of people around the world. The designs of organisations have changed fundamentally to reflect current technical and social realities, for example horizontal organisation, virtual relationships to and among customers: partnerships along the value stream; outsourcing; the increasing use of contract and transaction-based workers replacing loyalty and commitment-based relationships; and the building of work systems that include robotics, artificial intelligence and machine learning. The Fourth Industrial Revolution has been made possible by the generation of powerful internet-enabled digital platforms, for example Uber, Amazon, Airlines and Facebook, connecting people, information, advertisers, employers and customers. Digital platforms have become major enablers of the communication and coordination underpinning economic transactions and work systems. Digital platforms are co-evolving with the strategies and designs of organisations and work systems and of the economies and societies. The scope for relevant technical and market optimisation, integration and design now extends well beyond company boundaries to include industry and cross-industry ecosystems. Large elements of the global economy are linked together by technology platforms that enable the members of the ecosystem to operate in a complementary way and generate product and service innovations with sweeping involvement of and impact across many stakeholders. IT platforms have become the information processors and the integrators of activities that are carried out by customers and temporary teams cutting across organisational, sector and geographic boundaries. These teams are labelled 'smart' because the technology provides unprecedented access to data, information and analyses for coordinated and complementary activity. The capabilities inherent in digital platforms are integral to significantly increased collective intelligence. Work relationships are increasingly transactional, contractual, temporary and virtual. Many organisations are populated by small numbers of critical employees, connected to contractors and outsourcers, all with tasks and roles defined by the ecosystem-wide network.

Exercise

1 Describe your experience of work during COVID-19.
2 What was your emotional experience of working online?
3 Describe how your working relationships were enhanced or deteriorated during the pandemic.
4 What is your learning as a result of this?
5 What are your views on the potential disruption of work practices and relationship with digitalisation?

Part IV

Systems psychodynamics developments, definitions and professional development

Part IV of this volume is concerned with professional development, with developments in theory and practice, and with arguing for systems psychodynamics to be regarded as a paradigm.

Chapter 14, *Professional Development for Systems Psychodynamics Consultants*, written together with Anne Benson, Chair of the Professional Development Group at the Tavistock Institute of Human Relations, notes that professionals who practise in this field – theorists and consultants – are concerned with questions of what makes for an effective consultant and what makes for an effective consultancy intervention. Usual taxonomies and listing of competencies, the identification of skills and the framing of domains do not fully describe what systems psychodynamics consultants do. The interest of systems psychodynamics–trained consultants in the unconscious can make their work to the newcomer seem esoteric and obscure, because the unconscious, by its very nature, is unknown, difficult to grasp or see, often metaphorical rather than literal and frequently non-verbal. When the unconscious comes into view, it is experienced as magical, mysterious and potentially disturbing. Hence, unconscious dynamics in organisational contexts are not easily written into lists. Nevertheless, as difficult and imperfect as it might be, this chapter identifies the capabilities required for systems psychodynamics practice and the chapter indicates ways in which these capabilities can be developed. The chapter attempts to define the territory of systems psychodynamics consultancy practice by providing a useful frame for knowledge, skills and attitudes in values and ethics, practice theories, consultancy process, tasks and capabilities. The systems psychodynamics consultant must combine problem-solving, vision, determination, technical expertise and interpersonal and political skills. The chapter outlines basic competences of effective consultants as clarifying goals, team-building activities, communication skills, negotiation skills, and influencing skills to gain commitment to goals. Perceptions, beliefs and assumptions of systems psychodynamics consultants are vital aspects that form part of a professional practitioner's kit bag. These skills and competences are not founded on codified expertise, knowledge or techniques that can be instrumentally applied or learned through conventional educational or training interventions, because

DOI: 10.4324/9781003368663-19

self-awareness and the capacity for self-reflection are pre-requisites and are usually acquired through personal psychotherapy and attendance at group relations conferences, as well as formal programmes in Tavistock work.

Chapter 15 covers developments and definitions of systems psychodynamics and observes that the systems psychodynamics community of professional practitioners have over the past 60–70 years developed a new paradigm for understanding social and organisational life and the nature of work. The paradigm has stood the test of social and economic changes in the world from industrial society to the post-industrial society of the network and values organisation, virtual working, the information society and the post-COVID society. The systems psychodynamics paradigm serves as an incorporated model with several theories and categorisations of phenomena from other disciplines to construct a model of the world, of societies and organisations, individuals and groups and the theory of practice. The chapter supports our knowledge base informing our practice in keeping with our theoretical position on transdisciplinarity and confirms our commitment to our values of participative democracy.

Chapter 16 covers theoretical developments in the systems psychodynamics paradigm. This chapter describes some contemporary views about the systems psychodynamics paradigm. It has been a difficult task to choose to include people in this chapter as there are many people in this field who have contributed and continue to contribute to the development of new approaches and theories. Many other thinkers' writings can be found in the OPUS journal *Organisational and Social Dynamics*.

Appendix I

Systems psychodynamics – organisational resources

In this appendix, we introduce the reader to organisations that practise systems psychodynamics and group relations. Systems psychodynamics and group relations have continued to spread and develop across the globe.

Appendix II

Literature review on systems psychodynamics

The literature of systems psychodynamics continues to grow. We provide a brief overview of some of the literature over the recent period.

Chapter 14

Professional development for systems psychodynamics consultants

David Lawlor and Mannie Sher with Anne Benson

This chapter explores the capabilities required to be an effective systems psychodynamics consultant. It then considers the nature of the professional development needed to develop and sustain these capabilities.

Practitioners, theorists and researchers working in organisational development consultancy have debated for many years what makes an effective consultant, resulting in multiple taxonomies, lists of competencies, identification of domains and Venn diagrams. (Cheung-Judge and Holbeche, 2015; Cummings, 2008; Jones and Brazzel, 2014).

The challenge we face with such taxonomies is that the listing of competencies, the identification of skills and the framing into domains, is inevitably reductionist and feels insufficient to describe what systems psychodynamics consultants do. Are we therefore saying that what we do is so esoteric or ephemeral that it cannot be named, systematised or made straightforward? There is something in the esoteric nature of our work, significantly because of our interest in the unconscious. The unconscious by its very nature is unknown, difficult to grasp or see, often metaphorical rather than literal and frequently non-verbal. When the unconscious comes into conscious awareness, it is often experienced as magical and mysterious. Thus, it is not surprising that the capabilities required to work with unconscious dynamics in organisational contexts are not easily written into lists.

However difficult and imperfect it might be, we must work to identify the capabilities required for our practice and signal the ways to develop those capabilities, not to do so is negligent. If we avoid a clear articulation of our practice, we risk obfuscation, which supports exclusivity and can lead to a closed system. As Roberts (2019) reminds us, over time closed systems die.

As is often the case, it is the next generation who push those before them to provide clarity, show their colours and define the territory. Nutkevitch (2016) described the student body on their programme pushing and challenging programme directors for clarity about the integration of psychoanalytic and systems thinking. Similarly, Tschudy (2014, p. 158) described a group of newcomers to the field of OD demanding clarity among the confusing array of terms and practices. They wanted answers to the questions.

DOI: 10.4324/9781003368663-20

1 What do OD practitioners do?
2 What kinds of skills do you need to do it?
3 How does it all fit together?

Responding to this demand, Tschudy and colleagues created an OD map of the territory with seven primary parts. An adapted version of Tschudy's map provides a useful frame in which to locate the knowledge, skills and attitudes required for systems psychodynamics consultants.

1 Values and ethics
2 Practice theories
3 The consultancy process
4 Tasks associated with different aspects of the process
5 Capabilities required

Despite the above caveats, we think the following list of attitudes and abilities are fundamental to the consultant's role of supporting the consultative relationship. We will suggest that the systems psychodynamics consultant must combine problem-solving, vision, determination, technical expertise and inter-personal and political skills.

The following is a typical taxonomy of skills and competencies from the organisational development literature. The role of consultants as facilitators is extensively discussed within a rational framework. For example, Buchanan and Boddy (1992) list competencies of effective consultants as:

 I Clarifying specific goals
 II Team-building activities
III Communication skills
IV Negotiation skills
 V Influencing skills (to gain commitment to goals)

It can be deduced from these arguments that limitations in change management are associated with the managerial perceptions of the need for change, the opportunity to change and about the way to change. This renders perceptions, beliefs and assumptions of systems psychodynamics consultants as vital aspects to be understood.

Bennis (1993) defined four competencies for consultants to be successful in helping organisations to achieve effectiveness, improvement, development and enhancement. In his view, the four essential competencies for success include the following:

 i Broad knowledge of the intelligence from the behavioural sciences and theories and methods of change
ii Operational and relational skills, such as the ability to listen, observe, identify and report, and to form relationships based on trust

iii   Sensitivity and maturity, including self-recognition of motivators and the perceptions that others have of these motivators

iv   Authenticity in living and acting in accordance with humanistic values

In addition to the change agent competencies described above, Bennis (1993) also found that consultants intervene at different levels of an organisation at different times while working with people and building relationships within the target organisation. To be effective at these different levels, a change agent must rely on skills from both project management and organisational development (OD) – including planning, managing tasks, leading project teams, and interfacing with the users in the organisation – and on general knowledge of IT, business and human behaviour (Bloom, 1989; Johnson and Fredian, 1986; Koehler, 1987).

A set of common principles exists between the OD practitioner and the project manager according to Adams et al. (1997). These include communication, teamwork, process management, leadership, training and continuous learning. Clarke and Meldrum (1999) identified five aspects for the successful creation of the capacity for change management: vision, ambition and personal risk, positioning, subversion and political awareness. Some authors have also stressed the meaning of leadership of change (Hooper and Potter, 2000) in identifying the appropriate change agents. They demonstrate that leadership of change means 'developing a vision of the future, crafting strategies to bring that vision into reality and ensuring that everybody in the organization is mobilizing their energies towards the same goals, the process called emotional alignment'. Heifetz and Laurie (1997) argued that the most difficult challenges facing leaders today are making sure that people in the organisation can adapt to change and that leaders can envisage where the organisation is currently placed in the market and where it should be in the future.

These consultative skills are broadly synonymous with process consultation: listening, providing feedback, counselling, coaching and inter-group dynamics (Schein, 1988). Various traits and skills are as follows: self-identification, courage and outspokenness, belief in people, openness to lifelong learning, ability to deal with complexity and uncertainty and their powerful strategic vision (Caldwell, 2003). Other characteristics include flexibility, personal drive, desire to lead, honesty and integrity, cognitive ability, self-confidence, knowledge of the business (Kirkpatrick and Locke, 1991) and risk-taking (Dulewicz and Herbert, 2000). But these skill and competencies are not founded on codified expertise, knowledge or techniques that can be instrumentally applied or learnt through conventional educational or training interventions (Bennett and Leduchowicz, 1983).

We also elucidate the skills and competencies that are intrinsic to the systems psychodynamics model. For instance, the overall task during the entry and contracting stage is to decide whether to work with the client or not. To take this decision, the consultant needs to have the following skills and competencies:

a   Clarify who is the main client

b   The clients main objectives and motives

c   Agree objectives and overall scope for the consulting work
d   Plan the general sequence and duration of a specific phase of work
e   Agree how the work will be communicated to others
f   Consider who might be in steering roles in relation to diagnosis and mutual planning of an intervention
g   Assess access to people and sections of the organisation for stages 3 and 4 (below)
h   Agree finances, logistics, frequency of contact, confidentiality
i   Clarify roles of consultant and client in relation to specified phases of work

With each stage, we will show the skills that are needed by a systems psychodynamics consultant. The stages are the following: stage 1: scouting; stage 2: entry and contracting; stage 3: diagnosis; stage 4: planning and negotiating intervention; stage 5: taking action; and stage 6: evaluating action.

As with any approach to framing and shaping theory and practice, people from different institutions argue and, not to leave the politics out if it, compete over ownership and origins of ideas. Debate ranges around fidelity to 'the model', uniqueness of the model, the extent to which the model is live and dynamic, adapting to changing times and contexts.

Values and ethics

In thinking about being a consultant, we position values ethics and practice theories at the top of the map. They guide and influence all other elements on the map.

Inclusion and diversity

Implied in participative democracy is a commitment to inclusion which extends to a desire for diversity. As systems psychodynamics consultants, we strive to work in ways that move issues of inclusion and diversity beyond a rhetoric of 'embracing difference' to a more in-depth exploration and understanding intended to address and redress inequalities. We challenge the normative view of gender, race, class, sexualities, geography and wealth status and consider the impact of these for the role holder's authority and the authorisation of the role holder by others. We recognise that the very fabric of the structures and processes at work in organisations and systems is racialised and gendered (Turner, 2021; Salami, 2020; Vlasic, 2019). Therefore, we seek to develop people's capacity to critically reflect on the meaning embedded into the systemic structures and their impact on the work that is carried out within them and for the people carrying out the work.

Dialogue and deliberation

Dialogue and deliberation are dynamic processes that can build and strengthen relationships, bridge gaps, resolve conflicts, generate innovative solutions to problems and inspire collaborative action. Dialogue and deliberation processes provide a plethora of opportunities for people to stand back and become more fully engaged with each other and in the decision-making processes of an organisation.

Dialogue allows people to share their perspectives and experiences about difficult issues. It is not about judging, weighing or making decisions, but about understanding and learning, finding common ground, re-evaluating assumptions. Dialogue dispels stereotypes, builds trust, and enables people to be open to perspectives that are very different from their own. Deliberation is a related process with a different emphasis; it promotes the use of critical reasoning and logical argument in group decision-making. Instead of decision-making by power, coercion, or hierarchy, deliberative decision-making emphasises the importance of examining all sides of an issue fairly, collecting and considering the relevant facts, and carefully weighing the pros and cons of various options. This is not to deny the context of the decision-making process where the authorised leader may have to make decisions without having time to consult as widely as they would wish. This involves paying attention to Hirschhorn's concept of primary risk and its relation to the primary task.

Developing capacity for sustainability

Another value underpinning our work as consultants is working to develop the internal capacity of the organisations, teams, and systems in which we work. Our intention is always to work towards our own redundancy. We want to develop and leave capacity and capability within the system, not to render ourselves indispensable.

The process of consultancy

The section above has given a brief overview of the different theoretical perspectives that inform our practice. This section outlines what we do, and how we are, when we take up our role as systems psychodynamics consultants. For the purposes of writing and teaching, it is helpful to consider our consultancy practice in phases. However, we know that consultancy projects rarely follow a linear or circular pattern.

Practice theories: transdisciplinarity

One of the distinguishing features and core values of the Tavistock Institute since its inception has been its commitment to working across disciplines. Recently, Laasch, Moosmayer and Antonacopoulou et al. (2020) conceptualise this by talking about a transdisciplinary approach. This sits allied to, yet distinct from, multidisciplinary and interdisciplinary approaches. See table below:

Type	Definition
Multidisciplinarity	The process whereby researchers or practitioners from different disciplines work independently or sequentially, each from a discipline-specific perspective to address a common problem
Interdisciplinarity	The process whereby researchers from different academic disciplines work together to address a common problem and yet continue to do so largely from their respective disciplinary perspectives
Transdisciplinarity	The process whereby researchers from different disciplines work together to develop and use a shared conceptual framework that integrates discipline-specific concepts, theories and methods to address a common problem

As consultants, we draw from multiple theories and disciplines to inform and develop our practice. These include the social sciences, psychoanalysis, open systems theory, action research, complexity theory, anthropology, political sciences; organisational theory, change theory, ecology, the creative arts, neuroscience, and embodied practice. As it is impossible, or available only to few among us, to be expert in all these disciplines, we rarely work alone. We work as a minimum in pairs or teams, valuing participative democracy, dialogue, and deliberation within our working relationships. We grapple with all the complexities this brings; it is not easy.

Developing the capabilities of systems psychodynamics consultants

The Tavistock Institute supports the development of capacity and capabilities in others. Since 1957 with the first Leicester Conference, the Tavistock Institute has been providing professional development opportunities for people to develop as systems psychodynamics consultants. Our development offer has increased over the years and now includes programmes focusing on developing and deepening consultancy practice, working with board dynamics, working with the creative arts as a mechanism for organisational change, developing coaching and supervisory practice and developing young leaders. Our offers include the two-week immersive residential and fully experiential Leicester Conference, certificated modular programmes spanning 6 to 12 months, regular virtual and face-to-face meetings of communities of practice, half-day virtual learning events and an alumni community.

Like the consultancy practice itself, the Tavistock Institute's approach to developing the capabilities to practice are underpinned by a set of values and ethics and core theories concerning education, learning and development. The values and ethics of our approach to development match those of our practice, that is participative democracy, inclusion and diversity, dialogue and deliberation and developing capacity for sustainability and action research.

The creation and 'holding of space'

Winnicott's 'holding environment' for creativity and transitioning; Bion's 'space for knowing', not just knowing about; Bowlby's attachment theory and the requirement for a secure base for maturation and development characterise all Tavistock Institute experiential learning that is interwoven into its professional development programmes.

Experiential learning

Experiential learning operates at different levels, learning from previous experiences, providing new experiences and learning from them, here-and-now learning in the group relations tradition; observing oneself and one's state of mind in the programmes and reflecting on it is key to experiential learning.

Different forms of knowledge

The Tavistock Institute values knowledge from different sources; the challenge is about integrating cognitive, rational ways of knowing and knowledge from the unconscious, the role of emotions in knowing and learning, notions of somatic resonances.

Parallel process

The designs of the programmes are to enhance participants' deepening awareness of consultancy practice. Therefore, the dynamics in the programmes are valuable in understanding organisational dynamics. Here, we see the idea of the temporary organisation in which here-and-now dynamics can be experienced and understood.

Tasks and capabilities

As systems psychodynamics consultants, we need the capacity and capabilities to identify, understand and work with the task. The nature and location of the task can be understood in different ways. There is the task associated with and owned by the individual, team, organisation or system you are consulting to, what they are doing. There is the task or purpose of the consultancy project, and there are the tasks associated with the different phases of the consultancy process outlined in Figures 14.1 and 14.2.

In relation to the consultancy process, Izod and Whittle (2014) identified the dynamics strongly associated with each phase of the process, that is the unconscious processes likely to accompany the conscious rational task being undertaken. For example, during the initial stages of arriving and contracting the dynamics of power and containment might be at play, this may then lead into dynamics around capability, credibility and competition as the work of gathering data and understanding what is going on gets underway. As interventions are designed and implemented, the dynamics of risk and accountability might come to the fore, alongside those associated with transitions and liminality: as the work continues dynamics of sustainability and learning emerge, and the dynamics associated with loss and endings as the work ends (Izod and Whittle, 2014). In the same way that the process itself is not linear, the different dynamics might arise and reappear at different times; for example, the dynamics around loss may be present very early in the work.

Self as instrument

The use of self as instrument is a core capability (Izod and Whittle, 2014). Our ability to attune to our inner processes, to notice and recognise our emotions and our embodied experience is vital. When we can notice these experiences, more data is available to us. For example, when we are working with a team around an upcoming merger, we might feel a tightening in our stomach or notice that we are suddenly feeling sad. This might lead us to wonder whether people are feeling anxious about the merger. The moment we notice our stomach knot, that is what was happening, who was saying what, might give us an idea about what specifically is causing the anxiety. Our feelings of sadness might be an indication of unspoken or unspeakable sadness in the team.

To develop our capacity to use ourselves as instruments, we need to know ourselves well. We need to be aware of our own histories and how they have influenced us, what biases, vulnerabilities and preferences we hold. We need knowledge of our own valencies and defensive routines, how and when are they triggered. Such knowledge and awareness will help us distinguish between what belongs to us and what to the client system. It will also help us notice when we are being drawn into a dynamic unhelpfully and how we can intervene more usefully.

Use of self as instrument extends beyond our ability to attune to our own physical, emotional and cognitive processes. It also includes our presence, how we take up our authority in the work. How we listen and how we respond. It refers to how we take up our place within the territory as a whole, which is made up of values and ethics, practice theories, the process of consultancy, task and associated dynamics, capabilities.

Boundary, authority, role and task (BART)

Systems psychodynamics consultants work with issues of boundary, authority, role and task. These four constructs are the site of analysis and understanding in group relations work and are applicable to consultants working in and with teams, organisations or systems (Green and Molenkamp, 2005). Boundaries are encountered all the time, and consultants are more aware of some than others. For example, the deadline for submission of a proposal looms large and present; however, consultants may be less consciously aware of boundaries relating to whose opinions get sought or where conversations take place. Training in systems psychodynamics consultancy requires the exploration of **boundaries** in relation to:

1 Self and other
2 How permeable are the boundaries
3 Being too far inside or too far outside the boundary
4 Taking up a position on the boundary
5 Boundaries within and between:

   a   The individual and the group
   b   Thoughts and feelings
   c   The socio-technical system
   d   The organisation and its ecological context

6 The consultant's experience of crossing a boundary

Authority involves a scrutiny of different sources from above, alongside, below and within (Obholzer, 2019). The development of systems psychodynamics consultants entails reflection on how they take up their authority, what enables and hinders this, how they respond to others taking up their authority.

Role occurs at the intersection between a person, their system and the context (Long, 2016). Role is how the consultant is authorised to intervene. Role needs to be understood in relation to formal (job) and informal (social or sentient) roles. Role involves conscious and unconscious processes of how the role is given and taken (Reed and Bazalgette, 2006).

Task: In their development, systems psychodynamic consultants need to understand and distinguish different layers of **task**, notice which task is being worked on and by whom. Attention also needs to be given to anti-task activity.

Power

How power is understood and exercised is implicit in the values and ethics of systems psychodynamics consultants. Participative democracy, inclusion, diversity of voice, opinion, experience and dialogue are intrinsic to systems psychodynamics consultancy. Understanding and working with the dynamics of power is a key capacity. Systems psychodynamic consultants need to be explicit and aware of how power is exercised. Awareness of the exercise of power is likely to lead to deeper and meaningful relationships with the client systems.

A systems psychodynamics consultant would need to be aware of issues in the wider society around power imbalances. Power imbalances are highly contested topics that at times may lead to activity that conflicts with espoused values. Systems psychodynamics consultants need to pay attention to their sources of power, how these are acquired and maintained and become aware of how they exercise it. Consultants need to recognise and understand the factors, current, historical, inter-personal and systemic, that contribute to power relations, and how these are maintained and changed.

The development of consultants involves seeing power as systemic, a network of relations encompassing a whole social system (Balan, 2010). This theoretical construct suggests that individuals are not simply the objects of power, but they are the site where the power and the resistance to it are exerted. Dynamically, power refers to power *relations* between people, as opposed to an amount possessed by people. Power is ubiquitous and found in every kind of relationship (op cit). Consultants work with relationships between individuals that are imbued with societal, cultural, historical and political legacies. Therefore, power relations need to be understood systemically within this context and not simply as isolated interactions between separate individuals or groups. One of the better ways of understanding power relations is by attending group relations conferences.

Containment: the creation and holding of space

Organisational change inevitably raises anxieties, and systems psychodynamics consultants need to be acquainted with the concept of containment. Containment is the provision of a safe space where they can speak about their concerns (Kahn, 2001). To enable consultants to develop these capabilities, training to be a consultant includes:

i   Creating learning opportunities for experimentation
ii   Exploring
iii Taking risks
iv   Exposing vulnerabilities
v   Making connections between thoughts, feelings and behaviours
vi   Exposing and challenging assumptions
vii Tolerating difficulties
viii Applying theory and experience to consultancy interventions

These are the types of space necessary to develop the capabilities of systems psychodynamics consultants and programme design will reflect this, for example, the use of social dreaming matrices, embodied or artistic, non-verbal practices. Development programmes in systems psychodynamics foster knowing and experiencing and provide opportunities to observe, notice and understand the defensive deployment of knowing about intellectually.

Experiential learning

To develop the capabilities required for systems psychodynamic consultancy practice, and the capacity to know and not simply know about, experiential learning is core. Experiential learning informs current approaches to developing systems psychodynamic consultants. Programmes include significant elements of 'here-and-now' work, that is working with the dynamics between and within staff and participants as a total system in the here-and-now. Through experiential learning, participants learn and know the dynamics associated with boundary, authority, role, task and power in the group and by extension in organisations. These aspects of programmes draw on the methodology from group relations conferences. They might include small study groups, large study groups or inter-group events. The role of staff in experiential events is to draw attention to the process of what is happening in service of the primary task of the group and to hold the boundaries of the group in relation to the time, the task and the territory.

Experiences in these events can be confusing; usual norms of a 'teacher' leading and directing activity are disrupted; powerful feelings of anger, frustration, excitement, shame, fear, incompetence, competition, isolation, loss and desire can be experienced, enacted and defended against individually and collectively. The learning is profound and sustained when participants can:

1   Experiment with taking and giving authority; leadership and followership
2   Explore boundaries between inside and outside phenomena and events
3   Notice their own responses and those of others
4   Make connections between:

   a   Unconscious and conscious dynamics
   b   Feelings, thoughts and behaviours
   c   The individual and the group
   d   The group and its context

5   Observe when the group is on- and off-task
6   Tolerate difficult or uncomfortable experiences long enough to explore and understand them
7   Apply these insights to consultancy practice

Reflective practice

Systems psychodynamic consultants need to be reflective practitioners. Programmes for consultants include elements intended to develop capability in reflection and application in the workplace. Reflective practice is a way of identifying learning from experiential activities or from other work or life experiences and using this learning to inform future practice. Schon (1987) is credited with articulating the theory around reflective practice, "a dialogue between thinking and doing through which I become more skilful" (Schon, 1987, p. 31). Reflective practice is a way of surfacing tacit knowledge and a way of distinguishing espoused theory, that which we say we do or believe we do, and theory in action, that which we actually do (Argyris and Schon, 1974). The experiential approaches described above are designed to enable and support the development of reflective practice.

Exemplar of reflective practice

Organisational consultancy: working with the dynamics

A programme for consultants and change agents in advanced consultancy skills in Tavistock institute systems psychodynamics

The necessary skills, methods, aims and working practices of Tavistock Institute systems psychodynamics approaches of organisational consultancy include:

- Developing the capacity for reflection
- Understanding the emotional experience of task-related work so that these can be better understood and mastered
- Examining how individuals and teams debate, communicate and behave, sometimes unconsciously, within organisations in ways that can help or hinder the work of the organisation
- Paying attention to how organisations behave as whole systems in their environments
- Skilful negotiation in crossing the boundary and contracting

The task of the programme is to:

- Explore the roles and tasks of advanced organisational development and change consultants and managers
- Examine how to add depth and advanced practice skills to the roles and tasks within consultancy practice
- Think together in a safe space to deepen advanced consultation skills
- Encourage a culture of curiosity and enquiry within the programme
- Develop the necessary skills to be an advanced practitioner
- Learning will be based upon consultancy and management practice, theoretical input and experiential learning

The objective of the programme is to deepen consultancy skills as a systems psychodynamics organisational development and change consultant. The approach is to provide opportunities for deep or holistic learning that focuses on principles, links and meaning, valuing uncertainty, with the participants as active explorers. The programme provides opportunities to:

- Discuss consultation dilemmas faced by organisational development and change consultants and managers
- Problem-solve, plan and collaborate on consultation issues and dilemmas
- Bring aspects of consultative practice that arouse curiosity and the seeking of new ideas on how to work with current organisational dilemmas
- Examine the roles that consultant are often unwittingly 'invited into' by the system and how task-orientated or anti-task they might be
- Work on the advanced practitioners' skills to achieve capacities and abilities to work with micro-, meso- and macro-level contexts within systems

Design – how the programme works

The programme comprises modules that can be accessed in-person or online at the Tavistock Institute of Human Relations in London. The first module comprises introductions, expectations and examination of the learning needs of the participants, practice-based small group sessions and opportunities for sharing and discussing consultancy dilemmas.

Throughout the programme, several events are provided such as:

1 Theoretical input via reading seminars and exploring the application of ideas
2 Experiential events such as small study groups, social dreaming matrices, sensing walks, and regular reviews of each event in the module as the programme progresses.
3 The presentation of consultancy practice in order to deepen the learning and the application of advanced systems psychodynamics theory and practice.
4 The opportunity to receive in-depth feedback on taking a role as a consultant

Building on the Tavistock tradition of self-regulation and semi-autonomous work groups, the design of the programme facilitates participants' involvement in both the presentation and assessment of the material. In order to facilitate the deepening of consultancy skills, the group builds a challenging and supportive culture. The group reflects on its learning and thereby develops its work.

For more details, see: https://www.tavinstitute.org/what-we-offer/professional-development/organisational-consultancy-working-with-dynamics/.

Different forms of knowledge

Implicit in this chapter is the idea that there are different forms of knowledge and different ways of knowing. In Western cultures with the enduring influence of the 18th-century period of Enlightenment, cognitive, rational, technical knowledge is valued over other ways of knowing. As we have argued, systems psychodynamics consultants need to access and use other forms of knowledge that derive from unconscious processes, our emotions and our bodies, experiences and histories.

Newer understandings from complexity theory and neuroscience further support the need for recognising and valuing other forms of knowledge. Complexity theory (see Chapter 10) points to the idea of emergent and changing knowledge. The capacity to tolerate not knowing, and the ability to work with uncertainty are consultancy capabilities to be worked with. Recent understandings from neuroscience support ideas from psychoanalytic theory that many of our ways of relating are laid down before the development of the neocortex, the part of the brain responsible for cognition and reasoning. We also now have a greater understanding that aspects of our behaviour, especially when under stress, are not within our conscious control (Music, 2011). Current work around trauma recognises the role of the body in holding and enacting powerful knowledge (Van der Kolk, 2014). Emotions, often seen as having no place in the workplace, are known to provide valuable data and to enhance our decision-making (Damasio, 2000, 2006).

Programmes designed to develop systems psychodynamics consultants should therefore include elements that enable participants to access different forms of knowledge and different ways of knowing. Experiential learning as described above does this. Increasingly elements of embodied practice are included within development programmes. Gestalt, mindfulness and yoga enable greater connection between the mind, body and emotions. They enable our capacity to be present, making us more available to attune to what is happening within ourselves and with those around us. The capacity to be fully present supports the ability to stay with difficulties or discomfort. Theoretically, this is called working with and in the countertransference (see Lawlor and Sher, 2021, Chapter 3). Skill in working with the countertransference enables systems psychodynamics consultants to provide the containing environment required by the client system. Embodied practice also supports personal wellbeing and resilience, invaluable for consultants and clients.

Parallel process and double task

Systems psychodynamics consultants work with the notions of parallel process, which is often referred to projective identification, and the double task. Parallel process is a psychoanalytic concept in which the relational processes operating between the client and therapist are brought unconsciously into supervision (Pickvance, 2017). Cardona (2020) talks about the team as a sponge, meaning that the feelings and behaviour of teams vary and are influenced by the nature of the task they are engaged with. For example, teams working with children in the care system may find themselves especially impacted around endings, which may evoke unconscious anxieties and behaviours associated with the child's early and current feelings of abandonment.

Consultants find it useful to work with ideas of parallel process (projective identification, mirroring) in consultancy projects. Therefore, programmes in consultancy practice provide opportunities for developing skills in recognising, hypothesising about and working with these concepts. The here-and-now and other experiential activities described above work with these theories. At its simplest, the hypothesis is that the same dynamics that occur in organisations, systems or teams will play out within the temporary organisation of the programme and are thus available for study and learning. The specific composition of the group will bring opportunities to experience and learn using parallel process, projective identification, transference, countertransference and mirroring.

Bridger (1990) introduced the idea of the double task. He worked with the notion that at any one time an organisational group or team is attending to at least two tasks, the business task and the relational task. He proposed the idea when working in organisations, 'business-as-usual' and the emotional and conflictual elements at play should be observed and worked with at the same time. This process of integrating the 'business task' at hand and the emotional and relational activity in the group remains a key element of development programmes for systems psychodynamics consultants.

Ongoing development

This section has spoken primarily about development programmes. These are vital, foundational experiences and opportunities to learn and develop the craft of systems psychodynamics consultancy. We recommend that anyone seriously wanting to incorporate this approach into their practice participates in such a development programme. However, the work is not done once the programme is over. Like any craft, the learning and development continues over a lifetime. Using supervision, engaging in personal therapy or other self-understanding or development work, working alongside experienced others, the ongoing use of reflective practice, participating in alumni communities of practice, attending group relations conferences, presenting at and attending conferences, seeking connections and dialogue with other disciplines and practices, experimenting, reading and writing are all critical to one's ongoing development as a systems psychodynamics practitioner.

Summary

The next generation agitates for clarity, showing their colours and defining the territory. They demand clarity of the array of terms and practices. A useful frame to locate the knowledge, skills and attitudes focuses on values and ethics; practice theories; the consultancy process; and tasks and capabilities. The systems psychodynamics consultant must combine problem-solving, vision, determination, technical expertise and inter-personal and political skills. Competencies of effective consultants include clarifying goals; team-building activities; communication skills; negotiation skills; influencing skills to gain commitment to goals. Limitations in change management are associated with the managerial perceptions of the need for change, the opportunity to change and about the way to change. Perceptions, beliefs and assumptions of systems psychodynamics consultants are vital aspects to be understood. Four competencies for consultants include broad knowledge of the intelligence from the behavioural sciences and theories and methods of change; operational and relational skills, such as the ability to listen, observe, identify and report, and to form relationships based on trust; sensitivity and maturity, including self-recognition of motivators and the perceptions that others have of these motivators; authenticity in living and acting in accordance with humanistic values. Effective skills are required in planning, managing tasks, leading project teams and interfacing with the users in the organisation – and on general knowledge of IT, business and human behaviour. They must have vision, ambition and personal risk, positioning, subversion and political awareness. Leadership of change means 'developing a vision of the future, crafting strategies to bring that vision into reality and ensuring that everybody in the organization is mobilizing their energies towards the same goals, the process called emotional alignment'. The most difficult challenges are adapting to change. Listening, providing feedback, counselling, coaching and inter-group dynamics skills are relevant as are self-identification, courage and outspokenness, belief in people, openness to lifelong learning, ability to deal with complexity and uncertainty and their powerful strategic vision. Other characteristics include flexibility, personal drive, desire to lead, honesty and integrity, cognitive ability, self-confidence, knowledge of the business and risk-taking. These skills and competencies are not founded on codified expertise, knowledge or techniques that can be instrumentally applied or learnt through conventional educational or training interventions.

Exercise

1 Identify the gaps between your initial consultancy training and the ideas contained in this chapter?
2 Identify how you might fill the gap?
3 Which areas do you think you need to concentrate on?
4 Discuss with your peers how they see your development as a systems psychodynamics consultant.
5 How well are you acquainted with the theory?

Chapter 15

Systems psychodynamics – developments and definitions

David Lawlor and Mannie Sher

Here, we summarise and review the concepts and working practices of the systems psychodynamics model of organisational consultancy and its current applications. Previously, we have clarified that the systems psychodynamics literature pertaining to consultancy work and organisational theory is made up of many strands and theories (Lawlor and Sher, 2022). We have claimed that *psychoanalytic theory* as a means of understanding organisational process has a privileged place alongside *open systems* theory. These two bodies of knowledge come together in the descriptions of *projective and introjective process* that occur in organisations and in the individuals within them. However, the application of these ideas as a consulting methodology is poorly theorised. We detailed how consultancy in the systems psychodynamics tradition brings these two bodies of knowledge together for the sake of making better sense of the vicissitudes of organisational life. Specifically, the relationship between introjection and projection in the consulting relationship is not usually made explicit in the literature.

We have put forward the view that the model of systems psychodynamics consultancy is limited if it does not contain psychoanalytic and group relations perspectives. We have described how consultancy work that does not have an in-depth understanding and application of unconscious processes in individuals, groups and the wider environment can have limited success in solving complex and enduring people and systemic problems. Therefore, systems psychodynamics theory and practice embody the application of the combined theories of psychoanalysis and systems theories. To be sure, the rather limited contribution of developments within the socio-technical literature in the UK has led to an over-emphasis on the clinical aspects of the theory, that is addressing the 'what is wrong?' question. We have attempted to redress this imbalance by high-lighting how psychoanalytic theory and formulations would have limited application if they were not connected to the structural properties of the organisational and environmental systems, and answer the 'how to render the organisation's/society's performance more effectively for its citizens?' We have outlined how the socio-technical systems and design theory best provide this structural contribution because it considers every organisation to be made up

DOI: 10.4324/9781003368663-21

of people – the social system – using tools, techniques and knowledge – the technical system – to produce goods or services valued by customers, or users, and to the satisfaction of stakeholders – the environmental system. Systems psychodynamics theory demonstrates how organisations should be optimally designed and how the design impacts both the organisation's performance and the satisfaction of its members. The systems psychodynamics model shows that *changing* the design of the technical system affects the social system and vice versa. Systems psychodynamics argues that the most effective arrangements would be those that integrate the demands of both the technical and the social systems. This is known as *joint optimisation*, which is always *work in progress*. Peak performance as a goal can only be aspired to when the needs of both systems are recognised and met. In organisational design, **work design** is the application of socio-technical systems principles and techniques to the humanisation of work.

We have described how the multidisciplinary, transdisciplinary and multi-theoretical nature of the systems psychodynamics model makes an evaluation of the model a complex task. We have shown how the model is a complex in-terweaving of different theories that are all brought to bear when a consultant is working with a client system. We have demonstrated the use of the different concepts that make up the model when working in organisational consultancy. We have discussed the application of psychoanalytic theory and the appropri-ateness of open systems thinking for organisational theorising. The systems psychodynamics model as integrated psychoanalytic theory and open systems theory leads us to assert that systems psychodynamics constitutes a distinct paradigm. We offer Johnson and Duberley's (2000) interpretation of Kuhn's formulation of a paradigm as a:

> … *set of beliefs, values, assumptions and techniques centred around successive exem-plars of successful practical application. A paradigm serves as a regulative frame-work of metaphysical assumptions 'shared by members of a given community' (Kuhn, 1970) which specifies the character of the world and its constituent objects and pro-cesses and which acts as a 'disciplinary matrix' by drawing the boundaries for what a community's work is to look like. As such, paradigms are 'universally recognised scientific achievements that for a time provide model problems and solutions to a community of practitioners' (Kuhn, 1970). Each 'practitioner community' is charac-terised by a consensus, into which neophytes are socialised through their disciplinary training. This consensus is grounded in a tradition that bases their work around a shared way of thinking and working within an established network of ideas, theo-ries and methods. Each paradigm therefore has its own distinctive language which offers a unique means of classifying and construing the objects encountered during scientists' engagements with the world.*
>
> (Pg. 68)

The authors of these volumes, using the above definition, have shown that the systems psychodynamics community of professional practitioners has over the last 70+ years developed a new paradigm for understanding organisational life and the nature of work. The paradigm has stood the test of social and economic changes in the world from industrial society to the post-industrial society based on the network and values organisation, virtual working, the information society and the post-COVID society. The paradigm serves as an incorporated model with several theories and categorisations of phenomena from other disciplines to construct a model of the world, of societies, of organisations, individuals and groups and a theory of practice.

The theory of practice has presented problems for research. The development of theory and practice has led to different strands that can be identified as 'systems psychodynamics'. These different strands have placed different emphasis on the differing theoretical concepts underpinning their practice. Miller (1993) makes this same point, 'there has been no single systems psychodynamics role model'. Jaques (1951), Sofer (1961) and Rice (1963) described their positions differently. Commonalties are more important. Miller argues that the differing projects that the systems psychodynamics practitioners were engaged in led to the generation of different theories, as the demands of the 'laboratory of real life' required solutions from the action research/consultation processes in which they were involved.

We have shown that it is possible to bring the different strands of practice and theory together to make it possible to position oneself within the systems psychodynamics paradigm without necessarily adhering to all the theoretical propositions.

The literature below posits the core concepts of systems psychodynamics practice:

The individual and the mechanisms of defence	Klein (1959)
	Menzies (1960)
	Hirschhorn (1988)
Role	Reed and Armstrong *(1988)*
Group processes	Bion (1961)
Use of social systems as defences against anxiety	Jaques (1955a)
	Menzies (1960)
	Krantz (2010)
Boundary	Rice (1965)
	Miller and Rice (1967)
Systemic	Miller (1990)
Open system	Miller and Rice (1967)
	von Bertalanffy (1950)
Socio-technical system	Trist and Bamforth (1951)
Organisation-in-the-mind	Lawrence (1979)
	Hutton (1995)
	Armstrong (1995)
Authority and power	Rice (1965)
	Reed and Armstrong (1988)
	Jaques (1989)

The systems psychodynamics paradigm is the 'container' that supports consultancy practice:

Working with groups is a core practice and involves:

i   A temporary holding environment and container for client anxieties
ii   Working with or in the transference and countertransference
iii Working-through
iv   Defining and clarifying boundaries
v   Designing new forms of organisation
vi   Designing experiential learning events

Therefore, we claim that the systems psychodynamics model is a paradigm by virtue of:

a   Working with groups as a preferred method of diagnosis and intervention. This practice draws upon Bion (1961) and group relations, that is the 'Leicester Conference – a working conference for the study of organisational life'. This involves a distinctive form of process consultancy, in which the consultant works interpretatively with the 'material' presented by the client group
b   Serving as a temporary holding environment and container for client anxieties (individuals, teams, management and leadership groups)
c   Working with or in the transference – all the thoughts feelings and fantasies that are invoked in the client-consultant relationship. The consultant uses this experience to understand organisational life that is outside the client's awareness
d   Working with the countertransference; that is, offering a working hypothesis, and using one's own feelings, fantasies, impulses and behaviour as indicators of having become not only in, but of the client system
e   Working with projective identification, introjective identification and re-projection via an interpretation or working hypothesis or as an intervention
f   Working through, helping the client recognise resistance to change and the associated fears to change processes
g   Defining and clarifying boundaries. It is assumed that articulating and enacting a coherent array of roles and task systems is functional for organisational work
h   Designing new forms of organisation based on an open systems model (Miller and Rice, 1967) considering complexity theory (Gell-Mann, 1994; Gleick, 1987)
i   Designing experiential learning events; training in group relations

These elements make up the 'container' that is the systems psychodynamics paradigm. We argue that the systems psychodynamics paradigm includes the environment. The role of the environment must take its place alongside the study of technical systems and the psychodynamics of individuals, teams, groups and stakeholders. It is called the socio-ecological perspective, and if the interplay between environment and organisation is ignored, not spoken about, it will go underground and become part of the unconscious substratum of unknowable aspects of people's experiences. Authors sometimes leave out most fundamentally the concept of the *environment* that processes and concepts operate in. In such cases, the conceptual boundary around the core concepts and core practice do not allow for the environmental context in which practice takes place.

The work in the socio-ecological domain answers the identification of the environment in the systems psychodynamics model. Trist and Murray (1993) specifically make the connection between the work on socio-technical systems with the development of the socio-ecological model. They refer to the turbulent field that most organisations now find themselves in and make the point that over-bounded systems can no longer survive in the modern world of what is today referred to as globalisation:

> No organisation, however large, can go it alone in a turbulent environment. Dissimilar organisations become directly correlated. They need to become directly correlated. They need to be linked in networks. A new focus of the Tavistock Institute's (systems psychodynamics) work has been, therefore, the development of collaborative modes of intervention for the reduction of turbulence and the building of inter-organisational networks that can address 'meta-problems' at the 'domain' level.........The socio-ecological approach is linked to the socio-technical because of the critical importance of self-regulating organisations for turbulence reduction. It is further linked to the socio-psychological approach because of the need to reduce stress and regression. Primitive levels of behaviour can only too easily appear in the face of higher levels of uncertainty.
>
> (Trist and Murray, 1993)

Our books explore the more applicable metaphors of systems, individuals, groups, organisations and environments, operating like neural pathways with overlapping boundaries. Boundary location is then less determinate. Boundaries are truly permeable. The consequence for an individual is that work must be carried out in a multiplicity of roles and tasks and the membership of multiple overlapping systems. These books demonstrate that our perspectives and understandings must go beyond the kind of boundary constraints that we are familiar with. To have effectively intervened, the consultant would have to move outside the client boundary into boundaries of other systems that are impinging on the tasks of his client group. This is the work that consultants do. Working within a distinct boundary often prevents us from moving outside into wider, more complex systems and their sometimes, hidden influences.

The use of any metaphor or symbol for organisational life can easily lead to a reification process. Instead of regarding a group or boundary as heuristic concepts, one to be worked with and developed through thought and dialogue, they quickly can become fixed and institutionalised and be rendered meaningless and dead. We are not suggesting that the consultant should move directly into working with another group that is not the client, but more that the consultant might enable the client to think about and take action with the whole system.

Holding in mind all three domains that make up the systems psychodynamics model – the *socio-psychological, socio-technical and socio-ecological* – creates real difficulties for practitioners. It is as if three domains are too much to encompass in the consultant's 'methodological kit bag' and their core practice. The consultant may be driven into one domain to occupy professionally, and thus 'turns a blind eye' to what does not have to be faced elsewhere.

Definitions

Petriglieri and Petriglieri (2020) states:

> *Systems psychodynamic scholarship focuses on the interaction between collective structures, norms, and practices in social systems and the cognitions, motivations, and emotions of members of those systems. It is most useful to investigate the unconscious forces that underpin the persistence of dysfunctional organizational features and the appeal of irrational leaders. It is also well equipped to challenge arrangements that stifle individual and organizational development.*

They write:

> *The insights that taking a psychodynamic lens make available, reviewers told us, are compelling but not convincing, more poetic than precise. On the one hand, those are fair characterizations of the main protagonist and construct of psychodynamics – the unconscious – whose work is always to compel and seldom to convince. On the other hand, systems psychodynamic scholarship can help scholarship reconcile these dualities. ..... the best scholarship in this vein has the precision of poetics — rather than the precision one might associate with a scale. The kind of precision that does not sacrifice richness and leaves room for contradiction.*
>
> *Just because it is an interpretive, and at times critical, perspective, it does not mean that everything goes in systems psychodynamic theorizing. Quite the contrary. Its interpretive methods call for ruthless self-examination, as well as, and as a form of, data analysis.*

For these and other reasons, systems psychodynamics has been largely disregarded. Blignaut (2021) agrees with Gabriel and Carr (2002) when they say:

> *It is our contention that psychoanalysis opens valuable windows into the world of organisations and management, offering insights that are startlingly original, have extensive explanatory powers and can find ample practical implementations. And I*

am also sorry that the following has not happened: It is also our contention that as scholars of management and organisations move beyond the standard platform of organisational theory, centred on rationality, hierarchy and authority and become more interested in symbolic, irrational, emotional and discursive dimensions of organisational life, the insights of psychoanalysis will become more mainstream to the field and its applications more widespread.

Due to the key theoretical and practical application of psychoanalysis, the assumption can be made that the focus is on the individual. But systems psychodynamics is, 'a term used to refer to the collective psychological behavior', (Neumann, 1999, p. 57) within and between groups and organisations.

Systems psychodynamics, therefore, provides a way of thinking about energizing or motivating forces resulting from the interconnection between various groups and sub-units of a social system.

(Fraher, 2004; Neumann, 1999, p. 57)

Systems psychodynamics recognises that human beings inside and outside of their organisations are emotional beings with personal and family histories.

In all of these instances, then, work is a range of activities driven by complex motives, which may express both instrumental rationality and hidden unconscious desires, or the latter masquerading as the former.

Yiannis and Carr (2002)

Developments

The field of systems psychodynamics has broadened its range since the initial work on organisational dynamics and consultancy projects. Eric Miller was one of the initiators of the process when applying a systems psychodynamics view to the understanding of society (Khaleelee and Miller, 1985). They put forward the view that society could be understood as an intelligible field of study. The paper argues that in contrast to our membership of other groups, the inescapable group is society, a system in which all of us participate actively or passively. The question posed is does society have an unconscious. The use of splitting and projection is different when applied to society. Projections can be placed into whole categories as individuals may have little or no contact with such entities. Brunning and Khaleelee (2021) further develop these arguments in their *Danse Macabre and Other Stories: A Psychoanalytic Perspective on Global Dynamics* (Brunning and Khaleelee, 2021).

Revisiting primary task

Hoggett (1996) argued that the definition of ***primary task*** as the task that must be carried out for the institution to survive is limiting the definition to certain interest groups. Who defines the 'task' seems to be the point he is making. Within the group relations model, it would be those 'authorised' in role to make such decisions, but this may evade the issue of how they are authorised and whom this authorisation represents. Hoggett and Nestor (2021) question the traditional interpretation of the primary task and argue that the *purpose* of the system should also be considered. In the context of climate change, they cite Daum (2019) who asks both businesses and individuals confronting increasing precarity, 'what must I do in order to survive?' He usefully distinguishes between 'what and how' questions on the one hand, and 'why' questions on the other. 'Why' questions are about purpose and meaning both for organisations and for individuals. Hoggett and Nestor (2021) state that one of the core mantras of the group relations world is the primary task of the organisation, which is typically defined as 'that which it must undertake in order to survive'. They argue that unwittingly group relations has colluded with Lawrence's (2000), 'politics of salvation', with 'survival no matter what the cost' rather than with 'survival for what purpose?' As many writers (e.g. Krantz, 1989, 1990, 2008; Roberts, 2019) have argued, the challenge is to go beyond task to purpose, beyond what/how to why, beyond business-as-usual to transformational change. They propose that survivalist mind-sets are influencing the increasing insistence upon business-as-usual and its adoption as an ideology. Armstrong (2005) in reflecting on the term 'primary task' points out the term has considerable heuristic value, helping to sharpen and clarify the relation between organisational processes of import, conversion and export. He then questions if this helps us understand the meaning of the organisation, or as he puts it, 'the what-ness, the is-ness' of the organisation. He goes on to describe the concept of practice, based on MacIntyre's (1985) conceptualisation. Practice he suggests is the animating spirit, which gives psychic resonance to the organisation. This breathes life into the organisation and gives meaning to the primary task.

It is within this context of present-day practice of the systems psychodynamics tradition that the authors have written this book. From this overview of the literature, and an examination of practice, the authors have developed a methodology informed by the systems psychodynamics model. The model is also capable of examining how teaching and learning about consultancy is constructed through language and social processes to collectively construct norms and expectations, define and legitimise knowledge, build affiliation and position participants as they take up roles through social interaction.

Leadership and power

Postmodern and critical perspectives are theories that focus on power and domination and on challenges to hierarchy, bureaucracy and management control. Within the systems psychodynamics set of theories, power can appear to be a relatively unexplored concept. Gabriel (2011) argues that while contemporary ideas on leadership are varied and diverse with an emphasis on dispersed, diffused leadership, there is a coherent view of leadership from a psychoanalytic perspective. Freud (1921) demonstrated that leadership involved a powerful relation between leaders and followers; one based on identification of followers with the leader and their idealisation. Following Bion's (1961) analysis of group dynamics, he emphasised that leaders fulfil vital emotional functions for their followers, paramount among which is the containment of anxiety and other toxic emotions. Both Freud and Bion emphasise the tendency of leaders to awaken in their followers, fantasies and desires first experienced in childhood, in those early relations with parents, which act as templates for our subsequent encounters with authority and power. Gabriel (2011) defines leadership as being made up of imagining, willing, inspiring and driving. This is a definition that emphasises leaders as agents for change engaged in relations with others. 'Imagination' means being able to envisage new possibilities, new products, new ideas, new methods, new alliances, new ways of using words and language and even new needs and desires. 'Willing' means that the dream is not an 'idle' fantasy but becomes a strong motivator towards action. Imagining and willing together are essential for leadership. According to Gabriel, a leader will 'drive' others by emotionally engaging with them, being able to communicate, elaborate and share a vision, inspiring them and winning them over, but also occasionally by cajoling and exhorting them. 'Engaging' with others is a feature of all aspects of leading, including imagining. Leaders do not just sit and dream, waiting for a vision to arrive. Still less do visions arise from vision statements carefully prepared by hired consultants. Instead, visions emerge from active engagement with others, understanding of collective aspirations and wishes and flights of imagination that push the bounds of possibility. Armstrong (2005) seems to be making a similar point but with a different use of language when he suggests that leadership requires the capacity for 'discernment', the act of bringing into view and articulating what is often tacit within an organisation in relation to its implicit order, the ways in which it embodies meaning in its work.

Psychoanalysis and the study of organisations

The contributions of psychoanalysis to the study of organisations have been varied. Some of them have sprung from a hermeneutic perspective using psychoanalytic theories to examine organisational artefacts, some have embraced more pragmatic quasi-therapeutic approaches to account for persistent organisational irrationalities and dysfunctions, while others have adopted an approach consistent with Critical Management Studies (CMS), seeking to denaturalise and critique mainstream theories and to discover some emancipatory possibilities. These psychoanalytic approaches share an emphasis on unconscious organisational processes and an interest in irrational, fantastic qualities of organisational life.

Gabriel and Carr (2002) see as central the concept of transference, which can be a determining factor in relationships with leaders, peers and subordinates in organisations. Due to the emotional and irrational aspects of the transference dynamics, there can be a distortion of the emotions in these relationships (Baum, 1987; Diamond, 1988; Gabriel, 1999; Oglensky, 1995). As we have seen, organisations have defences against anxieties which the task of organisations can mobilise.

The containment of anxiety is a fundamental task in every organisation. A disproportionate amount of anxiety can lead to more defensive behaviour and structures, that is less permeable boundaries, practices and procedures that inhibit the carrying out of the primary task, while insufficient anxiety leads to complacency, inertia and gradual decay, a withdrawal from the primary task (Baum, 1987; French and Vince, 1999; Gould et al., 1999; Hirschhorn, 1988; Stacey, 1992; Stein, 2000). The task of a systems psychodynamics consultant is to pay attention to how this inevitable anxiety is being managed and thought about and help the system contain the anxieties.

Long (2001) argues that for the organisational consultant, working with organisations may require interventions from a variety of perspectives and the practice of organisational research or consultancy must draw on many sources. These might include data gathering, analysis and interpretation drawn from social science, psychology and economics. Theoretically, consultants might draw on systems theory, management theory and theories about human behaviour in general. Many are now drawing on psychoanalytic theory and practice in their consulting work (Hirschhorn and Barnett, 1993; Klein et al., 1998; Miller, 1993; Obholzer and Roberts, 1994). Long suggest that this practice involves the analytically trained practitioner in cultivating a state-of-mind capable of entertaining and understanding the state-of-mind of the other.

Systems psychodynamics focuses upon the use of psychoanalytic insights through interventions aimed at building better functioning organisations often with an emphasis upon group processes and/or analysing the emotional dynamics of the 'leaders' of the organisation. The emphasis is one of seeking to eliminate some of the unnecessary suffering and hardships and fostering learning, creativity and cooperation.

Postmodern perspectives: Stewart Clegg

Stewart Clegg (1990), in his work *Modern Organizations*, characterises postmodern organisations as:

1 Flexible structures needing workers with multiple skills who are capable of continual learning
2 Market niches replace mass consumption
3 Smaller is better' if organisations are doing what they do best

4 Bureaucracy is replaced by workplace democracy in which all employees are valuable sources of decision-making
5 Market needs are primary
6 Teams replace the emphasis on the individual contributor
7 Top-down management is made obsolete by self-managing teams
8 Quality is a part of all processes, not the 'inspected-for-quality' mentality of the past
9 Management is a responsibility fulfilled at a point in time rather than a permanent occupation
10 Rewards are more group and team-based than based on the individual
11 Trust is fundamental among all managers and employees, with an emphasis on broad support for planning and decision-making

These ideas are reminders of the seminal work conducted by Trist and Emery on socio-psychological, socio-technical and socio-ecological systems in autonomous working groups and large systems (Trist et al., 1990, 1993, 1997).

The future

This book is being written in the extraordinary years of 2020 onwards when the world is in the midst of a global pandemic and a European war. The pandemic has accelerated the need to move to new ways of working and the functioning of organisations. In many ways, this has accelerated and amplified changes that were already happening. The possibilities presented by advanced technology were already being exploited beforehand with more business being conducted virtually and the digital age well and truly established. The idea of virtual teams, virtual organisations and the disappearance of the office (maybe temporarily or maybe forever) have suddenly become a reality for many. Gallagher (2021), in *Hybrid working 2.0: Humanising the office* an analysis of office working in Australia, offers the following insights:

1 Flexible working to be the predominant way of working for knowledge workers, driven by work/life balance. Not having flexible options at work is emerging as a deal breaker, with 43% of knowledge workers prepared to walk. Current flexible working arrangements are not working. Flexible workers are significantly less productive than workers of fixed location because flexible working is too complicated. Flexible workers are struggling to figure out not only the where and when of work but also knowing what to do and how to work with their team.
2 Most organisations will become hybrid, in the way that most workers will be flexible. But strategy is conspicuously missing from current approaches. Hybrid models must elevate to more than solving logistical challenges to focus on the purpose of work.

3 Hybrid working 2.0 differentiates work according to the comparative advantage of the location. Remote working increases individual productivity; the office is where people come to work together through meaningful interactions. Productivity is boosted, and creativity is amplified.
4 Hybrid working 2.0 is a business imperative that drives values creation and accommodates workers' expectations of flexible arrangements. It is a win-win.
5 The 'new office' is central to hybrid working, which will be an anchor for your organisation to support organisational culture and new ways of working. A new focus on activity-based human interactions helps organisations determine the work ideally suited for the office, in hybrid mode, and remote.

Gallagher recommends four core strategies for organisations to shift to hybrid working 2.0:

1 Co-design a hybrid working model – work with your employees to align their expectations of flexible working with organisational needs that drive value creation
2 Program meaningful activity-based human interactions in the new office – establish new rituals and programmed activities that repurpose the office
3 Design the right space – optimise space around activities for the meaningful interaction of people
4 Develop a hybrid working charter – develop core hybrid working principles that guide decisions

Yang et al (2021) showed that firm-wide remote work caused the collaboration network of workers to become more static and siloed with fewer bridges across the organisation. At the same time, there were a decrease in synchronous communication and an increase in asynchronous communication. Together, these effects may make it harder for employees to acquire and share new information across the network.

The implications of these causal effects are:

1 Less diversity of expertise and perspectives on solving complex problems
2 Poorer ideation
3 Reduced transfer of knowledge, that is workplace learning
4 Reduced quality of workers' output

We imagine that similar findings would be found outside Australia. We believe that this calls for a reapplication of socio-technical systems design and the use of participative design to engage the workforce in truly humanising the workplace.

The differences and inequalities that have long existed are amplified and illuminated. For many, the workplace cannot become virtual, and for those where it can, the debate rages over whether it should. These changes in the technical or physical aspects of working life are simultaneously occurring amidst experiences of heightened emotion, increased anxiety and continuing uncertainty. Some individuals and organisations are creating and taking opportunities, the entrepreneurial spirit is booming in some parts of society, while in others there are grieving, exhaustion and experiences of redundancy, poverty and increased deprivation.

In many ways, the pandemic has further illuminated the increasing polarisation in society, a phenomenon noted pre-pandemic (Carothers and O'Donohue, 2019; Dartington, 2020; McNeil-Willson, 2020). Emanating from Cartesian dualism, Eurocentric patriarchy supports binary thinking (Salami, 2020). Polarisation reduces the space for dialogue and deliberation, for nuance, for difference or the holding of multiple perspectives. It looks for certainty for right and wrong; it increases opportunities for 'us and them'; in fact, it demands an 'us and them'.

The effects of the pandemic and the war in the Ukraine, and our responses to it and its ongoing legacy will significantly impact individuals, workplaces, communities and nations across the world in ways that we cannot yet know. For systems psychodynamics consultancy to remain an influential shaper of the field, we need to hold to our values and expand our tradition.

Below, we consider some of the elements of this change and the implications for systems psychodynamics consultancy.

Trends and possible futures

Systems psychodynamics consultants pay attention to trends and possibilities for the future of work, organisational life and the workforce. The pandemic has sparked much debate, speculation, and thinking about what working lives will look like in the future (Boland et al, 2020; Gobrin, 2021). Consultants need to ensure that practice remains relevant and how to influence, how and where to develop and adapt, including how to prepare future practitioners.

Church and Burke (2017) identified three future drivers:

1 The changing nature of work. They suggested that the boundaries around companies, defining how people do their day-to-day activities, what they do and how they connect in various social systems, have and will continue to change.
2 The changing nature of data; the importance of it, the speed, variety, authenticity, and volume of information both public and private will drive change.
3 The changing dynamics of the workforce, the shifting ethnic and generational demographics, values, structures, expectations and social

responsibility requirements of the new workforce include much discussion about generational differences between boomers, millennials, Gen Y, Gen Z and the newly emerging of Gen Alpha (Baum, 2020).

They also note four trends:

1 **A shift to platforms over products.** New forms of organisation are emerging because of e-commerce; structures are looser, more fluid, virtual and dynamic. The boundaries of what is and what is not part of the organisation are less clear (Krantz, 2013, 2014). For example, eBay and Uber provide centralised hubs or headquarters and large networks of transactions on a platform provided by the company with users operating independently of the company.
2 **A shift to digital over mechanical.** As technology becomes increasingly integrated into our lives, the need for agility and speed in the way businesses respond to information demands that they adopt a digital mind-set and set of processes.
3 **A shift to insights over data.** New types of organisational entities are producing volumes of data. The expectation for how data is harnessed and used is changing dramatically. The collection and processing of this information alone is not enough. In today's business, landscape organisations are focusing increasingly on generating insights from the data to inform business decisions and future direction.
4 **A shift to talent over employees.** This trend sits at the front of many HR and OD agendas. They highlight the philosophical distinction between talent management – a disproportionate focus on the few, and traditional OD, a concerted focus on the many (Church and Burke, 2017).

Similarly, Stubbings and Williams (2018) identify five overarching trends as the forces reshaping society and with that the world of work:

1 Technological breakthrough and rapid advances in technological innovation
2 Demographic shifts and the changing size, distribution and age profile of the world's population
3 Rapid urbanisation and significant increase in the world's population moving to live in cities
4 Shift in global economic power and power shifting between developed and developing countries
5 Resource scarcity with depleted fossil fuels, extreme weather, rising sea levels and water shortages

The responses to these challenges and opportunities will determine the future world that we will live in, the socio-ecological context (Trist et al., 1997). People will continue to be anxious and threatened at times and defend themselves against such threats, the socio-psychological context. People will continue to be variously ambitious, competitive, envious and compassionate. Understanding how people interact, the conscious and unconscious dynamics that exist between individuals and groups, how power and authority are assigned, taken up and exercised, the interconnectedness and interdependencies between people and systems including our eco-systems, and how all of these interact with the changing nature of the task to be performed will remain vital.

The importance of systems thinking for the future is emphasised (Church and Burke, 2017). Capabilities of adaptability, flexibility, creativity and agility are seen as the way forward for leaders, for leaders to develop in their workforce and for individuals to develop for themselves (Bushe and Nagaishi, 2018). Questions relating to boundary, authority, role, task and power will remain relevant, useful and important to ask. What will be essential to keeping systems psychodynamics practices alive, relevant and influential will be the ability to stay alert to the different answers evoked by such questions as they emerge over time.

Church and Burke (2017) argue that socio-technical understandings about how we function in our new and emerging work contexts will remain important. They suggest revisiting and revitalising these understandings in the light of current trends. There is a need for the practice and theoretical development of these concepts into an understanding of the joint optimisation of the socio-psychological, technical and digital systems for the future. Systems psychodynamics consultants will need to develop their theory and practice to incorporate the influence and impact of the digital world. Consultants are increasingly facing the need to understand the dynamics of virtual and networked organisations and how to helpfully intervene. Consultants know their current expertise has much to offer the future. However, unless systems psychodynamics consultants also develop their confidence, competence and authority in relation to digitalisation, the world of big data and advancing technology, they may find they are marginalised. This includes developing a capacity to incorporate the use and potential of new technology and the needs and expectations of new generations of consultants into the systems psychodynamics pedagogy for development programmes.

Changing power dynamics

We see from Freud that infants' acknowledgement of the parents as leaders generates the oedipal triangle. With greater knowledge, greater powers, power of life and non-life, access to resources and development, threats to independence and autonomy, influences the development of ambivalence (loving and hating feelings) towards parents and authority figures. The growth of populism appeals to basic primitive group feelings. These include the denial of dependency and interdependency, which, in turn, leads to counterdependency, that is we don't want other people; sibling rivalry; everybody must have prizes; divisions into us and them; the 'othering' of asylum seekers; going over the heads of the elite – appealing to the mob and the undifferentiated mass. These social issues mobilise the most primitive aspects of the group and are examples of Klein's paranoid-schizoid state of mind.

In relation to the exercise of power, do leaders view their followers as reflected images of glory and narcissism of themselves in the same way that parents think of their children reflecting them? Is it possible that the biological drive to propagate one's genes is visible in the mirroring of a fantasised ideal self in one's followers in their identification via projection with the leader? Political leaders such as Putin and Trump could be seen to be exemplars of this process.

The systems psychodynamics approach to understanding people in their work contexts developed in the post-Second World War era. Like many other enterprises emerging in the West during this time, its early pioneers were predominantly white, middle class, Oxbridge or equivalent, educated men. The resurgence of the Black Lives Matter movement in April 2020 and the #Metoo movement in 2017 demands the re-examination and recognition of how our systems and structures privilege some and oppress others.

With these sensitivities around how women and race are experienced, there can emerge a dynamic of being over careful so as not to cause offence. This is an important dynamic as it can make it hard to talk about the pain of racism, slavery or gender politics and their legacies. We see the rise of stranger fear; the other; the dynamics of superiority/inferiority. We have recently witnessed some police forces in America seemingly getting away with murder, the rise of Anti-Semitism, exceptionalism; Islamophobia (see Small Axe films – Steve McQueen – https://www.bbc.co.uk/iplayer/episodes/p08vxt33/small-axe). At play, seem to be primitive inter-group dynamics; projections of unwanted negative feeling aspects of the self, such as dirty, impure, ignorant, out of control sexuality, immorality, violence, greed, destruction, specialness, inferiority, abhorrence, fear, hatred, loathing, contempt, vilification, the primitive.

We also see the painful and persistent attempts to counter racism. We also see the need for a strong family system, a family system that was often and routinely broken to produce more slaves; it is difficult to recover from the damaged introjective models that have been forced into us by an oppressive and exploitative system. The introjects cause psychic damage to society and individuals because they are introjecting bad objects, that is negative and persecutory definitions of themselves. One way of understanding Black Lives Matter is that it is an attempt to deal with the introjects by reasserting the intrinsic worth of black people. This has many historical roots, and in living memory, we remember the civil rights movement, the campaigns against apartheid in South Africa, the Black Power and Black Panthers of the sixties. This reaction to the negative introjects is an attempt to preserve their humanness and dignity. The demand is that we re-examine and critically engage with our historical and current legacies of competing world economic forces and ideologies, the structures that govern decision-making, the distribution of wealth, our education systems, our histories, what constitutes knowledge. Systems psychodynamics consultants do not want to dismiss or negate what continues to be relevant and useful. However, it is imperative that we pay attention to these demands. To not do so, would conflict with values and ethics. In the application of theories and practice around power, authority, role, defences against anxiety, organisational structure, organisational design, leadership, followership and programme design, consultants could be asking questions:

1 Who is benefitting?
2 Who is being oppressed?
3 Whose bodies and voices are seen and heard?
4 Whose bodies and voices are not seen or heard?
5 Which systems or processes are we strengthening?
6 Which are we challenging or changing?
7 What sources of knowledge are we privileging and what are we devaluing, dismissing or not using?

Although systems psychodynamics consultants practice across the world and there are development programmes in every continent, the profession remains predominantly white. The reasons for this are multilayered and mirror the reasons for the inequities that exist across our society. To play our part in redressing this, we need to pay conscious and critical attention to our programme design and content, our marketing and recruitment practices, our faculty configurations and the wider organisations in which our programmes sit.

We need to incorporate the digital into the socio-technical and expand the sources of knowledge that inform our practice. We can continue to look to knowledge from the arts, creative and embodied practices, and knowledge from Black people and feminists, African and Eastern philosophies, personal narratives, knowledge from disenfranchised groups.

Dartington (2020) argued that the incorporation of aspects of Buddhist practice and Stoic philosophy would bring a renewed emphasis on an ethical understanding of individual agency. He also called for the need for all organisations to have a social purpose beyond survival and that this is incorporated into the systems psychodynamics concept of primary task in relation to an open system.

Such expansion of our knowledge base informing our practice is in keeping with our theoretical position of transdisciplinarity. It also enables continued commitment to our values of participative democracy in our changing world. Continued commitment to transdisciplinarity, alongside ethical positioning, will provide a grounded and containing stance. From such a stance, systems psychodynamics consultants will be well equipped to usefully influence and contribute to the future wellbeing of people, for communities and for organisational life.

It's hard to face being fully human

By Leslie Brissett

Background and context

The following case study covers the period December 2020 to January 2022. The client system, anonymised, is a large professional membership-serving organisation in the field of psychology in the UK. The organisation was stimulated by the Black Lives Matter movements that emerged during the COVID-19 pandemic to reflect on itself and its relationship to race, both as a professional representational body and the staffing matters it faced as an employer. The organisation of approximately 60,000 is organised into several sub-groups, divisions, sections and special interest groups, as well as regional offices and structures.

An approach was made by a pair of female professional members from one of the divisions for some collaboration with The Tavistock Institute of Human Relations, as the leading force in group relations methodologies, to support the division and the organisation to think about race in the professional field. The pair asked that the organisation work with the Tavistock Institute to create a group relations learning experience for its members and staff. The primary task of the event was to study the nature and impact of race in the professional field. The aim of the event would be to consider the meaning for the profession, and the membership as individuals, and how the organisation is serving its membership.

The journey as adventure

I was appointed the Director of the conference and therefore invited the staff to take up consultant roles. The professional pair who made the initial approach to the Institute were invited to take up roles in the directorate. One of the pair, a South Asian woman, was an experienced Group Relations Conference consultant, and the other, a white British woman, was new to group relations, but was deeply skilled and embedded in the professional field. The white British woman was designated as a staff member for membership. The Directorate devised and negotiated with the division and the organisation the methods and approaches we were suggesting for sponsoring, designing and delivering the group relations conference. This required finding and securing budgets and explicit commitments to the work of the conference. We finalised and explored the capacity of the organisational system to take part in a group relations learning event. This included supporting members in taking up member role as freely as possible. A group of members from the organisation formed a steering group for the development of the conference. The steering group's task was to conduct conversations with staff in the organisation and with the members around race, representation and the meanings held and attributed to race in this unique context.

Things did not progress well. Repeatedly, issues were not progressed or discussed at the appropriate levels within the organisation, and decisions that were made were not adhered to or seemed to be forgotten.

The journey as disaster

Eventually, after 15 months of monthly meetings and discussions at various levels of the organisation, we experienced the mantra: 'this is how we do things here' as part of the defensive system used to mask (or explain) what was experienced by us as a directorate as marginalising, dominating and obstructing. We hypothesised that this was possibly racially motivated. My presence as a black male leader perhaps recalled the actual murder of George Floyd, also a black male, since meanings are attached to black male bodies and trigger unconscious fear, shame and guilt at the historic abuse that black males have suffered at the hands of 'white' systems. Our hypothesis is that facing and working with such historical abuses was dealt with by denial, avoidance and rationalisation within this professional system.

Nirmal Puwar (2004) describes the idea of 'space invaders' from a psychosocial perspective. She claimed that notions of entitlement had its roots in specific places and roles. Principally, her research addressed women in the UK parliament, and it was tested and studied in other contexts. She posits that women and other racialised identities were out of place as they were not the traditional white bodies meant to perform the roles of parliamentarians or other leadership positions. These racialised and gendered bodies were seen against the backdrop of the invisible and traditional occupiers of these spaces, that is white and male. This process of being rendered visible when one ought to be Invisible made them stand out, and that process of standing out was experienced as an assault by the onlooker.

As a black male conference Director, accompanied by a South Asian female and a white female, the organisation could not work with these dynamics or think about its implications. Consequently, the organisation did not fully support the conference and it did not take place. The Directorate experienced this as sabotage.

Going from bad to worse

After the conference was cancelled, a meeting was held to 'conduct a post-mortem' about what went wrong. The 'post-mortem' meeting agreed that the Directorate would collaborate with the organisation's management to write to those members who had registered that the conference was cancelled and how they would be reimbursed. As agreed, I did the first draft and sent it to one of the organisation's senior managers. In the draft, I set out the experience in the run-up to the conference and the number of misunderstandings and the feelings associated with them and our hypotheses about the racialised underpinnings of the organisation's behaviour. The purpose of stating our hypotheses was to be transparent and provide evidence about the dynamics of race in the field and to keep the space open to create dialogue and the capacity to think about what had happened. There was no response to the first draft for ten days, which made me curious. And then I received an email that began with: 'you have made accusations that would require a complaints investigation', and ended with, 'we will use our standard wording'. I was not surprised at this unilateral action, disregard of our agreement and the inability to collaborate, but this level of disrespect did concern me. I wrote back suggesting that we still had time to honour our commitments and work through the strong feelings that were clearly located in the organisation. To this day, I still await a response...

The 'somatic norm' is the term used to describe the assumption that black or female people ought to fulfil certain roles. In this case, the colour of the consultants seemed intolerable, and the issues of race could not be thought about, and therefore, the process of extrusion was enacted.

Consulting to an organisation on issues and dynamics of racialised identities is a stressful and challenging process for the client organisation. This applies to the individuals – consultants and consultees – taking part in the consultation. The consulting assignment can be thought of as the overlap of two triangular relationships: the first triangle is formed by everyone in the system: everyone has a triangular relationship with race: personal, familial and cultural representational fields that form a picture in the mind of race for them ('race-in-the-mind'). That first triangle is overlaid with the second triangle formed of the context of the assignment, where the consultant's triangle meets each client's triangle and the organisation's triangle. It is a complex picture that appears fractal-like, and each person must navigate the pressure to locate themselves at any one point in the intervention. In this complex three-cornered relationship, one element is always in danger of being excluded. This seemed to be the dynamic that we were all caught in while attempting to run group relations conferences on racial dynamics.

Concluding thoughts on systems psychodynamics, boundaries, authority, leadership and role and the development of theory

How does systems psychodynamics stand up in the contemporary world? Within traditional models of organisation, there tends to be an emphasis on a binary view of the world. We either do this or we do that. It can be seen from the chapter on complexity and working with large complex systems that this stance is both outdated and illusionary. Whereas in the systems psychodynamics framework, the attempt is to hold many differing perspectives in mind simultaneously, hopefully this leads to a state of mind where one is holding different perspectives on organisational dilemmas. The attempt is to move away from a reductionist stance to an all-inclusive multidimensional view. The dominant model for organisations is to envision one of constant and perpetual growth. This can lead to organisations both exploding and imploding due to this imperative. A more nuanced approach is to strive for balance; what is it that we can realistically achieve at this point and what we should let go off is a painful question that needs to be confronted. This leads us to consider the issues of control. As Gabriel (1999) points out, theories of organisation and management have been preoccupied with control. He goes on to show that management is predominated by the notion of extending control to all aspects of life. But he also usefully points out that the desire for control is motivated by feelings of insecurity, uncertainty and impending chaos (Drucker, 1980, 1995; Watson, 1994). With the advent of complexity theory, we are now more attuned to the reality that control is often illusionary. Complexity theory is now embedded in the work of systems psychodynamics consultancy. Given the turbulent environments that most organisations now inhabit, confusion and insecurity is a day-to-day experience. As Gould said:

Organisations were, to be sure, never closed systems, but in more stable times with much slower rates of change, they were experienced as self-contained and self- perpetuating. By contrast, contemporary post-industrial organisations often have quite the opposite character. They are experienced as unstable, chaotic, turbulent, and often unmanageable.

(Gould, 1993, p. 50)

The traditional model of capitalist culture is that life's goals are achieved through the acquisition of external material. The realisation of the catastrophic impact of climate change is forcing individuals, societies and organisations to consider how sustainable their organisational practices are. The need to effect significant changes in behaviour inevitably brings resistance. It is here with the understanding of unconscious defence mechanisms and social defence mechanisms that systems psychodynamics has much to offer. To survive, we are going to have to look at radical innovation and accept that we must live with the resources at our disposal and restore and repair the damage that we as a species have inflicted on the planet. Psychoanalytic insights into the dynamics of guilt and reparation are particularly pertinent. Along with this goes perhaps the recognition that life's purpose being about acquiring wisdom and inner peace. But this is not to deny the material reality that most people on the planet live at subsistence levels and that the developed world consumes most of the planet's resources.

Boundaries

As we have already noted, organisational boundaries are experienced very differently from the 50s and 60s when Miller, E. J. and Rice, A. K., (1967) first drew our attention to them. Organisational boundaries are more complex as we noted in Chapter 9 *On Working with Large Complex Partnerships*. The removal or blurring of boundaries, which separated organisations, or the setting up of internal markets, which erect new internal boundaries, has all required a re-examination of how boundary-crossing is negotiated and understood. The outsourcing of work and tasks to other agencies has gained more traction over the recent two decades and again changes the nature of the boundary. The idea that an organisation is detached from its environment by a fixed and immovable position is increasingly untenable. Therefore, boundaries are less fixed, more negotiable, weaker and potentially at risk, and more permeable than in the original open systems theory. All these developments mean that systems psychodynamics is continually being asked to examine its theories and practice. These developments in the environment demand that the adherence to open systems theory, task, role and boundary must be viewed as exploratory concepts rather than fixed and static ideas. But what must be borne in mind is that individuals in role will require containment and the shifting of boundaries can entail significant anxiety and may lead to a retreat from the boundary and the task. The recognition of social defences against anxiety is still a relevant and useful set of ideas that constantly need to be revisited. We can see that everything has a boundary, defining what is inside and what is outside. These boundaries provide 'containers' that hold the work, time, territory and task. They help to provide clarity of roles, resources and responsibility. Boundaries enable communication, collaboration, connection and competition across them. At the same time, it is possible to attack, defend, cut off and stagnate within a boundary. They can be impermeable or permeable. From systems thinking and complexity theory, we see that boundaries are complex. We see that they seem to have become less fixed, more permeable, more vulnerable, and more negotiable, but they may not be. The crossing of a boundary may induce anxiety. This anxiety can encourage defensive behaviours and practices, which do not support cross-boundary working. The crossing of boundaries can induce multiple responses and feelings. These feelings may be heightened, sometimes difficult, but it is always useful to notice the response in oneself and in others. One may feel that one is being too far in or being too far out when crossing a boundary.

Authority and leadership

When working from a systems perspective, we see that leadership takes place at every level within a system. It is not solely the province of people holding senior positions in a hierarchy, or those with the word 'leader', 'head of' or 'director' in their title. Within the systems psychodynamics framework, leadership is a relational activity. Also, the role of follower is as important as that of leader. Staff at every level can take leadership or followership roles. Leadership is the most important determinant of the development and maintenance of an organisation's culture. Every interaction at every level shapes the culture of an organisation; staff are very mindful of how those in leadership roles behave and exercise authority and power and will take their cue from them.

It is evident that the world of organisations is complex within a turbulent environment. Leadership in a complex world is an emotionally demanding task. The brokering of relationships and connections, seeing difference, contradictions and multiple perspectives as helpful is a key attribute for those taking up a leadership role. Understanding that we can be mobilised in the 'field' or, in other words, in interaction with the organisational system, is a necessary feature of today's leaders. Given insight from complexity, we must accept that there is no ultimate truth, no single right solution; only multiple, possible next steps. This requires leaders to ask the question *'How do things get done around here?'* Wherever one starts investigating in the system and noticing where that leads you, one needs to have an ability to notice patterns, search for hidden assumptions and meaning, recognising that not knowing is a capability, having curiosity about states of mind. A key skill for those in authority and leadership roles is a capacity for critical reflection on the states of mind of groups, individuals and sub-systems. This entails working with the connection between the self and the system. Following this reflective state, one can then hopefully have some recognition of one's impact on groups and the culture.

Authority is an embodied experience, which often is exciting and frightening at the same time, which sometimes can be a spiritual experience, and which often is non-verbal or hard to articulate. In making sense of our experiences in any role we have taken up, meaning can emerge that informs us that we are authors of our own actions.

Collective leadership

Collective leadership means everyone taking responsibility for the success of the organisation (and system) as a whole, not just their own area. Collective leadership and cultures are characterised by everyone focusing on continual learning and through this on the improvement of care, services or operations. It requires high levels of dialogue, debate and discussion to achieve shared understanding about quality issues and possible solutions.

Self-leadership

The ability to bring out the best in individuals in any circumstances for the ultimate aim of realising better outcomes is a key aspect of systems psychodynamics consultancy. The systems psychodynamics approach is that leadership solutions are partial; they are part of an ongoing emerging learning process to which there is no concrete and finite answer. Leadership is more than the personal characteristics, behaviour and actions of individuals (fitting in with our heroic narratives in history, stories and films). It is the relationship between the individual and the follower that establishes good leadership. Leadership to be truly leading, then, needs good quality followership. Complex tasks in organisations cannot be accomplished without widely distributing responsibility for leadership among people/employees in the organisation. The aim is to maximise human potential of an organisation. This work involves an understanding of the relationship between the individual and the group. The systems psychodynamics approach to leadership is therefore:

1 Focused on challenges (the task to be performed) rather than upon the person
2 Collective and less individual
3 Multifaceted and less one-size-fits-all

Role

Why is understanding role important? We have referenced systems and systems thinking. One of the key things to understand about how a system functions is that if you make a change in one area, it has a ripple effect on the rest of the system, much like the domino effect. In a system, a role has a function; it can be a catalyst or a blockage (a visionary or a gatekeeper). A role when coloured by the sentient system responds to the emotion in the system. Within the systems psychodynamics framework, there is a way to explore the importance of role in an organisation. Whereas an analytical approach isolates elements, a systems psychodynamics approach is holistic and takes relations or interconnections and interdependence into consideration. Role is sometimes seen as prescriptive, described and defined by others, static. When a person joins a group or organisation, they enter a system in a context. As well as the person bringing their own personality, values, skills, etc., to a role, a role also belongs to and is shaped by its system and context. Therefore, roles are relational; thus, our actions are always from role in relation to another or other roles. Role-taking relates to the idea of the system in the mind of both the role holder and is influenced by the pushes and pulls of the system in the mind of others.

The question of the mind-body split is still a question for debate; the systems psychodynamics paradigm is always paying attention to the tendency to split so that the human (and social) dualism of the organism can be seen and worked with as a totality. This can be seen most clearly when we emphasise paying attention to the emotional experience one is having. Emotional experiences are felt as somatic processes, that is anxiety as a physical and a mental state. The oscillating movements of individualism, the me-oriented culture versus individuality within a group context, is a perennial tension and takes us back to Bion's basic assumption theories. The learning of facts and computational learning is contrasted with how to be wise and gain the ability to operate effectively in the world.

There is a desire for certainty that all things are knowable and can be planned for, whereas the reality, in this complex world, is that we have to acknowledge and accept uncertainty. The linear model is giving way to a more circular and rhythmic process: detachment and objectivity giving way to involvement, engagement and subjectivity, learning from experience and the significance of emotions in organisation life.

The fusion of systems thinking and psychoanalysis

At the heart of systems psychodynamics is the fusion of systems thinking and psychoanalysis. As we have seen, the management of anxiety is a core task in every organisation. Gabriel (2016) gives a comprehensive overview of the application of psychoanalysis to organisation studies, (http://www.yiannisgabriel. com/2016/01/psychoanalysis-and-organization-studies.html).

He offers an overview of the current state of psychoanalytic contributions to the study of organisations and indicates some areas for future research. He reminds us that from the work of Menzies and others following her ground-breaking work, we have seen that disproportionate anxiety leads to defensive routines, while inadequate anxiety breeds complacency, inertia and gradual decay (Baum, 1987; French and Vince, 1999; Hirschhorn, 1988). Systems psychodynamics gives consultants the theory and practice to work at recognising and differentiating defences, which enhance the capacity to manage insecurity and threat, and to build a containing structure and culture. The literature of systems psychodynamics continues to explore how the combination of psychodynamic practice and theory alongside systems theory and complexity can aid our understanding of contemporary organisations and the dilemmas they face in an ever-increasing turbulent and uncertain environment.

Exercise

1   The Tavistock model is sometimes described as 'old fashioned', 'stuck in the past', 'worshipping its ancestors'. After reading this chapter, what stands out for you as the key developments in the theory and practice?
2   How would you integrate these developments in your day-to-day practice?
3   What would be the challenges for you?
4   What kind of training and development do you think you would need to practice in the Tavistock paradigm?
5   How would you describe your organisation's primary task; its reasons for survival?
6   How would you describe your organisation's purpose? What meaning does it have?
7   What are the risks of taking up ethical issues with your client systems?
8   Given the dominance of the idea of distributed leadership and authority, how easy is it to find where power lies?

Chapter 16

Theoretical developments in the systems psychodynamics paradigm

David Lawlor and Mannie Sher

David Armstrong

David Armstrong is a social psychologist by background; from 1959 to 1967, he was a junior project officer at the Tavistock Institute of Human Relations, working on action research projects under the leadership of Eric Trist. Subsequently, he worked as a senior research fellow at Chelsea College, the University of London, and from 1978 to 1994 as a consultant at the Grubb Institute of Behavioural Studies. In 1994, he joined the staff of Consultancy Service at the Tavistock Clinic, where he continues to practice as an associate member of staff. A collection of his papers, edited by Robert French, Organization in the Mind: Psychoanalysis, Group Relations and Organizational Consultancy, was published by Karnac in 2005. In 2014, with Michael Rustin he co-edited Social Defences Against Anxiety: Explorations in a Paradigm (London: Karnac).

He has worked in action research and organisational consultancy for more than thirty years. His key skills are in helping leaders and managers to develop their ability to understand and make use of organisational dynamics in identifying new approaches to challenges they and their organisations are facing.

He has a particular interest in the management of change and visioning and strategic leadership. David has worked in this field with senior executives and executive teams in business, government, health and education in the UK and worldwide. His experience includes working with executives in pharmaceuticals, investment banking, NHS Trusts, local government, higher education, prison governors and for senior civil servants.

He is a thought leader in the field and has published widely on psychoanalysis. His work (particularly his writing on The Organisation in the Mind) has extended and promoted the Tavistock systems-psychodynamic perspective and has had a hugely significant impact in the field and beyond the consultancy world. One the most significant contribution has been his work on the emotional factors in the life of an organisation. Obholzer draws our attention to David's work on emotions in organisations.

The place of emotions in organisational life, its relationship to thinking and its potential for insight and as a basis for intervention – these have been the core

DOI: 10.4324/9781003368663-22

elements of David Armstrong's' attention and work. He has used the lens offered by psychoanalytic thinking and practice, particularly the work of Wilfred Bion, to shed fresh light on the dynamics of group and organisational life and on the practice of organisational consultancy.

(Obholzer, 2005)

Armstrong maintains that the origins of the Tavistock traditions that led eventually to the coinage of 'systems psychodynamics' came out of a practice of 'social engagement', as social scientists, but also as citizens or soldiers responding to the immediate challenges and concerns of a society at war, and then at postwar reconstruction. All the great advances, both in practice and in theory, that help to make up systems psychodynamics – the focus on the group, on action research, on an existential involvement alongside the client, and then group relations, socio-technical systems, and social defences – all owe their origin and emergence to this engaged practice.

The future developments of the field will come and only come from 'our engagements in the new organisational and social challenges 75 years on'. Armstrong thinks these challenges will be more inter-organisational and societal than they were, partly consequent of the new technological revolutions, for example AI; partly on the organisational dilemmas of globalisation, partly on what seems an increasingly psychotic turn in socio-political relations and behaviour.

The emergence of social dreaming may represent a significant methodological lever in this new context, both as a probe into social experience and as a generative symbolic vehicle.

This links also to why Armstrong fears and greatly regrets signs of some weakening in the more psychoanalytic strands in thinking, if only for the reason, that Larry Hirschhorn states in his introduction to the first volume of this trilogy that phantasy ('fantasy', for Larry) is perhaps the most generative human mode – like a kind of mental equivalent of toolmaking.

Harold Bridger (1909–2005) (https://www.ispso. org/the-field/distinguished-members/)

Bridger was part of a remarkable group of social scientists at the Tavistock Institute that – since its creation following the Second World War – has made an enduring contribution to the field. These social scientists include Wilfred Bion, Eric Trist, Tommy Wilson, A.K. Rice, Elliot Jaques, Fred Emery, Pierre Turquet, Eric Miller, Isabel Menzies Lyth, Gordon Lawrence, Frank Heller and Lisl Klein (writes Dr Mark Stein, The Guardian, 12 July 2005).

Bridger's first major contribution occurred during the Second World War when he worked alongside Wilfred Bion. Bridger's projects during this time – at the War Office Selection Boards, Northfield Hospital and Civil Resettlement Units – were landmark achievements that strongly influenced his later thinking and career.

Following the war, Bridger was invited to become one of the twelve founder members of the Tavistock Institute, thus beginning a remarkable association with that institution that lasted over half a century. Bridger also trained as a psychoanalyst, undergoing analysis with Paula Heimann and being supervised by Melanie Klein and John Rickman, all during one of the most exciting and turbulent periods in the history of the British Psychoanalytical Society.

Bridger's distinctive contribution lay in several areas. First, he developed and refined the 'double-task' approach: this involved scrutinising and working with the organisation's primary task, as well as examining and working with the 'process', the secondary task; drawing on his psychoanalytic training, he paid particular attention to the unconscious dimensions of the process. Bridger made a pioneering contribution to understanding and working with the interface between the primary and secondary tasks, dealing with the complex issues that emerge there, and designing methodologies and 'working conferences' that facilitate the mutual development of both tasks.

Second, drawing on the psychoanalytic work of Winnicott, Bridger developed the idea of 'the transitional approach to change'. Central to this notion is the idea that change can only be successful if it involves 'transitional' places to learn and develop, as well as test out new arrangements, relationships and working practices.

Third, he developed 'working conferences' – 'transitional institutions' operating on 'double-task' lines – that ran, and continue to run, on a regular basis for the development of managers; these are intended to allow people the space to develop their thinking about organisations in a new way. Bridger, who developed an exceptional skill in the design and running of these, focused squarely on bringing participants' current dilemmas and issues into the working conference.

Larry Hirschhorn

Larry Hirschhorn, Principal and one of the Centre for Applied Research (CFAR) five founders, is a recognised expert on the psychodynamics of organisations and has consulted to executive teams in a broad range of industries, helping them refine their group process so they can make better decisions. Trained as an economist, Larry's consulting approach is grounded in the realities of the client's business model, their interest in identifying avenues to profitable revenue, and the relationships between behaviour, group dynamics and business success. He has developed many of the proprietary tools the firm uses to help clients develop strategy, implement change and improve collaboration. He is a prolific writer, with four books and many articles in scholarly and consumer business publications to his credit. In 2008, he won the Eliot Jaques award from the Society of Consulting Psychology for his article, 'The Fall of Howell Raines and the *New York Times*'. He is a member, founding member and former president of ISPSO – the International Society for the Psychoanalytic Study of Organizations. Larry earned a BA in Economics from Brandeis University and a Ph.D. in

Economics from the Massachusetts Institute of Technology. He is the founder and director of *Dynamics of Consulting*, a CFAR sponsored program for experienced consultants and coaches. He was an adjunct faculty member in the School of Human and Organization Development at Fielding Graduate University, a faculty member in the school of Organization Dynamics at the University of Pennsylvania, and an adjunct professor at the Wharton School. He is the author of *The Workplace Within: The Psychodynamics of Organizational Life* (1988), *Reworking Authority* (1997), *Managing in the New Team Environment* (2002) a *Beyond Mechanization: Work and Technology in a Post-Industrial Age* (1984) and *Cutting Back: Retrenchment and Redevelopment in Human and Community Services* (1983).

Hirschhorn has continued to work on developing the systems psychodynamics theory and practice. Hirschhorn (2018) argues that our inherited categories for examining group relations, boundary, authority, role and task are inadequate to the task of understanding what he calls developmental projects. The latter are work settings in which participants are creating something novel, as they would in developing a drug, designing a product or producing a new play. He suggests that knowledge work challenges the BART (boundaries, authority, role and task) framework. He argues that we need the concept of the 'developmental project' (DP) to describe the distinctive features of knowledge work. People working in a DP face an existential risk, they move through stages and phases that disrupt the experience of continuity, they use boundary objects to integrate their different disciplinary foci around a shared image of the final product, and they experience moments of truth when victories and crises put them in touch with the underlying challenges they face. He suggests that the DP has several features that are the analogues of 'BART', including scaffolding, edges, promises and deadlines. These features, in addition to boundary objects, help participants contain the experience of the existential risk they face, but may also become sources of social defence. For example, scaffolds can create the illusion of continuity, the boundary object can be used as a fetish, and deadlines may replace a vision of the ultimate product. He examines some of these propositions through a case study of a research team in a university. He suggests that such projects entail existential rather than routine risks, use boundary objects rather than the work process to focus attention, create a social system in which management and authority are loosely connected, and rely on 'edges' rather than boundaries to mobilise resources. He explores these issues by referencing some published cases of developmental work, for example, the failed project Taurus, an undertaking to computerise trading on the London Stock exchange. He presents a case in which he participated as a researcher and consultant, of a multidisciplinary team in a university setting building a computer simulation of 'forced migration'. He proposes how the new dimensions of developmental projects might distort working; for example, the boundary object can become a fetish object and edges can distort commitments and confuse authorisation.

In another paper, Hirschhorn (2020) extends the systems psychodynamics model and suggests what he describes as some novel extensions of the classical systems psychodynamics model of organisational dynamics. He points out that the classical model privileges the emotion of anxiety as the primary trigger for psychosocial experiences in organisations. He argues that it has been limiting, since there are several other important emotions that shape how people take up their work and their roles in organisations. In his paper, he demonstrates how open systems theory and socio-technical thinking emerge logically from the anxiety model by highlighting how organisations become functional, and work becomes satisfying. He goes on to explore how desire as a feeling for the future stimulates feelings such as danger, dread and excitement. When these feelings become dispositive, they generate experiences associated with anxiety, and the primary risk, as well the potential for a developmental politics. Politics can be developmental rather than defensive when executives create settings where conflict is seen as transaction and rationality as an achievement.

He aims to extend the systems psychodynamics model by including other emotions that groups and organisations experience. He lays out a succession of four extensions of the model, each depending on the one before it. The first two track the development of the systems psychodynamics model from its origins in anxiety to its extension in the concept of socio-technical systems. The last two extensions introduce new terms and ideas highlighting how the psychodynamics of organisations shapes strategic choice and developmental change.

First, he examines how the role of anxiety shapes our core understanding of organisation psychodynamics. Then, he shows how open systems theory adds to the original conception by delineating a model of the well-functioning organisation in which anxiety is contained. He also shows how socio-technical system thinking amplifies the idea of the well-functioning organisation by considering the issues of alienation and work satisfaction. He then makes a link that argues that in settings where work is satisfying, the good experience stimulates the desires of workers and members, who, by virtue of their psychological investment in the organisation, can envision new ways to do work and new work to do. This then leads to a proposition that desire and its link to a potential new task stimulate politics and an experience of a primary risk. A case is made for the idea of developmental defences and structures and he proposes a next step for a psychoanalytically informed theory of organisation development. He asks can organisations tolerate the friction sufficiently to take advantage of desire and its consequences?

He summarises his argument as follows:

In this paper I have presented an extended version of the original Tavistock model. I did this by showing how its evolution, through open systems thinking to socio-technical theory, is linked together conceptually. I then added some new elements to the model by highlighting how the role of desire when linked to a conception of a new task, triggers a developmental process and feelings such as danger, excitement and dread. I suggested that these feelings created a sense of primary risk and a politics of choice. When executives cannot cope with theses politics, they erect social defences

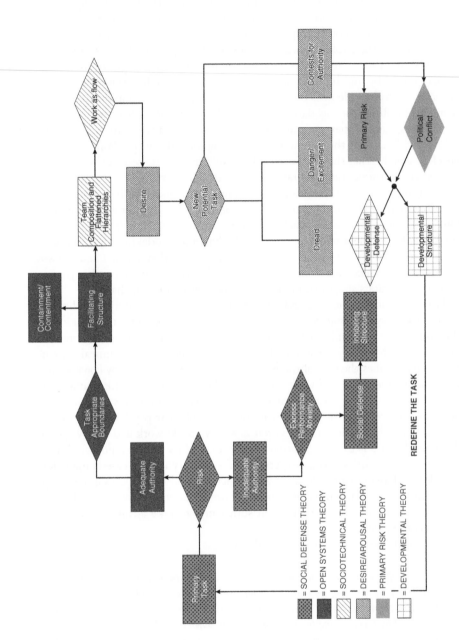

Figure 16.1 Hirschhorn's Development Propositions. Reproduced with permission from the author.

against making reasonable decisions by depersonalizing opponents, stereotyping them as immoral or suppressing conflict by ritualizing decision forums. I argued that when they cope they are more likely to make decisions that lead to a new conception of the enterprises' primary task. I propose that a next step for extending the Tavistock model is to define and describe the setting that promotes a developmental culture. I suggest that this culture is based on five norms: privileging ideas; making conflict overt; regarding conflict as a transaction; understanding the rationality is an achievement and creating a public space for real work.

He then presents a final diagram to illustrate his development propositions (Figure 16.1).

Next steps for systems psychodynamics

Hirschhorn (personal communication) proposes that systems psychodynamics can develop by considering three distinct issues: creative work and the developmental project, shifting from anxiety to excitement and restoring a focus on the individuality of the leader.

The developmental project

Systems psychodynamics draws our attention to the way in which anxiety and work are coupled in settings where operations and activities are ongoing. We examine how the risk associated with the work stimulates anxiety and how managers then create appropriate boundaries to contain it. We typically ask, what is the primary task, how does it create anxiety and how do the leaders and managers create a structure, with its appropriate roles, so that people can work effectively. This framework, while fundamental, is partial. It does not describe what happens when people are engaged together in developmental work. A developmental project is a setting in which people are building something new, whether, for example, it be a new product, a computer application, a drug or a theatrical production. The risk and its attendant anxiety in these settings are existential. People do not face the challenge of preventing performance reductions, but of preventing utter failure. A reviewer may pan a Broadway production after the very first night of its performance, thus shutting it down, a drug may confer no benefit in an investigative trial, a computer application may attract few buyers.

Hirschhorn argues that in these settings, the concept of the 'primary task' is insufficient for describing how people focus their energies, attention and talents. Instead, we should highlight what anthropologists call a 'boundary object' (Hirschhorn (2018, 2020). For example, in the case of the theatrical production the boundary object is represented in a succession of 'drafts' from the initial story idea through a script and its revisions to the final dress rehearsal and its production on opening night.

The boundary object is the crucible for the work and shapes crucially how people take up their roles. For example, in conventional systems psychodynamics we privilege role clarity. We want people to stay in their own 'lanes' while respecting the authority that others derive from their respective roles. But in developmental projects, the overarching prospect of utter failure overrides the configuration of roles. Instead, the mantra, in settings where safety is paramount, should govern conduct here: *'If you see something, say something'*. When it doesn't, small mistakes or missed opportunities, for example, a scene in a play that does not work, a character that is too loosely drawn, creates a confounding and amplifying debt, which corrupts later drafts of the boundary object. Small mistakes are multiplied in their effects. This means that to succeed, everyone must have 'their eyes on the prize'. Success is paramount. If 'purpose', in the sense of, 'why we are here' is held in the mind, then that affords the basis for stepping out of one's lane when necessary. Challenging another in their role performance because you think they are undermining the purposes of the organisation takes guts is creative and can win you enemies. This is different from multiskilling, which is built into the organisation design and depends less on individual discretion. The concept of 'if you see something, say something' cuts across the division of labour and its representation in the configuration of roles.

Excitement versus anxiety

In conventional systems psychodynamics, we focus on anxiety and its containment. We privilege the idea of equanimity, a setting of sufficient stability so that everyone can do their best work. But any common-sense psychology suggests that people seek excitement and thrills as an antidote to what is dull and routine in their lives. Therefore, scenes of danger in movies are attractive, people love roller coasters, why they watch a burning building from a safe distance, and why they start new businesses. In an article, Hirschhorn and Horowitz (2014) proposed that extreme sports were one prototype for understanding the phenomenology of excitement. A hang glider describes the pleasures of immersion when, as he integrated 'gravity, wind, lift and sink', he felt unified with the forces of nature. The windsurfer describes the pleasure of intense focus where though everything is happening fast, 'it's kind of like slow motion'. The stock trader said that in trading 'you dug down to the bottom of yourself', you 'cut away all the layers of insulation' and were in a state that was both 'less and more conscious' at the same time. What these quotes suggest is that excitement is a necessary prelude to certain psychological achievements; feeling merged, in control, exposed, whole, and truthful. Excitement in this sense signals the possibility of these achievements. Sexual love may be the underlying prototype for all these experiences.

In his classic *The Soul of a New Machine*, Kidder (1981) provides a model of excitement for a work group. Tasked with producing a new mainframe computer under difficult conditions with limited resources, a team of engineers achieved a sense of cohesion 'in which the entire group, especially, its managers seemed to be operating on instinct. Only the smallest visible arrangements existed among them'.

Our next step for systems psychodynamics is to explore these emotional dynamics and their impact on the life of enterprises. How and why do people seek out exciting work? What are the dynamics that hold a group together under conditions of excitement? What social defences might emerge to grey out the emotions associated with risky work? For example, business plans that pretend to forecast future revenues, or an artificial division of labour that separates disciplines that should be integrated, for example the software engineer, the marketer, the interface designer and the ergonomics engineer.

Refocusing on the individuality of the leader

Systems psychodynamics is a system framework, but it needs to restore a focus on the character of the individual leader. It is too facile to say that groups get the leaders they deserve, as if groups create leaders. We know enough from our everyday experience in organisations and politics that individual leaders make a difference. They bring drive, passionate and deep practical knowledge to an enterprise. The best leaders shake up organisations to meet challenges and perform at their best to do what Zaleznik calls 'Real Work'. Yet, it is also true that under the impress of their own psychodynamics, leaders can destroy organisations. It is useful to distinguish between two types of leaders: the attached leader who identifies deeply with the organisation's real work and its vicissitudes and the detached leader who views the enterprise as an abstraction; as a vehicle for converting expenses into profits without considering the people, with their strengths and limitations, who make this happen. One interesting question is how does a leader's biography and character lead him towards one or the other disposition. There is a long tradition of thinking about leaders from a psychoanalytic perspective. Think Erik Erikson, Abraham Zaleznik, Harry Levenson and Manfred Kets de Vries. Systems psychodynamics needs to integrate this body of work into its ongoing development as a theory and practice.

Lucian Hudson

Chair of Council, Tavistock Institute of Human Relations; Director of Communications, Durham University

A reflective practitioner's perspective: what does it mean to be Tavistock Institute trained?

Since 2000, I have been the professional lead and communications director in seven large, complex organisations, high-profile and increasingly more market driven. In my role, Aristotle's notion of the whole being more than the sum of its parts is brought into sharp relief. I work both with whole systems and with constituent parts. I work with changing, competing and conflicting agendas, yet my role requires that we consider institutions as a 'whole', led with constancy of purpose and publicly accountable. Even if thought of as whole, these organisations do not exist in isolation, their boundaries are porous and shifting. They are part of wider ecosystems. When under threat or trying to gain competitive advantage, organisations are insecure and imperilled egos, driven by the forces of life and death, asserting a keen sense of their own identity – yet they live with the continuing conundrum of working with and beyond silos, setting and resetting strategies, structuring and restructuring, ostensibly to achieve greater effectiveness and efficiency.

I develop as practitioner by getting the job done, adapting and iterating as appropriate. My practice is significantly enhanced by reflection and interpretation and reinterpretation of what I do when accounting for my work and developing others. It is enriched by the experiential learning provided by The Tavistock Institute of Human Relations, use of its approaches, methodologies and techniques, and frequent contact with its community of 'Tavistockians' – refugees, orphans, prophets, sages and hybrids – long before hybridity became fashionable.

All the organisations I have worked for – in media, government, business, civil society and education – are ambivalent about the need for change. However, having to adapt to survive, they acknowledge and often proclaim its necessity. Leaders speak of a 'burning platform' or a 'burning vision' – sometimes both. When in crisis, acute or chronic, these organisations harness communications expertise, to respond to crisis, also to anticipate and avoid a crisis. They can use crisis to transform an organisation. They use communications to make sense of mess and disorder and craft coherence.

I deliver on the task by working with and through others. I depend significantly on asking questions, guiding, advising, influencing and inspiring others to own the changes that are required for the organisation to survive and thrive. How I take up my role as an internal and external consultant has become more integral in delivering a professional service and gives me my authority within the wider system. I sum up the difference my Tavistock training with 6 Cs: curiosity; containment; care (accurate empathy, what Carl Rogers calls unconditional positive regard); creativity in co-creation with groups; confluence (shared sense-making and understanding); and challenge (timely use of questioning, probing, testing assumptions, offering working hypotheses).

My authority is derived not only from exercising technical and professional skills (e.g. being an expert in my field, devising and implementing campaigns or managing reputation risk), but enabling leaders and their teams, trying to avoid the 'lure of a cure' or being 'the one who is supposed to know', balancing that quest for results with asking, Why? What if? and How about? Enabling here means working with the dynamics of a group to create the conditions for participants to assess risk and opportunity, especially in managing brand and reputation (insofar as these lend themselves to 'management'). The prerequisite for creative work is confluence, especially developing shared understanding, and containment, particularly of anxiety, holding a space in which trust and rapport can develop. Only then can challenge and creativity take root and possibilities be explored which best secure preferred outcomes. In so doing, those involved take responsibility for the role that they have in communicating and engaging with external and internal stakeholders.

When I was the communications director of the Foreign & Commonwealth Office, I led a change programme to make communications 'mainstream'. This meant ensuring that responsibility for public engagement at all overseas embassies was more visible through commentary by our senior diplomats on social media. Our diplomats were confident in sharing their assessments on key developments internally, but historically were much more circumspect offering public comment for fear of cutting across agreed messages communicated centrally. Through an innovative process of facilitating discussion on the scope and limits of their engagement, highlighting the opportunities and challenges of interaction on social media, we established that there was room for manoeuvre in their taking up a more public role. The understanding that we reached was that if they kept to overarching policy messages, they could speak based on their local knowledge and report on activities where they had first-hand experience. A high-profile topic was collaboration to tackle climate change and their convening power in bringing together interested parties. That greater transparency showed public diplomacy in action and reflected positively on everybody's efforts.

Systems thinking acknowledges that communication happens whether we intend it or not, and it can take different forms. One of the most distinctive aspects of my Tavistock learning is becoming more aware how in groups, mental constructs emerge from a group's interactions, both in structured and semi-structured settings, and in the interstices between such meetings, side conversations, watercooler chats, fleeting exchanges, verbal and non-verbal. We make meaning and significance, together, as part of a group and apart from it.

Power relations are complex and evolving. Visions, strategies and plans co-exist with hierarchy, structures and reporting lines, and explicitly shape the functioning and development of organisations. Even more important is what is tacit and invisible, rooted in culture, adherence to values and norms, practiced behaviours, and the multiplicity of groups and networks who through their actions and habits determine just how much is delivered, in what manner and with what degree of priority.

Tensions encountered in pursuit of my role spur creativity. The grit in the oyster produces the pearl. Difference makes the difference. I am both at the edge of an organisation and at its centre, thinking, feeling and working both with its centripetal and centrifugal forces, its above-the-surface knowledge of itself, and its below-the-surface realities, emerging and hidden. I mind the gap that all too easily grows between what an organisation formally espouses and actually practices. I try to articulate or have articulated what alignment and coherence exists or might be possible, depending on consent, compliance and more active cooperation. What is co-created has more chance of sustained success than what is imposed. Holding a conversation, moving it on and changing it are communication skills increasingly needed in the modern workplace.

It is often said that actions speak louder than words. Actions are context-specific, though, and are framed with reference to paradigms, concepts, narratives and metaphors that are spoken and unspoken. What constitutes action is itself a communication. My function provides some of the vectors that shape discourse. These influence how we think and feel and construct our sense of what constitutes reality and possibility.

The shift over the past twenty years in communications and marketing has been from emphasis A, 'putting lipstick on a pig' (perceptions and expectations do persist that those in our role are 'spin-doctors' and/or a leadership's Praetorian Guard) to emphasis B, catalysts for organisational development. In practice, the two co-exist but the ratio between the two varies, depending on the extent those in leadership roles are strategic or tactical, aiming for the longer term or securing short-term advantage. These choices are not binary. My proactive role entails presenting an organisation from the inside out but also presenting the external environment from the outside in and presenting the organisation to itself, both as whole and in its constituent parts. 'Speaking truth to power' is one of the most challenging aspects of my role, and 'power' is often distributed.

My work is invariably transient, transactional and time- and context-specific, yet it also hints at an implicate order beneath appearances. As a professional, I indeed 'profess' an abiding faith that shared understandings and agreements are beneficial and can prove durable. That faith is tested. The risk is being captured by or capturing only one end of the polarities. My agency and freedom lie in where I relate in that spectrum and how I navigate between the polarities, often framing or re-framing either/or choices as both/and.

W. Gordon Lawrence (https://www.ispso.org/the-field/distinguished-members/)

W. Gordon Lawrence when working at the Tavistock Institute in the early 1980s became convinced that there was a social and political context to people's dreams. He was heavily influenced by reading *The Third Reich of Dreams* by the German journalist Charlotte Beradt (1968), who asked her medical friends in the 1930s to collect the dreams of patients who consulted with them. All these patients were Jewish. The dreams were telling them of their horrendous future in Nazi Germany. Gordon saw that it was possible to dream socially, to dream not about me, but what is happening to the human condition. In the spring of 1982, with a psychoanalyst friend, Patricia Daniels, he began holding weekly social dreaming sessions at the Tavistock Centre, these sessions were called 'A Project in Social Dreaming and Creativity'.

Social dreaming has been developed to surface the unconscious and creative thoughts about issues in management teams, the preoccupations of disparate groups about social issues, at Conferences to surface the unconscious issues which are stalking the thoughts of participants. Gordon was interested in bringing social dreaming into the worlds of education and work, as demonstrated in his 1998 book *Social Dreaming @ Work* and by his own attempts to create businesses that could bring social dreaming into the workplace. By the time of the publication of *Social Dreaming @ Work,* Gordon had started up Symbiont Technologies with Marc Maltz and Martin Walker in the USA. Gordon's work of promoting social dreaming continues through the activities of the Gordon Lawrence Foundation (http://socialdreaming. squarespace.com/gordonlawrence), the Social Dreaming International Network (https://socialdreaminginternational.net/), the Tavistock Institute and other organisations.

The contribution of Susan Long – systems psychodynamics today (https://www.ispso.org/the-field/distinguished-members/)

Susan Long is Director, Research and Scholarship at the National Institute of Organisational Dynamics Australia (NIODA). She was formerly Professor of Creative and Sustainable Organisation at RMIT, Royal Melbourne Institute of Technology, University in Melbourne.

Currently, she supervises research students and conducts organisational research. Susan also teaches and supervises doctoral candidates at different universities including a Professional Doctorate conducted at the Melbourne Institute of Creative Arts Therapy and supported through NIODA, teaches in the INSEAD Master of Coaching and Consulting program in Singapore and also works as part of the MSc Leading at the Edge program conducted by the Grubb Institute in Australia.

As an organisational consultant in private practice, Susan works with organisational change, executive coaching, board development, role analysis, team development and management training. She originally trained as a clinical psychologist and psychotherapist.

Susan's experience of working with people as individuals and in groups and organisations gives her a broad perspective on management practices. Susan's capacity as a teacher and organisational consultant/ researcher has led her to be invited onto the boards of prestigious organisations and elected onto the committees of professional bodies.

She is a member of Comcare's advisory board for the Centre of Excellence for Research into Mental Health at Work and a former member of the Board of the Judicial College of Victoria. She was Founding President of Group Relations Australia and a past president of the International Society for the Psychoanalytic Study of Organisations. Her participative research has attracted grants through the Australian research Council and industry. She has published ten books and many journal articles.

Long suggests that systems psychodynamics and its sister discipline socioanalysis are going through exciting times. The disciplines are evolving, extending and best of all, connecting with other disciplines.

Beginning in the mid-20th century, ideas and practices from psychoanalysis, especially from Wilfred Bion (1961, 1970), were combined with systems thinking at the Tavistock Institute in London. This led to a discipline eventually named as systems psychodynamics (Fraher, 2004; Gould et al., 2001). As such, it grew and informed organisational consulting and research; group relations practices; and group and social dynamics thinking across the globe. Socioanalysis was coined as a descriptor by members of the Australian Institute for Socioanalysis, extending systems psychodynamics to broad social issues. The examination of unconscious processes in human social systems is central to these disciplines.

In the 21 century, their ideas and practices have become applied more broadly. Take for instance the application to climate change issues. The physical and environmental sciences have given warnings of catastrophic change for decades, increasingly so as ocean temperatures have risen, species loss has increased, and CO_2 emissions have changed the atmosphere. We live now in what is called the Anthropocene age; a geological epoch identified by the ways in which humans have altered whole world climatic, ecological and atmospheric systems. However, just informing our societies has not brought about effective transitions or changes to collective behaviours.

Systems psychodynamics is enquiring into the reasons why governments, corporations and individuals have done so little about reducing emissions despite these warnings. What are the human factors that stand in the way of our own good? In this field, there was initially an exploration of a collective perversity that was demonstrated in the response to climate science findings; denial being central to this, but also a global turning away from the recognition that some countries and peoples will suffer more from the effects of climate change than others, together with the greed of large corporations and the perhaps willing inability of cultures to extract themselves from their dominance. This was the diagnosis of our psycho-social condition (Long (2015); Hoggett (2010); Weintrobe (2016).

Increasingly though, systems psychodynamics is now exploring the ways in which we must radically change our perspective of ourselves (Weintrobe (2020). Hoggett (2022) points to the eco-psycho-social state that we exist in and can no longer ignore (Hollway (2022); Hollway et al. (2022). I am calling the study of this state, eco-socioanalysis. Humanity needs to explore its inner nature and how this sits within broader earth systems (Rozak (1995, 2022); Long and Lockhart (2022). If modern humanity was predicated upon an extraction mentality – taking from the earth and other creatures whatever it wanted – post-modern humanity must recognise that it is not a master of all things, but just one part of a broader earth system. Instead of following a parasitic pathway, we need to find symbiotic relations with other creatures and the earth itself. This requires new mind-sets at governmental, social and organisational levels.

In the related area of eco-semiotics – that examines the various signs in nature between species and the natural environment – systems psychodynamics contributes by asking the question 'how does unconscious communication relate to human eco-socioanalytic systems?' The concept of the unconscious has evolved since first introduced by the philosopher Friedrich Schelling in the early 19th century (Long, 2016; McGrath, 2013). Applied by Schelling to systems in nature and to theology, the idea has become mostly identified with Sigmund Freud and psychoanalysis. Jumping off from Freud's investigations into group psychology (Freud, 1921), several social scientists and psychoanalysts have formulated ideas about unconscious processes in groups and organisations. The idea of the associative unconscious (Long and Harney, 2013) comes into the field of semiotics and explores a network of signs and symbols within and between individuals, accessed only through communication because no one individual can access the whole societal unconscious field by themselves. It is as if there is an unconscious network linking people from within any interacting social system. How different unconscious networks do or do not interlink globally is an area of study on socioanalytic dialogue between different cultures (Boccara, 2014). Additionally, through systems psychoanalytic links to semiotics, we might study not only the associative unconscious in human social systems, but links between these and other systems in nature. Another frontier is the work of neuro-psychoanalysis (Leuzinger-Bohleber et al., 2017).

Increasingly psychoanalysts have found contemporary neuroscience as supporting many of the ideas in psychoanalysis. One idea taken up by some neuro-psychoanalysts is that consciousness stems primarily from the emotional centres of the old brain and the reticular activating system rather than the cerebral cortex. In simpler terms, consciousness emerges from emotional life rather than logical reasoning. This resonates strongly with, for example, Wilfred Bion's psychoanalytic theory of thinking. What does this mean for systems psychodynamics and socioanalysis? Well, it supports work that calls for an examination of the emotional life of the organisation rather than simply pursuing rational directions that are most often rationalisations serving individual and group political and parasitical interests.

Now is the time for systems psychodynamics to join with other disciplines to explore a world that is in many ways seamless, despite our post-Cartesian efforts to divide it up.

Burkard Sievers (https://www.ispso.org/the-field/distinguished-members/)

Burkard Sievers was Professor Emeritus of Organization Development in the Schumpeter School for Business and Economics at Bergische University Wuppertal in Germany. In his research, he focuses on unconscious dynamics in management and organisation from a socioanalytic and systemic perspective.

His writing on 'motivation as a surrogate of meaning', 'leadership as perpetuation of immaturity', 'trusting in trust against all reason' and 'the management of wisdom in organisations' and his love for magic dragons (curing the monster) has earned respect in the critical management academic community.

His consultancy work with regard to exploring the impact of encapsulated historic guilt/shame re the Nazi third Reich atrocities into present-day German corporations is unparalleled, as are his explorations into the meaning of finance in globalised markets from a socioanalytic perspective.

Burkard founded the German group relations institute 'Mundo' and directed its annual German GR conferences 'Menschen in Organizationen' and later the series of international group relations conferences 'Trans-European Management' for over two decades, inviting international staff from across the globe to explore the effects of the fall of the Berlin Wall and the opening of Eastern Europe on business & society, from an experiential systems psychodynamics perspective.

Burkard had a close working relationship with Gordon Lawrence and frequently invited him for Social Dreaming Workshops to Germany.

Grounded in organisational symbolism, Sievers depicts the potential meaning of work in the broader context of life and death. Thus, Siever's book is a fundamental critique of motivation, participation and leadership research (Sievers, B. (ed.) (2009).

With human mortality in mind, organisation and management appear in a different light: motivation as a surrogate for meaning, participation and management as a quarrel about immortality, and leadership as a perpetuation of immaturity. Sievers advocates a 'management of wisdom'.

Systems psychodynamics – organisational resources

AGSLO (Sweden)

https://agslo-se.translate.goog/?_x_tr_sl=sv&_x_tr_tl=en&_x_tr_hl=en-GB&_x_tr_pto=sc

Since 2000, AGSLO has been a foundation with the aim of promoting the study of social processes in groups and organisations, by, among other things, organising group relations conferences and other activities with pedagogical or informative content. The AGSLO Foundation comprises a board with a minimum of 10 members, as well as a maximum of one foundation council with a minimum of 10 and a maximum of 50 members. The board, which is based in Stockholm, manages the foundation and manages its operations.

The Foundation Council meets at least once a year, where views on the Foundation's activities can be discussed, and the members of the Foundation Council can collect and provide information so that, based on their position in society, they can contribute to promoting the Foundation's purpose by marketing the Foundation and its activities.

The board appoints its own members and elects positions of trust. The board also proposes new foundation councils, which can be elected at the annual foundation council meeting.

The A. K. Rice Institute for the study of social systems

https://www.akriceinstitute.org/

The A. K. Rice Institute for the Study of Social Systems (AKRI) is the educational, not-for-profit organisation for group relations in the USA. The Institute's educational mission is the study of how unconscious thoughts and feelings significantly impact our lives when we are in groups – from family to workplace to nation. AKRI aims to deepen our understanding of complex social behaviours by providing experiential learning opportunities called Group Relations Conferences, as well as through research, publications, symposia, professional meetings, organisational consulting, experiential workshops, leadership training, and group relations consultant certification.

Bayswater Institute

https://www.bayswaterinst.org/

The Bayswater Institute promotes organisational and institutional wellbeing through the integration of human considerations with technical and economic ones in the design and development of work organisations and other institutions. Group relations events include Managing Complexity in Organisations. The Bayswater Institute provides a range of research, consultancy and professional development services to individuals, groups and organisations as they implement change in a complex, constantly shifting world. The Institute uses Double Task to develop their client's capabilities to work in and understand groups of all kinds and levels. With their GroupAware programme, they recognise it as a significant contribution to personal development, efficiency and resilience. GroupAware provides a new way of seeing teams or groups and provides insights into more effective team working. GroupAware empowers people at all levels of organisations. This leads to improved team performance, deeper reflective practice and the resilience to catalyse change in a complex world.

Belgirate conferences (the international group relations network)

Siv Boalt Boëthius and Stefan Jern (2011) recapture and reflect upon the history of early international group relations work by presenting some aspects of the first four international group relations symposia. The symposia were intended to offer space for international cooperation, scientific and professional presentations and experiential work in a frame where transference was to be minimised in favour of collegial work. They also suggest that the possibility to understand and manage inter-institutional transference, rivalry and conflict was probably also on the hidden agenda. These events took place between 1988 and 1998. They were: The International Symposium in Oxford (1988), The Temporary Learning System in Spa in Belgium (1990), The International Group Relations and Scientific Conference in Lorne, Australia (1993), and The International Group Relations Symposium in Maryland, USA (1998). These events may be characterised by the ways they were initiated and designed and by their dynamics. Each may be seen as representing a development of various ideas, which to a certain extent have been integrated in the present Belgirate Conferences.

Since the first Belgirate meeting in 2003, these three-yearly meetings have become *the* place where professionals who work in Group Relations Conferences everywhere in the world come to exchange ideas about theory, practice, and the characteristics of the group relations professional community. Each conference has produced a book (Brunner et al., 2006; Aram et al., 2009; Aram et al., 2012, 2015, 2019), which, like the conferences, has two major purposes: the first to introduce what is new, exciting and/or controversial in this field, and the second to explore our conscious and unconscious professional discourse, namely, the politics of our ideas, the language in use, terms, ethical values (explicit or implicit), the nature of the concepts used, or never used, theoretical writings; metaphors and their hidden meanings, the tools and methods in use (or never used) in the practice, the nature of the work, in short, the professional culture of group relations.

Similarly, the books that have followed the Belgirate meetings have become the publishing home for much of the group relations literature in the past decade-and-a half. They have supplanted compilations and anthologies that used to be published (e.g. the USA AK Rice Institute's *Group Relations Reader* series). And in virtually all instances, the Belgirate presentations are not published elsewhere.

The Il Nodo group

https://www.ilnodogroup.it/chi-siamo/

The Il Nodo Group is a social enterprise in Italy founded in 2007 and made up of people from different cultural and professional backgrounds who intend to promote an ethical and democratic approach to the problems of functioning of groups and work organisations. The Social Enterprise, through its members, carries out training, consultancy and research activities.

The object of observation of their studies and interventions in organisations are the conscious and unconscious relational processes between individuals, between and in work groups. This approach assumes that organisations are social systems that not only operate according to rational criteria but are strongly influenced by emotional factors that interfere at various levels.

The international society for the psychoanalytic study of organisations

https://www.ispso.org/

The International Society for the Psychoanalytic Study of Organizations is a professional organisation with 320 members from around the world. The largest contingents are from Eastern and Western Europe (103), the USA (100), Australia (50) and the UK (44). The Society seeks to help establish and sustain a community of thinkers and practitioners who share an interest in examining organisations from a psychoanalytic perspective. It helps scholars and practitioners from different disciplines, countries and with varying political persuasions to develop and communicate ideas, including those focused on applying research and theory to practice. It provides a public forum for discussing, presenting and distributing papers that explore the field of the psychoanalytic organisational studies. Its purpose is to explore how psychoanalytic thinking can further our understanding of organisations and the wider social influences that impact on them. The insights gained are used to promote and support the development of healthier, more humane and better performing organisations.

National Institute of Organisation Dynamics Australia (NIODA) and socioanalysis

In Australia, socioanalysis is the term, which describes systems psychodynamics. Formal education in systems psychodynamics was founded in Australia at Swinburne University, Melbourne, by Associate Professor John Newton in 1981. Over the next 20 years, John, and from 1990, Professor Susan Long, developed a suite of organisation dynamics postgraduate degrees ranging from a Graduate Certificate through to Professional Doctorate and PhD level.

The National Institute of Organisation Dynamics Australia (NIODA) currently offers internationally renowned post-graduate education and research in organisation dynamics, and decades of experience consulting with Australian organisations. The study of organisation dynamics brings together socio-technical and psychoanalytic disciplines to explore the unconscious dynamics that exist in every group, team or organisation. Learning more about these theories, and reflecting on the experience of them, can support leaders and managers to unlock great potential in their organisations, tackling issues through a whole new light. Socioanalysis is the activity of exploration, consultancy and action research, which combines and synthesises methodologies and theories derived from psychoanalysis, group relations, social systems thinking, organisational behaviour and social dreaming.

Socioanalysis offers a conception of individuals, groups, organisations, and global systems that take account of conscious and unconscious aspects and potentialities. From this conception are born methods of exploration, which can increase capacities through making conscious what was unconscious for individuals, groups, and organisations, and through releasing energy and ideas that help create individual and organisational direction and meaning. Socioanalysis has at its heart a query as to what is the psychological truth for an individual, group, organisation, or other social system, and how may this best be brought to light as a means for creative transformation and growth?

Group relations

GroupRelations.com (http://www.grouprelations.com/index.php) is a resource for people who are interested in the dynamics of people and organisations. It contains information about the theory behind group relations; a calendar and details about upcoming group relations training and events; news; group relations publications; and people and organisations who work in group relations. Under organisations, brief details about group relations organisations worldwide are provided. There is also a discussion forum for debate on the theory, design, research and application of group relations in organisations and wider society. The website is run by the Tavistock Institute, but other organisations and individuals contribute information. Email r.kelly@tavinstitute.org for details. Anyone can submit a message to the forum. www.GroupRelations.com is a useful educational resource.

Group relations Australia

https://www.grouprelations.org.au/

The purpose of GRA is to promote the study of group dynamics and the interactions between conscious and unconscious processes in organisations, groups and society. This approach is a more in-depth way to gain a deeper understanding of why certain structures exist in society, such as racism, sexism, bullying and corruption, to name a few.

The aim is to achieve this understanding through conferences, seminars, workshops, training and the publication of articles through the journal *Socioanalysis*. *Socioanalysis* was first published in 1999, co-edited by Prof Susan Long and Dr Allan Shafer – under the auspices of the then Australian Institute of Socio-Analysis, now published by Group Relations Australia. It was published initially with the hope that it would provide a contact point for those who wished to read and write about socioanalytic work and ideas. *Socioanalysis,* some 22 years later, is a recognised and highly regarded scholarly journal – still edited by Prof Susan Long – with quality international papers covering a wide spectrum of topics in the fields of socioanalysis, group relations and systems psychodynamics. Along the way it has included some specially edited editions on current themes, most recently in Volume 18 in 2017, focused on *Seeking Asylum.*

Group relations international

https://www.grouprelations.org/about-us

Group Relations International (GRI) serves as a home for people who have experienced the power of group relations work, particularly in combination with spirituality and social justice. GRI wants to nurture the Group Relations networks by offering a place to co-create as individuals and/or organisations. They are open to collaboration around group relations conferences and application events, writing, reflecting and meeting.

Group relations programme (the Tavistock institute)

https://www.tavinstitute.org/what-we-offer/group-relations/

Dr Leslie Brissett is the director of the group relations programme, which offers opportunities to learn about group, organisational and social dynamics; the exercise of authority and power; the interplay between tradition, innovation and change; and the relationship of organisations to their social, political and economic environments.

The focus of group relations conferences is on the relatedness of individual to group, organisation and environment and hence has synergies with other work of the Tavistock Institute including organisational redesign and organisation culture. Participants may expect to develop their capacities to manage themselves in the multiple roles necessary for contemporary leadership and hence the conferences provide a useful steppingstone in the process of leadership development and strategy development.

The learning at the conferences, which are educational and are part of the Tavistock Institute's professional development stream, emphasises increased insight into irrational, or unconscious processes we get involved in as we take up our roles in various groups. The basis of group relations theory is that 'groups' move in and out of focusing on their task and back and forth between a number of different defensive positions based on unarticulated 'group' desire and anxiety.

'Group Relations' aims to help groups improve the focus on their tasks, improve performance, better utilise group members' potentials and reduce the constraining effects of competing dynamics.

Group Relations is a method of study, training and development that was developed by the pioneers of the Tavistock Institute including Ken Rice, Eric Miller, Pierre Turquet, Isabel Menzies Lyth and Gordon Lawrence. The method of group relations study is usually in conference design of varied lengths, some of which are residential, others not. Group Relations conferences, as other methodologies developed at the Tavistock Institute, are rooted in action research and hence offer opportunities for people to learn through experience.

The Tavistock Institute's Group Relations Programme organises and runs several different forms of Group Relations conferences – some are open to everyone; others are in-house events for organisational clients. The best-known of these conferences is the Leicester conference.

Group relations (Tavistock and Portman NHS Trust)

https://tavistockandportman.nhs.uk/news-and-events/group-relations-conferences/

Tavistock and Portman NHS Trust run a number of in-house Group Relations conferences with a variety of themes and topics; these are mostly aimed at their student group. Attendance at a Group Relations conference is part of the curriculum of many Tavistock and Portman programmes.

OFEK

http://www.ofekgroups.org/en/index.php?option=com_frontpage&Itemid=1

OFEK – Organization-Person-Group – the Israeli Association for the Study of Group and Organizational Processes was founded in 1985 and today functions as a community interest company. OFEK strives to promote in Israel the field of experiential learning of group and organisational processes in the Tavistock group relations approach. The study of these processes is of special importance in Israel, where belonging to groups and identifying with them are central features of social life. OFEK's approach combines psychoanalytic with systemic understanding of groups, organisations and social processes. This unique combination allows for an understanding of organisations as open systems, and stresses emotional, irrational and unconscious elements in group and organisational processes. OFEK's fundamental assumption is that ignoring these components undermines the efficiency of groups and of individuals in taking up roles in organisations. People and organisations today must adapt to a changing, more complex reality than in the past. Hence, acquiring skills in identifying unconscious processes in groups, and understanding the complex relations between the individual and the system, contributes directly to the ability to take up roles creatively, from a position of authority and responsibility.

OPUS – an organisation for promoting understanding of society

https://www.opus.org.uk/

Sir Charles Goodeve founded it in 1975 with the object of promoting understanding of society and of organisations within society. He believed that, if we were better able to understand the processes operating in industry and society – particularly those causing conflict – then our decisions could become more rational, we would become more effective managers of ourselves and others and we would be able to act with greater authority and responsibility as citizens. In establishing OPUS as a non-political organisation, with charitable status, Sir Charles was supported and encouraged by his links with the Tavistock Institute (TIHR) and the Industrial Society. It was recognised that the study and promotion of a better understanding of society – how it works, how the individual relates to it – with a particular emphasis on conflict, formed a distinctive field of endeavour which could most effectively be tackled from an autonomous basis. Its overall aim is on helping the individual to act with authority and responsibility in the role of citizen.

OPUS aims to be an organisation of people who believe that it is important that we and others develop a deeper understanding of organisational and societal processes and the ways in which we relate to them; and that we use such understanding to act with authority and responsibility in our various roles. OPUS exists to promote the development of the reflective citizen. The objective of OPUS is to promote and develop the study of conscious and unconscious organisational and societal dynamics through educational activities, research; consultancy and training; and a scientific meetings programme.

OPUS listening posts

OPUS Listening Posts are a psycho–social research project that result in analyses and hypotheses regarding societal dynamics that are not available from any other source. They are based on the notion that a group of people meeting together allows the unconscious expression of some characteristics of the wider social system. The experience of the Listening Post is itself, therefore, relevant to an understanding of society beyond individual and personal preoccupations.

The development of systems psychodynamics and its reach both academically and practically can be seen by the continuous output of journal articles and books. The OPUS journal, *Organisational and Social Dynamics* is a forum for the publication of academic and reflective writing that is relevant and accessible to an international readership. Writers from psychoanalytic, group relations, and systems perspectives can address emerging issues in societies and organisations throughout the world. The journal aims to sustain a creative tension between scientific rigour and popular appeal, both developing conversations with the professional and social scientific world and opening these conversations to practitioners and reflective citizens everywhere.

Partners in confronting collective atrocities (PCCA)

http://p-cca.org/

Partners in Confronting Collective Atrocities uses group relations methodologies in developing strategies to engage with the legacy of past atrocities that can contribute to opening the possibility of a more hopeful future. The aim of the organisation is to work through the effects of the Holocaust and of past and present national and international conflicts that lead to destructive escalation, in the service of a better understanding among national groups worldwide.

The institute of leadership transformation, South Africa (TILT)

https://tiltinternational.com/index.html

The work of Jean Cooper at The Institute of Leadership Transformation (TILT) in teaching and consulting work is rooted in the fields of systems psychodynamics, group relations and complexity theory. He often partners with the Tavistock Institute of Human Relations, the pioneers in the field. TILT specialises in executive coaching, leadership development and organisational change in the context of South Africa. TILT also run training groups and provide professional supervision to other consultants and coaches. The approach views organisations as complex, imperfect systems with both conscious and unconscious dimensions. TILT takes the organisation's primary task and strategic objectives as departure points and the clients and TILT measure their success in terms of the organisation's increased effectiveness and performance.

Literature review on systems psychodynamics

Journals

Human relations

Human relations is an international peer-reviewed journal publishing the highest quality original research to advance our understanding of social relationships at and around work. Human relations encourages strong empirical contributions that develop and extend theory, as well as more conceptual papers that integrate, critique and expand existing theory. Human relations addresses the social relations in and around work – across the levels of immediate personal relationships, organisations and their processes, and wider political and economic systems. It is international in its scope. The journal is grounded in critical social science that challenges orthodoxies and questions current organisational structures and practices. It promotes interdisciplinarity through studies that draw on more than one discipline or that engage critically across disciplinary traditions. It deploys any social science method used in a rigorous manner. It promotes studies that draw out the practical implication of their results in a manner consistent with critical engagement with practice as opposed to advice to particular actors or groups.

Organisational and social dynamics

O&SD aims to create a deeper understanding of organisational and social processes and their effects on individuals, and to provide a forum for both theoretical and applied papers addressing emerging issues in societies and organisations from a psycho-social perspective. The editors seek to sustain a creative tension between scientific rigour and popular appeal, by developing conversations with the professional and social scientific worlds and opening them to practitioners and reflective citizens everywhere.

Contributions include: theoretical argument and discussion, case studies of consultations or action research projects, reviews of books, plays and other artistic works providing insight into organisational and social dynamics, analyses and reviews of contemporary social and political events, personal polemics and reflections, dialogues exploring opposing views.

Journal of Applied Behavioral Science (JABS)

The *Journal of Applied Behavioral Science (JABS)*, peer-reviewed and published quarterly, is the leading international journal on the effects of evolutionary and planned change. Founded and sponsored by the NTL Institute, *JABS* is continually breaking ground in its exploration of group dynamics, organisation development, and social change. *The Journal of Applied Behavioral Science* (JABS) brings to scholars and professionals the latest theory and research on processes and techniques of change in groups, organisations and larger systems, and academic-practitioner collaborations. The journal also informs professionals and organisations on issues in group, organisational and system dynamics.

Socioanalysis

Socioanalysis is a recognised and highly regarded scholarly journal, edited by Prof Susan Long, with quality international papers covering a wide spectrum of topics in the fields of socioanalysis, group relations and system psychodynamics.

Recent publications

E. J. Miller, *From Dependency to Autonomy: Studies in Organization and Change* (1993)

In this collection Eric Miller drew on the experience of three decades as organisational consultant to various sorts of institutions, employing approaches drawn from psychoanalysis, systems theory and the group relations movement, whilst working at the Tavistock Institute. Miller drew on the experience of 3 decades as organisational consultant to various sorts of institutions, employing approaches drawn from psychoanalysis, systems theory and the group relations movement. Among the sites analysed in these papers are an airline; hospitals for incurables, the elderly, the mentally ill; a diocese; a prison; a diplomatic mission; manufacturing companies and rural sites. Throughout his case studies he addresses issues of dependence, independence and counter dependence Millers aim was to help people to gain greater influence over their environments. Miller focused constantly on values and concepts in action.

Yiannis Gabriel, *Organizations in Depth: The Psychoanalysis of Organizations* (1999)

This book is a comprehensive and systematic examination of the insights psychoanalysis can offer to the study of organisations and organisational behaviour. Richly illustrated with examples, Yiannis Gabriel's exhaustive study provides fresh understandings of the role of creativity, control mechanisms, leadership, culture and emotions in organisations.

Core theories are explained at length and there is a chapter on research strategies. Extensive reference is made to practical cases, and there is a review of the key debates.

Robert French & Russ Vince, *Group Relations, Management, and Organization* (1999)

In *Group Relations, Management, and Organization* (1999), Robert French and Russ Vince bring together a collection of important essays by an international group of authors. The authors represent different cultures, roles and institutional backgrounds, as well as a variety of perspectives on the past, present, and future of group relations and its current impact on management, organisations, institutions and societies. The importance of the book is in the perspective that it offers on the traditions of group relations and the changes that are taking place within this field. The book provides the reader with reflections and insights which are highly relevant to an in-depth understanding both of the role of manager and to the dynamics of organising and consulting.

Laurence Gould et al., (2001). The Systems Psychodynamics of Organizations: Integrating the Group Relations Approach, Psychoanalytic, and Open Systems Perspectives. Karnac Books, London.

This authoritative source book on the learning and creative application of the systems psychodynamic perspective defines the field, presenting the key concepts, models, and social methodologies that derive from it, together with their theoretical and conceptual underpinnings in psychoanalysis, group relations and open systems theory.

Clare Huffington, David Armstrong, William Halton, Linda Hoyle and Jane Pooley, *Working Below the Surface: The Emotional Life of Contemporary Organisations (Tavistock Clinic Series)* (2004)

This Tavistock Consultancy Service book identifies the distinctive competences in the human dimension of enterprise and the dynamics of the workplace. The intention is to identify and explore some of the key themes that have emerged, such as the emotional world of the organisation and the dynamics of resistance to change, and how these affect and influence the understanding of leadership and management in contemporary organisations.

Karen Izod and Sue Whittle, *Mindful Consulting* (2009)

This earlier book coincided with an increasing recognition that the challenges facing society and organisations are not amenable to 'quick fixes'. The approaches to consultancy which underpin the cases presented here are particularly relevant in this new context. The contributors are graduates of AOC [The

Tavistock Institute Masters Programme in Advanced Organisational Change and Consulting} and their associates; and the work they describe here is a testament to the quality of that programme and the learning that participants got from it. One thread which runs through the book is consultancy as learning: learning for both the client and the consultant. The contributors to this book are both accomplished and experienced as consultants, and in a continuous process of development. They are open to reflection, critique of their work, and learning from and with their clients. This notion of learning on the part of client is important too. An effective consultancy intervention is one which not only helps the client to address a particular issue or problem, but which also develops the capacity of the client organisation and individuals in it to respond to change and development in the future.

Susan Long, *Socioanalytic Methods Discovering the Hidden in Organisations and Social Systems* (2013)

With *Socioanalytic Methods (2013)*, Susan Long explores the study of groups, organisations, and society using a systems psychoanalytic framework: looking beneath the surface (and the obvious) to see the underlying dynamics and how these dynamics are interconnected. Long examines several of the methodologies used in socioanalytic/systems psychodynamics work. Even though the beginnings of socioanalytic/systems psychodynamics investigation lay in the mid-20th century, a broad look across several methodologies has not been done before, despite separate publications dealing with different methods. In addition, several new methods have been developed in recent years, which the present work incorporates. Connecting all these methods is their aim of 'tapping into' the dynamic operation of what the author calls 'the associative unconscious' within and between social systems. The associative unconscious is the unconscious at a systemic level. Each of the methods discussed in this book accesses the associative unconscious in different ways.

Mannie Sher, *The Dynamics of Change: Tavistock Approaches to Improving Social Systems* (2013)

Mannie Sher focuses on the hallmark of approaches of the Tavistock Institute, combining research in the social sciences with professional practice in organisational and social change. It shows how consultant and client system are partners in the process of organisational analysis and design. This book includes descriptions of several major assignments in which Sher's understanding of 'Tavistock' systems psychodynamic models is applied. It refers to the historical connections between the Tavistock Institute and social science pioneers. Sher offers an overview of the central features of systems psychodynamics, the ubiquitous presence of anxieties and the mobilisation of institutional and social defence systems against them, a set of inspired ideas that have defined 'Tavistock' social science research methodologies, organisational change initiatives, and executive coaching encounters for over a century. This book aligns theory and practice. Sher describes examples of work explaining how systems psychodynamics concepts influence practice for the benefit of clients and the social good. According to reviewers, the book shows precisely and with great subtlety what is necessary for effective leadership. The capacity to decide and to wait, to think and to feel, to ponder and to act intuitively, to be deeply connected to present realities and yet always aware of overarching objectives – these qualities are more than personal competencies: Mannie Sher demonstrates how such capacities can be embedded in work as diverse as a GP's clinic, a bank's boardroom and an entire regulatory system. The book is of interested to people in leadership roles, and to everyone keen to understand how human beings can possibly cope, with wisdom and good humour, with the challenges of responsible roles in modern organisations.

Robin C. Stevens and Susan Rosina Whittle, *Changing Organizations from Within Roles, Risks and Consultancy Relationships* (2013)

This book is unusual in providing a range of authentic insider accounts. The editors define 'insiders' as employees who lead and support change efforts within their own organisations, and those psychoanalytically aware external consultants – external 'insiders' – who work closely with organisations and use the dynamics of transference and projection in their relationships with clients to illuminate organisational issues. The book's editors and several of the authors are graduates, or have been faculty members, of the Tavistock Institute Advanced Organizational Consultation programme, with experience of running development programmes for consultants and of coaching insiders. *Changing Organizations from Within* examines the pulls on role and identity that can easily undermine competence and practice. Understanding the system psychodynamics present in organisations helps consultants and change agents to make use of an insider perspective without becoming enmeshed in the client organisation's regressive and inertial dynamics. The authors provide practical advice to help insiders navigate organisational space, make sense of tricky situations, and work more mindfully to help organisations change.

Karen Izod and Susan Rosina Whittle, *Resourceful Consulting: Working with Your Presence and Identity in Consulting to Change* (2014)

Izod and Whittle show that consultants and practitioners working with change can feel at a loss as to how to help their clients move forward. Organisations get stuck in routine ways even when they have innovations in mind. Consultants get stuck in familiar interventions which no longer prove stimulating or effective. Such challenges to practice can preoccupy and reinforce these stuck positions.

Drawing on their experiences of working with the professional development of consultants and change-agents over many years, this book provides an asset-based approach to consulting, where the resources to work at this 'stuckness' come from the way that we think about and use ourselves: our Identity and our presence. They propose that developing capacities to recognise and analyse *who* we bring into our consulting, and *how* we bring ourselves is central to resourceful practice. Without a skilful integration of these resources, the potential for change can be compromised. In handbook format, the book is structured in seven sections: Potential Space, Identity, Presence, Role Space, Practice, Change, and Future Developments. Focussing on practitioners' preoccupations, the authors offer models, theories, tales and activities to help describe and analyse their Identity and their Presence. They tell stories which question how Practice supports or compromises change, and suggest playful experimentation as a route to Change, and the development of a more resource-ful approach to consulting practice.

David Armstrong and Michael Rustin, *Social Defences against Anxiety: Explorations in a Paradigm* (2014)

In *Social Defences Against Anxiety: Explorations in a Paradigm* (2014) the introduction is excellent at conveying the concepts and the subsequent developments following Isabel Menzies Lyth's original work. Isabel Menzies Lyth was a pivotal and highly original thinker in group and organisational dynamics, specifically concerning the theme of social defences against anxiety. In this volume, David Armstrong and Michael Rustin do justice to her work by bringing together an impressive range of therapists, consultants, and academics, who further her thinking and take this approach into several new areas. The book critically engages one of its foundational concepts: collective unconscious defences against shared anxiety.

Susan Long, *The Perverse Organisation and Its Deadly Sins* (2018)

It is invidious to single out individuals, but below we highlight some of the key texts that have enlarged and extended the theory and practice of systems psychodynamics. Susan Long, with *The Perverse Organisation and its Deadly Sins (2018)*, made an important and significant contribution by examining the nature of perversity and its presence in corporate and organisational life. Four chapters examine the 'corporate sins' of perverse pride, greed, envy and sloth, each taking case studies from major organisations suffering their effects. Finally, the book enquires into the nature of the consumer/provider pair as a centrepiece of the perverse cultural dynamics of current organisational life. The emphasis in the book is on perversity displayed by the organisation as such, rather than simply by its leaders, or other members, even though they may embody and manifest perverse primary symptoms to the extent that they at times engage in corrupt or criminal behaviour. What is explored is a group and organisation dynamic, more deeply embedded than conscious corruption. Within the perverse structure some roles become required to take up corrupt positions. They become part and parcel of the way things work. The person may condemn certain practices, but the role requires them. Tensions between person and role may mean that the person in role acts, as they would not while in other roles. Such tensions may lead to the dynamics of perversity. This book is important reading for managers, consultants, and all who are interested in the dynamics propelling what seem to be the out-of-control dynamics within contemporary organisational life. It helps us understand how many people in positions of trust may end up abusing those positions. It looks at how we may be collectively perverse despite our individual attempts to be otherwise. It is a psychoanalytically inspired and politically informed look at contemporary organisational life which takes us from the mysteries of the New York Stock Exchange via Calisto Tanzi (Italy's Robert Maxwell) to the dynamics of envy in professional associations.

Susan Long, John Newton and Burkard Sievers, *Coaching in Depth* (2018)

With *Coaching In Depth* (2018), Susan Long, John Newton and Burkard Sievers introduce us to the management consultancy technique of Organizational Role Analysis (ORA); a technique with the immensely practical purpose of helping managers to stay 'in role and on task'. The ORA method is grounded in a process of consultation that derives from the conjunction of open systems theory and psychodynamic understandings of human behaviour. It enables the collaborative resolution of the mental and emotional tensions represented in the client's work role as they strive to manage the dynamics between their organisation-in-the-mind and the organisation-in-reality.

Halina Brunning, *Executive Coaching* (2006)

In *Executive Coaching* Halina Brunning (2006), and her colleagues explore in depth the field of coaching from a psychodynamic perspective and integrate this with examples that bring the uncertainties and realities of today's organisations to life. It looks beneath the surface and beyond the one-to-one coaching relationship, which enables the coaching client to deepen their emotional intelligence and their understanding of political and unconscious dynamics in organisations. The case studies clearly demonstrate that this is an effective methodology for enhancing their effectiveness in their roles. Those using systems psychodynamics and psychoanalytic approaches were engaged in coaching long before the term became fashionable, with many having decades of in-depth experience in this field.

Tim Dartington, *Managing Vulnerability* (2018)

Tim Dartington declares that clinicians, managers and researchers – as well as politicians and religious leaders – are worrying about a lack of compassion and humanity in the care of vulnerable people in society. Dartington explores the dynamics of care. He argues that we know how to do it, but somehow we seem to keep getting it wrong. Poor care in hospitals and care homes is well documented, and yet it continues. Care for people in their own homes is seen as an ideal, but the reality can be cruel and isolating. The author describes research over forty years in thinking why institutional and community care are both subject to processes of denial and fear of dependency. His examples include children in hospital, people with disabilities living in the community, and the care of older people and those with dementia.

Dartington was a researcher at the Tavistock Institute of Human Relations in the 1970s and worked there with Eric Miller and Isabel Menzies Lyth. He has continued to carry out consultancy and research in health and social care from a systems psychodynamics perspective and has written on the organisational issues in the delivery of care.

Dartington's book is a unique, intelligent and passionate text about the many ways we – as individuals and as society try to evade, actually hate, facing the facts of helplessness. Public services designed to provide rapid positive outcomes become clumsy when dealing with deterioration, yet that is where our humanity is tested. Dr Sebastian Kraemer points out that Tim Dartington reveals the wisdom of decades of experience as a Tavistock social scientist, with painful examples from his consultancy practice of life at the front line, then gives a brilliant account of his attempts to get coherent help for his wife, Anna, as she became demented in middle age. With comments from Anna herself, this is very moving and learned account of defences against vulnerability laced with deadpan irony creates irresistible and instructive reading for all who use or provide public services. Dartington brings to light the social and psychological matrix that shapes our systems of care and how today's cultural context, which so often devalues dependence, creates debilitating cross currents for leaders and managers of organisations providing care. The book provides a penetrating account of how emotions associated with the work of caring find their way into the structure, informal processes, and functioning of modern caring institutions.

David Armstrong (eds Robert French and Russ Vince), *Organization in the Mind: Psychoanalysis, Group Relations and Organizational Consultancy* (2018)

David Armstrong has been a leading figure internationally in the fields of organisational consultancy and group relations for many years. French and Vince have gathered, for the first time, his key writings in this area. This is essential reading for managers and leaders, as well as organisational consultants, academics and students of organizations. Armstrong has been a powerful influence in shaping our understanding of the organization- in-the-mind, organisational consultation, and role analysis. In this collection, he puts many of his most important contributions in public view.

Paul Hoggett, (ed.) *Climate Psychology: On Indifference to Disaster: Studies in the Psychosocial* (2019)

Paul Hoggett edits and investigates the psycho-social phenomenon which is society's failure to respond to climate change. It analyses the non-rational dimensions of our collective paralysis in the face of worsening climate change and environmental destruction, exploring the emotional, ethical, social, organisational and cultural dynamics to blame for this global lack of action.

The book features eleven research projects from four different countries and is divided in two parts, the first highlighting novel methodologies, the second presenting new findings. Contributors to the first part show how a 'deep listening' approach to research can reveal the anxieties, tensions, contradictions, frames and narratives that contribute to people's experiences, and the many ways climate change and other environmental risks are imagined through metaphor, imagery and dreams.

Using detailed interview extracts drawn from politicians, scientists and activists as well as ordinary people, the second part of the book examines the many ways in which we both avoid and square up to this gathering disaster, and the many faces of alarm, outrage, denial and indifference this involves.

Halina Brunning, *Psychoanalytic Essays on Power and Vulnerability* (2019)

In *Psychoanalytic Essays on Power and Vulnerability edited by Halina Brunning (2019)*, Brunning explores the interconnectedness of power and vulnerability from its expression in early mother-child relationships through to its effects in organisational life and in broad societal and global dynamics. The stance is from the systems psychodynamics or socioanalytic perspective: examining the underlying and largely unconscious drivers of overt behaviours. The chapters throw light on how the balance between power and vulnerability is revealed and shifted; held or shattered; with resounding consequences. The book is an important addition to understanding more about the complexities of organisations and society. Two hypotheses are explored: It is possible to discern psychodynamic evidence that unresolved humiliation trauma is being re-evoked and recycled by attempts to find solutions and cures through the tyranny of austerity measures. But the question is asked whether these are 'chosen trauma' (Volkan, 2010) which may be at the heart of the foundation matrix (Foulkes, 1973) of the European Community. The exploration of political and economic leadership in the crisis in the European Union builds on the notion of society as a large group proliferating crises of identity. From a systemic perspective it is possible to analyse the nation states of Europe protesting with regressive nationalism, refusing collaboration by engaging in economic warfare while at the same time attempting rescue packages. The protest could be seen as defensive denial of their humbling at the hands of the over-ambitious aspects of the European single currency project and the demise of the potency of the nation state. The concluding section reflects on these issues and tries to distinguish the recycling of humiliation trauma from defence against the experience of being humbled.

Claudia Nagel, *Psychodynamic Coaching: Distinctive Features* (2019)

In *Psychodynamic Coaching: Distinctive Features* (2019), Claudia Nagel presents a comprehensive overview of the unique features of psychodynamic coaching. As leaders and managers acknowledge the need to understand themselves and their context by looking underneath the surface to improve their decision-making, psychodynamic approaches offer unique insight. *Psychodynamic Coaching: Distinctive Features* covers not only the major theory but also the practice of coaching, giving guidance from beginning to end of the client relationship. Constructive, holistic and accessible, it demonstrates the impact and dynamics of the unconscious whilst illustrating the power of understanding human behaviour in the complexity of the modern world.

Brissett, Sher & Smith, *Dynamics at Boardroom Level: A Tavistock Primer for Leaders, Coaches and Consultants* (2019)

In *Dynamics at Boardroom Level: A Tavistock Primer for Leaders, Coaches and Consultants* (Brissett et al., 2019) this book asks how can boards and members of boards reach their full potential? The Tavistock Institute of Human Relations (TIHR) has been at the forefront of thinking about organisations since its inception in 1947. The corporate world is undergoing increasing pressure to demonstrate a sustainable, generative and meaningful impact on society and employees whilst delivering improved services and products. There is a useful framework of theory and practice that broadens vision and deepens thinking about what is happening in boardrooms. The book opens the door to the reader to a new world of board dynamics, edited by those who really understand the deeper workings of the complex human system and its work at board level. This edited volume brings together the insights and contemporary case studies from participants on the Tavistock Institute's Dynamics @ Board Level programme that draws on the thinking of Tavistock scholars and practitioners and their work on the dynamics of task, role, authority and power.

Anton Obholzer and Vega Zagier Roberts (eds), *The Unconscious at Work, Second Edition* (2019)

The Unconscious at Work, Second Edition, draws on a body of thinking and practice which has developed over the past 70 years, often referred to as 'the Tavistock approach' or 'systems-psychodynamics'. All the contributors are practising consultants who draw on this framework, bringing it alive and making it useful to any reader – manager, leader or consultant, regardless of whether they have any prior familiarity with the underlying concepts – who is curious about what might be driving the puzzling or stressful situations they find in their workplace.

The First Edition was addressed to people working in 'the human services': health, social care and education. Since it was published in 1994, there has been growing interest in the business world, and in understanding more about the 'irrational' side of organisational life. The Second Edition includes an entirely new section where the key ideas are revisited and illustrated with case studies from a wide range of business organizations, from large corporations to start-ups and family businesses.

Francesca Cardona, *Work Matters: Consulting to Leaders and Organizations in the Tavistock Tradition* (2020)

In *Work Matters: Consulting to Leaders and Organizations in the Tavistock Tradition (2020)*, Cardona points out that work is complicated: it can be fulfilling and exciting, or disappointing and disruptive. She shows that we spend most of our adult lives at work; it shapes our identities and provides a context for our creativity and talents. It can be the source of great pleasure – and of profound distress. In *Work Matters*, organisational consultant Cardona examines our changing relationship with work today. Drawing on case studies from a wide range of individuals and organisations, she considers the dynamics at play in our working lives. Cardona examines how to navigate times of transition, and the balance of power in the workplace, while also addressing latent issues such as the effects of shame, the cost of ill-conceived organisational structures and tasks, the interface between the personal and the professional, and the manager's most precious skill: the ability to be psychologically present. Finally, Cardona casts an eye on the consultant's role in helping organisations move forwards in ways that are professionally and personally rewarding.

Halina Brunning and Olya Khaleelee, *Danse Macabre and Other Stories: A Psychoanalytic Perspective on Global Dynamics* (2021)

Danse Macabre and Other Stories: A Psychoanalytic Perspective on Global Dynamics by Halina Brunning and Olya Khaleelee (2021) examines the world using a systemic and psychoanalytic lens, including concepts of splitting, separation, projection, displacement, and the return of the repressed. It considers what impact the disappearance of some iconic and psychic containers has on individuals functioning and why we choose populist leaders to shore up our own social defences. Brunning and Khaleelee question why the world feels so threatening when the objective facts suggest that overall much is improving for the global citizen. Brunning and Khaleelee have created a coherent framework to conceptualise global dynamics within a matrix form. The matrix contains dialectic dynamic forces for both good and evil, love and hate, creation and destruction. They take a closer look at the plethora of phenomena which they see arising therein. Whilst the matrix holds steady, inside it is a world in constant flux, reconfiguring and rearranging itself, as if in a kaleidoscope, with inevitable and unavoidable turbulence, but Brunning and Khaleelee hypothesise that there is an underlying pattern that is available to be discerned and studied. Aware of this turbulence, Brunning and Khaleelee wish to share their view of the world in the hope of offering a containing reflection, capable of calming the nerves of the readers as well as their own.

Anton Obholzer, Workplace Intelligence: Unconscious Forces and How to Manage Them (2021)

This book provides a range of insights into the unconscious processes at play in the workplace and an introduction to a balanced approach to organisations. Obholzer explores key concepts, showing how our emotions and early experiences inform the roles we play at work, as well as how we react to other people. It encourages close observation and reflection and utilisation of this knowledge for managing ourselves and others fruitfully. It also provides managers with the methods to intervene and tackle these issues, elaborating on topics from leadership and group dynamics to meetings and work-life balance. Gilles Amado points out that Anton Obholzer illustrates not only the numerous psychic phenomena operating under the surface of organisations, but also subtly shows ways to make sense of the consulting and intervention processes in which his psychoanalytic and anthropological expertise, along with his well-known humour, provides aid.

Gabriella Braun, All That We Are: Uncovering the Hidden Truths behind Our Behaviour at Work (2022)

Gabriella Braun asks the question who do you bring with you to work? She suggests that try as we might, we cannot leave part of ourselves under the pillow with our pyjamas when we go to work. We bring all that we are. In this collection of stories, Gabriella Braun shares insights from over twenty years of taking psychoanalysis out of the therapy room and into the staff room. She shows us why a board loses the plot, nearly causes their company to collapse, and how they come through. We see the connection between a head teacher's professional and personal loss. We understand seemingly unfathomable behaviour – why a man lets his organisation push him around, a lawyer becomes paranoid, a team repeatedly creates scapegoats, and founders of a literary agency feud. At a time when we are re-thinking the workplace, *All That We Are: Uncovering the Hidden Truths Behind Our Behaviour at Work (2020)* shows that by taking human nature seriously, we can build more humane organisations where people and their work can thrive.

References

Abraham, F., (2013). The Tavistock group. *In:* M. Witzel and M. Warner (eds.), *The Oxford Handbook of Management Theorists.* Oxford: Oxford University Press. http://www.tavinstitute.org/projects/the-tavistock-group/

Ackoff, R. L., and Emery, F. E., (1972). *On Purposeful Systems: An Interdisciplinary Analysis of Individual and Social Behavior as a System of Purposeful Events.* New Brunswick, NJ: Aldine Transaction.

Ackoff, R., (1974). The social responsibility of operational research. *Journal of Operational Research Society,* 25, 361–371. Englewood Cliffs, NJ: Prentice-Hall.

Adams, J. R., Bilbro, C. R., and Stockert, T. C., (1997). *Principles of Project Management Collected Handbooks from the Project Management Institute.* Newton Square, PA: Project Management Institute.

Adorno, T. W., Frenkel-Brunswik, E., Levinson, D., and Sanford, N., (1950). *The Authoritarian Personality.* New York: Harper & Row.

Alderfer, C. P., (1980). Consulting to underbounded systems. *In:* C. P. Alderfer and C. L. Cooper (eds.), *Advances in Experiential Social Processes* (Vol. 2). New York: John Wiley, pp. 267–295.

Aldrich, H., (1976). Resource dependence and inter-organization relations. *Administration and Society,* 7(4), 419–454.

Aldrich, H., and Whetten, D. A., (1981). Organizational sets, actions sets, and networks. *In:* P. Nystrom and W. H. Starbuck (eds.), *Handbook of Organizational Design.* London: Oxford University Press, pp. 385–408.

Allen, P. M., (1998a). *Modelling Complex Economic Evolution; Evolving Complexity in Social Science in Systems: New Paradigms for the Human Sciences.* Berlin, London: Walter de Gruyter.

Allen, P. M., (1998b). Evolutionary complex systems: Models of technological change, complexity in social science. *In:* G. Altman, and W. Koch, (eds.), *New Paradigms for the Human Sciences.* Berlin, London: Walter de Gruyter.

Allen, P. M., (1997). *Cities & Regions as Self-Organizing Systems: Model of Complexity Environmental Problems & Social Dynamics Series,* Vol 1. Gordon & Breach Science Publication.

Allport, G. W., (1948). Foreword. *In:* G. Lewin (ed.), *Resolving Social Conflicts: Selected Papers on Group Dynamics.* New York: Harper & Row, pp. vii–xiv.

Alvesson, M., and Deetz, S., (1996). Critical theory and postmodernism approaches to organizational studies. *In:* S. Clegg, W. R. Nord and C. Hardy, (eds.), *Handbook of Organization Studies.* London: Sage Publications, pp. 191–217.

Alvesson, M., and Blom, M., (2019). Beyond leadership and followership: Working with a variety of modes of organizing. *Organizational Dynamics,* 48, 28–37.

Anderson, P., (1999). Complexity theory and organization science: *In: Organization Science,* Vol. 10, No. 3. Special issue: *Application of Complexity Theory to Organization Science,* Pg. 216–232.

Anderson, S. B., Braskamp, L. A., Cohen, W. M., Evans, J. W., Gilmore, A., Marvin, K. E., Shipman, V. C., Vanecko, J. J., and Wooldridge, R. J., (1982). Evaluation research society standards for program evaluation. *New Directions for Program Evaluation,* 7–19.

Aram, E., and Noble, D., (1998). Working with small business managers in conditions of ambiguity and uncertainty. *The Complexity & Management Working Papers Series no: 18.* The University of Hertfordshire Business School Working Papers Series. *Available from:* Uhra.herts.ac.uk

Aram, E., and Noble, D., (1999). Educating prospective managers in the complexity of organisational life: Teaching and learning from a complexity perspective. *Management Learning,* 30(3), 321–342.

Aram, E., (2000). Virtual dynamics and socio-technical systems. *In:* E. Coakes, D. Willis, and R. Lloyd-Jones (eds.), *The New Socio Tech: Graffiti on the Long Wall.* London: Springer Verlage. 160-169

Aram, E., (2001). *The Experience of Complexity: Learning as the Potential Transformation of Identity.* Unpublished doctoral thesis, University of Hertfordshire.

Aram, E., Baxter, R., and Nutkevitch, A. (Eds.), (2009). *Adaptation and Innovation: Theory, Design and Role-Taking in Group Relations Conferences and their Applications. Belgirate: Volume II.* London: Karnac.

Aram, E., (2010). *The Aesthetics of Group Relations, a Talk Given at the AK Rice Institute's 40th Anniversary Symposium.* Chicago, IL. https://www.akriceinstitute.org/

Aram, E., (2011). *Introduction to Complexity, a Talk Given As Part of the TIHR Lunch Time Food for thought Series.* https://www.tavinstitute.org/projects/an-introduction-to-complexity-theory/

Aram, E., (2012). *Complexity – Going Deeper, a Talk Given as Part of the TIHR Lunch Time Food for Thought. Available from:* https://www.tavinstitute.org/projects/complexity-going-deeper/

Aram, E., Baxter, R., and Nutkevitch, A. (Eds.), (2012). *Belgirate III: Tradition, Creativity and Succession in the Global Group Relations Network.* London: Karnac Books.

Aram, E., and Sher, M., (2013). Group relations conferences, *In:* S. Long (ed.), *Socioanalytic Methods: Discovering the Hidden in Organisations and Social Systems.* London: Karnac, pp. 257–277.

Aram, E., (2015a). *Complexity and Boards: Course reading.* Dynamics @ Board Level. Tavistock Institute of Human Relations. Unpublished.

Aram, E., (2015b). *Does Love Matter? Fear and Compassion in Organisations and Leadership, Part of the Lunch Time Talk Series. Available from:* https://www.tavinstitute.org/projects/does-love-matter-fear-and-compassion-in-organisations-and-leadership/

Aram, E., (2015c). *Remembering, Learning and the Media: A Thought Piece. Available from:* https://www.tavinstitute.org/news/remembering-learning-media/

Are robots stealing our jobs? (2018). CIPD podcast (episode 142) *Available from:* www.cipd.co.uk/podcasts/digital-transformation

Argyris, C., and Schon, D. A., (1974). *Theory in Practice: Increasing Professional Effectiveness.* San Francisco: Jossey-Bass.

Argyris, C., (1983). Action science and intervention. *Journal of Applied Behavioural Science*, 19(2), 115–135.

Argyris, C., (1993). On the nature of actionable knowledge. *The Psychologist*, 6(1), 29–32.

Argyris, C., Putnam, R. W., and Smith, M. C., (1985). *Action Science: Concepts, Methods, and Skills for Research and Intervention*. San Francisco: Jossey Bass.

Armstrong, D., (2005a). *Organization in the Mind: Psychoanalysis, Group Relations and Organizational Consultancy*. London: Karnac.

Armstrong, D., (2005b). The recovery of meaning. *In:* Eds: Robert French, *Organization in the Mind: Psychoanalysis, Group Relations and Organizational Consultancy*. London: Karnac, pp. 55–68.

PorraArmstrong, D., and Rustin, M. (Eds.), (2014). *Social Defences against Anxiety: Explorations in a Paradigm*. London: Karnac.

Armstrong, D., (2015). The authority of the dream. *Socioanalysis*, 17, 1–11.

Armstrong, D., (2019). *The Practice of Social Dreaming: Guiding Principles*. Available from: https://www.tavinstitute.org/wp-content/uploads/2019/05/The-Practice-of-Social-Dreaming-Guiding-Principles.pdf

Arthur, W. B., (1999). *Coming from Your Inner Self, Conversation with W. Brian Arthur*, Xerox PARC, April 16, by Joseph Jaworski, Gary Jusela, C. Otto Scharmer. *In:* https://www.presencing.org/aboutus/theory-u/leadership-interview/W_Brian_Arthur

Ashby, W. R., (1956). *An Introduction to Cybernetics Chapman and Hall*. London.

Ashby, W. R., (1960). *Design for a brain: The origin of adaptive behavior*. London: Chapman & Hall.

Attwood, M., Pedler, Pritchard, M., and Wilkinson, D., (2003). *Leading Change: A Guide to Whole Systems Working*. Bristol: Policy Press.

Austrom, D., and Ordowich, C., (2019). Calvin Pava. Sociotechnical system design for the digital coal mines. *In:* D. Szabia, W. Pasmore, M. Barnes, and A. Gipson (eds.), *The Palgrave Handbook of Organizational Change Thinkers*. Chapter 75. Palgrave Macmillan, pp. 1293–1323.

Austrom, D., Ordowich, C., and Painter, B., (2022). *Co-Designing the Workspace, a New Value Proposition for STS Designing*. Available from: https://stsroundtable.com/resources/sodf-materials/0; https://www.jungmasterclass.com/p/the-interpretation-of-dreams

Avis, J., (2018). Socio-technical imaginary of the fourth industrial revolution and its implications for vocational education and training: A literature review. *Journal of Vocational Education & Training*, 70(3), 337–363.

Axelrod, R., (1990). *The Evolution of Cooperation*. London: Penguin.

Axelrod, R., and Cohen, M. D., (2001). *Harnessing Complexity*. New York: Basic Books.

Axelrod, R., (1997). *The Complexity of Cooperation: Agent-Based Models of Competition and Collaboration*. Princeton University Press.

Babington-Smith, B., and Farrell, B. A. (Eds.), (1979). *Training in Small Groups: A Study of Five Methods*. Oxford: Pergamon.

Baburoglu, O., (1992). Tracking the development of the Emery–Trist systems paradigm. *Systems Practice*, 5(3), 263–290.

Bain, A., (1982). The Baric experiment: The design of jobs and organization for the expression and growth of human capacity. *Tavistock Institute Occasional Paper. No. 4.*

Bain, A., (1998). Social defences against organizational learning. *Human Relations*, 51(3), 413–430.

Balan, S., (2010). *M. Foucault's view on power relations*. Institute of Philosophy and Psychology. C.R. Motru. *Available from:* https://cogito.ucdc.ro/nr_2v2/M.%20FOUCAULT%27S%20VIEW%20ON%20POWER%20RELATIONS.pdf

Balazs, K., and Kets de Vries, M. F. R., (1997a). *Bang and Olufsen: A company in transition*. IN-SEAD case study.

Balazs, K., and Kets de Vries, M. F. R., (1997b). The downside of downsizing. *Human Relations*, 50(1), 11–50.

Balazs, K., and Kets de Vries, M. F. R., (1998). Beyond the quick fix: The psychodynamics of organizational transformation and change. *European Management Journal*, 16(5), 611–622.

Balazs, K., and Kets de Vries, M. F. R., (1999a). Transforming the mind-set of the organisation: A clinical perspective. *Administration Society*, 30(6), 640–675. *Available from:* INSEAD, France. https://knowledge.insead.edu

Balazs, K., and Kets de Vries, M. F. R., (1999b). *Creating the "Authentizotic" Organization: Corporate Transformation and Its Vicissitudes — A Rejoinder*. *Available from:* https://www.google.co.uk/url?sa=t&rct=j&q=&esrc=s&source=web&cd=7&ved=2a-hUKEwjbivaIg5_pAhVcThUIHargA5UQFjAGegQIBRAB&url=https%3A%2F%2Fflora.insead.edu%2Ffichiersti_wp%2Finseadwp1999%2F99-02.pdf&usg=AOvVaw0nIDCPoqhwvpw6d9Q4m73s

Bargal, D., and Bar, H., (1992). A Lewinian approach to intergroup workshops for Arab-Palestinian and Jewish youth. *Journal of Social Issues*, 48(2), 139–154.

Barker, C., Pistrang, N., and Elliot, R., (1994). *Wiley Series in Clinical Psychology. Research Methods in Clinical and Counselling Psychology*. Oxford, England: John Wiley & Sons.

Barley, S. R., and Kunda, G., (2001). Bringing work back in. *Organisation Science*, 12(1), 76–95.

Barth, F., (1964). Competition and symbiosis in north east Baluchistan. *Folk*, 6(1), 15–22.

Barrett, F. J., and Fry, R. E., (2005). *Appreciative Inquiry: A Positive Approach to Building Cooperative Capacity*. Chagrin Falls, OH: Taos Institute.

Barton, J., and Selsky, J. W., (2000). The third track of the open-systems-thinking school: An application of domain theory to New Zealand ports. *Systemic Practice and Action Research*, 13, 257–277.

Baum, H., (1987). *The Invisible Bureaucracy: The Unconscious in Organisational Problem Solving*. New York: Oxford University Press.

Baum, H., (2020). A changing world of work. What can we learn from the service sector about employing Millennials (and Gen Z)? *Organizational Dynamics*, 43(3), 1–8.

Baum, H. S., (1989). Organizational politics against organizational culture: A psychoanalytic perspective. *Human Resource Management*, 28(2), 191–207.

Baum, T., and Hai, N., (2020). Hospitality, tourism, human rights and the impact of COVID-19. *International Journal of Contemporary Hospitality Management*, 32(7), 2397–2407.

Baxter, M., (2019). *Does the UK really need more robots? In RPA the UK is a leader. Information Age*. *Available from:* www.information-age.com/about-information-age/

Beckhard, R., (1967). The confrontation meeting. *Harvard Business Review*, 45(2), 149–155.

Bednar, P., and Welch, C., (2020). Socio-technical perspectives on smart working: Creating meaningful and sustainable systems. *Information Systems Frontiers*, 22, 281–298.

Beech, N., Burns, H., de Caestecker, L., MacIntosh, R., and MacLean, D., (2004). Paradox as invitation to act in problematic change situations. *Human Relations*, 57(10), 1313–1332.

Beer, M., Spector, P., Lawrence, P., et al., (1985). *Human Resource Management: A General Manager's Perspective*. New York: Free Press.

Beinum, H. van., (1990). *Observations on the Development of a New Organisational Paradigm*. Stockholm: The Swedish Centre for Working Life.

Bendel, J., (2018). Deep adaptation: A map for navigating the climate tragedy. Initiative for leadership and sustainability, *Occasional Paper 2, University of Cumbria*. *Available from:* https://iflas.blogspot.com/2018/07/new-paper-on-deep-adaptation-to-climate.html

Bennett, R., and Leduchowicz, T., (1983). What makes for an effective trainer? *Journal of European Industrial Training*, 7(2), 3–46.

Bennis, W., (1993). *An Invented Life, Reflections on Leadership and Change*. Reading, MA: Addison-Wesley.

Benson, J., (2018). *Working More Creatively with Groups*. London: Routledge.

Beradt, C., (1966). *The Third Reich of Dreams*. New York: Quadrangle Books.

Berg, D. N., (1998). Resurrecting the muse: Followership in organizations. *In:* E. Klein, F. Gabelnick, and P. Herr (eds.), *The Psychodynamics of Leadership*. Madison, CT: Psychosocial Press, pp. 27–52.

Bergiel, J. B., Bergiel, B. E., and Balsmeier, W. P., (2008). Nature of virtual teams: A summary of their advantages and disadvantages. *Management Research News*, 31(2), 99–110.

Bick, E., (1964). Notes on infant observation in psychoanalytic training. *International Journal of Psycho-analysis*, 45. Reprinted in *Collected Papers of Martha Harris and Esther Bick*, ed. M. H. Williams. Perthshire: Clunie Press, 1987, pp. 240–258.

Bing, P., (1947). Task Perception and Interpersonal Relations in Industrial Training: The Development of a Training Project in the Hosiery Industry. *Human Relations*, Part 1, 1, 121–130; Part 2 No 2, 373–412.

Bion, W. R., (1961). *Experiences in groups and other papers*. London: Tavistock Publications, [Reprinted London: Routledge, 1989; London: Brunner-Routledge, 2001.]

Bion, W., (1961). Experiences in Groups. New York: Basic Books (See selections from: Experiences in Groups, *In:* A. D. Coleman and W. H. Bexton (eds.), Group Relations Reader 1, A. K. Rice Institute Series, Washington DC, 1975.

Bion, W., (1962a). Learning from experience. *International Journal of Psychoanalysis*, 43, 306–310.

Bion, W., (1962b). *Learning from Experience*. London: Karnac.

Bion, W., (1967). Attacks on linking, *In: Second Thoughts: Selected Papers on Psychoanalysis*. London: Heinemann Medical (reprinted London: Mansfield Reprints, 1984).

Bion, W., (1967). *Second Thoughts*. London: Maresfield Library: Karnac.

Bion, W. R., (1970). *Attention and Interpretation*. London: Tavistock Publications.

Bion, W., (1977). *Seven Servants*. New York: Jason Aronson.

Bion, W., (1980). *Bion in New York and Sao Paulo*. (ed.) F. Bion, Perthshire: Clunie Press.

Bion, W., (1984). *Elements of Psychoanalysis*. London: Heinemann.

Bion, W. R., (1991). *A Memoir of the Future*. London: Karnac.

Biran, H., (2007). The dreaming soldier. *In:* W. G. Lawrence (eds.), *The Infinite Possibilities of Social Dreaming*. London: Karnac, pp. 29–45.

Blakely, R., (2020). *The Appliance of Science: Professor Creates Lab Robot that Never Stops*. *Available from:* The Times www.thetimes.co.uk/article/the-appliance-of-science-professor-creates-lab-robot-that-never-stops-gdj739mn8

Blignaut, S., (2021). Exploring systems psychodynamics: The weird and wonderful world of the unconscious. *Available from:* https://sonjablignaut.medium.com/exploring-systems-psychodynamics-the-weird-and-wonderful-world-of-the-unconscious-89d15eb9c872

Block, P., (2000). *Flawless Consulting* 2nd edn. San Francisco: Pfeiffer.

Bloom, N., (1989). Select the right manager for success. *Personnel Journal,* 68(8), 77–81.

Boccara, B., (2014). *Socio-Analytic Dialogue: Incorporating Psychosocial Dynamics into Public Policies.* Maryland: Lexington Books.

Boëthius, S. B., and Stefan, J., (2011). *Early International Group Relations Symposia - from Oxford to Belgirate. What has been learnt and how do we keep the lamp trimmed and burning? Available from*: https://www.researchgate.net/publication/280933709_Early_International_Group_Relations_Symposia_-_from_Oxford_to_Belgirate_What_has_been_learnt_and_how_do_we_keep_the_lamp_trimmed_and_burning

Boland, S., et al., (2020). *Reimagining the Office and Work Life after Covid 19.* McKinsey and Company. *Available from:* https://www.mckinsey.com/business-functions/organization/our-insights/reimagining-the-office-and-work-life-after-covid-19#

Bollas, C., (1992). *Being a Character: Psychoanalysis and Self Experience.* London: Routledge.

Bolton, and Roberts, V. Z., (1994). Asking for help: Staff support and sensitivity groups re-viewed. *In:* A. Obholzer and V. Z. Roberts (eds.), *The Unconscious at Work.* New York: Routledge, pp. 156–165.

Borda, F., and Rahman, M. A. (Eds.), (1991). *Action and Knowledge: Breaking the Monopoly with Participatory Action Research.* New York: Intermediate Technology Publications/Apex Press.

Boulton, J., Allen, P., and Bowman, C., (2015). *Embracing Complexity: Strategic Perspectives for an Age of Turbulence.* Oxford: Oxford University Press.

Bourke, I., (2022). Interview with Sally Weintrobe. *Available from*: https://www.newstatesman.com/author/india-bourke

Bradbury, K., Mirvis, P., Neilsen, E., and Pasmore, W. A., (2008). Action research at work: Creating the future following the path from Lewin. *In:* P. Reason and H. Bradbury, (eds.). *Handbook of Action Research.* (2nd edn. London: Sage, pp. 77–92.

Braun, G., (2022). *All That We Are: Uncovering the Hidden Truths Behind Our Behaviour at Work.* London: Piatkus.

Bridger, H., (1990). *Courses and Working Conferences as Transitional Learning Institutions Available from:* http://moderntimesworkplace.com/archives/ericsess/sessvol1/HaroldBp221.opd.pdf *In:* Trist, E., and Murray, H., (1990). Eds The Social Engagement of Social Science, a Tavistock Anthology, Volume 1: The Socio-Psychological perspective. University of Pennsylvania Press.

Bridger, H., (1990). The discovery of the therapeutic community: The northfield experiment. *In:* E. Trist, and H. Murray (eds.), *The Social Engagement of Social Science, a Tavistock Anthology, Volume 1: The Socio-Psychological perspective.* London: London Free Association Press, pp. 68–87. *Available from:* http://moderntimesworkplace.com/archives/ericsess/sessvol1/Bridgerp68.opd.pdf

Brissett, L., Sher, M., and Smith, T., (2020). *Dynamics at Boardroom Level: A Tavistock Primer for Leaders, Coaches and Consultants.* London: Routledge.

Britton, R. S., (2021). *Personal Communications.*

Brunner, L. D., Nutevitch, A., and Sher, M. (Eds.), (2006). *Group Relations Conferences: Reviewing and Exploring Theory, Design, Role-Taking and Application.* London: Karnac Books.

Brunning, H., and Perini, M. (Ed.), (2010). *Psychoanalytic Perspectives on a Turbulent World*. London: Karnac Books.

Brunning, H., (2011). *Psychoanalytic Reflections on a Modern World*. London: Karnac Books.

Brunning, H., (2013). *Psychoanalytic Essays on Power and Vulnerability*. London: Karnac Books.

Brunning, H. (Ed.), (2006). *Executive Coaching Systems-Psychodynamic Perspective*. London: Karnac Books.

Brunning, H., and Khaleelee, O., (2011). *Danse Macabre and Other Stories: A Psychoanalytic Perspective on Global Dynamics*. London: Phoenix Publishing House.

Brynjolfsson, E., and McAfee, A., (2014). *The Second Machine Age: Work, Progress, and Prosperity in a Time of Brilliant Technologies*. New York: WW Norton.

Brynjolfsson, E., and McAfee, A., (2017). The business of artificial intelligence. *Harvard Business Review July 2017* (reprint BG1704 available at HBR.org).

Buchanan, D., and Boddy, D., (1992). *The Expertise of the Change Agent, Public Performance and Backstage*. New York: Prentice Hall.

Bunker, B., and Alban, B., (1997). *Large Group Interventions: Engaging the Whole System for Rapid Change*. San Francisco: Jossey-Bass.

Burke, W. W., and Litwin, G. H., (1992). A causal model of organizational performance and change. *Journal of Management,* 18(3), 523–545.

Burke, W. W., and Biggart, N. W., (1997). Inter organizational relations. *In:* D. Druckman, J. E. Singer, and H. Van Cott (eds.), *Enhancing Organizational Performance*. Washington, DC: National Academy Press, pp. 120–149.

Burke, W., Lake, D., and Waymire, J. (Eds.), (2008). *Organization Change: A Comprehensive Reader*. San Francisco: Jossey Bass.

Burke, W. W., and Noumair, D. A., (2015). *Organisation Development: A Process of Learning and Changing*. London: FT Press.

Burke, W., (2017). *Organisation Change Theory and Practice,* 5th Edition. New York: Sage.

Burnes, B., (2004a). Kurt Lewin and complexity theories: Back to the future? *Journal of Change Management,* 4(4), 309–325.

Burnes, B., (2004b). Kurt Lewin and complexity theories: Back to the future? *Journal of Change* Emery, F., and Trist, E., (1960). Report on the Barford Conference for Bristol/Siddley, Aero-Engine Corporation. Document no. 598. London: Tavistock. *Management,* 4:4, 309–325. *Available from:* https://www.researchgate.net/publication/228990434_Kurt_Lewin_and_complexity_theories_Back_to_the_future

Burnes, B., (2004c). Kurt Lewin and the planned approach to change: A reappraisal. *Journal of Management Studies,* 41, 977–1002. *Available from:* https://www.researchgate.net/publication/228990434_Kurt_Lewin_and_complexity_theories_Back_to_the_future

Burnes, B., (2007). Kurt Lewin and the Harwood studies: The foundations of OD. *Journal of Applied Behavioural Science,* 43(2), 213–231.

Burnes, B., (2013). Looking back to forward. *In:* R. T. By and B. Burnes (eds.), *Organisational Change, Leadership and Ethics*. London: Routledge, pp. 243–258.

Burnes, B., and Cooke, B., (2012). Review article: The past, present and future of organization development: Taking the long view. *Human Relations,* 65(11), 1395–1429.

Burns, T., and Stalker, G. M., (1961). *The Management of Innovation*. London: Tavistock.

Burton, R., (1932). *The Anatomy of Melancholy*. London: Dent.

Bushe, G.R., (2010). Generativity and the transformational potential of appreciative inquiry. *Organizational generativity: Advances in appreciative inquiry*, 3, 1–13.

Bushe, G, and Nagaishi, M., (2018). Imagining the future through the past: Organization development isn't (just) about change. *Organization Development Journal*, Fall, 23–36.

Business, Energy and Industrial Strategy Committee, (2019). *Businesses Face being Left Behind by Transition to New Technologies*. parliament.uk *Available from:* www.parliament.uk/business/committees/committees-a-z/commons-select/business-energy-industrial-strategy/news-parliament-2017/automation-and-future-of-work-report-published-17-19/

Caldwell, R., (2003). Models of change agency, a fourfold classification. *British Journal of Management*, 14, 131–142.

Cameron, K., and Lavine, M., (2006). *Making the Impossible Possible: Leading Extraordinary Performance*. San Francisco, CA: Berrett-Koehler.

Cameron, K., (1986). Effectiveness as paradox: Consensus and conflict in conceptions of organizational effectiveness. *Management Science*, 32, 539–553.

Cameron, E., and Green, M., (2015). *Making Sense of Change Management*. London: Kogan Page.

Capra, F., (1996). *The Web of Life*. London: Harper Collins.

Capra, F., (2002). *The Hidden Connections: A Science for Sustainable Living*. London: Harper Collins

Cardona, F., (2020). *Work Matters: Consulting to leaders and organizations in the Tavistock Tradition*. London: Routledge.

Carothers, T., and O'Donohue, A., (2019). *Democracies Divided: The Global Challenge of Political Polarization*. Washington DC: Brookings Institution Press.

Carr, A., and Zanetti, L., (1999). Metatheorising the dialectics of self and other: The psychodynamics in work organizations. *American Behavioral Scientist*, 43(2), 324–345.

Carr, A., (1993). The psychostructure of work: Bend me, shape me, anyway you want me, as long as you love me it's alright. *Journal of Managerial Psychology*, 8(6), 2–6.

Carr, A., (1998). Identity, compliance and dissent in organisations: A psychoanalytic perspective, *Organization*, 5(1), 81–89.

Castells, M., (2000). *The Rise of the Network Society* (2nd Ed.). Oxford: Blackwell.

Castells, M., (2007). Communication, power and counter-power in the network society. *International Journal of Communication*, 1(1), 238–266.

Checkland, P., (1999). *Systems Thinking, Systems Practice*. Chichester: Wiley & Sons.

Cherns, Albert., (1976). The Principles of Socio-technical design. *Human Relations*, 29, 783–792.

Cheung-Judge, L. M-Y., and Holbeche, L. (Eds.), (2011). *Organisational Development*. London: Kogan Paul.

Cheung – Judge, M., and Holbeche, L., (2015). *Organization Development: A Practitioner's Guide for OD and HR*. London: Kogan Page.

Chevalier, J. M., and Buckles, D. J., (2013). *Participatory Action Research, Theory and Methods for Engaged Inquiry*. London: Routledge.

Child, J. (2005). *Organization: Contemporary Principles and Practice*. Oxford: Blackwell.

Church, A., and Burke, W., (2017). Four trends shaping the future of organisations and organization development. *OD Practitioner*, 49(3), 14–22.

Cilliers, F., and Koortzen, P., (2005). Working with conflict in teams: The CIBART model. *HR Future*, October, 51–52.

Clark, D., (2019, November 21). *United Kingdom: People Living Alone in 2019, by Age and Gender. Statista, Available from:* www.statista.com/statistics/281616/people-living-alone-in-the-united-kingdom-uk-by-age-and-gender/

Clark, T., and Fincham, R., (2002). *Critical Consulting: New Perspectives on the Management Advice Industry.* Oxford: Blackwell.

Clarke, M., and Meldrum, M., (1999). Creating change from below, early lessons for agents of change. *The Leadership & Organizational Development Journal,* 20(2), 70–80.

Clarke, P. A., (1972). *Action Research and Organizational Change.* London: Harper & Row.

Clegg, C. W., (2000). Socio-technical principles for system design. *Applied Ergonomics,* 31(5), 463–477.

Clegg, S. R., Cunha, J. V. D., and Cunha, M. P., (2002). Management paradoxes: A relational view. *Human Relations,* 55(5), 483–503.

Clegg, S. R., Kornberger, M., & Pitsis, T., (2005). *Managing & Organizations: An Introduction to Theory and Practice.* London: SAGE.

Coch, L., and French, J., (1948). Overcoming resistance to change. *Human Relations,* 1, 512–532.

Coghlan, D., and Jacobs, C., (2005). Kurt Lewin on reeducation. Foundations for action research. *The Journal of Applied Behavioral Science,* 41(4), 444–457.

Coghlan, D., and Brannick, T., (2005). *Doing Action Research in Your Own Organization* (2nd ed.). London: Sage.

Coghlan, D., and Shani, A. B., (2010). Editors' introduction: Organization development: Toward a mapping of the terrain. *In:* D. Coghlan and, A. B. Shani (eds.), *Fundamentals of Organization Development.* (Vol. 1). London: Sage, pp. xxiii–xxviii.

Coghlan, D., and Coughlan, P., (2010). Notes toward a philosophy of action learning research. *Action Learning: Research and Practice,* 7(2), 195–205.

Coghlan, D., (2011). Organization development and action research. *In:* D. Boje, B. Burnes and J. Hassard (eds.), *The Routledge Companion to Organizational Change.* Abingdon: Routledge, pp. 45–58.

Cohen, L., and Manion, L., (2007). *Research Methods in Education.* Sixth edition. Routledge.

Collier, J., (1945). United States Indian administration as a laboratory of ethnic relations. *Social Research,* 12(3), 275–276.

Collier, D., (2011). Understanding process tracing. *PS: Political Science and Politics,* 44(4), 823–830, University of California, Berkeley. *Available from:* http://polisci.berkeley.edu/sites/default/files/people/u3827/Understandi...

Collins, D., (2000). *Management Fads and Buzzwords: Critical-Practical Perspective.* London: Routledge.

Conner, D. R., (1993). Managing change: A business imperative. *Business Quarterly,* 58(1), 88–92.

Cooke, B., (1999). Writing the left out of management theory: The historiography of the management of change. *Organization,* 6(1), 81–105.

Cooper, R., and Foster, M., (1971). Socio-technical systems. *American Psychologist,* 26(5), 467–474.

Carothers, T., and O'Donohue, A. (Eds.), (2019). *Democracies Divided: The Global Challenge of Political Polarization.* Brookings Institution Press. http://www.jstor.org/stable/10.7864/j.ctvbd8j2p Planned Change

Crosby, G., (2021). *Why Kurt Lewin's Social Science Is Still Best Practice for Business Results, Change Management, and Human Progress.* London: Routledge.

Costa, M., (2020). Putting Black-owned businesses in the spotlight. *Raconteur*, 28th July 2020, p. 5.

Cummings, T. G., (1978). Self-regulating work groups: A socio-technical synthesis. academy of management. *The Academy of Management Review*, 3(3), 625–634.

Cummings, S., Bridgman, T., and Brown, K. G., (2016). Unfreezing change as three steps: Rethinking Kurt Lewin's legacy for change management. *Human Relations*, 69(1), 33–60.

Cummings, T., Ed., (2008). *Handbook of Organization Development*. Los Angeles: Sage.

Cummings, T. G., and Worley, C. G., (2009). *Organisation Development and Change, 9th edn*. Mason, OH: South Western /Cengage Learning.

Cunningham, B. C., (1993). *Organizational Development and Action Research*. New York: Praeger.

Curl, A., (1947). Transitional communities and social re-connection: A follow-up study of the civil resettlement of British prisoners of war Part 1. *Human Relations*, 1, 42–68.

Czander, W. M., (1993). *The Psychodynamics of Work and Organizations*. New York: Guilford Press.

Damasio, A. (2000). *The Feeling of What Happens: Body, Emotion and the Making of Consciousness*. London: Vintage Books.

Damasio, A., (2006). *Descartes Error*. London: Vintage Books.

Da Vinci, L., (1938). *The Notebooks of XIX Philosophical Maxims. Morals. Polemics and Speculations*. Translated by Edward MacCurdy. Republished, Konecky & Konecky, 2002.

Dartington, T., (2018). *Managing Vulnerability the Underlying Dynamics of Systems of Care*. London: Routledge.

Dartington, T., (2020). Greed, hatred and delusion in organisational life. *Organisational and Social Dynamics*, 20(1), 106–117.

Daum, M., (2019). Owning our part: from denial-based business to a regenerative economy. *Organisational and Social Dynamics*, 19(2), 249–263.

Davies, P., ed., (1994). Nicolis, G., Physics of far-from-equilibrium systems and self-organisation. *In: The New Physics*. Cambridge University Press.

Davis, L., (1993). The coming crisis for production management. *In:* E. Trist and H. Murray (eds.), *The Social Engagement of Social Science* (Vol. 2). Philadelphia: University of Pennsylvania Press, pp. 303–312.

Davies, R., (2015). *Industry 4.0 Digitalisation for productivity and growth. Briefing*. European Parliamentary Research Service.

Dawson, P., (1994). *Organizational Change: A Processual Approach*. London: Paul Chapman Publishing.

Dawson, S., (1992). *Analysing Organisations*, 2nd ed. London: Macmillan.

de Guerre, D. W., (2002). Action research as process: The two stage model for active adaptation. *Cell*, 514, 214–1692.

de Guerre, D. W., (2002). Doing action research in one's own organization: An ongoing conversation over time. *Systemic Practice and Action Research*, 15(4), 331–349.

De Sitter, L. U., Hertog, J. F., and Dankbaar, B., (1997). From complex organizations with simple jobs to simple organizations with complex jobs. *Human Relations*, 50(5), 497–536.

Denison, D. R., Hooijberg, R., and Quinn, R. E., (1995).Paradox and performance: Toward a theory of behavioural complexity in managerial leadership. *Organization Science*, 6(5), 524–540.

Deutsch, M., (1968). The effects of cooperation and competition upon group process. *Group Dynamics: Research and Theory*, 3, 461–482.

Diamond, M., (1988). Organizational identity: A psychoanalytic exploration of organizational meaning. *Administration & Society*, 20(2), 166–190.

Diamond, M., (1993). *The Unconscious Life of Organisations: Interpreting Organisational Identity*. New York: Quorum.

Diamond, M., (1998). The symbiotic lure: Organizations as defective containers. *Administrative Theory and Praxis*, 20(3), 315–325.

Dixon, N., (1976). *On the Psychology of Military Incompetence*. London: Futura Publications.

Diytoolkit, (2020). *Theory of Change. Available from:* https://diytoolkit.org/tools/theory-of-change/?cn-reloaded=1

Dhondt, S., Oeij, P., and Pot, F., (2021). Digital transformation of work: Spillover effects of workplace innovation on social innovation. *In:* J. Howaldt, C. Kaletka, and A. Schroder (eds.), *A Research Agenda for Social Innovation*. Cheltenham: Edward Elgar, pp. 99–113.

Doran, G. T., (1981). There's a S.M.A.R.T. way to write management's goals and objectives. *Management Review,* 70(11), 35–36.

Doyle, M., Claydon, T., and Buchanan, D., (2000). Mixed results, lousy process: The management experience of organizational change. *British Journal of Management*, 11(3), 59–87.

Dreyfus, H. L., and Rabinow, P., (1982). *Michel Foucault: Beyond Structure and Hermeneutics*. New York: Harvester.

Drucker, P., (1980). *Managing in Turbulent Times*. New York: Harper & Row.

Drucker, P., (1992). *Managing for the Future*. New York: Harper Collins.

Drucker, P., (1995). *Managing in a Time of Great Change*. New York: Truman Talley Books/Dutton.

Duberley, J., and Johnson, P., (2000). *Understanding Management Research*. London: Sage.

Dulewitz, V., and Herbert, P., (2000). Predicting advancement to senior management from competencies and personality data. A seven-year follow up study, *British Journal of Management*, 10(1), 13–23.

Durkheim, E., (1933 [1893]). *The Division of Labour in Society*. New York: Macmillan.

Durkheim, E., (2020). *Ryan Schram's Anthrocyclopaedia. Available from:* https://anthro.rschram.org/emile_durkheim

Eason, K., (2011). Before the Internet: The relevance of socio-technical systems theory to emerging forms of virtual organisation. *In: Knowledge Development and Social Change Through Technology: Emerging Studies. Information Science Reference,* Hershey: USA: *Available from:* https://www.academia.edu/18003551/New_Sociotechnical_Insights_in_Interaction_Design?email_work_card=view-paper

Daum, M., (2019). Owning our part: from denial-based business to a regenerative economy *Organisational and Social Dynamics,* 19(2), 249–263.

Eijnatten, F. M. van., (1993). *The Paradigm that Changed the Work Place*. Assen: Van Gorcum.

Eijnatten, F. M. van., (1998). Developments in socio-technical systems design (STSD). *In:* P. J. D. Drenth, H. Thierry, and Ch. J. de Wolff (Eds.), *Handbook of Organizational Psychology*, Vol. 4: Organizational psychology. Sussex: Psychology Press/Taylor & Francis Group, pp. 61–88.

Eisenstein, C., (2020). *The Coronation. Available from:* https://charleseisenstein.org/essays/the-coronation/

Elias, N., (1987). *Involvement and Detachment.* London: Basil Blackwell.

Emde, R. N., (1980). Toward a psychoanalytic theory of affect: II. Emerging models of emotional development in infancy. *In:* S. Greenspan and G. Pollock (eds.), *The Course of Life: Psychoanalytic Contributions Toward Understanding Personality Development. Vol. I: Infancy and Early Childhood.* Washington, DC: U.S. Government Printing Office, pp. 85–112.

Emery, F. E., (1959). Characteristics of socio technical systems. *In:* E. Trist (ed.), (1981). *The Evolution of Socio-technical Systems: A Conceptual Framework and an Action Research Program.* Toronto: Ontario Quality of Work Life Centre, p. 11.

Emery, F., (1959). *Characteristics of Socio-Technical Systems.* London: Tavistock Institute Document 527. *Revised in: The Emergence of a New Paradigm of Work. Canberra: Centre for Continuing Education, Australian National University,* 1978. Also in: *Design of Jobs,* edited by L. E. Davis and J. C. Taylor. Harmondsworth: Penguin Books, 1972. Vol. 11, pp. 157–186.

Emery, F., (1969). Introduction. *In:* F. Emery (ed.), *Systems Thinking.* Vol 1. Penguin, Harmondsworth.

Emery, F. E., (1977). *Futures We Are In.* Leiden: Martinus Nijhoff.

Emery, F. E., (1981). Educational paradigms: An epistemological revolution. *Human Futures,* 1(17). *In:* Trist, E., Murray, H., and Emery, F. E. (eds.), (1997). *The Socio-Ecological Perspective.* (Vol. III). Philadelphia: University of Pennsylvania Press.

Emery, F., (1993). The characteristics of socio-technical systems. *In:* E. Trist, and H. Murray (eds.), *The Social Engagement of Social Science Vol 2: The Socio-technical Perspective.* Philadelphia: University of Pennsylvania Press, pp. 157–186.

Emery, F., and Trist, E., (1960). *Report on the Barford Conference for Bristol/ Siddley, Aero-Engine Corporation.* Document no. 598. London: Tavistock.

Emery, F. E., Trist, E. L., Churchman, C. W., and Verhulst, M., (1960). *Socio-technical systems. Management Science Models and Techniques,* vol. 2 Oxford, UK: Pergamon (pg. 83–97).

Emery, F. E., and Thorsrud, E., (1964). *Form and content of Industrial Democracy. Some experiments from Norway and other European countries.* Oslo: Oslo University Press.

Emery, F., and Trist, E., (1965). The causal texture of organisational environments. *Human Relations,* 18(1), 21–32. *Also in:* E. Trist, F. Emery and H. Murray (1997). *The Social Engagement of Social Science,* Vol. 3. Philadelphia: University of Pennsylvania Press, pp. 53–64.

Emery, F. E., and Trist, E. E., (1969). Socio-technical systems. *In:* F. E. Emery (ed.), *Systems Thinking: Selected Readings.* Harmondsworth: Penguin Books, pp. 281–296.

Emery, F. E., and Trist, E., (1973). *Towards a Social Ecology.* New York: Plenum.

Emery, F. E., and Emery, M., (1974). *Responsibility and Social Change.* Canberra: Australia National University, Centre for Continuing Education.

Emery, F. E., and Emery, M., (1997). Toward a logic of hypotheses: Everyone does research. *Concepts and Transformation,* 2(2), 119–144. (also published in London: Tavistock (1969), and in Assen: Van Gorcum (1969).

Emery, M., (1993). *Participative Design for Participative Democracy.* Canberra: Australia National University, Centre for Continuing Education.

Emery, M., and Purser, R., (1996). *The Search Conference. A Powerful Method for Planning Organisational Change and Community Action.* San Francisco: Jossey-Bass Inc.

Emery, M., (1997). *Open Systems Is Alive and Well.* Presented at Academy of Management national meetings, Boston.

Emery, M., (1999). *Searching: The Theory and Practice of Making Cultural Change.* John Benjamins, Amsterdam.

Emery, M., (2000). The current version of Emery's open systems theory. *Systems Practice Action Research,* 13(5), 623–644.

Emery, M., (2022). *The Evolution of Open Systems Theory. Available from:* https://www. socialsciencethatactuallyworks.com/_files/ugd/d59011_3214407c6aad4b628b8b3c90 cfb55f7b.pdf

Eoyang, G., and Holladay, R., (2013). *Adaptive Action: Leveraging Uncertainty in Our Organization.* Stanford, CA: Stanford University Press.

Erikson, E. H., (1950). *Childhood and Society.* New York: Norton.

Erikson, E., (1958). *Young Man Luther: A Study in Psychoanalysis and History.* Austen Riggs Monograph. New York: Norton

Erikson, E., (1993). *Gandhi's Truth: On the Origins of Militant Nonviolence.* New York: W. W. Norton & Company.

Etchegoyen, R. H., (1991). *The Fundamentals of Psychoanalytic Technique* (P. Pitchon, Trans.). London: Karnac.

Feibleman, J., and Friend, W., (1945). The structure and function of organization. *The Philosophical Review,* 54(1), 19–44.

Fenichel, T., (2019). *Schelling, Freud and the Philosophical Foundations of Psychoanalysis: Uncanny belonging.* London: Routledge.

Filfilam, K., (2020). Empathy and compassion crucial in COVID-19 era. *Raconteur, Business Continuity and Growth,* August 2nd, p.1.

Fisher, D., Rooke, D., and Torbert, W. R., (2000). *Personal and Organizational Transformations through Action Inquiry.* Boston: Edge/work Press.

Follett, M., (1998). *The New State: Group Organization: The Solution of Popular Government.* University Park, PA: The Pennsylvania State University Press.

Fosha, D., Siegel, D., and Solomon, M., Eds (2009). *The Healing Power of Emotion. Affective Neuroscience, Development and Clinical Practice.* New York: W.W. Norton and Company

Foster, M., (1972). An introduction to the theory and practice of action research in work organizations. *Human Relations,* 25, 529–556.

Foucault, M., (1970). *The Order of Things: An Archaeology of the Human Sciences.* Vintage Books, New York, NY (original work published 1966).

Foucault, M., (1972). *The Archaeology of Knowledge.* London: Tavistock (original French version 1969).

Fox, W. M., (1995). Socio-technical system principles and guidelines: Past and present. *Journal of Applied Behavioral Science,* 31(1), 95–105.

Fraher, A. L., (2004). Systems Psychodynamics: The Formative Years of an Interdisciplinary Field at the Tavistock Institute *History of Psychology,* 7(1), 65–84.

Friedman, G., (2014). Workers without employers: Shadow corporations and the rise of the gig economy. *Review of Keynesian Economics* 2(2), 171–188.

Freire, P., (1970). *Pedagogy of the Oppressed.* New York: Herder & Herder.

French, R., and Simpson, P., (1999). Our best work happens when we don't know what we're doing it. *Journal of Socio-Analysis,* 1(2), 216–230.

French, R., and Vince, R. (Eds.), (1999). *Group Relations, Management, and Organization.* Oxford: Oxford University Press.

French, W., and Bell, C., (1999). *Organization development*. 6th edn. Upper SADDLE River, NJ: Prentice-Hall.

Freud, S., (1915). *The Unconscious. In: Standard Edition*, 14, 159–204.

Freud, S., (1921). Group psychology and the analysis of the ego. *In: Penguin Freud library*, Vol. 12, Harmondsworth: Penguin Books, 1984.

Freud, S., (1923). The infantile genital organization. *In: Standard Edition*, XIX, pp. 143–144.

Freud, S., (1924). *A General Introduction To Psychoanalysis*. Horace Liveright, Inc. trans. Joan Riviere.

Freud, S., (1963). Analysis terminable and interminable. *In:* P. Rieff (ed.), *Therapy and Technique*, Collier, New York, NY (original work published 1937).

Freud, S., (1985a). *Civilization and its discontents, Civilization, Society and Religion,* Vol. 12. Pelican Freud Library, London, pp. 245–340. A original work published 1930.

Freud, S., (1985b), Group psychology and the analysis of the ego *In: Civilization, Society and Religion*. Vol. 12. Pelican Freud Library, London, pp. 91–178 (original work published 1921).

Freud, S., (1988). *New Introductory Lectures On Psychoanalysis*. Vol. 2. Pelican Freud Library, London A original work published 1933.

Friedman, V. J., (2001). Action Science: Creating communities of inquiry in communities of practice. *In:* P. Reason and H. Bradbury (eds.). *Handbook of Action Research: Participative Inquiry and Practice*. London: Sage Publications, pp. 159–170.

Frohman, M. A., Sashkin, M., and Kavanagh, M. J., (1976). Action-research as applied to organization development. *Organization and Administrative Science*, 7, 129–161.

Frooman, J., (1999). Stakeholder influence strategies. *Academy of Management Review*, 24(2), 191–205.

Gabriel, Y., (1993). Organizational nostalgia: Reflections on the golden age. *In:* S. Fineman, (ed.), *Emotion in Organizations*. London: Sage, pp. 118–141.

Gabriel, Y., (1998). Psychoanalytic contributions to the study of the emotional life of organizations. *Administration & Society*, 30(3), 291–314.

Gabriel, Y., (1999). *Psychoanalytic Research in Organisations. Organisations in Depth*. London: Sage.

Gabriel, Y., (2011). Psychoanalytic approaches to leadership. *In:* A. Bryman, D. Collinson, K. Grint, B. Jackson, and M. Uhl-Bien (eds.), *The SAGE Handbook of Leadership*. London: Sage, pp. 393–405.

Gabriel, Y., (2016). Psychoanalysis and the study of organization. *In:* R. Mir, H. Willmott, and M. Greenwood (eds.), *The Routledge Companion to Philosophy in Organization Studies*. Abingdon, UK: Routledge, pp. 212–224.

Gabriel, Y., and Carr, A., (2002). Organizations, management and psychoanalysis: An overview. *Journal of Managerial Psychology*, 17(5), 348–365.

Gallagher, S., (2021). *Hybrid Working 2.0: Humanising the Office. Available from:* https://www.swinburne.edu.au/downloads/Swinburne_National_Survey_Report_v3.pdf

Gallessich, J., (1982). *The Profession and Practice of Consultation*. San Francisco: Jossey-Bass.

Gandini, A., (2019). Labour process theory and the gig economy. *Human Relations*, 72(6), 1039–1056.

Gazzaley, A., and Rosen, L. D., (2016). *Ancient Brains in a High Tech World*. Cambridge. MA: MIT Press Cambridge.

Gell-Mann, M., (1994). *The Quark and the Jaguar: Adventures in the Simple and the Complex*. New York: WH Freeman.

Gerlach, N., (1996). The business restructuring genre: Some questions for critical organisation analysis. *Organization*, 3, 3425–3453.

Gilley, A., (2005). *The Manager as Change Leader*. Westport, CT: Praeger.

Gilmore, T., and Krantz, J., (1990). The splitting of leadership and management as a social defence. *Human Relations*, 43(2), 183–204.

Gleick, J., (1987). *Chaos: Making a New Science*. New York: Viking Press. .

Gloster, M., (2000). Approaching Action Research from a Socioecological Perspective. *Systemic Practice and Action Research*, 13(5), 665–682.

Gobrin, A., (2021). The future of work: How to prepare for the post-pandemic workplace. Forbes human resources council. *Available from: The Future of Work: How to Prepare for The Post-Pandemic Workplace (forbes.com)*

Gold, M., (1992). Metatheory and field theory in social psychology: Relevance or elegance? *Journal of Social Issues*, 48(2), 67–78.

Goldstein, J., (1999). Emergence as a construct: History and issues. *Emergence*, 1(1), 49–72.

Golembiewski, R. T., and Sun, B. - Chu., (1990). Positive-findings bias in QWL studies: Rigor and outcomes in a large sample. *Journal of Management*, 16(3), 665–674.

Goodwin, B., (1995). *How the Leopard Changed Its Spots*. London: Phoenix.

Goodwin, B., (1997). *Strategy & Complexity Seminar. Available from:* http://www.lse.ac.uk/lse/complex

Goody, J., (1973). Evolution and communication: The domestication of the savage mind. *British Journal of Sociology*, 24(1), 1–12.

Gould, L., Stapley, L., and Stein, M. (Eds.), (2001). *The Systems Psychodynamics of Organisations*. London: Karnac.

Gould, L., (1993). Contemporary perspectives on personal and organizational authority: the self in a system of work relations. *In:* L. Hirschhorn, and C. A. Barnett (eds.), *The Psychodynamics of Organizations*. Philadelphia, PA: Temple University Press, pp. 49–66.

Gould, L., Ebers, R., and Clinchy, R., (1999). The systems psychodynamics of a joint venture: Anxiety, social defences, and the management of mutual dependence. *Human Relations*, 52(6), 697–722.

Graen, G. B., and Scandura, T. A., (1987). Toward a psychology of dyadic organizing. *Research in Organizational Behavior*, 9, 175–208.

Green, Z., and Molenkamp, R., (2005). *The BART System of Group and Organizational Analysis Boundary, Authority, Role and Task. Available from:* https://www.it.uu.se/edu/course/homepage/projektDV/ht09/BART_Green_Molenkamp.pdf

Greenson, R. R., (1967). *The Technique and Practice of Psychoanalysis*. New York: International Universities Press.

Greenwood, D., and Levin, M., (2007). *Introduction to Action Research*. 2nd edn. Thousand Oaks CA: Sage Publications.

Greenwood, D., (2007). Pragmatic action research. *International Journal of Action Research*, 3(1 and 2), 131–148.

Greenwood, D. J., (1991). Collective reflective practice through participatory action research: a case study from the Fagor cooperatives of Mondragón. *In:* D. A. Schön (ed.), *The Reflective Turn: Case Studies in and on Educational Practice*. New York, Teachers College Press, pp. 84–107.

Griffith, T. L., and Dougherty, D. J., (2001). Beyond socio-technical systems: introduction to the special issue. *Journal of Engineering Technology Management*, 18, 2007–2218.

Grint, K., (2020). Leadership, management and command in the time of the coronavirus. *Leadership*, 16(3), 314–319.

Grote, G., and Guest, D., (2017). The case for reinvigorating quality of working life research. *Human Relations*, 70(2), 149–167.

Grotstein, J., (2000). *Who Is the Dreamer Who Dreams the Dream: A Study of Psychic Presences*. London: The Analytic Press.

Gustafson, J. P., and Cooper, L., (1985). Collaboration in small groups. *In:* A. D. Colman and M. H. Geller (eds.), *Group Relations Reader 2*. Washington, DC: A. K. Rice, pp. 139–150.

Guest, D., Knox, A., and Warhurst, C., (2022). Humanizing work in the digital age: Lessons from socio-technical systems and quality of working life initiatives. *Human Relations*, Research Article, *Available from:* https://journals.sagepub.com/doi/full/10.1177/00187267221092674

Gustavsen, B., (1985). *Workplace Reform and Democratic Dialogue: Economic and Industrial Democracy*, Vol. 6. London: Sage.

Gustavsen, B., (2001). Theory and practice: The mediating discourse. *In:* P. Reason and H. Bradbury (eds.), *Handbook of Action Research: Participative Inquiry and Practice*. London: Sage Publications, pp. 17–26.

Gustavsen, B., (2003). New forms of knowledge production and the role of action research. *Action Research*, 1(2), 153–164.

Treasury, H. M., (2020). *Magenta Book: Central Government Guidance on Evaluation. Available from:* https://www.gov.uk/government/ /the-magenta-book.

Habermas, J., (1971). *Knowledge and Human Interests*. Boston, MA: Beacon Press.

Hagel, J., Seely Brown, J., and Davison, L., (2009). The big shift: Measuring the forces of change. *Harvard Business Review*, July-August, 87(7/8), 86–89.

Hall, C. S., and Lindzey, G., (1978). *Theories of Personality*. 3rd ed. New York: John Wiley & Sons.

Halton, W., (1994). Some unconscious aspects of organisational life: Contributions from psychoanalysis. *In:* A. Obholzer, and V. Roberts (eds.), *The Unconscious at Work*. London: Routledge, pp. 11–18.

Hämäläinen, R. P., and Saarinen, E., (2008). Systems intelligence - the way forward? A note on Ackoff's Why few organizations adopt systems thinking. *Systems Research and Behavioral Science*, 25, 821–825.

Harrison, O., (2008). *Open Space Technology: A User's Guide* (Third ed.). Oakland, CA.

Harrison, A., Krantz, J., and Gilmore, T., (2011). *Regeneration in Organisations: Psychoanalytic Perspectives*. Panel Session: How the Meaning of Relatedness is Changing in Contemporary Organisations, ISPSO. Melbourne.

Hawken, P., (1993). *The Ecology of Commerce*. New York: Harper Business.

Heifetz, R., (1994). *Leadership without Easy Answers*. Cambridge, MA: Belknap.

Heifetz, R., and Laurie, D., (1997). The work of leadership. *Harvard Business Review*, January–February, 124–135.

Hsieh, T., (2010). *Delivering Happiness: A Path to Profits, Passion and Purpose*. New York: Grand Central Publishing.

Heller, F., (2004). Action research and research action: A family of methods. *In:* C. Cassell, and G. Symon, (eds.), *Essential Guide to Qualitative Methods in Organisational Research*, London: Sage, pp. 349–360.

Heller, F., Nelson, A., Russell, S., and Sher, M., (2005). *Research-dynamic Consultancy: A Tavistock Approach*. Paper to British Academy of Management, Oxford 13–15 September 2005.

Hendry, C., (1996). Understanding and creating whole organizational change through learning theory. *Human Relations*, 48(5), 621–641.

Herbst, P. G., (1993). Designing with minimal critical specifications. *In:* Trist and H. Murray (eds.), *The social engagement of social science: A Tavistock anthology. Volume II the socio-technical perspective*. Philadelphia, PA: University of Pennsylvania Press, pp. 294–302.

Heron, J., (1996). *Co-operative Inquiry: Research into the Human Condition*. London: Sage Publications.

Heron, J., and Reason, P., (2001). The practice of co-operative inquiry: Research with rather than on people. *In:* P. Reason and H. Bradbury (eds.), *Handbook of Action Research: Participative inquiry and practice*. London: Sage Publications, pp. 179–188.

Heron, J., and Reason, P., (2008). Extending epistemology with a co-operative inquiry. *In:* P. Reason and H. Bradbury, (eds.), *Handbook of Action Research* (2nd edn). London: Sage, pp. 367–380.

Hills, D., (2018). Research into learning at the leicester conference. *Organisational & Social Dynamics*, 18(2), 167–190.

Hinshelwood, R. D., (1989). *A Dictionary of Kleinian Thought*. London: Free Association Books.

Hirschhorn, L., (2021). The death and life of Tony Hsieh: The dynamics of projection. *Available from:* http://learningfromexperiencelarryhirschhorn.blogspot.com/2021/03/the-death-and-life-of-tony-hsieh.html

Hirschhorn, L., (1988). *The Workplace Within*. Cambridge, MA: MIT Press.

Hirschhorn, L., (1990). Leaders and followers in a post-industrial age. *Journal of Applied Behavioral Science*, 26, 529–542.

Hirschhorn, L., (1999). The primary risk. *Human Relations*, 52(1), 5–23.

Hirschhorn, L., (2021). Extending the Tavistock model: Bringing desire, danger, dread, and excitement into a theory of organisational process *Organisational and Social Dynamics*, 21(1), 114–133.

Hirschhorn, L., (2018). Beyond BART (boundaries, authority, role and task): Creative work and the developmental project. *Organisational and Social Dynamics*, 18(1), 41–61.

Hirschhorn, L., and Barnett, C., (1993). *The Psychodynamics of Organizations*. Philadelphia, PA: Temple University Press.

Hirschhorn, L., and Gilmore, T., (1989). The psychodynamics of a cultural change: Learning from a factory. *Human Resource Management*, 28(2), 211–233.

Hirschhorn, L., and Horowitz, S., (2014). Extreme work environments: Beyond anxiety and social defense. *In:* D. Armstrong and M. Rustin (eds.), *Social Defenses Against Anxiety: Explorations in a Paradigm*. London: Karnac, pp. 189–212.

Hodges, J., (2017). *Consultancy, Organizational Development and Change*. London: Kogan Page.

Hoggett, P., (1996). *Review of the: The Unconscious at Work: Individual and Organisational Stress in the Human Services*, London: Routledge, 1994. http://human-nature.com/free-associations/hogg.html

Hoggett, P., (2010). Engaging with Climate Change Conference. *Available from:* https://www.youtube.com/watch?v=wsfwHvBJfwI

Hoggett, P. (Ed.), (2019). *Climate Psychology: On Indifference to Disaster (Studies in the Psychosocial)*. London: Palgrave Macmillan.

Hoggett, P., and Nestor, R., (2021). First genocide, now ecocide: An anti-life force in organisations? *Organisational & Social Dynamics*, 21(1), 97–113.

Hoggett, P., (2022). *Talk at the conference: '6 Months on from COP26 Psycho-Social Reflections: What have we learnt?'* See: https://www.bpc.org.uk/event/six-months-on-from-cop26-psychosocial-reflections-what-have-we-learnt/ Also see: https://www.climatepsychologyalliance.org/

Holland, J. H., and Miller, J., (1991). Artificial adaptive agents in economic theory. *In: American Economic Review, Papers and Proceedings*, 81, 365–370.

Holland, J. H., (1995). *Hidden Order: How Adaptation Builds Complexity*. Redwood City, CA: Addision Wesley.

Holland, J. H., (1998). *Emergence: From Chaos to Order*. Redwood City, CA: Addison Wesley.

Holland, J. H., (2006). Studying complex adaptive systems. *Journal of Systems Science and Complexity*, 19(1), 1–8.

Hollis, J., (2021). *The Interpretation of Dreams, Dreams as a Path to Personal Authority*. *Available from*: https://www.jungmasterclass.com/p/the-interpretation-of-dreams

Hollway, W., (2022). Towards an eco-psych-social analysis of climate change. *In: Palgrave Handbook of Psycho-Social Studies*. Cambridge: Palgrave Macmillan.

Hollway, W., Hoggett, P. Robertson, C., and Weintrobe, S., (2022). *Climate Psychology: A Matter of Life and Death*. Oxfordshire: Phoenix Publishing.

Holman, P., Devane, T., and Cady, S., (2007). *The Change Handbook*. 2nd edn. San Francisco: Berrett-Koehler.

Holman, P., (2011). *Engaging Emergence: Turning Upheaval into Opportunity*. *Available from*: http://peggyholman.com/wp-content/uploads/2010/06/211001pkSystems-Thinkerarticle.pdf

Hooper, R. A., and Potter, J. R., (2000). *Intelligent Leadership, Creating a Passion for Change*. London: Random House. http://www.tavinstitute.org/lectures_and_presentations/pdf/kurt-lewin-dynamic-approach-rule-2/https://www.bl.uk/business-and-management/editorials/kurt-lewins-field-theory

Huffington, C., Brunning, H., and Cole, C., (1996). *The Change Manual – Key Issues in Organisational Development and the Management of Change*. London: Karnac Books.

Huffington, C., Armstrong, A., Halton, W., Hoyle, L., and Pooley, J., (2004). *Working below the Surface. The Emotional Life of Contemporary Organisations*. London: Karnac.

Hutchins, E., (1991). The social organization of distributed cognition. *In:* L. B. Resnick, J. M. Levine, and S. D. Teasley (eds.), *Perspectives on Socially Shared Cognition*. Washington, DC: American Psychological Association, pp. 283–307.

Hutchinson, K., (2018). *Evaluation Failures: 22 Tales of Mistakes Made and Lessons Learned*. London: Sage.

Industry 4.0, 5 (2021). *Life–changing Ways Industry 4.0 will Change Society*. *Available from*: https://it-voices.com/en/articles-en/5-life-changing-ways-industry-4-0-will-change-society/

Ison, R., (2017). *Systems Practice: How to Act: In Situations of Uncertainty and Complexity in a Climate-Change World*. Open University, Milton Keynes.

Izod, K., and Whittle, S. R., eds., (2009). *Mind-ful Consulting*. London: Karnac.

Izod, K., and Whittle, S. R., eds., (2014). *Resource-ful Consulting: Working with your Presence and Identity in Consulting to Change*. London: Karnac.

Jackson, M. C., (1992). *Systems Methodology for the Management Sciences*. New York: Plenum Press,

Jackson, M. C., (2006). Creative holism: A critical systems approach to complex problem situations. *Systems Research and Behavioral Science System Residence*, 23, 647–657.

Jackson, M. C., (2019). *Critical Systems Thinking and the Management of Complexity.* Oxford: Wiley.

Jackson, M. C., (2020). How we understand "complexity" makes a difference: Lessons from critical systems thinking and the covid-19 pandemic in the UK. *Systems,* 8(4), 52. *Available from:* https://doi.org/10.3390/systems8040052

Janoff, S., and Weisbord, M., (1995). *Future Search: An Action Guide to Finding Common Ground in Organizations and Community.* San Francisco: Berrett-Koehler.

Jaques, E., (1948). Interpretive group discussion as a method of facilitating social change: A progress report on the use of group methods in the investigation and resolution of social problems. *Human Relations,* 1(4), 533–549.

Jaques, E., (1951). *The Changing Culture of a Factory.* London: Tavistock Publications. Reissued New York: Garland, 1987. (See: Working Through Industrial Conflict: the service department at the Glacier Metal Company, *In:* E. Trist and H. Murray (eds.), (1990), *The Social Engagement of Social Science, Vol. 1: The Socio-Psychological Perspective.* London: Free Association Books.

Jaques, E., (1953). On the Dynamics of Social Structure: A contribution to the psycho-analytical study of social phenomena deriving from the views of Melanie Klein. *In:* E. Trist, and H. Murry (eds.). (1990). *The Social Engagement of Social Science, Vol. 1: The Socio-Psychological Perspective.* London: Free Association Books.

Jaques, E., (1955). Social systems as a defence against persecutory and depressive anxiety. *In:* M. Klein, P. Heimann, and R. E. Money-Kyrle (eds.), *New Directions in Psychoanalysis.* London: Tavistock Publications, pp. 478–498.

Jaques, E., (1965). Death and the mid-life crisis, *In:* E. B. Spillius, (ed.). (1990). *Melanie Klein Today, Vol. 2: Mainly Practice.* London: Routledge.

Jaques, E., (1995a). Why the psychoanalytical approach to understanding organizations is dysfunctional. *Human Relations,* 48(4), 343–349.

Jaques, E., (1995b). Why the psychoanalytical approach to understanding organizations is dysfunctional. *Human Relations,* 48(4), 343–349.

Jesuthasan, R., and Boudreau, J., (2018). Reinventing jobs: A 4-step approach for applying automation to work. *Harvard Business Review Press.* Available from: https://hbsp.harvard.edu/product/10174-PDF-ENG

Johnson, G., (1987). *Strategic Change and the Management Process.* Oxford: Blackwell.

Johnson, H. H., and Fredian, A. J., (1986). Simple rules for complex change. *Training and Development Journal,* 40(8), 47–50.

Johnson, R. A., (1976). *Management, Systems, and Society: An Introduction.* Pacific Palisades: Goodyear Pub. Co., pp. 222–224.

Jones, B., and Brazzel, M., Eds., (2014). *NTL Handbook of Organizational Development and Change* (2nd ed). San Francisco: Wiley.

Jones, R., (2020). Homebuyers "plotting move to country" amid increased home working. The Guardian. *Available from:* www.theguardian.com/money/2020/may/08/homebuyers-plotting-move-to-country-amid-increased-home-working

Joseph, B., (1993). *Envy, public lecture.* In: Tavistock Series.

Kagan, J., (1994). *Nature of the child.* New York: Basic Books.

Kahn, W. A., (2001). Holding environments at work. *The Journal of Applied Behavioral Science,* 37(3), 260–279.

Kahn, W. A., (1995). Organizational change and the provision of a secure base: Lessons from the field. *Human Relations,* 48(5), 489–514.

Kanter, R., Moss., (1983). *The Change Masters.* New York: Simon & Schuster.

Kanter, R., Moss., Stein, B., and Jick, T., (1992). *The Challenge of Organizational Change.* New York: The Free Press.

Kauffman, S., and Macready, W., (1995). Technological evolution and adaptive organizations. *Complexity Journal*, 1(2), 26–43.

Kauffman, S., (1993). *The Origins of Order: Self-Organisation and Selection in Evolution.* New York: Oxford University Press.

Kauffman, S., (1995). *At Home in the Universe.* Oxford: Oxford University Press.

Kauffman, S., (2000). *Investigations.* Oxford University Press.

Keesing, R. M., (1972). Paradigms lost: The new ethnography and the new linguistics. *Southwestern Journal of Anthropology*, 28(4), 299–332.

Kelly, J. (2011). *New Yorkers are leaving the city in droves: Here's why they're moving and where they're going.* Forbes. *Available from:* www.forbes.com/sites/jackkelly/2019/09/05/new-yorkers-are-leaving-the-city-in-droves-heres-why-theyre-moving-and-where-theyre-going/#252d72af41ac

Kemmis, S., and McTaggart, R., (1992). *The Action Research Planner* (third edition). Geelong, Vic.: Deakin University Press.

Kernberg, O., (1998). *Ideology, Conflict, and Leadership in Groups and Organisations.* New Haven, CT: Yale University.

Kernberg, O. F., (1979). Regression in organizational leadership. *Psychiatry*, 42(1), 24–39.

Kets de Vries, M. F. R., (1980). *Organizational Paradoxes: Clinical Approaches to Management.* London: Tavistock Publications.

Kets de Vries, M. F. R., (1989). Leaders who self-destruct: The causes and cures. *Organizational Dynamics*, 17(4), 4–17.

Kets de Vries, M. A. (Ed.), (1991). *Organizations on the Couch.* San Francisco: Jossey-Bass.

Kets de Vries, M. F. R., (2000). The clinical paradigm: Manfred Kets de Vries' reflections on organisational theory – Interview by Erik van Loo. *Academy of Management Executive and European Management Journal*, 18(1), 2–21.

Kets de Vries, M. F. R., (2004). *Lessons on Leadership by Terror: Finding Shaka Zulu in the Attic.* Cheltenham, UK: Edward Elgar.

Kets de Vries, M. F. R., (2006). *The Leader on the Couch.* Chichester, UK: John Wiley & Sons.

Kets de Vries, M., and Miller, D., (1984). *The Neurotic Organization.* San Francisco: Jossey-Bass.

Kets de Vries, M. F. R. (Ed.), (1984). *The Irrational Executive: Psychoanalytic Explorations in Management.* New York: International Universities Press.

Kets de Vries, M. F. R., (2016). The psychodynamic approach. *In:* P. G. Northouse (ed.), *Leadership: Theory and Practice.* Western Michigan University, Seventh Edition, pp. 295–326. *Available from:* https://www.academia.edu/37183578/Business_Leadership?auto=download&email_work_card=download-paper

Kets de Vries, M. F. R., and Miller, D., (1985). Narcissism and leadership: An object relations perspective. *Human Relations*, 36(6), 583–601.

Kets de Vries, M. F. R., and Cheak, A., (2014). *Psychodynamic Approach* INSEAD Working Paper No. 2014/45/EFE, *Available from:* SSRN: https://ssrn.com/abstract=2456594 or http://dx.doi.org/10.2139/ssrn.2456594

Kets de Vries, M. F. R., and Schein, E., (2000). Crosstalk: Transatlantic exchanges. *The Academy of Management Executive*, 14(1), 30–51.

Khalsa, G., and Passmore, W., (1993). The contributions of Eric Trist to the social engagement of social science. *Academy of Management Review*, 18, 3, 546–569.

Kidder, T., (1981). *The Soul of a New Machine*. Boston: Little Brown, pp. 117, 151.

Kieser, A., (2002). On communication barriers between management science consultancies and business organizations. *In:* T. Clark and K. Robin Legge (eds.), *On Knowledge, Business Consultants and the Selling of Total Quality Management. Critical Consulting.* Oxford: Blackwell, pp. 206–227.

Kippenberger, T., (1998a). Planned change: Kurt Lewin's legacy. *The Antidote*, 14, 10–12.

Kippenberger, T., (1998b). Managed learning: Elaborating on Lewin's model. *The Antidote*, 14, 13.

Kirkpatrick, D., (1994). *Evaluating training programs: The four levels.* San Francisco: Berrett-Koehler.

Kirkpatrick, D., (1996). Revisiting Kirkpatrick's four-level-model. *Training & Development*, 1, 54–57.

Kirkpatrick, S. A., and Locke, E. A., (1991). Leadership, do traits matter? *Academy of Management Executive*, 5(2), 48–60.

Klein, E. B., Gablenick, F., and Herr, P. (Eds.), (1998). *The Psychodynamics of Leadership.* Madison, CT: Psychosocial Press.

Klein, L., and Eason, D., (1991). *Putting Social Science to Work.* New York: Cambridge University Press.

Klein, L., (2005). *Working Across the Gap.* London: Routledge.

Klein, L., (2008). *The Meaning of Work.* London: Routledge.

Klein, L., (2012). *Nobody Said It Would be Easy.* Book Guild Publishing.

Klein, M., (1948). *Contributions to Psychoanalysis*, 1921–1945. London: Hogarth Press.

Klein, M., (1957). *Envy and Gratitude.* New York: Basic Books.

Klein, M., (1959a). Our adult world and its roots in infancy. *Human Relations*, 12(4), 291–303.

Klein, M., (1959b). Our adult world and its roots in infancy. Republished (1963). *In: Our Adult World and Other Essays.* London: Heinemann; *also in:* Colman, A. D., and Geller, M. H., (1985). *Group Relations Reader 2*, A.K. Rice Institute, Jupiter, 5–19.

Kling, R., and Gerson, E., (1978). Patterns of segmentation and intersection in the computing world. *Symbolic Interaction*, 1(2) (Spring).

Kling, R., (1977). The organizational context of user-centered software design. *MIS Quarterly*, 1 (Winter), 41–52.

Kling, R., (2000). Learning about information technologies and social change: The contribution of social informatics. *The Information Society*, 16(3), 217–232.

Kochan, T. A., Lansbury, R. D. & MacDuffie, J. P. (2018). *After lean production: Evolving employment practices in the world auto industry.* Cornell U. Press.

Koehler, K. G., (1987). The key to successful project management. *CMA Communication*, 61(2), 13–14.

Kohlberg, L., (1981). *The Philosophy of Moral Development.* New York: Harper & Row.

Kotter, J. P., (1996). *Leading Change.* Boston: Harvard Business School Press.

Kotter, J. P., and Schlesinger, L. A., (1979). Choosing strategies for change. *Harvard Business Review*, (March/April), 106–114.

Kram, K. E., (1983). Phases of the mentor relationship. *Academy of Management Journal*, 26(4), 608–625.

Kram, K. E., (1996). A relational approach to career development. *In:* D. T. Hall & Associates, *The Career Is Dead: Long Live the Career.* San Francisco: Jossey-Bass, pp. 132–157.

Kramer, E. H., (2019). *The Impact of Digital Transformation on Sociotechnical Thinking*, Paper presented to 2019 Meeting of Global Network for SmarT Organization Design, Los Angeles, CA.

Krantz, J., and Gilmore, T. N., (1990). The splitting of leadership and management as a social defense. *Human Relations*, 43(2), 183–204.

Krantz, J., (1989). The managerial couple: Superior-subordinate relationships as a unit of analysis.' *Human Resource Management*, 28(2), 161–176.

Krantz, J., (1990). Lessons from the field: An essay on the crisis of leadership in contemporary organizations. *Journal of Applied Behavioural Science*, 26(1), 49–64.

Krantz, J., (2001). Dilemmas of organisational change: A systems psychodynamic perspective.

Krantz, J., (2006). Leadership, betrayal and adaptation. *Human Relations*, 59(2), 221–240.

Krantz, J., (2008). Sources of hope in contemporary organizations. *In:* A. Ahlers-Niemann, B. Sievers, R. Redding Mersky and U. Bremer (eds.), *The Normal Madness in Organizations: Socio-analytic Thoughts and Interventions.* Dusseldorf: EHP Verlag Andreas Kohlhage.

Krantz, J., (2010). Social Defences and twenty-first century organizations. *British Journal of Psychotherapy*, 26(2), 192–201.

Krantz, J., (2013). *Organisations: A Psychodynamic Contribution.* L. *Vansina* (ed.) London: Karnac, pp. 51–70.

Krantz, J., (2014). Social defences in the information age. *In:* M. Rustin and D. Armstrong (eds.), *Social Defences against Anxiety: Explorations in the Paradigm.* London: Karnac, pp. 192–200.

Kübler-Ross, E. (Ed.), (1969). "Approaching twenty-first century, information-based Organisations." *In: Humanness on Death and Dying.* New York: Macmillan.

Kuhn, T. S., (1970). *The Structure of Scientific Revolutions. Enlarged (2nd ed.).* Chicago, IL: University of Chicago Press.

Kurt, S., (2016). Kirkpatrick model: Four levels of learning evaluation. *In: Educational Technology,* October 24. *Available from:* https://educationaltechnology.net/kirkpatrick-model-four-levels-learning-evaluation/

Kyle, N., (1993). Staying with the flow of change. *Journal for Quality and Participation*, 16(4): 34–42.

Laasch, O., Moosmayer, D., Antonacopoulou, E., et al., (2020). Constellations of transdisciplinary practices: A map and research agenda for the responsible management learning field. *Journal Business Ethics*, 162, 735–757.

Lacan, J., (1966). Écrits: *English translation 1977*, London: Routledge.

Lacan, J., (1973). *The Four Fundamental Concepts of Psycho-Analysis.* English Translation 1979, Harmondsworth: Penguin.

Lad, L., (1985). *Policy-Making Between Business and Government: A Conceptual Synthesis of Industry Self-Regulation and Case Study Analysis of the Direct Selling Association Code of Conduct.* Unpublished doctoral dissertation, Boston University.

Lapierre, L., (1991). Exploring the dynamics of leadership. *In:* M. F. R. Kets de Vries, The Jossey-Bass management series. *Organizations on the Couch: Clinical Perspectives on Organizational Behavior and Change.* San Francisco: Jossey-Bass, pp. 69–93.

Lasch, C., (1980). *The Culture of Narcissism.* Abacus, London.

Latour, B., (1990). Technology is society made durable. *The Sociological Review*, 38(S1), 103–131.

Lawlor, D., and Sher, M., (2021). *An Introduction to Systems Psychodynamics Consultancy Research & Training Volume 1 "dawn"*. London: Routledge.

Lawrence, W. G., (1977). Management development ... some ideals images and realities. *In:* A. Coleman and M. Geller (eds.), (1985). *Group Relations Reader 2.* Washington, DC: A.K. Rice Institute Series.

Lawrence, W. G., (1986). Understanding organizational life. *In:* G. P. Chattopadhyay, Z. H. Gangjee, M. L. Hunt, and W. G. Lawrence (eds.), *When the twain meet.* Allahabad: A. H. Wheeler & Co., Private Limited, p. 59.

Lawrence, W. G., (1991). Won from the void and formless infinite: Experiences of social dreaming. *Free Associations*, 2(2), 259–294.

Lawrence, W. G. (Ed.), (1998). *Social Dreaming @ Work.* London: Karnac.

Lawrence, W. G., (1999). A mind for business. *In:* French, R., and Vince, R. (eds.), *Group Relations, Management, and Organization.* Oxford University Press, Oxford, pp. 40–53.

Lawrence, W. G., (2000). *Tongued with Fire: Groups in Experience.* London: Karnac.

Lawrence, W. G., (2003). Social dreaming as sustained thinking. *Human Relations*, 56(5), 609–623.

Lawrence, W. G. (Ed.), (2003). *Experiences in Social Dreaming.* London: Karnac.

Lawrence, W. G., (2004). *Introduction to Social Dreaming: Transforming Thinking.* London: Karnac Books.

Lawrence, W. G. (Ed.), (2007). *Infinite Possibilities of Social Dreaming.* London: Karnac.

Lawrence, W. G. (Ed.), (2010). *The Creativity of Social Dreaming.* London: Karnac.

Lawrence, W. G., (2012). *Social Dreaming: Making the Unconscious Available in Systems,* Presentation written for a Policy Seminar at the Tavistock Clinic, unpublished.

Lawrence, W. G., Bain, A., and Gould, L., (1996). The fifth basic assumption. *Free Associations*, 6(1), 28–55.

Lawson, C., (2010). Technology and the extension of human capabilities. *Journal for the Theory of Social Behaviour*, 40(2), 207–223.

Le Feuvre, C., (2012). The psychodynamics of climate change denial: The need for an ecopsychoanalysis. *Socioanalysis*, 14, 13–23.

Lear, J., (2006). *Radical Hope: Ethics in the Face of Cultural Devastation.* Harvard: Harvard University Press.

Leventhal, D., (1997). Adaptation on rugged landscapes. *Management Science*, 43, 934–950.

Levinson, H., (1972). *Organisational Diagnosis.* Cambridge, MA: Harvard University Press. Levinson, J., (1976). *Psychological Man.* Cambridge, MA: Levinson Institute.

Levinson, H., (1981). *Executive.* Harvard University Press, Cambridge, MA (original work published 1968).

Levinson, H., (1994). The practitioner as diagnostic instrument. *In:* A. Howard (Ed.), *Diagnosis for Organizational Change. Methods and Models.* New York: Guilford, pp. 27–52.

Levinson, H., (2002). Psychological consultation to organizations: Linking assessment and intervention. *In:* R. L. Lowman (ed.), *Handbook of Organizational Consulting Psychology.* San Francisco: Jossey-Bass, pp. 415–449.

Lewin, K., (1920). Die Sozialisierung des Taylorsystems: Eine Grundsätzliche Untersuchung zur Arbeits-und Betriebspsychologie [The socialization of the Taylor system: Systems and theory in psychology]. *Gestalt Theory*, 3, 129–151.

Lewin, K., (1939). When facing danger. *In:* G. W. Lewin (ed.), *Resolving Social Conflict.* New York: Harper & Row.

Lewin, K., (1943–1944). Problems of research in social psychology. *In:* D. Cartwright (ed.), *Field Theory in Social Science*. New York: Harper & Row.

Lewin, K., (1943a). Psychological ecology. *In:* D. Cartwright (ed.), *Field Theory in Social Science*. New York: Harper Row

Lewin, K., (1943b). The special case of Germany. *In:* G. W. Lewin (ed.), *Resolving Social Conflict*. London: Harper & Row.

Lewin, K., (1946a). Action research and minority problems. *Journal of Social Issues*, 1946, 2, 34–46.

Lewin, K., (1946b). Behavior and development as a function of the total situation. *In:* L. Carmichael (ed.), *Manual of Child Psychology*. New York: John Wiley and Sons, pp. 791–844.

Lewin, K., (1946c). Research on minority problems. *The Technology Review*, 48(3), 43–46.

Lewin, K., (1946). Action research and minority problems. *In:* G. W. Lewin (ed.), *Resolving Social Conflict*. London: Harper & Row.

Lewin, K., (1947a). Frontiers in group dynamics: Concept, method and reality in social science; social equilibria and social change. *Human Relations,* 1(1), 5–41.

Lewin, K., (1947b). Frontiers in group dynamics: II. Channels of group life; social planning and action research. *Human Relations*, 1(2), 143–153.

Lewin, K., (1947c). Group Decision and Social Change. *In:* T. H. Newcomb and E. L., Hartley (eds.), *Readings in Social Psychology*. New York: Henry Holt, pp. 197–211.

Lewin, K., (1947d). Studies towards the integration of the social sciences. *Human Relations*, I, 1–140.

Lewin, K., (1948). *Resolving Social Conflicts*. Washington, DC: American Psychological Association, 1948 (reprinted 2008).

Lewin, K., (1951). *Field Theory in Social Science: Selected Theoretical Papers* (ed. Cartwright, D). New York: Harper & Row.

Lewin, K., (1952). *Field Theory in Social Science: Selected Theoretical Papers*. London: Tavistock.

Lewis, M. W., (2000). Exploring paradox: Toward a more comprehensive guide. *Academy of Management Review*, 25(4), 760–776.

Lewin, K., Lippitt, R., & White, R. Patterns of aggressive behavior in experimentally created "social climates". *Journal of Social Psychology*, 1939, 10, 271–299.

Lippitt, R., (1959). Dimensions of the consultant's job. *Journal of Social Issues*, 15(2), 5–12.

Lippitt, R., Watson, J., and Westley, B., (1958). *The Dynamics of Planned Change*. New York: Harcourt, Brace and World.

Long, S., (1999). The tyranny of the customer and the cost of consumerism: An analysis using systems and psychoanalytic approaches to groups and society. *Human Relations*, 52(6), 723–743.

Long, S., (1999). Action research, participative action research and action learning in organizations. *In:* Y. Gabriel (ed.), *Organizations in Depth*. London: Sage Publications, pp. 262–266.

Long, S., Newton, J., and Sievers, B. (Eds.), (2006). *Coaching in Depth: The Organisational Role Analysis Approach*. London: Karnac.

Long, S., (2008). *The Perverse Organisation and Its Deadly Sins*. London: Karnac.

Long, S., (2019). Dreaming a culture. *Socio-Analysis*, 21, 59–70.

Long, S., et al., (1997). *Collaborative Action Research in an Organisation: Can Psychoanalytically Informed Thinking Deepen the Collaboration?* Paper presented at the ISPSO Symposium.

Long, S., (2001). Working with organizations: The contribution of the psychoanalytic discourse. *Organisational & Social Dynamics*, 2, 1–25. *Available from:* https://www.academia.edu/29165687/Working_with_Organizations_The_Contribution_of_the_Psychoanalytic_Discourse?email_work_card=title

Long, S. D., (2013). *Socioanalytic Methods Discovering the Hidden in Organisations and Social Systems*. London: Routledge.

Long, S. D., and Harney, M., (2013). The associative unconscious. *In:* S. Long (ed.), *Socioanalytic Methods*. London: Karnac, pp. 25–43.

Long, S. D., (2015). Turning a blind eye to climate change. *Organisational and Social Dynamics*, 15(2), 248–262.

Long, S., Ed., (2016). *Transforming Experience in Organisations*. London: Karnac.

Long, S. D., and Lockhart, M., (2022). Talk given at the 2022 OPUS Conference online. See: https://www.opus.org.uk/international-conference/

Lovelock, J., (2000). *Gaia: A New Look at Life on Earth*. New York: Oxford University Press.

Ludema, J., and Fry, R., (2008). The practice of appreciative inquiry. *In:* P. Reason and H. Bradbury, (eds.), *Handbook of Action Research*. 2nd edn. London: Sage, pp. 280–296.

Ludema, J. D., Cooperrider, D. L., and Barrett, F. J., (2001). Appreciative inquiry: The power of the unconditional positive question. *In:* P. Reason and H. Bradbury (eds.), *Handbook of Action Research: Participative inquiry and practice*. London: Sage Publications, pp. 189–199.

Luhmann, N., (1984). The self-description of society: Crisis fashion and sociological theory. *International Journal of Comparative Sociology, Leiden*, 25, 59.

Luhmann, N., (1990). *Essays on Self Reference*. New York: Columbia.

Luhmann, N., (2000). *Organisation und Entscheidung*. Opladen/Wiesbaden, Westdeutscher Verlag.

Luoma, J., (2007). Systems thinking in complex responsive processes and systems intelligence. *In:* R. P. Hämäläinen and E. Saarinen (eds.), *Systems Intelligence in Leadership and Everyday Life*. Systems Analysis Laboratory, Helsinki University of Technology, Espoo, pp. 281–294.

Luoma, J., Hämäläinen, R., and Saarinen, E., (2011). Acting with systems intelligence: integrating complex responsive processes with the systems perspective. *Journal of Operational Research Society*, 62, 3–11.

Lüscher, L. S., and Lewis, M. W., (2008). Organizational change and managerial sensemaking: working through paradox. *Academy of Management Journal*, 51(2), 221–240.

Maccoby, M., (1976). *The Gamesman: New Corporate Leaders*. New York, NY: Simon and Shuster.

MacIntyre, A., (1985). *After Virtue*. London: Duckworth.

MacLennan, B., (2012). *Evolutionary Psychology, Complex Systems, and Social Theory*. Knoxville: University of Tennessee Press.

Macy, J., (1995). Working through environmental despair. *In:* T. Roszak, M. Gomes and A. Kanner (eds.), *Ecopsychology: Restoring the Earth, Healing the Mind*. San Francisco: Sierra Club Books, pp. 240–259.

Maier, M., and Rechtin, E., (2000). *The Art of Systems Architecting*, 2nd Edition. Los Angeles, CA: University of Southern California.

Maitland, l., and Park, D., (1985). A model of corporate PAC strategy. *Academy of Management Proceedings.*

Majchrzak, A., Griffith, T., Reetz, D., and Alexy, O., (2018). Catalyst organizations as a new organization design for innovation: The case of hyperloop transportation technologies. *Academy of Management Discoveries,* 4(4), 472–496.

Malan, D. H., (1979). *Individual Psychotherapy and the Science of Psychodynamics.* London: Butterworth- Heinemann.

Malan, D. H., and Osimo, F., (1992). *Psychodynamics, Training and Outcome in Brief Psychotherapy.* London: Butterworth- Heinemann.

Mangham, I., (1988). Managing the executive process. *In:* A. A. Pettigrew (ed.), *Competitiveness and the Management Process.* Oxford: Blackwell.

Marcuse, H., (1955). *Eros and Civilization: A Philosophical Inquiry into Freud.* Boston, MA: Beacon.

Marmot, M., Allen, J., Boyce, T. Goldblatt, E., Morrison, J. (2020). *Health Equity in England: the Marmot Review 10 years on.* Published by The Institute of Health Equity.

Marrow, A. J., (1969). *The Practical Theorist: The Life and Work of Kurt Lewin.* New York: Teachers College Press.

Marshall, G., (1998). Qualitative comparative analysis. *In: A Dictionary of Sociology. Available from:* http://www.encyclopedia.com/doc/1O88-qualitativecomparatvnlyss.html

Martin, A. W., (2001). Large group processes as action research. *In:* P. Reason and H. Bradbury (eds.), *Handbook of Action Research.* London: Sage, pp. 200–208.

Marx, K., and Engels, F., (1844). *The Communist Manifesto.*

Matejka, K., and Ramona, J., (1993). Resistance to change is natural. *Supervisory Management,* 38(10), 10–11.

Mayne, J., (2008). *Contribution Analysis: An approach to exploring cause and effect,* ILAC methodological brief, *Available from:* http://www.cgiarilac.org/files/ILAC_Brief16_Contribution_Analysis_0.pdf

Mayo, E., (1933). *The Human Problems of an Industrial Civilization.* New York: The Macmillan Company.

McArdle, K., and Reason, P., (2008). Action research and organization development. *In:* T. Cummings (ed.), *Handbook of Organization Development.* Thousand Oaks, CA: Sage, pp. 123–136.

McCann, J. E., (1983). Design guidelines for social problem-solving interventions. *The Journal of Applied Behavioral Science,* 19(2), 177–189.

McCann, J., and Selsky, J., (1984). Hyperturbulence and the emergence of Type 5 environments. *Academy of Management Review,* 9(3), 460–470.

McLeod, S. A., (2015). *Unconscious mind.* Simply Psychology. www.simplypsychology.org/unconscious-mind.html

McConnell, J. W. Family Foundation (2010): *A Practitioner's Guide to Developmental Evaluation. Available from:* http://www.dmeforpeace.org/sites/default/files/Dozios%20et%20al_Practitioners%20Guide%20to%20Developmental%20Evaluation.pdf

McDermott, R., (1999). Why information technology inspired but cannot deliver knowledge management. *California Management Review,* 41(4), 103–117.

McDermott, R., Snyder, W. M., and Wenger, E., (2002). *Cultivating Communities of Practice: A Guide to Managing Knowledge.* Boston, MA: Harvard Business School Press.

McGrath, S. J., (2012). *The Dark Ground of Spirit: Schelling and the Unconscious.* London: Routledge. Roszak, T. *Available from:* Roszak https://www.context.org/iclib/ic34/roszak/)who

McKay, J., and Marshall, P., (2001). The dual imperatives of action research. *Information Technology and People,* 14(1), 46–59.

McKernan, J., (1991). *Curriculum Action Research. A Handbook of Methods and Resources for the Reflective Practitioner.* London: Kogan Page.

McNeil-Willson, R., (2020). *What Will 2020 Bring? Finding Our Way in a More Polarised World. Available from:* https://www.opendemocracy.net/en/global-extremes/what-will-2020-bring-finding-our-way-more-polarised-world/

McNiff, J., and Whitehead, J., (2005). *All You Need to Know About Action Research.* London, UK: London, UK: Sage, pp. 3–5.

McTaggart, R., (1996). Issues for participatory action researchers. *In:* O. Zuber-Skerritt (ed.), *New Directions in Action Research.* London: Falmer, 243–255.

Mead, G. H., (1934). *Mind, Self, and Society: From the Standpoint of a Social Behaviourist.* C. W. Morris, ed. Chicago: University of Chicago Press.

Medeiros-Ward, N., Watson, J. M., and Strayer, D. L., (2015). On supertaskers and the neural basis of efficient multitasking. *Psychonomic Bulletin & Review,* 22, 876–883.

Meltzer, D., (1984). *Dream Life: A Re-examination of the Psycho-Analytical Theory and Technique.* London: Clunie Press.

Menzies, I., (1960). A case study in functioning of social systems as a defence against anxiety. *Human Relations,* 13, 95–121. *Also in:* I. Menzies-Lyth (1988). *Containing Anxiety in Institutions: Free Association Books,* pp. 43–85.

Menzies Lyth, I. E. P., (1979). Staff support systems: Task and anti-task in adolescent institutions. *In: Containing Anxiety in Institutions: Selected Essays,* London: Free Association Books, 1988.

Menzies Lyth, I. E. P., (1983). Bion's contribution to thinking about groups. *In:* J. S. Grotstein (ed.), *Do I Dare Disturb the Universe?* London: Mansfield Library, pp. 661–666.

Menzies-Lyth, I., (1988). *Containing Anxiety in Institutions: Selected Essays.* London: Free Association.

Menzies Lyth, I., (1990). A psychoanalytic perspective on social institutions. *In:* E. Trist and H. Murray (eds.), *The Social Engagement of Social Science: A Tavistock Anthology. Vol. 1, The Socio-Psychological Perspective.* London: Free Association Books, pp. 463–475.

Menzies Lyth, I. E. P., (1991). Changing organisations and individuals: Psychoanalytic insights for improving organisational health. *In:* Kets de Vries (ed.), *Organisations on the Couch: Clinical Perspectives on Organisational Behaviour and Change.* San Francisco: Jossey-Bass, pp. 361–364.

Mersky, R., (2012). Contemporary methodologies to surface and act on unconscious dynamics in organisations: An exploration of design, facilitation capacities, consultant paradigm and ultimate value. *Organisational and Social Dynamics,* 1(25), 19–43.

Michaels, M., (2001). *The Quest for Fitness: A Rational Exploration into the New Science of Organization.* San Jose, CA: Writers Club Press.

Miles, R. H., (1980). *Macro-organizational Behavior.* Santa Monica, CA: Goodyear, pp. 182–184.

Miller, E. J., (1959). Technology, territory, and time: the internal differentiation of complex production systems. *Human Relations,* 12(3), 243–272.

Miller, E., (1976). *Task and Organization*. New York: Wiley.

Miller, E. J., (1990a). Experiential Learning in Groups I: The Development of the Leicester Model. *In:* E. Trist and H. Murray (eds.), *The Social Engagement of Social Science: A Tavistock Anthology Volume 1*. (Vol. 1, pp. 165–185). Philadelphia: University of Pennsylvania Press. *Also in:* The Social Engagement of Social Science, Vol. 1: The Socio-Psychological Perspective. London: Free Association Books.

Miller, E. J., (1990b). Experiential learning in groups 2: Recent developments in dissemination and application. *In:* E. Trist and H. Murry (eds.), *The Social Engagement of Social Science, Vol. 1: The Socio-Psychological Perspective*. Philadelphia: University of Pennsylvania Press. *Also in:* The Social Engagement of Social Science, Vol. 1: The Socio-Psychological Perspective. London: Free Association Books.

Miller, E. J., (1993). *From Dependency to Autonomy: Studies in Organisation and Change*. London: Free Association Books.

Miller, E., (1995). On the working note. *Journal of Managerial Psychology*, 10(6), 27–30.

Miller, E. J., (1999). *The Tavistock Institute's Contribution to Job and Organizational Design (Two Volumes)*. Aldershot: Aldgate.

Miller, E. J., and Gwynne, G., (1972). *A Life Apart*. London: Tavistock Publications.

Miller, E. J., and Rice, A. K., (1967). *Systems of Organization: The Control of Task and Sentient Boundaries*. London: Tavistock Publications (See selections from: Systems of Organisation, *In:* A. D. Coleman and W. H. Bexton (eds.), *Group Relations Reader 1*, A.K. Rice Institute Series, Washington DC, 1975; *See also:* Task and Sentient Systems and their Boundary Controls, *In:* E. Trist and H. Murry (eds.). *The Social Engagement of Social Science, Vol. 1: The Socio-Psychological Perspective*.

Mingers, J., (1995). *Self-Producing Systems: Implications and Applications of Autopoiesis*. New York: Plenum Press.

Mitleton-Kelly, E., (2012). *Ten Principles of Complexity & Enabling Infrastructures*. London School of Economics.

Mohr, B., and Dessers, E., eds (2019). *Designing Integrated Care Systems: A Socio-Technical Perspective*. Switzerland: Springer.

Money Kyrle, R., (1978). *Collected Papers*. London: Clunie Press.

Moore, J., (1996). *The Death of Competition: Leadership and Strategy in the Age of Business Ecosystems*. New York: Harper Business.

Morgan, G., (1986). *Images of Organisation*. London: Sage.

Morgan, G., (1993). Organisational choice and the new technology. *In:* E. L. Trist and H. Murray (eds.), *The Social Engagement of the Social Sciences: A Tavistock Anthology Vol. 2: The Socio-technical Perspective*. London and: Philadelphia: University of Pennsylvania Press, pp. 354–368.

Morin, E., (2005). *Restricted Complexity, General Complexity*. In Proceedings of the Colloquium 'Intelligence de la complexité: Épistémologie et pragmatique', Cerisy-La-Salle, France.

Motamedi, K. K., (1977). Adaptability and copability: A study of social systems, their environment, and survival. *Group & Organization Studies*, 2(4), 480–490.

Mumford, E., (1996). *Systems Design: Ethical Tools for Ethical Change*. London: Macmillan.

Mumford, E., (2003). *Redesigning Human Systems*. London: Idea Publishing Group.

Mumford, E., (2006). The story of socio-technical design: Reflections on its successes, failures and potential. *Information Systems Journal*, 16(4), 317–342.

Murnighan, J. K., and Conlon, D. E., (1991). The dynamics of intense work groups: A study of British string quartets. *Administrative Science Quarterly*, 36(2), 165–186.

Music, G., (2011). *Nurturing Natures: Attachment and children's' emotional and brain development*. Hove: Psychology Press Taylor.

Nadler, D. A., (1998). *Champions of Change: How CEOs and their Companies are Mastering the Skills of Radical Change*. San Francisco: Jossey-Bass.

Nadler, D. A., and Tushman, M., (1980). A model for diagnosing organizational behavior: Applying the congruence perspective. *Organizational Dynamics*, 9(2), 35–51.

Nagel, C., (2020). *Psychodynamic Coaching Distinctive Features*. London: Routledge.

Brissett Nelson, A., and Solvilc, P., (2004). *Research Action as a Consultancy Methodology 2nd International Conference on Management Consulting*: Lausanne (Conference Proceedings, pp. 95–99).

Netland, T. H., et al., (2008). *The New Importance of Socio-technical Systems Research on High-tech Production Systems*. SINTEF Technology and Society N-7465 Trondheim, Norway. *Available from:* https://www.researchgate.net/publication/254912675_The_new_importance_of_socio-technical_systems_research_on_high-tech_production_systems

Neumann, J. E., (1999). Systems psychodynamics in the service of political organizational change. *In:* R. French and R. Vince (eds.), *Group relations, management, and organization*. Oxford, England: Oxford University Press, pp. 54–69.

Neumann, J., (2005). *Kurt Lewin – Dynamic Approach Rule {online}*. Tavistock Institute. *Available from:* http://tihr-archive.tavinstitute.org/page/2/

Neumann, J., (2005). Kurt Lewin at the Tavistock Institute. *Educational Action Research*, 13, 119–136. *Available from:* https://www.researchgate.net/publication/238400476_Kurt_lewin_at_the_tavistock_institute

Neumann, J. E., (2011a). Kurt Lewin – 'Dynamic approach rule'. Lectures & Presentations. *Available from:* http://www.tavinstitute.org/projects/kurt-lewin-dynamic-approach-rule-2/

Neumann, J. E., (2011b). Kurt Lewin – 'Field theory rule'. Lectures & Presentations. *Available from:* http://www.tavinstitute.org/projects/field-theory-rule/

Neumann, J. E., (2012). Kurt Lewin – 'Contemporaneity rule'. Lectures & Presentations. *Available from:* http://www.tavinstitute.org/projects/kurt-lewin-contemporaneity/

Neumann, J. E., (2013a). Kurt Lewin – 'Constructive method rule'. Lectures & Presentations. *Available from:* http://www.tavinstitute.org/projects/kurt-lewin-constructive-method-rule/

Neumann, J. E., (2013b). *Action Research and Four Practical Principles Selected and Interpreted from Kurt Lewin*. Paper presented at the "Learning to Change: Capacity Building for Action Research" workshop, held on 7–10 May 2013, Lamezia Terme. Google Scholar

Neumann, J. E., (2013c). *Action Research and a Cycle for Planned Change*. Paper presented at the "Learning to Change: Capacity Building for Action Research" workshop, held on 7–10 May 2013, Lamezia Terme.Google Scholar

Neumann, J. E., (2018). The origins and status of action research April 1984. *The Journal of Applied Behavioural Science*, 20(2), 113–124. *Available from:* http://www.tavinstitute.org/projects/field-theory-rule/

Neumann, J. E., (2010). How integrating organizational theory with systems psychodynamics can matter in practice: A commentary on critical challenges and dynamics in multiparty collaboration. *The Journal of Applied Behavioral Science*, 46(3), 313–321.

Neumann, J., Kellner, K., and Dawson-Shepherd. Eds., (1997). *Developing Organisational Consultancy*. London: Routledge.

Neumann, J. E., Miller, E. J., and Holti, R., (1999). Three contemporary challenges for OD practitioners. *Leadership & Organization Development Journal*, 20(4), 216–221.

Newton, J., Long, S., and Sievers, B., Eds., (2006). *Coaching in Depth*. London: Karnac.

Nicholas, J. M., (1979). Evaluation research in organisational change interventions: Consideration and some suggestions. *Journal of Applied Behavioural Science*, 15(1), 23–39.

Nicolini, D., Sher, M., Childerstone, S., and Gorli, M., (2004). In search of the 'structure that reflects': Promoting organisational reflection practices in a UK health authority. *In:* M. Reynolds and R. Vince (eds.), 81–104. *Organising Reflection*. Ashgate, London, UK. *Also In:* Sher, M., (2013). *The Dynamics of Change: Tavistock approaches to improving social systems*. London: Karnac.

Nicolis, G., and Prigogine, I., (1989). *Exploring Complexity*. New York: W.H. Freeman.

Normann, R., and Ramirez, R., (1993). From value chain to value constellation: Designing interactive strategy. *Harvard Business Review*, 71 (July-August), 65–77.

Nutkevitch, A., (2016). *The Psychoanalytic "Hypen" Systemic Approach: Reflections and Conceptualisations*. Presented to The Gathering Copenhagen.

Nuvolari, A., (2004). Collective invention during the British industrial revolution: The case of the Cornish pumping engine. *Cambridge Journal Economics*, 28, 347–363.

O'Connor, C., (1993). Managing resistance to change. *Management Development Review*, 6(4), 25–29.

O'Mahony, S., and Bechky, B. A., (2006). Stretchwork: Managing the career progression paradox in external labour markets. *Academy of Management Journal*, 49(5), 918–941.

O'Neil, J., and Marsick, V., (2007). *Understanding Action Learning*. New York: American Management Association.

Oakden, J., (2014). *The use of Rich Pictures in Evaluation*. [Video of slide presentation]. *Retrieved from:* https://www.youtube.com/watch?v=q7CTREXtFuk and https://www.betterevaluation.org/en/evaluation-options/richpictures

Obholzer, A., and Roberts, V. (Eds.), (1994). *The Unconscious at Work*. London: Routledge.

Obholzer, A., (2021). *Workplace Intelligence: Unconscious Forces and How to Manage Them*. London: Routledge.

Obholzer, A., (1999). Managing the unconscious at work. *In:* French, R., and Vince, R. A. (eds.), *Group Relations, Management, and Organization*. Oxford: Oxford University Press, pp. 87–97.

Oglensky, B., (1995). Socio-psychoanalytic perspectives on the subordinate. *Human Relations*, 48(9), 1029–1054.

Oldham, G. R., and Hackman, J. R., (2010).

Orlikowski, W. J., (1993). The duality of technology: Rethinking the concept of technology in organizations. *Organization Science*, 3(3), 398–427.

Painter, B., (2009). *STS Theory – From the Industrial to the Knowledge Age*. *Available from:* http://moderntimesworkplace.com/good_reading/GRWorkRed/STS_Theory_-_From_Industrial_To_Knowledge_Age.pdf.

Painter, B., et al., (2016). Sociotechnical systems design: Coordination of virtual teamwork in innovation. *Team Performance Management*, 22(7/8), 354–369.

Pan, S. L., and Scarbrough, H., (1998). A socio-technical view of knowledge-sharing at buckman laboratories. *Journal of Knowledge Management*, 2(1), 55–66.

Panskepp, J., (2009). Brain emotional systems and qualities of mental life. From animal models to implications for psychotherapeutics. *In:* D. Fosha, D. Siegel, M. Solomon (eds.), *The Healing Power of Emotion. Affective Neuroscience, Development and Clinical Practice.* New York: W.W. Norton & Company.

Pasmore, W., (1988). *Designing Effective Organizations: The Socio-Technical Systems Perspective.* New York: Wiley.

Pasmore, W., (1994). *Creating Strategic Change Designing the Flexible, High-Performing Organization.* New York: Wiley.

Pasmore, W., (1995). Social change transformed: The socio-technical perspective. *Human Relations*, 48, 1, 1–21.

Pasmore, W. A., (2001). Action research in the workplace: The socio-technical perspective. *In:* P. Reason, and H. Bradbury (eds.), *Handbook of Action Research.* London: Sage, pp. 38–47.

Pasmore, W. A., and Friedlander, F., (1982). An action research program for increasing employee involvement in problem solving. *Administrative Science Quarterly*, 27, 343–362.

Pasmore, W. A., Francis, C., Haldeman, J., and Shani, A., (1982). Sociotechnical systems: A North American reflection on empirical studies of the seventies. *Human Relations*, 35(12), 1179–1204.

Pasmore, W. A., (2015). *Leading Continuous Change: Navigating Churn in the Real World.* Oakland, CA: Berrett-Koehler Publishers *Also see:* https://www.advancedchange.com/wp-content/uploads/2020/06/WP01-Leading-Continuous-Change.pdf

Pasmore, W., Winby, S., Mohrman, S., and Vanasse, R., (2018). Reflections: Sociotechnical systems design and organization change. *Journal of Change Management*, 19(2), 67–85.

Pasmore, W., et al., (2019). *Braided Organizations: Designing Human-Centric Processes to Enhance Performance and Innovation.* Charlotte, NC: Information Age Publishing.

Patton, M., (2010). *Developmental Evaluation Applying Complexity Concepts to Enhance Innovation and Use.* New York, NY: Guilford Press.

Patton, M. Q., (1997). *Utilisation-focused Evaluation: The New Century Text.* Thousand Oaks, CA: Sage.

Pava, C., (1983). Designing managerial and professional work for high performance: A sociotechnical approach. *National Productivity Review*, 2, 126–135.

Pava, C., (1983). *Managing New Office Technology: An Organizational Strategy.* New York: Free Press.

Pava, C., (1986). Redesigning sociotechnical systems design: Concepts and methods for the 1990s. *Journal of Applied Behavioral Science*, 22(3), 201–221.

Pava, C., (1986). New strategies of systems change: Reclaiming non-synoptic methods. *Human Relations*, 39(7), 615–633.

Pawson, R., and Tilley, N., (1997). *Realistic Evaluation.* London: Sage.

Pawson, R., (2013). *The Science of Evaluation: A Realist Manifesto.* London, SAGE.

Pedler, M., and Burgoyne, J., (2008). Action learning. *In:* P. Reason and H. Bradbury, (eds.), *Handbook of Action Research.* 2nd edn. London: Sage, pp. 319–332.

Peirce, C. S., (1878). The rules of philosophy. *In:* M. Konvitz and G. Kennedy (eds.), (1960), *The American Pragmatists.* New York: New American University, pp. 80–127.

Peters, M., and Robinson, V., (1984). The origins and status of action research. *Journal of Applied Behavioural Science*, 20(2), 113–124.

Petriglieri, G., and Petriglieri, J. L., (2020). The return of the oppressed: A systems psychodynamic approach to organization studies. *Academy of Management Annals*, 14. *Available from:* https://sites.insead.edu/facultyresearch/research/doc.cfm?did=66021

Pettigrew, A., (1973). *The Politics of Organizational Decision Making*. London, Tavistock Publications.

Pfeffer, J., and Salancik, G., (1978). *The External Control of Organizations*. New York: Harper & Row, Philadelphia.

Piaget, J., (1952). *The Origins of Intelligence in Children*. New York: International Universities Press.

Pickering, A., (2001). Practice and posthumanism: Social theory and a history of agency. *In:* T. Schatzki, K. K. Cetina, and E. von Savigny, (eds.), (2005). *The Practice Turn in Contemporary Theory*. London: Routledge, pp. 172–183.

Pickvance, D., (2017). CAT supervision: A relational model. *In:* D. Pickvance (ed.), *Cognitive Analytic Supervision*. London: Routledge, pp. 23–38.

Pine, F., (1985). *Developmental Theory and Clinical Process*. New Haven, CT: Yale University Press.

Poli, R., (2017). *Introduction to Anticipation Studies*. New York. Springer.

Porras, J., and Hirscheim, R., (2007). A lifetime of theory and action on the ethical use of computers. A dialogue with Enid Mumford. *JAIS*, 8(9), 467–478.

Porras, J.I. and Roberston, P.J., (1992). *Organizational Development: Theory, Practice, Research*. In: Dunnette, M.D. and Hough, L.M., Eds., Handbook of Industrial and Organizational Psychology, Consulting Psychologists Press, Palo Alto, pp. 719–822.

Pratt, J., Gordon, P., and Plamping, D., (1999/2005). *Working Whole Systems: Putting Theory into Practice*. Abingdon: Radcliffe.

Pribram, K. H., and McGuinness, D., (1975). Arousal, activation, and effort in the control of attention. *Psychological Review*, 82(2), 116–149.

Prigogine, I., and Stengers, I., (1985). *Order Out of Chaos*. London: Flamingo.

Purser, R., and Griffin, T., (2008). Large group interventions: Whole system approaches to organizational change. *In:* T. Cummings (ed.), *Handbook of Organization Development*. Thousand Oaks, CA: Sage, pp. 261–276.

Pusic, E., (1999). Organisational theory and participation. *In:* F. Heller, E. Pusic, G. Strauss and B. Willpert (eds.), *Organisational Participation: Myth and Reality*. Oxford: Oxford University Press, pp. 65–96.

Puwar, N., (Ed.), (2004). *Space Invaders: Race, Gender and Bodies Out of Place*. New York: Berg.

Quinn, R. E., and Cameron, K. S. (Eds.), (1988). *Paradox and Transformation: Toward a Theory of Change in Organization and Management*. Cambridge, MA, Ballinger Publishing Co/Harper & Row Publishers.

Quinlan, M., (2021). COVID-19, health and vulnerable societies. *Annals of Work Exposures and Health*, 65(3), 239–243.

Ramirez, R., and Selsky, J., (2014). Strategic planning in turbulent environments: a social ecology approach to scenarios. *Long Range Planning. Available from:* http://www.sciencedirect.com/science/article/pii/S0024630114000703

Rappaport, R. N., (1970). Three dilemmas in action research. *Human Relations*, 23(6), 499. Also in: McKernan, J., (1991). *Curriculum Action Research. A Handbook of Methods and Resources for the Reflective Practitioner*. London: Kogan Page.

Reason, P., and Bradbury, H., (2008). *Handbook of Action Research*. 2nd edn. London: Sage.

Reason, P., and McArdle, L., (2005). Action research and organization development. *In:* T. G. Cummings, and G. Christopher (eds.), *Organization Development and Change*, 9th Edition Worley South-Western Cengage Learning 5191 Natorp

Boulevard Mason, OH 45040 USA. *Available from:* http://www.peterreason.eu/
Papers/ActionResearchandOrganizationDevelopment

Reason, P., and Rowan, J., (1981). *Human Inquiry: A Sourcebook for New Paradigm Research.* London: Sage.

Reed, B. D., and Armstrong, D. G., (1988). *Notes on Professional Management.* London: Grubb Institute.

Reed, B., and Bazalgette, J., (2006). Organisational role analysis at the Grubb institute of behavioural studies: Origins and development. *In:* J. Newton, S. Long, and B. Sievers, (eds.), *Coaching in Depth.* London: Karnac, pp. 43–62.

Reed, J., (2007). *Appreciative Inquiry: Research for Change.* Thousand Oaks, CA: Sage.

Reich, W., (1970). *The Mass Psychology of Fascism.* New York, NY: Farrar, Strauss and Giroux.

Rittel, H. W. J., and Webber, M. M., (1981). *Dilemmas in a General Theory of Planning.* In: Systems Thinking; Emery, F. E., Ed.; Penguin: Harmondsworth, UK, 2, 81–102.

Revans, R., (1998). *ABC of Action Learning.* London: Lemos and Crane.

Reynolds, L., (1994). Understand employees' resistance to change. *HR Focus,* 71(6), 17–18.

Rice, A. K., (1953). Productivity and social organization in an Indian weaving shed; an examination of some aspects of the socio-technical system of an experimental automatic loom shed. *Human Relations,* 6, 297–329.

Rice, A. K., (1958). *Productivity and Social Organisation: The Ahmedabad Experiment: Technical Innovation, Work Organisation and Management.* London: Tavistock Publications. Reprinted: (2001). Abingdon: Routledge.

Rice, A. K., (1963). *The Enterprise and Its Environment.* London: Tavistock. Publications.

Rice, A. K., (1965). *Learning for Leadership Interpersonal and Intergroup Relations.* London: Routledge.

Rice, A. K., (1969). Individual, group, and intergroup processes. *Human Relations,* 22, 565 584.

Rieff, P., (1966). *The Triumph of the Therapeutic.* New York, NY: Harper & Row.

Rigg, C., (2006). *Action Learning: Leadership and Organizational Development in Public Services.* Abingdon: Routledge.

Rittell, H., and Webber, M., (1973). Dilemmas in a general theory of planning. *Policy Sciences,* 4, 155–169.

Robbins, S., and Judge, T. A., (2009). *Organizational Behavior: Concepts, Controversies, and Applications,* 13th edn. Upper Saddle River, NJ: Prentice-Hall.

Roberts, V. Z., (2019). Changing the stories we are 'in': Power, purpose and organization. *In:* A. Obholzer and V. Roberts (eds.), (2nd ed.), *The Unconscious At work.* London: Routledge.

Roberts, V. Z., and Brunning, H., (2007). Psychodynamic and systems-psychodynamic coaching. *In: Handbook of Coaching Psychology - A Guide for Practitioners.* Edited by Stephen Palmer and Alison Whybrow. London: Routledge.

Roethlisberger, F., and Dickson, W., (1939). *Management and the Worker.* Cambridge, MA: Harvard University Press.

Rogers, P., (2014). *Theory of Change.* UNICEF. *Available from:* https://www.betterevaluation.org/sites/default/files/Theory_of_Change_EN...

Rogers, P., (2104). *Ways of Framing the Difference Between Research and Evaluation.* *Available from:* https://www.betterevaluation.org/en/blog/framing_the_difference_between_research_and_evaluation

Roszak, T., Gomes, M., Kanner, A., and Brown, L. (Eds.), (1995). *Eco-Psychology: Restoring the Earth/ Healing the Mind*. Berkeley: Counterpoint Press.

Rosen, R., (1985). *Anticipatory Systems: Vol 1 Philosophical, Mathematical and Methodological Foundations;* IFSR International Series on Systems Science and Engineering. N.Y. Pergamon.

Rosenau, P. M., (1991). *Post-Modernism and the Social Sciences*. Princeton, NJ: Princeton University Press, pp. 3–24.

Roth, G. L., and Kleiner, A., (1998). Developing organizational memory through learning histories. *Organizational Dynamics*, 27(2), 43–61.

Sadler, P. (Ed.), (1998). *Management Consultancy: A Handbook of Best Practice*. London, Kogan Page.

Salami, M., (2020). *Sensuous Knowledge. A Black Feminist Approach for Everyone*. London: Zed Books.

Samuel, S., (2020). *Everywhere Basic Income Has Been Tried, in One map. Available from:* Vox www.vox.com/future-perfect/2020/2/19/21112570/universal-basic-income-ubi-map

Scarvia, B. A., Braskamp, L. A., Cohen, W. M., Evans, J. W., Gilmore, A., Marvin, K. E., Shipman, V. C., Vanecko, J. J., and Wooldridge, R. J., (1982). *Evaluation Research Society Standards for Program Evaluation. New Directions for Program Evaluation*, 7–19.

Schein, E., (1988). *Process Consultation, Its Role in Organizational Development*. Reading MA: Addison-Westley Publishing.

Schein, E. H., (1988). *Organizational Psychology*, 3rd edn. London: Prentice-Hall.

Schein, E. H., (1989). Organization development: Science, technology or philosophy? *MIT Sloan School of Management Working Paper*, 3065–89-BPS. *In:* D. Coghlan and A. Shani (2010). (Eds.) *Fundamentals of Organization Development*, 1:91–100. London: Sage.

Schein, E. H., (1996). Kurt Lewin's change theory in the field and in the classroom: notes towards a model of management learning. *Systems Practice*, 9(1), 27–47.

Schein, E. H., and Bennis, G. W., (1965). *Personal and Organizational Change through Group Methods*. New York: Wiley.

Schick, N., (2020). *Deep Fakes and the Infocalypse: What You Urgently Need to Know*. Monoray Hachette.

Schön, D. A., (1971). *Beyond the Stable State*. New York: Norton.

Schön, D. A., (1987). *Educating the Reflective Practitioner*. San Francisco: Jossey Bass Publishers.

Schön, D. A., (1991). *The Reflective Turn: Case Studies in and on Educational Practice*. New York: Teachers College Press.

Schon, D. A., (1995). Knowing-in-action: The new scholarship requires a new epistemology. *Change*, November/December, 27–34.

Schore, A., (2012). *The Science of the Art of Psychotherapy*. New York: W.W. Norton & Company.

Schumpeter, J., (2017). *Theory of Economic Development* (3rd ed). New York: Routledge.

Schwab, K., (2016). *The Fourth Industrial Revolution*. London: Penguin.

Schwartz, D. (1958). Uncooperative Patients? *The American Journal of Nursing*, 58(1), 75–77.

Schwartz, H., (1990). *Narcissistic Process and Corporate Decay*. New York, NY: New York University Press.

Schwartz, H., (1987). Anti-social actions of committed organizational participants: An existential psychoanalytic perspective. *Organization Studies*, 8(4), 327–340.

Scott, J., (2011). Light in my life. *Organisational and Social Dynamics*, 11(1), 21–40.

Scott, R., (1992). *Organizations: Rational, Natural and Open Systems*. Pg. 230. Englewood Cliffs, NJ: Prentice-Hall.

Searles, H. F., (1972). Unconscious processes in relation to the environmental crisis. *The Psychoanalytic Review*, 59(3), 361–374.

Segal, H., (1991). *Dream, Phantasy and Art*. London: Routledge.

Seiler, J. A., (1967). *Systems Analysis in Organizational Behavior*. R. D. Irwin, Homewood, Ill. Selener, D., (1997). *Participatory Action Research and Social Change*. Ithaca, NY: Cornell.

Selsky, J., Goes, J., and Baburoglu, O., (2007). Contrasting perspectives of strategy making: Applications in 'hyper' environments. *Organisation Studies*, 28(1), 71–94.

Sennett, R., (1998). *The Corrosion of Character: The Personal Consequences of Work in the New Capitalism*. New York, NY: Norton.

Shani, A., and Sena, J., (2000). Knowledge management and new product development: Learning from a software development firm. *Proceedings of the Third International. Conf. on Practical Aspects of Knowledge Management* (PAKM2000). Basel: Switzerland.

Shani, A. B. (Rami), and Pasmore, W. A., (1985). Organization inquiry: Towards a new model of the action research process. *In:* D. D. Warrick (ed.), *Contemporary Organization Development: Current Thinking and Applications*. Glenview, ILL: Scott Foresman and Company, pp. 438–448.

Shani, A. B., and Bushe, G. R., (1987). Visionary action research: A consultation process perspective. *Consultation: An International Journal*, 6(1), 3–19.

Shapiro, E. R., and Carr, A. W., (1991). *Lost in Familiar Places*. New Haven, CT: Yale University Press.

Sharpe, E., (1937). *Dream Analysis*. New York: Norton.

Shaw, P., (2002). *Changing Conversations in Organisations – A Complexity Approach to Change*. London: Routledge.

Shepard, H., and Katzell, R. A., (1960). *An Action Research Program for Organization Improvement*. Foundation for Research on Human Behavior. *Also in:* B. Cooke and J. Woolfram-Cox, (eds.). *Fundamentals of Action Research,* Vol II, pp. 317–334. London: Sage.

Sher, M., (2013). A tale of one city: Social dreaming and the social protest movement – occupy London at tent city. *Socio-analysis*, 15, 60–71.

Sher, M., (2013). *The Dynamics of Change: Tavistock Approaches to Improving Social Systems*. London: Routledge.

Sher, M., (2019). Social spaces for social dreaming. *In:* S. Long and J. Manley (eds.), *Social Dreaming: Philosophy, Research, Theory and Practice*. London: Routledge, pp. 155–166.

Siebel, T., (2019). *Digital Transformation: Survive and Thrive in an Era of Mass Extinction*. New York: Rosetta Books.

Sievers, B., (1986). Beyond the surrogate of motivation. *Organization Studies*, 7(4), 335–351.

Sievers, B., (1994). *Work, Death and Life Itself*. Berlin: Walter de Gruyter.

Sievers, B., (1999). Psychotic organization as a metaphoric frame for the socioanalysis of organizational and interorganizational dynamics. *Administration and Society*, 31(5), 588–615.

Sievers, B. (Ed.), (2009). *Psychoanalytic Studies of Organizations: Contributions from the International Society for the Psychoanalytic Study of Organizations (ISPSO) 1983-2008*. London: Karnac.

Siggelkow, N., and Levinthal, D. A., (2003). Temporarily divide to conquer: Centralized, decentralized, and reintegrated organizational approaches to exploration and adaptation. *Organization Science*, 14(6), 650–669.

Silverstone, R., and Hirsch, E., (1992). *Consuming Technologies: Media and Information in Domestic Spaces*. London/New York: Routledge.

Sinofsky, S., (2021). *Creating the Future of Work*. *Available from:* https://medium.learningbyshipping.com/creating-the-future-of-work-449c66707e35

Sitter, L., de, Hertog, J. den, and Eijnatten, F. van., (1990). *Simple Organisations, Complex Jobs: The Dutch Socio-technical Approach*. Paper presented at the Annual Conference of the American Academy of Management, San Francisco.

Smelser, N., (1998). Vicissitudes of work and love in Anglo-American Society. *In:* Smelser, N.A (ed.), *The Social Edges of Psychoanalysis*. Berkeley, CA: University of California Press, pp. 93–107.

Smelser, N., (2008). Social transformations and social change. *International Social Science Journal*, 50(156), 173–178.

Smith, W. K., and Lewis, M., (2011). Toward a theory of paradox: A dynamic equilibrium model of organizing. *Academy of Management Review*, 36(2), 381–403.

Smith, M. K., (2001). *Kurt Lewin: Group, Experimental Learning and Action Research*. The Encyclopaedia of Informal Education, pp. 1–15. *Available from:* http://www.infed.org/thinkers/et-lewin.htm

Snowden, D. J., and Boone, M. E., (2007). A leader's framework for decision making. *Harvard Business Review*, 85, 69–76.

Sofer, C., (1961). *The Organisation from Within: A Comparative Study of Social Institutions Based on a Socio-therapeutic Approach*. London: Tavistock.

Sonenshein, S., (2010). We're changing – or are we? Untangling the role of progressive, regressive, and stability narratives during strategic change implementation. *Academy of Management Journal*, 53(3), 477–512.

Sorge, A. T., and van Witteloostuijn, A., (2004). The (non) sense of organizational change: An essay about universal management hypes, sick consultancy metaphors, and healthy organization theory. *Organization Studies*, 25(7), 1205–1231.

Spohrer, J. Siddike, A. K., and Kohda, Y., (2017). *Rebuilding Evolution: A Service Science Perspective*. Proceedings of the 50th Hawaii International Conference on System Sciences, pp. 1663–1672.

Stacey, R. D., (1991). *The Chaos Frontier: Creative Strategic Control for Business*. Oxford: Butterworth Heinemann.

Stacey, R., (1992). *Managing Chaos: Dynamic Business Strategies in an Unpredictable World*. London: Kogan Page.

Stacey, R. D., (1992). *Managing the Unknowable: The Strategic Boundaries Between Order and Chaos*. San Francisco: Jossey Bass.

Stacey, R. D., (1993). *Strategic Management and Organizational Dynamics*. London: Pitman.

Stacey, R. D., (2000). *Strategic Management and Organisational Dynamics: The Challenge of Complexity*. Third edition. London: Pearson Education.

Stacey, R. D., (2001). *Complex Responsive Processes in Organizations: Learning and Knowledge Creation*. London: Routledge.

Stacey, R. D., (2003a). *Complexity and Group Processes: A Radically Social Understanding of Individuals*. New York: Brunner-Routledge.

Stacey, R. D., (2003b). Learning as an activity of interdependent people. *Learning Organization*, 10, 325–331.

Stacey, R., (2006). Complexity at the 'edge' of the basic-assumption group. *In:* L. J. Gould, L. F. Stapley, and M. Stein (eds.), *The Systems Psychodynamics of Organizations: Integrating the Group Relations Approach, Psychoanalytic, and Open Systems Perspectives: Contributions in Honour of Eric J. Miller.* London: Karnac Books, pp. 91–114.

Stebbins, M. W., and Snow, C. C., (1982). Processes and payoffs of programmatic action research. *The Journal of Applied Behavioral Science*, 18(1), 69–86.

Steers, R. M., and Porter, L. W., (1991). *Motivation and Work Behavior.* McGraw-Hill, pp. 215, 322, 357, 411–413, 423, 428–441 and 576.

Steier, F., Brown, J., and Silva, F., (2015). *The World Cafe in Action Research Settings.* In: The SAGE handbook of action research. London: SAGE, pp. 211–219.

Stein, H., (1998). *Euphemism, Spin, and the Crisis in Organizational Life.* Westport, CT: Quorum Books.

Stein, H., (2001). *Nothing Personal, Just Business.* Westport, CT: Quorum Books.

Stein, H. F., (1996). She's driving us nurses crazy!: On solving the wrong problem as a consulting organizational psychologist. *Consulting Psychology Journal: Practice and Research*, 48(1), 17–26.

Stein, M., (1997). Envy and leadership. *European Journal of Work and Organisation Psychology*, 6(4), 453–465.

Stein, M., (2004). The critical period of disasters: Insights from sensemaking and psychoanalytic theory. *Human Relations*, 57(10), 1243–1246.

Stein, M., (2000). After Eden: Envy and the defences against anxiety paradigm. *Human Relations*, 53(2), 193–211.

Stein, M., (2000). The risk taker as shadow: A psychoanalytic view of the collapse of barings bank. *Journal of Management Studies*, 37(8), 1215–1229.

Stein, M., (2003). Unbounded irrationality: Risk and organizational narcissism at long term capital management. *Human Relations*, 56(5), 523–540.

Stein, M., (2005). The Othello Conundrum: The inner contagion of leadership. *Organization Studies*, 26(9), 1405–1419.

Stein, M., (2007). Oedipus Rex at Enron: Leadership, oedipal struggles, and organizational collapse. *Human Relations*, 60(9), 1387–1410.

Stern, E., (2012). *Impact Evaluation - A Guide for Commissioners and Managers. Available from:* https://assets.publishing.service.gov.uk/media/57a0896de5274a31e000009c/60899_Impact_Evaluation_Guide_0515.pdf

Stokes, J., (1994). What is unconscious in organisation? *In:* R. Casemore et al. (eds.), *What makes Consultancy Work?* London: South Bank University Press.

Stubbings, C., and Williams, J., (2018). *Workforce of the Future PWC. Available from:* https://www.pwc.com/gx/en/services/people-organisation/publications/workforce-of-the-future.html

Sturdy, A., (2002). Front-line diffusion: The production and negotiation of knowledge through training interaction. *In:* T. Clark and R. Fincham (eds.), *Critical Consulting: New Perspectives on the Management Advice Industry.* Oxford: Blackwell, pp. 130–152.

Susman, G. I., and Evered, R. D., (1978). An assessment of the scientific merits of action research. *Administrative Science Quarterly*, 23, 582–601.

Susman, G. I., and Chase, R. B., (1986). A sociotechnical analysis of the integrated factory. *Journal of Applied Behavioral Science*, 22(3), 257–270.

Taleb, N. N., (2013). *Antifragile: How to Live in a World We Don't Understand*. London: Allen Lane.

Taylor, F. W., (1911, reprinted 1914). *The Principles of Scientific Management*. New York: Harper and Brothers.

Taylor, F. W., (1911 [1967]). *The Principles of Scientific Management*. New York: WW Norton & Company.

Taylor, D. C., Taylor, C. E., and Taylor J. O., (2012). *Empowerment on an Unstable Planet: From Seeds of Human Energy to a Scale of Global Change*. New York: Oxford University Press.

Taylor, K., and Marienau, C., (2016). *Facilitating Learning with the Adult Brain in Mind*.

The Global Risks Report., (2017). *Available from:* https://www.weforum.org/reports/the-global-risks-report-2017

Thompson, J., (1967). *Organizations in Action*. New York: McGraw Hill.

Thorsrud, E., (1977). Democracy at work: Norwegian experiences with non-bureaucratic forms of organization. *Journal Applied Behavioural Science*, NTL Institute, 13(3), 410–421.

Tichy, N. M., (1983). *Managing Strategic Change*. New York: John Wiley.

Timmins, G., (1993). *The Last Shift: The Decline of Handloom Weaving in Nineteenth-Century Lancashire*. Manchester: Manchester University Press.

Tobach, E., (1994). Personal is political is personal is political. *Journal of Social Issues*, 50(1), 221–244.

Tomkins, L., (2020). *Where Is Boris Johnson? When and Why It Matters that Leaders Show Up in a Crisis. Available from:* Leadership https://doi.org/10.1177/174271502 0919657

Torbert, W. R., (2001). The practice of action inquiry. *In:* P. Reason and H. Bradbury (eds.), *Handbook of Action Research: Participative Inquiry and Practice*. London: Sage Publications, pp. 250–260.

Torbert, W., (2004). *Action Inquiry*. San Francisco: Berrett-Koehler.

Törmänen, M., (2017). *Virtual Teams: Considerations, Advantages and Disadvantages*. School of Business and Management Major: Supply Management Year: University in Lappeenranta, Finland Master's Thesis.

Toulmin, S., and Gustavsen, B., (1996). *Beyond Theory: Changing Organizations through Participation*. Amsterdam: John Benjamins.

Trist, E., (1973). The establishment of problem-oriented research domains. *In:* F. Emery and E. Trist (eds.), *Towards a Social Ecology*. New York: Plenum/ Rosetta, pp. 91–102.

Trist, E., (1976). Action research and adaptive planning. *In: Experimenting with Organizational Life*. Springer, Boston, MA.

Trist, E., (1977). A concept of organisational ecology. *Australian Journal of Management*, 2(2), 161–175.

Trist, E., (1979). The environment and system response capability: A futures perspective. *Futures*, 12, 113–127.

Trist, E., (1983). Referent organizations and the development of inter-organizational domains. *Human Relations*, 36, 269–284. (See Trist, E.L.: Reference Organizations and the Development of Inter-Organizational Domains, Vol. III: The Socio-Ecological Perspective, Tavistock Anthology. University of Pennsylvania Press.) *Available from*: www.moderntimesworkplace.com

Trist, E., (1983). Afterword. *In:* C. Pava (ed.), *Managing New Office Technology: An Organizational Strategy*. New York: Free Press, pp. 163–175.

Trist, E., and Bamforth, K., (1951). Some social and psychological consequences of the longwall method of coal getting: An examination of the psychological situation and defences of a work group in relation to the social structure and technological content of the work system. *Human Relations*, 4(1), 3–38.

Trist, E., and Murray, H., eds (1990). *The Social Engagement of Social Science, Tavistock Anthology, Volume I: The Socio-Psychological Perspective*. University of Pennsylvania Press. *Available from:* www.moderntimesworkplace.com

Trist, E., and Murray, H., eds (1993). *The Social Engagement of Social Science, Tavistock Anthology, Volume II: The Socio-Technical Systems Perspective*. University of Pennsylvania Press: *Available from:* www.moderntimesworkplace.com

Trist, E. L., Emery, F. E., and Murray, H., eds (1997). *The Social Engagement of Social Science, Tavistock Anthology, Volume III: The Socio-Ecological Perspective*. University of Pennsylvania Press: *Available from:* www.moderntimesworkplace.com

Trist, E. L, Emery, F., and Murray, H., (1990, 1993, 1997). *The Social Engagement of Social Science: A Tavistock Anthology. Vols. I- III*. Philadelphia, PA: University of Pennsylvania Press.

Trist, E. L., (1981). The evolution of socio-technical systems: A conceptual framework and action research programme. *Occasional Paper No. 2, Ontario Quality of Working Life Centre*. Ontario, Canada. *Also in: Journal of Issues in the Quality of Working Life*. Occasional Paper, Issue 2.

Trist, E., and Murray, H. (Eds.), (1990). Historical overview: The foundation and development of the tavistock institute to 1989. *In:* E. Trist and H. Murray (eds.), *The Social Engagement of Social Science: A Tavistock Anthology*, Vol. 1.

Trist, E., and Murray, H. (Eds.), (1990). Historical overview: The foundation and development of the Tavistock Institute to 1989. *In:* E. Trist and H. Murray (eds.), *The Social Engagement of Social Science: A Tavistock Anthology*, Vol. 1.

Trist, E., Higgin, G., Murray, H., and Pollock, A., (1963). *Organisational Choice: Capabilities of Groups at the Coal Face Under Changing Technologies: The Loss, Rediscovery and Transformation of a Work Tradition*. London: Tavistock Publications.

Trist, B., Trist, E., and Murray, H., (1997). *The Social Engagement of the Social Sciences: A Tavistock Anthology London Vol. 3: The Socio-ecological Perspective*. Philadelphia: University of Pennsylvania Press.

Truex, D., Baskerville, R., and Klein, H., (1999). Growing systems in an emergent organization. *Communications ACM*, 42(8), 117–123.

Tscudy, T., (2014). An OD map: The essence of organization development. *In:* B. Jones and M. Brazzel, (eds.), *NTL Handbook of Organizational Development and Change* (2nd Ed). San Francisco: Wiley.

Turner, D., (2021). *Intersections of Privilege and Otherness in COUNSELLING AND Psychotherapy*. London: Routledge.

Turner, D., (2021). *Intersections of Privilege and Otherness in Counselling and Psychotherapy*. London: Routledge.

Tushman, M. L., and Romanelli, E., (1985). Organizational evolution: A metamorphosis model of convergence and reorientation. *Research in Organizational Behavior*, 7(2), 171–222.

Tushman, M., Smith, W. K., Wood, R. C., Westerman, G., and O'Reilly, C., (2010). Organizational designs and innovation streams. *Industrial and Corporate Change*, 19(5), 1331–1366.

Ulrich, D. (1998). *Human Resource Champions*. Boston, MA: Harvard Business School Press.

Vallas, S. P., and A. Kovalainen (Eds.), (2019). *Work and Labor in the Digital Age, Research in the Sociology of Work*. Bingley: Emerald.

Van Alstyne, M., (1997). The state of network organization: A survey in three frameworks. *Journal of Organizational Computing*, 7(3).

van Beinum, H., (1990). *Observations on the Development of a New Organizational Paradigm*. Stockholm: Arbetslivscentrum. Philadelphia: John Benjamins.

Van Beinum, H., (1990). On participative democracy. *In: The Social Engagement of Social Science Volume 3, The Socio-Ecological Perspective.* London: Inaugural address given on acceptance of the position of professor in the psychological, organisational and societal significance of participative democracy, in respect of the Cleveringa Chair, University of Leiden, 26th November, 1990. *Available from:* http://www. moderntimesworkplace.com/archives/ericsess/sessvol3/ZKVANBEIp570.pdf

van Beinum, H., Faucheux, C., and van der Vlist, R., (1996). Reflections on the epigenetic significance of Action Research. *In:* S. Toulmin and B. Gustavsen (eds.), *Beyond Theory: Changing Organizations through Participation* (Vol. 2).

Van der Kolk, B. (2014). *The Body Keeps the Score: Mind Brain and Body in the Transformation of Trauma*. London: Penguin Books.

Varela, F., and Maturana, H., (1992). *The Tree of Knowledge*. Shambhala.

Vickers, G., (1965). *The Art of Judgement*. London: Chapman and Hall.

Vince, R., and Broussine, M., (1996). Paradox, defense and attachment: Accessing and working with emotions and relations underlying organizational change. *Organization Studies*, 17(1), 1–21.

Vlasic, A., (2019). Going to the root: How white caucuses contribute to racial justice. *The Arrow: A Journal of Wakeful Society: Culture and Politics*.

Vo, A. T., Christie, C. A., (2018). Where impact measurement meets evaluation: Tensions, challenges, and opportunities. *American Journal of Evaluation*.

Von Bertalanffy, L., (1950). An outline of general system theory. *British Journal for the Philosophy of Science*, 1, 114–129.

Von Bertalanffy, L., (1950). The theory of open systems in physics and biology. *Science*, 3, 23–29.

Vygotsky, L., (1978). *Mind in Society: The Development of Higher Psychological Processes*. Cambridge, MA: Harvard University Press.

Waclawski, J., and. Church, A. H., (2002). *Organization Development: A Data-Driven Approach to Organizational Change*. San Francisco: Jossey-Bass.

Waddell, D., (2007). *Contemporary Management*. North Ryde, NSW: McGraw-Hill Irwin.

Waelder, R., (1967). Inhibitions, symptoms and anxiety: Forty years later. *The Psycho-Analytic Quarterly*, 36, 1–36.

Waldrop, M. M., (1992). *Complexity: The Emerging Science at the Edge of Order and Chaos*. New York: Simon and Schuster.

Wang, B., Liu, Y., Qian, J., et al., (2021). Achieving effective remote working during the COVID-19 pandemic: A work design perspective. *Applied Psychology*, 70(1), 16–59.

Warhurst, C., Mathieu, M., and Dhondt, S., (2020). *Industrie 4.0, Policy Brief #2, Beyond 4.0. Available from:* https://beyond4-0.eu/news/1

Warhurst, C., and Knox., A (2022). Manifesto for a new quality of working life. *Human Relations*, 75(2), 304–321.

Watkins, K. M., and Mohr, B., (2001). *Appreciative Inquiry: Change at the Speed of Imagination*. San Francisco: Jossey-Bass.

Watson, T. J., (1994). *In Search of Management: Culture, Chaos and Control in Managerial Work*. London: Routledge.

Weber, L., (2017). The end of employees. *The Wall Street Journal. Available from:* https://www.wsj.com/articles/the-end-of-employees-1486050443

Webster, G., and Goodwin, B., (1996). *Form and Transformation: Generative and Relational Principles in Biology*. Cambridge University Press.

Wegner, D. M., et al., (1987). Paradoxical effects of thought suppression. *Journal of Personality and Social Psychology*, 53, 5–13.

Weick, K. E., (2001). *Making Sense of the Organization*. Oxford: Blackwell.

Weintrobe, S., (2016). Psychoanalysis as social intervention: Why silence is not an option. *Quarterly Bulletin of the American Psychoanalytic Association*. Spring/summer 2013 issue

Weintrobe, S., (2020). *Climate Crisis and Consciousness: Re-imagining Our World and Ourselves*. London: Routledge.

Weintrobe, S., (2021). *Psychological Roots of the Climate Crisis, Neoliberal Exceptionalism and the Culture of Uncare*. London: Bloomsbury.

Weisbord, M., (1987). *Productive Workplaces*. San Francisco: Jossey-Bass.

Weiss, C. H., (2013). Evaluation of programs. *Reading: Universal Journal of Educational Research*, 1(4), 323–327.

Weiss, C. H., (1972). *Evaluation Research: Methods for Assessing Program Effectiveness*. Englewood Cliffs.

Werr, A., and Stjernberg, T., (2003). Exploring management consulting finns as knowledge systems. *Organizational Studies*, 24(6), 881–908.

Westen, D., (1999). The scientific status of unconscious processes: Is Freud really dead? *Journal of the American Psychoanalytic Association*, 47(4), 1061-

What Works Network: Available from: https://www.gov.uk/guidance/what-works-network

Whittle, S. R., and Stevens, R. C., eds., (2013). *Changing Organizations from Within: Roles, Risks, and Consultancy Relationships*. Farnham: Gower.

Wheatley, M., (1992). *Leadership and the New Science*. Oakland CA: Berrett-Koehler Publishers.

Wheelen, T. L., and Hunger, J. D., (1983). *Strategic Management and Business Policy*. Reading, MA: Addison-Wesley.

Whitworth, B., (2009). A brief introduction to socio-technical systems. *In: Encyclopaedia of Information Science and Technology*, Second edition, Edited by Claude Ghaoui, Hershey: Idea Group Publishing.

Whyte, W. F., (1964). On street corner society. *In:* E. W. Burgess, and D. J. Bogue (eds.), *Contributions to Urban Sociology*. Chicago, IL: The University of Chicago Press.

Whyte, W. F., (1969). *Organizational Behavior: Theory and Application*. Homewood, Ill.: R.D. Irwin.

Winby, S., and Moorman, S., (2018). Digital sociotechnical system design. *The Journal of Applied Behavioral Science*, 54(3).

Winnicott, D. W., (1947). Hate in the countertransference. *In: Collected Papers: Through Paediatrics to Psychoanalysis*. London: Hogarth Press and the Institute of Psychoanalysis, 1958.

Winnicott, D. W., (1965). *The Maturational Processes and the Facilitating Environment*. New York: International University Press.

Winnicott, D. W., (1971). *Playing and Reality*. London: Tavistock Publications (Reprinted Harmondsworth: Penguin Books, 1980).

Winnicott, D., (1975). *Through Paediatrics to Psychoanalysis*. New York: Basic Books.

Winter et al., (2014). Beyond the organizational 'container': Conceptualizing 21st century sociotechnical work. *Information and Organization*, 24(4), 250–269. *Available from:*https://www.academia.edu/27265291/Beyond_the_organizational_container_Conceptualizing_21st_century_sociotechnical_work

Woodman, R. W., and Wayne, S. J., (1985). An investigation of positive findings: Bias in evaluation of organisation development interventions. *Academy of Management Journal*, 28, 889–913.

Woodward, J., (1958). *Management and Technology.* London: H.M.S.O.

Work: A Tavistock Approach to Making Sense of Organizational Life. London: Routledge, pp. 58–70.

Wright, S., and Morley, D., (1989). *Learning Works: Searching for Organizational Futures.* Toronto: ABL Group, York University.

Wrzesniewski, A., and Dutton, J. E., (2001). Crafting a job: Revisioning employees as active crafters of their work. *Academy of Management Review*, 26(2), 179–201.

Yaeger, T., Sorensen, P., and Bengtsson, U., (2005). Assessment of the state of appreciative inquiry: Past, present and future. *In:* R. Woodman and W. A. Pasmore (eds.), *Research in Organization Change and Development*, Vol. 15. Oxford: Elsevier, pp. 197–319.

Yang, L., Holtz, D., Jaffe, S. et al., (2021). The effects of remote work on collaboration among information workers. *Nature Human Behaviour. Available from:* https://doi.org/10.1038/s41562-021-01196-4

Zaleznik, A., (1966). *Human Dilemmas of Leadership.* New York: Harper Collins.

Zaleznik, A., (1977). Managers and leaders: Are they different? *Harvard Business Review*, 55, May-June, 47–60.

Zaleznik, A., (1989a). *The Managerial Mystique.* New York, NY: Harper and Row.

Zaleznik, A., (1989b). The mythological structure of organizations and its impact. *Human Resource Management*, 28(2), 267–278.

Zaleznik, A., and Kets de Vries, M. F. R., (1975). *Power and the Corporate Mind.* Oxford: Houghton Mifflin.

Zaleznik, A., (1990). The leadership gap. *The Executive*, 4(1), 7–22. *Available from:* www.jstor.org/stable/4164929

Zaleznik, A., (1991). Leading and managing: Understanding the difference. *In:* M. F. R. Kets de Vries, The Jossey-Bass management series. *Organizations on the Couch: Clinical Perspectives on Organizational Behavior and Change.* San Fransico: Jossey-Bass, pp. 97–119.

Zarka, M., Kochanovskaya, E., and Pasmore, W., (2019). *Braided Organizations: Designing Augmented Human-Centric Processes to Enhance Performance and Innovation.* Charlotte NC: Information Age Publishing.

Zhu, Z., (2007). Complexity science, systems thinking and pragmatic sensibility. *Systems Research and Behavioral Science*, 24(4), 445–464.

Zizek, S., (1989). *The Sublime Object of Ideology.* London: Verso.

Zuber-Skerritt, O., (1992). *Professional Development in Higher Education: A Theoretical Framework for Action Research.* London: Kogan Page.

Zuboff, S., (2005). Big other: Surveillance capitalism and the prospects of an information civilization. *Journal of Information Technology*, 30(1), 75–89.

Zuboff, S., (2019). *The Age of Surveillance Capitalism: The Fight for a Human Future at the New Frontier of Power.* New York: Hachette Book Group.

Index

Note: **Bold** page numbers refer to tables; *italic* page numbers refer to figures.

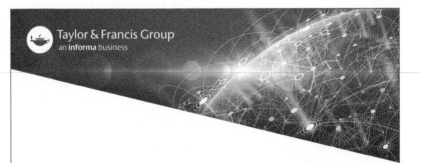

Taylor & Francis eBooks

www.taylorfrancis.com

A single destination for eBooks from Taylor & Francis
with increased functionality and an improved user
experience to meet the needs of our customers.

90,000+ eBooks of award-winning academic content in
Humanities, Social Science, Science, Technology, Engineering,
and Medical written by a global network of editors and authors.

TAYLOR & FRANCIS EBOOKS OFFERS:

A streamlined
experience for
our library
customers

A single point
of discovery
for all of our
eBook content

Improved
search and
discovery of
content at both
book and
chapter level

REQUEST A FREE TRIAL
support@taylorfrancis.com

Printed and bound by CPI Group (UK) Ltd, Croydon, CR0 4YY

09/07/2024

01017196-0016